962.004   163793
  Mur

      Murray.
      Sons of Ishmael.

SONS OF ISHMAEL

AMS PRESS
NEW YORK

ARAB OF SOUTH SINAI

SONS OF ISHMAEL

A STUDY OF THE EGYPTIAN BEDOUIN

By

G. W. MURRAY

"And God was with the lad; and he grew, and dwelt in the wilderness, and became an archer. And he dwelt in the wilderness of Paran, and his mother took him a wife out of the land of Egypt."
Genesis xxi, 20–21.

LONDON
GEORGE ROUTLEDGE & SONS, LTD.
BROADWAY HOUSE: 68-74 CARTER LANE, E.C.
1935

LORETTE WILMOT LIBRARY
NAZARETH COLLEGE

Library of Congress Cataloging in Publication Data

Murray, George William, 1885-
　　　Sons of Ishmael.

　　　　Reprint of the 1935 ed. published by G. Routledge & Sons, London.
　　　Bibliography: p.
　　　Includex index.
　　　1. Bedouins in Egypt. 2. Egypt—Social life and customs. I. Title.
　　　DT72.B4M8　　1978　　962'.004'927　　74-15071
　　　ISBN 0-404-12115-2

Reprinted from an original in the collections of the University of Illinois Library, Urbana-Champaign

From the edition of 1935, London
First AMS edition published in 1978
Manufactured in the United States of America

AMS PRESS INC.
NEW YORK, N.Y.

PREFACE

AFTER a quarter of a century, handsomely measured, spent in the charting of the desert and the survey of mankind from Suakin to Baalbek, the time has come to pass my experience on, and, since I believe that the ordinary man's narrative loses in vigour if he attempts to see too far round his subject, I have not troubled to excise the occasional prejudices that may be discovered here and there in mine, betraying a rather nomadic point of view in the author.

A word as to the compilation of the book ; much is due to the wise men who have gone before me and written their own books, more to the unequalled experience of Wilfred Jennings Bramly, which has been placed unreservedly at my disposal, and a great deal to many Bedouin sheikhs and guides. I have for years relentlessly pursued the practice of taking a guide from one end of Egypt to the other. So the views of the 'Ababda on the Sinai Arabs, and of the Sinai Arabs on the 'Ababda, and both on the Awlad 'Ali, have all been available. In fact we have improved on Midshipman Easy's duel at Malta, and fired all ways round the triangle.

A correspondence of many years' standing with Professor C. G. Seligman, to me the pioneer in the discovery of the early Hamitic culture, has gradually been opening my eyes to the meaning of much that I had been thoughtlessly observing. The volume in its swaddling clothes has also been exposed to the gaze, not always admiring, of all the friends I thought likely to be constructive in their criticism. This book may be a poor thing but it is not my own ; it is a far far better book than I could have written unaided. To all my friends, much thanks. My critics may now do their worst, but full revenge for this book will never be taken till some Bedouin has written his view on England.

Finally I should like to record my gratitude to the editor and proprietors of the Cornhill Magazine for their permission to reprint the poem which follows.

THE BAD PENNIES

When Adam fled from Eden, and our good world began,
And peasants tilled the valleys—not so did every man;
For Sâlem was a robber, the first of all his clan,
And he called his sons Salâma, Selîm, and Suleyman.

Salâma was a sailor in the days of the great rain;
With donkeys, doves, and dragons he prayed for land in vain—
He stole his master's daughter, he stole his camels twain,
And on the slopes of Ararat the tribe began again.

With all men's hands against them, their hands 'gainst every man,
Still do they rob the stranger from Tangier to Ispahan,
And guard the guest in honour, that ragged roving clan,
(But now they burn tobacco—and powder when they can)
And name their sons Salâma, Selîm, and Suleyman.

In the last and longest Autumn, when the earth's turn comes to die,
All the woods and harvests withered, all the seas and rivers dry,
Vast and dim shall spread the desert, not a sound and not a cry,
With a pale sun hardly shining, in a cold and cloudless sky.

Through the dust that once was cities, over sand where rivers ran,
Camel-bells shall tinkle faintly, of the world's last caravan.
Searching yet for vanished footsteps, stalks Salâma in the van;
Next him, chiding on the camels, laden down with pot and pan,
Follows greybeard Father Sâlem, last Selîm and Suleyman.

G. W. MURRAY.

TABLE OF CONTENTS

CHAPTER		PAGE
	PREFACE	v
	INTRODUCTION	1

PART I

I THE DESERT IN ANCIENT TIMES 7
The Dessication—Hamitic Africa—The "Troglodytes"—Early Semitic Arrivals—The Pharaohs' Hunt for Gold—The Hyksos—The Hebrews—The Libyan Invasion—Ptolemaic Trade Routes—Roman Patrols—Nature of the Northern Littoral—The Blemmyes—The Arab contrasted with the African Bedouin.

II THE ARAB INVASION 24
The Conquest of Egypt—The Yemenites and Ishmaelites—The Invasion of North Africa—The Berbers—Warfare with the Beja—The Beni Hilal and Beni Suleim—'Aidhab—The Bedouins in the Middle Ages—Return of the Arabs from the West—Muhammad 'Ali and the Bedouins—Present-day Conditions.

PART II

III THE TRIBE 35
Composition of a Tribe—Pedigrees—The Food-Covenant—Adoption—Communism within the Tribe—Vassals—Outcasts—*Hiteim*—Inter-tribal Relations—Power of the Sheikh—Tribal Brands—Disputes about the Right to Hire Camels

IV LIFE IN THE TENTS 48
Childhood—Young Girls—Status of Women—Relics of "Mother-right" — Slavery — Hospitality — Occupations—Song and Dance—Medicine among the Arabs—Dress—Weapons—The Tent—Its Furniture—The Beja Hut.

V FOOD 85
Food always eaten in Common—Men and Women feed apart—Baking Bread—Bread from the Seed of Wild Plants—Meat—Expedients in Time of Famine—Food Taboos.

VI DOMESTIC ANIMALS 93
No Trace of former Totems—Possible former Belief that Animals contained the Souls of the Dead—Milk Customs—Sheep—Goats—Dogs—Horses—Saddles—Donkeys.

TABLE OF CONTENTS

CHAPTER		PAGE
VII	THE CAMEL	103

The Camel unknown in Ancient Egypt—Its value to the Bedouin—Regarded as almost Human by the Pagan Arabs—Not a Totemic Animal—Points of a good Camel—Its Intelligence—Camels as Draught Animals—Its Dentition—Names applied to it at Different Ages—Time it can go without Watering—Racing on Camels—Different Breeds of Camels—Anecdote of the Zareiqa—Camel Saddles.

VIII THE CHASE 117

Tracking—Leopards and Cheetahs—Catching Hyenas—Ibex-hunting with Dogs—Walking down a Gazelle—The Wheel-trap—Wild Sheep—Addax—The Wild Boar—The Wild Ass—Ostrich-hunting—Hare-hunting—Catching Quail—Falconry.

IX RAIDING AND WARFARE 133

The Bedouin Arabs A Nation—Organization of a Raid—Office of the *'Aqid*—Antiquity of Raiding—Raid of the Blemmyes on Tor—Warfare of the Towara and the Ma'aza—Raid of the 'Ababda on the Beni Wasil—Raid of the 'Atawna on the 'Ababda—Battles of Meisa and Murrat—Battle of Tor—Raid of the Haweitat on the Muzeina.

PART III

X BELIEFS 149

Allah—Welis and Sanctuaries—Jinn—*Umm el-Gheith*—Sacred Stones—Relics of a Serpent Cult—Sacred Trees—Divination—The Bedouin Calendar—Lucky and Unlucky Days—Names of Stars.

XI RITES AND CEREMONIES 168

Rites de Passage—Pregnancy—Birth—Naming—Circumcision—Hair and Hair Sacrifice—Marriage—Burial Cairns—Customs connected with Blood—Vestiges of Christianity among the Beja.

XII THE LAW OF BLOOD-VENGEANCE 200

Preliminary Remarks—Their Law only a Civil Code—Individuals not recognized—Blood-revenge usually a Private Affair—The *Diya* or Blood-money—A Sinai Blood-revenge—Surrender of the Homicide to the Dead Man's Relations.

XIII LAWS OF THE TENT AND OF WOMEN . . . 212

The Law of the Tent—The *Dakhîl*—The Tent as Sanctuary—Possible origin of This—Refusal to Enter a Tent an Insult—The Story of the *Marqub*—Rape—Abduction—Adultery—Divorce.

TABLE OF CONTENTS

CHAPTER		PAGE
XIV	LEGAL PROCEDURE	227

The Judge as a Consultant—Rules of Evidence—The Oath—The *Mubasha'*—Judgment—Assessment of Wounds—The Guardian—Inheritance—Recovery of Debt—Taking Camels without Leave—Flotsam and Jetsam.

PART IV

| XV | ARABS OF SINAI AND THE EASTERN DESERT . . | 243 |

'Ayaida — Badara — Haweitat — Laheiwat — Masa'id — Arabs of Qatia—Suwarka—Terabin—Tiyaha—Towara—The Jebeliya or Serfs of the Monastery—The Ma'aza of Egypt—Hiteim.

| XVI | THE WESTERN BEDOUIN (EL-MUGHARBA) . . | 271 |

General Remarks—The Arab and the Libyan—The Sa'adi Tribes and the Murabitin — Bedouins of the Northern Littoral—Awlad 'Ali—Jawabis—Jumei'at—Samalus—Shiheibat.

| XVII | BEDOUIN SETTLED IN THE NILE VALLEY . . | 284 |

'Abs — 'Afeinat — 'Amayim — 'Aqeila — 'Atiyat — Awlad Suleiman—Bahja—Baraghith—Bar'asa—Beni 'Una—Beni Wasil—Billi—Dhu'afa—Fawakhir—Fawayid—Ferjan—Fezara—Hanadi—Harabi—Hawara—Hawata—Hawazma — Ja'afira — Jebeliya — Jahama — Jawazi — Juheina — Luzd — Mugharba — Mujabara — Qadadfa — Qat'an — Tarhuna.

| XVIII | THE BEJA . . . . | 301 |

General Remarks—The Beja a Relic of the Earliest Invaders of the Nile Valley—The 'Ababda—The Hamedorab.

	PEDIGREE OF THE 'ABABDA	302
XIX	EPILOGUE	309
APPENDIX	WESTERN DESERT LAW	313

The Bloodwit—Difference between Intentional and Unintentional Killing—Killing of or by a Woman—Distribution of the Bloodwit—Taking Refuge (*Nazala*)—Outlawry—Oath to be taken when Evidence is Lacking—Killing of a Mediator—Killing of a Thief—Killing of an Adulterer—Slaying by Contrivance—Instigation of Murder—Slaying by a Minor—Slaying of a Relative—Neglect of a Guest—Responsibility of a Host—Death in Prison—Death from Fright—Causing Miscarriage—Overlaying—Slaying by or of a Dangerous Animal—Rape—Assessment of Wounds—False Evidence—Stealing—Civil Claims—Land.

| INDEX | . . . . | 329 |

LIST OF ILLUSTRATIONS

Plates

		FACING PAGE
	Arab of South Sinai	*Frontispiece*
I	Sinai Scenery	8
II	Mountains of the Eastern Desert	16
III	Young Sinai Girls	48
IV	Sinai Maidens	54
V	'Ababda Types	56
VI	Arab Types	62
VII	Beja Dancing	64
VIII	Arab with *Kefiya* and '*Uqal*	70
IX	Arab Woman's Mask (*Burqu'*)	72
X	Arab Tents	80
XI	The Beja Hut	86
XII	Camels	104
XIII	'Ababda Youths	118
XIV	Etbai Scenery	120
XV	Arab of the 'Aleiqat	136
XVI	Sheikh Zeidan Mudakhil	144
XVII	Tombs of Saints	152
XVIII	Jebeliya Woman Unveiled	168
XIX	Coiffure of the Beja	182
XX	Sheikh 'Ilwani's *Harim*	184
XXI	Cairns	198
XXII	Sheikh Mudakhil Suleiman	208
XXIII	Sinai Women	224
XXIV	An Old Ma'aza	240
XXV	Young Arab of the Towara	248
XXVI	Young Arab of the 'Aleiqat	256
XXVII	Sheikhs of the Muzeina	264
XXVIII	Arab of the Rashaida (Hiteim)	270
XXIX	Jumei'at Types	280
XXX	Bisharin Types	296
XXXI	A Bishari	304

LIST OF ILLUSTRATIONS

IN THE TEXT

FIG.		PAGE
1	Arrival of the Aamu	15
2	The *Rababa*	63
3	The *Holal*	74
4	Beja Sword and Scabbard	77
4a	Bishari Spear	77
5	Beja Daggers	79
6	Sinai Camel-stick	80
7	Beja Head-rest	82
8	Sinai Tobacco Pipe	84
9	The Escape from the Tiyaha	115
10	The "Wheel-trap"	122

MAPS

Egypt	4
Arab Tribes of Sinai	247
Bedouin Tribes in Northern Egypt	285
Desert Wells	312

WORKS FREQUENTLY CITED

Quoted as

BATES, O. *The Eastern Libyans* . . . . . . Bates
BLACKMAN, W. S. *The Fellahin of Upper Egypt*, London, 1927. Blackman
BURCKHARDT, J. L. *Notes on the Bedouins and Wahabys*,
   London, 1830 . . . . *Notes*
—— *Travels in Nubia*, London, 1819 . . . . *Nubia*
—— *Travels in Syria and the Holy Land*, London, 1822 . *Syria*
BURTON, R. F. *Pilgrimage to Al Madinah and Mecca*,
   Memorial Edition, 1893 . . . . . . *Pilgrimage*
DOUGHTY, C. *Arabia Deserta*, London, 1926 . . . Doughty
DUMREICHER, A. *Trackers and Smugglers in the Deserts of
   Egypt*, London, 1931 . . . . . . Dumreicher
IBN BATTUTA. *Travels in Asia and Africa* (H. A. R. Gibb's
   Translation), London, 1929 . . . . . Ibn Battuta
IBN KHALDUN. *History of the Berbers* (ed. de Slane), Algiers,
   1852–6 . . . . Ibn Khaldun
JARVIS, C. S. *Yesterday and To-day in Sinai*, London, 1931 . Jarvis
JAUSSEN, A. *Coutumes des Arabes au Pays de Moab*, Paris, 1908 Jaussen
KENNETT, A. *Bedouin Justice*, Cambridge, 1925 . . . Kennett
KLUNZINGER, C. B. *Upper Egypt*, London, 1878 . . . Klunzinger
MACMICHAEL, H. A. *A History of the Arabs in the Sudan*,
   Cambridge, 1922 . . . . MacMichael
MUNZINGER, W. *Ostafrikanische Studien*, Schaffhausen, 1863 Munzinger
MUSIL, A. *The Manners and Customs of the Rwala Bedouins*,
   New York, 1928 . . . . *Rwala*
NA'UM BEY SHUQEIR. *Tarikh Sina wa'l 'Arab*, Cairo, 1916 Shuqeir
ROBERTSON SMITH, W. *Kinship and Marriage in Early Arabia*,
   Cambridge, 1885 . . . . *Kinship*
ROBINSON, E. *Researches in Palestine*, vol. i, London, 1841 . Robinson
SELIGMAN, C. G. *Some Aspects of the Hamitic Problem in
   the Anglo-Egyptian Sudan*, *JRAI*, xliii, 1913 . . . Hamites

SONS OF ISHMAEL

INTRODUCTION

" What, unless biological science is a mass of errors, is the cause of human intelligence and vigour ? Hardship and freedom."—The Time Machine.

THROUGHOUT this book the name " Bedouin " is used as a translation of the Arabic word *badawy* meaning " inhabitant of the desert ". Just as the title " sailor " should be reserved for a blue-water mariner, so " Bedouin " ought really to be kept for one who travels or resides on the true desert itself, while all those numerous gipsy-like vagabonds who hang round the outskirts of the cultivation and live by blackmailing the peasants or stealing from them, should be looked down upon as longshore men, beachcombers, anything you please except the real article.

Merely to inhabit a desert demands much skill, craft in both senses of the word, some experience and a lot of travel. There, one must " do, not be ", so " Bedouin " conveys rather the idea of a profession or trade. It has nothing to do with race, and is by no means synonymous with " Arab ", which should signify an inhabitant of, or immigrant from, Arabia, whether Bedouin or not.

In Egypt, and indeed throughout North Africa, there are numerous true Bedouin tribes of purely African (Hamitic) stock, such as Beja, Berber, Tuareg, to whom the term " Arab " is often misapplied.

That, in remote times (pre-historic in the fullest sense of the word) these early Semites and Hamites may have had a common origin and culture [1] is reasonably probable. Again, of the two, the Hamites are presumably the closer to the southern Indo-Europeans, but the cradle-lands of all of them are still unknown. Egypt is their meeting ground, and the circumstances of desert life have preserved for us considerable samples of the two races, still hardly emerging from their

---

[1] Elliot Smith says, " But the modern Arab . . . and wandering Bedouin, who make their way into Egypt, present so close a likeness to the Proto-Egyptian racial type that it would be a matter of some difficulty to distinguish between their osseous remains." *The Ancient Egyptians,* 86.

primitive cultures of the late Stone Age. When one compares the manners and customs of the two, item by item, much is discovered common to both, that has not been superimposed from outside. Also, residuals remain which may aid in the closer definitions of the original Hamitic and Semitic cultures. For our Bedouins (allowing for Armenoid admixture) are the yet living ancestors of some of the most civilized races, Egyptians, Arabs, and Jews, and so deserve a much more detailed and critical study than I have been able to achieve here.

The material is herewith presented as a set of parallel analyses of their cultures and beliefs, pointing out step by step where they agree or disagree. A brief description of each tribe by itself follows in which some repetition becomes inevitable.

History largely fails in dealing with these nomads, and they wander so widely that geography is of little moment, I have therefore contented myself with the briefest of notes on the latter subject as introduction. Though eked out from classical sources, the account is, of course, almost restricted to descriptions of customs current at the present day, or within the memory of those now living. My own knowledge of these people extends over more than twenty-five years in time, and I have derived much valuable assistance from those like Jennings Bramly Bey of much greater experience.

By the end of my book, if he wade so far, I hope the reader will be able not only to visualize the people, their appearance and their actions, but also in some measure to be able to think with a mind like theirs, if he wants to. A Bedouin mind, though certainly unimaginative, is a possession not to be despised, and the Sherifs of Mecca used regularly to send their children to the black tents to acquire one. For a nomad's thoughts are of altogether different quality to those of a peasant, just as the peasant's differ from the townsman's. Civilized man is for ever straining after unattainable ideals, while varying those ideals pretty rapidly. Divine discontent is the poetical name for the dæmon that drives him, and he is always imperfect and unhappy. A sphere, where all the laws have been made, all the useful knowledge attained, and all the inhabitants perfectly adapted to live and move therein, may appear to him fossilized and tiresome. Life may only vary in the desert from the monotonous to the macabre; yet retreat there has been fashionable since the days of

St. Anthony. Hermits need not immure themselves within four walls, monasteries may be of the spirit and the whole wide desert may serve as a *laura* in which the twentieth century can contemplate some of its remote predecessors. Even if that spectacle be not altogether edifying, yet the struggle against nature always invigorates. The Bedouin has none of those fears of the dark ; of being alone ; of wide spaces, that disgrace the peasant. Rather does he err in the other extreme and is afraid to sleep below a roof. His highest ideal of co-operation is the pack controlled by a leader ; the herd influenced by a panic seems his natural prey. In the last resort when the fires of the world burn low, the Bedouin-minded will be found to survive the peasants or the town dwellers.

Moreover it has been said that the noblest thing about man is that he can contemplate his own extinction with equanimity. That problem is often forced upon his attention at sea, on high mountains, and in the desert.

Something (as little as possible) must now be said of the scene, for the prejudice has to be fought down that our desert is wholly composed of sand, gravel, and scattered oases. Were this really so, there would be few Bedouin for me to write about and no book, for the listless oasis-dwellers, poor-spirited from isolation and malaria, are in no way nomadic, and so fall outside the scope of this essay. South of the narrow littoral where rain falls, the western desert of Egypt, which Herodotus named Libyan, must plead guilty to the arraignment. It is even duller to travel over than to write about. But the coastal belt has a beauty of its own in its skies and its wild flowers, and there, before each capricious winter rainfall, some forty thousand almost sedentary Arabs hopefully sow a scanty barley crop. This district, the Marmarica of the Romans, is dotted with thousands of large cisterns cut into the rock in ancient times, and the clearing out and re-cementing of these will certainly allow a larger area to be brought again under cultivation.

South of the barley belt, a limestone plateau extends for forty or fifty miles till it falls away in the bold cliffs bordering the northern edge of the great Qattara depression. In spring, there is sometimes grazing for the camels of the Arabs on this steppe ; in summer it is deserted.

SONS OF ISHMAEL

At the foot of the cliffs, stretches the lifeless Qattara depression, seven thousand square miles of scrub and mud-flat, all below sea-level. Southwards again there is nothing but the pitiless waste of the Sahara. Leaving the five oases buried in desolation, let us fly hurriedly to the east.

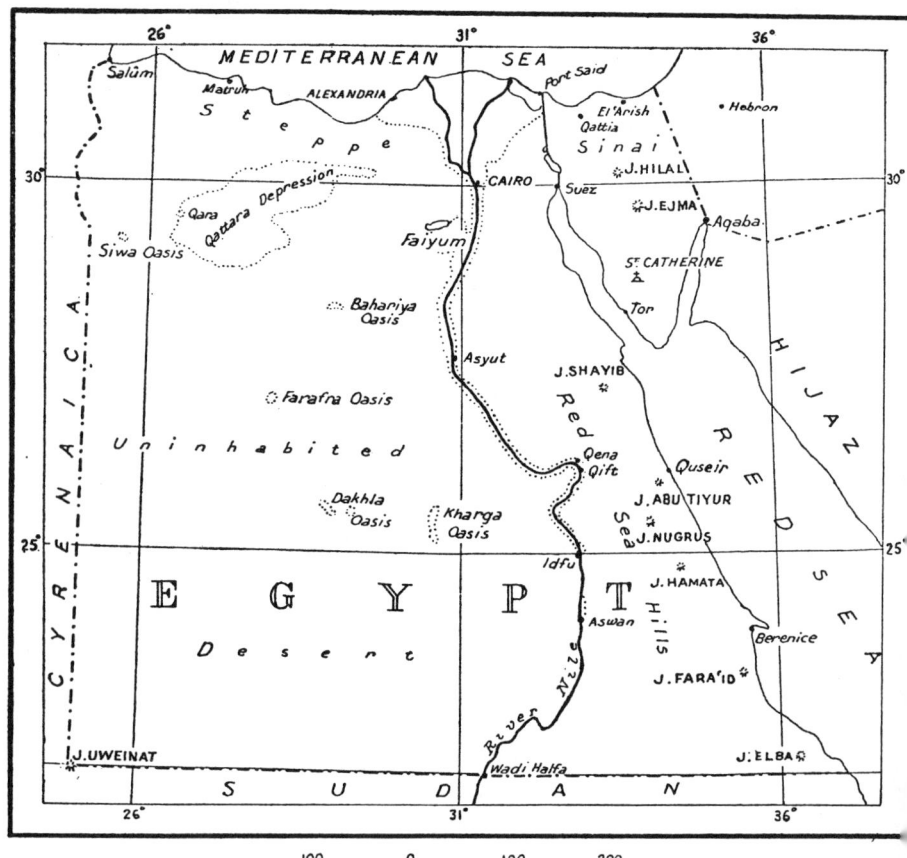

The first surprise is the Nile. It comes as a shock to see a great river, with a thin fringe of palm trees, rolling through such a solitude, while the desert below now begins to be streaked with valleys. For immediately to the east of the river, the country rises abruptly into plateaux, limestone in the north and sandstone in the south. Unlike the Libyan Desert, where the wind has generally eroded all traces of the former drainage lines, this eastern wilderness

INTRODUCTION

is dissected deeply. At rare intervals, wells and waterholes occur in the wadi-floors making travel possible.

But the glory of the Eastern Desert is the mountain range that fences it off from the sea, the African Cordillera.

Just inside the extreme south-east corner, where the Sudan frontier reaches the coast, rise the Elba mountains green with verdure, in vivid contrast to the thousands of square miles of waterless desert which ring them round. Here lies the stronghold of the fuzzy-headed Bisharin, full of legend and mystery, where Kuka, their ancestor sits turned to stone in a cave that no European has ever seen.

From the highest pinnacle of wooded Elba, the eye travels over the desert north of the audacious peaks of Berenice's Bodkin and the Mons Pentadactylus, now Jebel Fara'id, on the tropic of Cancer. On their northern horizon lies the rose-red whaleback of Hamata, who stares in turn at the fin on the back of his brother leviathan Nugrus, only fifty miles away. Nugrus sees the small jagged peak of Abu Tiyur near Quseir, once the only town between Suez and Suakin. Little Abu Tiyur looks humbly towards the vast Shayib, 7,200 feet, the highest hill in Egypt, whose glance ranges over two hundred miles from the Nile at Qena to the chapel-crowned St. Catherine above the Convent of Mount Sinai, across the Gulf of Suez. St. Catherine sees the flat-topped Jebel 'Ejma and 'Ejma looks north again to Hilal. Hilal stares over the frontier to the same green hills of Hebron that Joshua and Caleb spied out in the Promised Land.

Nine eyeshots thus cover the whole seven hundred miles and a great breadth beside. So eight Bedouin shepherds, four Arab and four African, might see all that is worth seeing in our Eastern Desert and Sinai, but some of them would have to climb hard to gain their eyries.

Sinai, in its northern moiety, is yet another limestone plateau sloping gradually to the Mediterranean from a bold salient escarpment called the Tih, facing south. Here, owing to the greater altitude, more rain falls than in the low country west of Alexandria. Near the coast and the Suez Canal, lies a good deal of sand, and in numerous places the wind has scooped out these dunes down to the subsoil water-level, so that in the hollows grow large groves of date-palms. There is some population at Qatia, and more at El-'Arish, where the great wadi of that name " the river of Egypt ", reaches the Mediterranean.

PART I

Chapter I
THE DESERT IN ANCIENT TIMES

" I hold rather that the Egyptians did not come into being with the making of that which Ionians call the Delta; they ever existed since men were first made; and as the land grew in extent many of them spread down over it, and many stayed behind."—Herodotus.

The Desiccation—Hamitic Africa—The "Troglodytes"—Early Semitic Arrivals—The Pharaohs' Hunt for Gold—The Hyksos—The Hebrews—The Libyan Invasion—Ptolemaic Trade Routes—Roman Patrols—Nature of the Northern Littoral—The Blemmyes—The Arab contrasted with the African Bedouin.

"Happy are those nations that have no history," and history in the desert does not gallop, but crawls at a camel's pace. Whole centuries pass without events. Yet to those who can wait long enough things happen even in the desert, and if we accelerate our magic carpet sufficiently in time, more may be seen than an interminable series of petty raids for camels.

For climate is subject to variations, periodic rather than annual, and round a desert which is not absolutely sterile, a succession of only two or three years with rain may produce alarming consequences. Then the neighbouring cultivators are suddenly assailed by vast clouds of locusts, immeasurably more numerous than the trivial swarms of the year before, and, in a twinkling, ruin takes the place of plenty. A far more dangerous situation comes about when a generation of good years is succeeded by a period of drought. Sooner or later an explosion, only to be likened to that of a volcano, results and the desert discharges floods, not indeed of lava, but of fierce nomads not to be withstood by anything less than the strength of a militant civilization.

Such a vent of racial dispersion exists in the Arabian peninsula, dormant for the moment, and the former existence of others in the Sahara may be inferred from the widespread litter of Hamitic languages and cults which they have spewed all over Africa. (Indeed, until quite lately, the "Green

Mountain" (Jebel Akhdar) behind Derna in Cyrenaica represented a pretty active little crater of this kind).

Northern Egypt must then have resembled the present Negeb of Southern Palestine, where chalky hills covered with dwarf oak and scrub rise from broad plains of alluvium, rich with grass after the winter rain, but in summer, dry, dusty, and subject to aerial erosion.

In Southern Egypt the limestone gives place to sandstone, and here, in Palæolithic and Neolithic days, a great natural frontier ran right across Africa, busy with "factories" where the more fortunate flint-owning races of Middle Egypt and Cyrenaica probably traded hand-axes and scrapers with the even less civilized tribes of Nubia and Inner Libya.

Ten to fifteen thousand years ago, rain very gradually ceased to fall on the low-lying parts away from the coasts, desert conditions began to spread little by little and presently, urged by the north-westerly gales, the long parallel lines of dunes which now streak the Libyan Desert set out on their long march from the Qattara Swamps to the oases at a glacier-crawl of less than ten yards a year.

East and west of the Nile, the grass and scrub slowly vanished, the trees withered, the game migrated, and the cattlemen and hunters deserted the drying plains for the marshes of the Nile Valley, which until then they had looked upon as rather dangerously full of elephants, lions, and the like.

The last desert areas to be abandoned were, curiously enough, those most inaccessible to-day—the sheets and rolling dunes of sand which, unlike the gravel, retained something of the scanty rainfall.[1] These are dotted to-day with the grinding stones and spearheads left by the men of the past.

Down in the valley they took to cultivation and fishing, and were soon cankered with the beginnings of civilization. For the noble and lazy nomad may turn into an industrious *fellah*, but he can never turn back. Hardihood to support starvation, thirst, the fatigue of travel, the hammer-blows of the sun, the blasts of the sandstorm is not acquired in one but many generations. The Bedouins of to-day are the unspoilt descendants of Ishmael; their blood is pure.

[1] "For many months of every year in the rainy season these wide sand-belts of Arabia are the home of the tenting Badawin and their flocks and herds: they contain the whole secret of nomad life, for nowhere are the pastures richer than in their folds, and without them the pastoral life of the Arabs would be impossible." Philby, *The Heart of Arabia*, 149.

Plate I

Mount Sinai (Jebel Musa)

Wadi Gharba

SINAI SCENERY

So the upland plains were abandoned to the wind, now laden with sand, which soon removed every vestige of soil from the surface. Only such mammals as were adapted to rainless conditions remained : the wild ass, gazelle, ibex, Barbary sheep, addax and oryx antelope, ostrich, and cheetah. All these, except perhaps the oryx, survived to within human memory; while the giraffe, which can live several months without drinking, visited the southern deserts in good years. The leopard, a hill-animal, is gone from Egypt, but haunts the mountain peaks of Sinai.

Some remnants of this former abundant Saharan fauna lingered long ; the elephant survived in the Atlas till Roman times and dwarf crocodiles are still found from time to time in the wadis of Air and Ahaggar. Fish of the genus *Cyprinodon* occur in the Khor Arba'at near Port Sudan, the lakes of Siwa Oasis, and, in Algeria, in the oasis of Zab and the Wadi Gir. I have seen toads in the Egyptian oases and also in Jebel Asotriba just south of the Egypto-Sudan frontier.

Some early rock-drawings of elephants near Aswan have been weathered to the same colour as the rock on which they were hammered out and may perhaps date back to a wetter period.[1] But after the final setting-in of the great drought, there is abundant proof that the climate of Egypt has remained virtually unchanged throughout the whole historic period. For, near Aswan in the same region as the rock-drawings mentioned above, the Archæological Survey of Nubia discovered pre-dynastic bodies perfectly preserved by the dry sand alone without artificial aids, while in Sinai the First Dynasty inscription of Semerkhet at Jebel Maghara (in very soft sandstone) " does not appear in the least weathered since it was cut ". These relics of the past would not have come down to us at all, if there had been regular rainfall at any time during the last five thousand years. Again in the days of Rameses II, a lack of water in the desert led to the temporary abandonment of the gold-mines; while to make another great leap through the centuries, Strabo records as a marvel " that it rained in Upper Egypt in his time ".

Until the completion of this desiccation, so remote in time by ordinary standards, though really quite late in the long history of the human race, the whole of North Africa

---

[1] G. W. Murray and O. H. Myers, " Some Pre-dynastic Rock-Drawings," *JEA.*, xix, 129-132.

with the Arabian peninsula must have formed one great grassland or steppe, roamed over by intensely nomadic families of hunters and herdsmen following the rainfall like the animals they tamed or slew.

Even at this early stage, they could not have been wholly homogeneous; the more active plainsmen must have soon become differentiated from the stay-at-home mountainfolk, just as elsewhere the ship-owning people sailed right away into a different culture from the timid fish-eaters of the coast. But most of their skulls exhibit an extreme dolichocephaly, and all their languages which survive to-day are of the same type, Hamitic. Of this, the Semitic family, important as it is, seems to be only a later specialized group.

With the gradual intensification of the drought, their mass movements became more and more restricted, and the tribes began to solidify into races; while the hardening of the conditions under which they lived so sharpened their wits, that the progressive families, who settled in the rich valleys hitherto avoided on account of the wild beasts they contained, soon began to cultivate.

Two racial groups began to form; the "Arabs", isolated between the Nile and the Euphrates, who had been influenced by the "Armenoids", a hook-nosed race from the north-east, and the "Libyans" of the Sahara who became tinged to a darker hue with negro blood in the south, and whitened along the coast as the result of European inroads.[1]

Everywhere some of the more conservative, inspired with a native distrust of the nascent civilizations of the valleys and a deepseated passion for personal liberty, coupled with a contempt for any possessions that might hamper their freedom, held to the high desert at all costs, where their equally conservative descendants of to-day still attempt the simple life of their forefathers. They were not yet in possession of the camel, but if their humble ass was not exactly a ship of the desert, he was certainly a most serviceable beast. "Donkeys and determination" had to be their motto, and, since the donkey is not an animal on which to carry out raids, they must perforce have abstained from the organized plunder of their more industrious neighbours. Later on, when the horse came in, the Egyptian quadrilateral became a desert stronghold,

---

[1] The acute mind of Herodotus may have intended to make this racial distinction when he christened the deserts east and west of the Nile (not the Red Sea) Arabian and Libyan respectively.

THE DESERT IN ANCIENT TIMES

protected on the north by the wellnigh impregnable Delta, on the east by the Red Sea, and on the west by the dunes. Certainly it was open to invasion from the Sudan down the Nile, yet the gateway there is so well guarded by art and nature that it has only once been forced—in the twenty-fifth Dynasty. But, however strong its walls, this Egyptian fortress was exposed at every corner to bold raids from the hills beyond the desert.

At different times, Libyans burst in upon the Nile Valley from the "Green Mountain" in Cyrenaica ; Nubians from the hills of Darfur took possession of the cataracts ; while wave upon wave of Ethiopians chased each other north-westwards from the mountains of Abyssinia. All these were North African races, even if mixed with foreign blood, and their raids and incursions made little physical and cultural difference. But the foreign invasions from the north-east were of vastly greater importance. All Egypt fell a prey to the Hyksos at the end of the Twelfth Dynasty ; while in the seventh century of the Christian era, the Arabs made a lasting conquest and stamped their language and religion not only upon Egypt, but upon all North Africa.

The neolithic ancestors of the Egyptians left nothing behind them on the surface but their implements of stone, wrought from chert and flint in the north ; from quartz, quartzite, sandstone, slate, and various igneous rocks in the south. West of the Nile, rock-paintings discovered by Count Almasy at Jebel 'Uweinat, show a chocolate-coloured race, with a taste for steatopygy in their women, owning cattle and armed with the bow. The climate of 'Uweinat must have permitted their survival down to dynastic times, for one of the chiefs is depicted smiting his enemy in true Pharaonic style. Yet Miss Caton Thompson found no trace of dynastic remains in Kharga prior to the twenty-seventh Dynasty.[1]

East of the Nile in the Red Sea hills, a scanty rainfall has enabled a race resembling the pre-dynastic Egyptians to remain to our times,[2] in spite of repeated Arab invasions. These are the Beja tribes of 'Ababda, Bisharin, Hadendawa, and Beni 'Amir ; the middle two speaking a Hamitic language

---

[1] G. Caton Thompson, *Man*, June, 1932. A stela of the Libyan Twenty-Second Dynasty has been found in Dakhla.
[2] G. W. Murray, "The Northern Beja," *JRAI.*, lvii, 39–53.

akin to those spoken by the Masai of East Africa, the Shilh of Morocco, the Guanche of the Canary Islands and the Hottentots of South Africa.[1]

The discovery of a pre-dynastic burial on the Red Sea coast [2] shows that these Hamites were there from a very early date.

The earliest known inhabitants of the Nile Valley itself, the " Badarians " and their Proto-Egyptian successors, were men of short stature and slender build ; their hair was dark and curly, yet by no means " woolly " ; there was a short tuft of beard beneath their chins, and their skulls were long, narrow, and " coffin-shaped " with a prominence of the occiput at the back of the head. In all these characteristics they resembled the modern Beja east of the Nile.

Various survivals, which can only be referred to a period when a common " Hamitic " culture existed over all North-East Africa, have been exposed by diligent research, particularly among the warlike Masai and kindred tribes of the south. A mode of circumcision, a peculiar type of bow, the " wheel-trap ", a method of time-reckoning and the foppish care lavished on the male coiffure, all establish some connection between these modern peoples and the Ancient Egyptians or their neighbours ; while the remarkable discovery of two wooden arm-clamps, such as the Masai warriors wear to-day, was made by the Archæological Survey of Nubia in an undisturbed grave of early dynastic date at Shellal. We can therefore safely assume that the early Badarian and pre-dynastic cultures of Upper Egypt were purely African.[3]

A vague memory, too, seems to have lingered among some of the Egyptians that their ancestors had come from Punt (Eritrea or Somaliland), or some country adjacent thereto. For the name Punt was usually written without the sign which designated a foreign country, and most significantly the natives of Punt are depicted as wearing the curious plaited beard turned up at the end, which the Egyptians of the First Dynasty had worn, and which later was usually associated with the gods and the dead who had become deified.

But not all of the forty-odd tribes who settled in the

---

[1] C. Meinhof, *Die Sprachen der Hamiten*.
[2] G. W. Murray and D. E. Derry, *Man*, Sept., 1923.
[3] For a summary of all this evidence see " Modern Survivors from Punt ", by H. Frankfort and " Egyptian Influence in Negro Africa ", by C. G. Seligman, both essays in *Studies Presented to F. Ll. Griffith*.

valley and founded the nomes of Egypt are likely to have been homogeneous. No doubt the then inhabitants of the western half of the Delta resembled the Libyans, as they do to-day, and the easterners the Arabs. For on the celebrated slate palette of the protodynastic King Narmer, a hook-nosed " Armenoid " native is seen running away, and another protodynastic palette shows booty from " Tehen " (Libya), oxen, asses, sheep, and trees.

Some of the early inhabitants of the Egyptian deserts were known to the Ancient Egyptians by the name of ʽ*antiu* or ʽ*anu*, often mistranslated " Troglodytes ".[1] This word ʽ*anu* was probably only a general term for " Bedouin ", for the Libyans were sometimes called ʽ*anu-Tehennu*, yet it was commonly employed to designate the aquiline " Armenoid " race whose descendants have so greatly altered the population of northern Africa. A First Dynasty representation of a desert-man from near the First Cataract depicts him as one of these ʽ*anu* or Arabs, and so too Semerkhet, a Pharaoh of the same dynasty, is shown smiting an ʽ*anu* at Jebel Maghara in Sinai, and taking away his spear ; the first recorded blow in a long Hamito-Semitic conflict that was later carried on between the Arabs and the ʽAbabda down to our father's time.

Other early undated people on the Sudan frontier buried oxen in graves [2] and set up sacred monoliths, just such pillars as were abominated by the early Hebrews. These kinsmen the Egyptians left behind in the Eastern Desert were peaceful on the whole. Few in numbers, roaming over vast solitudes, they seem to have offered no opposition to the gold-hunting Pharaohs of the Old and Middle Kingdoms ; in the words of Strabo, " they were neither numerous nor warlike, but were accounted so by the ancients, because they attacked travellers." [3]

This primitive race, of whom the mountain ʽAbabda and Beni ʽAmir of to-day are survivors, has remained uncontaminated in the Eastern Desert, down to the present day.

Pepi I, a king of the Sixth Dynasty, about 2375 B.C. dispatched an expedition against the *Heriu-sha* or " sand-dwellers ", who must have inhabited the North Sinai coast,

---

[1] The word has nothing to do with caves but seems to refer to a special sort of bow.
[2] G. W. Murray, *JEA.*, xii, 248–9.
[3] *Strabo*, xvii, 53.

and against the *Aamu*.[1] Later, in the time of Pepi II of the same dynasty, the Aamu murdered an official called Enenkhet on the Red Sea coast while he was building ships for a voyage to Punt.[2] What these *Aamu* were like is known exactly from some paintings in a Twelfth Dynasty tomb, about 1900 B.C., at Beni Hasan, where thirty-seven *Aamu* are shown bringing tribute to the Governor of the White Oryx Nome.

Their chief's title and name is given as Absha, " prince of the desert," a title used afterwards by the Hyksos. He is depicted as leading a tame ibex, and Petrie says of him,

> " The Chief's face is obviously Semitic, being closely like that of the Bedawin of the present day ; the narrow line of beard down the jaw, rising toward the corner of the mouth and then sloping away to the chin, the long aquiline nose, and the general expression are all familiar in the Arab face " . . . " After the chief comes a follower leading an oryx ; then four armed men with bow, boomerangs, and spears ; two children on an ass laden with rugs ; a boy with a spear ; four women gaily dressed in coloured garments, patterned with stripes, chequers, and frets ; another ass laden with baggage, a spear, and a shield ; a man with a water-skin on his back, playing a lyre ; and lastly, a bowman with a boomerang. Here is no sign of inferior civilization. The clothing is quite as much as the Egyptians used, the decoration of it is more profuse than on the Egyptian dress, the arms are the same as in Egypt, the bow and boomerang, and the spear is not common so early in Egypt ; the sandals are as good as the Egyptian pattern, and the women have socks. Though a different civilization, it is in no way inferior to the Egyptian in the arts of life which were needful to such a people." [3]

As long ago as the Twelfth Dynasty, nearly four thousand years ago, the Hamito-Semitic frontier in the Eastern Desert stood much where it does to-day, for while the artists at Beni Hasan were depicting the arrival of these hook-nosed Aamu bringing tribute, not fifty miles to the southward, a portrait of a Beja with thin nose, chin-tuft beard, and mop of hair was being inscribed on the walls of a tomb chapel at Meir.

At the close of the Middle Kingdom, a fearful storm burst upon an unprepared Egypt. The Hyksos tribes of Western Asia had realized the value in war of the horse. The raiding by one tribe of the next, when weapons are equal,

---

[1] Generally translated " Asiatics ". [2] Breasted, *Ancient Records*, i, 163.
[3] *History of Egypt*, i, 180–1.

THE DESERT IN ANCIENT TIMES

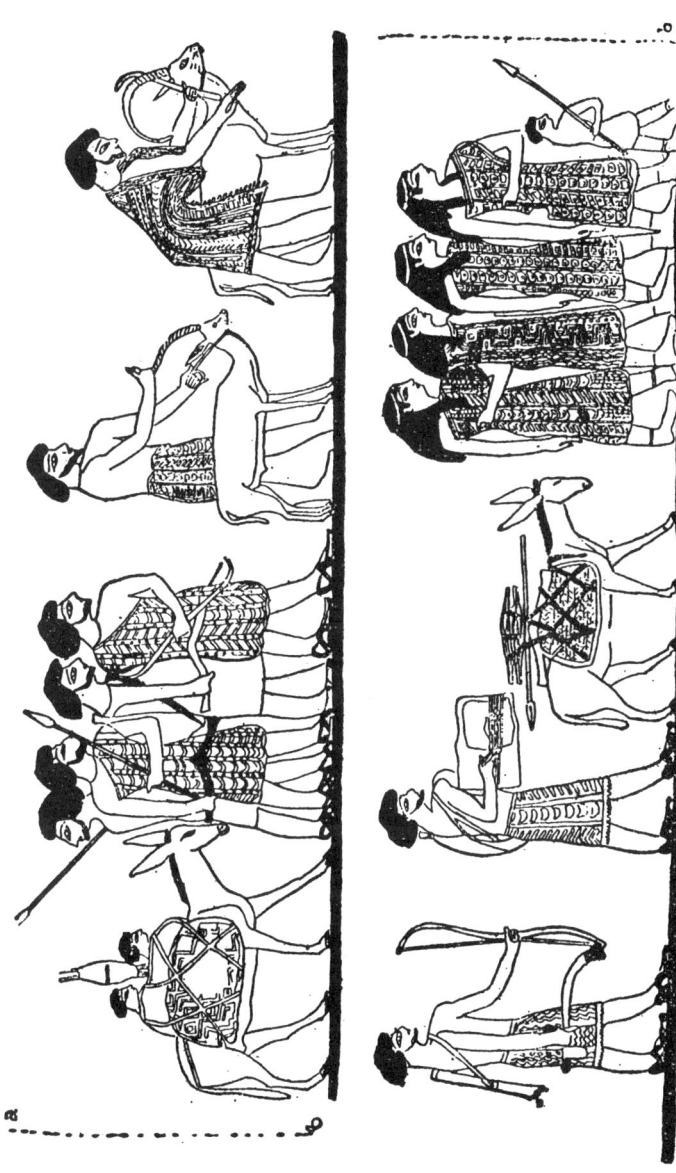

Fig. 1.—Arrival of the Aamu (after Newberry, *Beni-Hasan*, i, pl. 30).

is moderated as a rule by the fear of retaliation. But a sudden great improvement in communications may corrupt good manners, and when a tribe discovers it can raid unsuspecting people at a distance, who can't raid back, the game becomes popular. Just as wolves combine, so tribes coalesce ; nations are born, kings replace sheikhs, history is made.

Fired by dreams of easy booty, these Hyksos flooded into Egypt, and were not expelled till the Egyptians had obtained and mastered the new weapon. So the horse came to Egypt, but he has never figured largely in our desert history ; conditions were too hard for him.

The Hyksos were driven out about 1600 B.C., and the monarchs of the New Empire again exploited the Eastern Desert for gold and ornamental stones.

Sometime in this period of the New Empire, a tribe of Semitic-speaking Bedouin,[1] who had settled in Goshen, resented the arbitrary rule of the Pharaoh, and left Egypt for the land of their forefathers. Of their Exodus and their conquest of Palestine, the detailed story survives, though written from tradition long years after the events it narrates. The exact route the Hebrews followed through the peninsula of Sinai seems to have been clear to the mind of the scribe who wrote it down (though not to us).

Faithfully, too, there has been preserved for us the rigid Mosaic code, and the Hebrews' lapses from the stark new religion of Yahweh to their earlier and easier worship of stocks and stones. We possess indeed in the Pentateuch an inimitable picture of the Bedouin phase of their existence that passed away when the children of Israel crossed Jordan more than three thousand years ago.

Their exodus has been often repeated, notably in our grandfathers' days by the Hanadi, for the ebb and flow of nomads into Egypt is always going on. But the Hebrews may well claim to be the Chosen People, for never since their day has a tribe of feckless squatters from the Wadi Tumilat been moulded by events into any resemblance to the most persistent race that history has ever known. And, since the fall of Jericho, the jealous hand of Ishmael has always been lifted unsparingly against his half-brother Isaac.

During all this ebb and flow the main Western Desert

---

[1] " Semitic is a linguistic term, and cannot be used as a racial designation. The Arabs are a Semitic people, and belong to the Mediterranean race ; the Jews are a Semitic people, and belong to the eastern branch of the Alpine race."—Elliot-Smith, *Human History*, 162.

PLATE II

MOUNTAINS OF THE EASTERN DESERT

[face p. 16

THE DESERT IN ANCIENT TIMES

remained quite uninhabited, while the Mediterranean coast and the oases were peopled by a Hamitic stock, of which the ancient Egyptians recognized three or four types, though the Arabs later lumped them all together as Berbers.

1. The Tehenu, the almost sedentary population of what is now the province of Beheira and the coast. They spoke a distinct language of their own and did not share the Egyptian veneration for the cow.[1] Their modern successors have been much modified by the mediæval Arab invasions, and perhaps by earlier Semitic drifts to the westward in ancient times.

2. The Temehu, a pastoral cattle-owning race who inhabited the oases, and perhaps extended into the Northern Sudan.[2] They were slightly negroid in type but not so dark as their successors, the present Tebu, who now only occasionally visit the extreme south-west of Egypt after rain.

3. More warlike " Libyans " from further west, called Lebu or Rebu by the ancient Egyptians.

Aided by another warlike nomadic tribe from the west, the Meshwesh, and Sardinian pirates, these Libyans began to invade Egypt during the Nineteenth Dynasty, but they were vigorously repelled by Merenptah. Later, by more or less peaceful penetration one of the Meshwesh was enabled to assume the title of Pharaoh in the Twenty-second.

These nomadic swarmings into the cultivated lands after drought, too bloodless to be dignified with the title of " invasions ", are none the less terrible scourges to the fellahin. Ellsworth Huntington describes a modern one as follows :—

> " The next day at about half-past eight in the morning, one of the great desert tribes came streaming in from the south-east. Thousands and thousands of camels passed by. Far as the eye could see they stretched away into the wilderness. Scattered at intervals of one or two hundred feet they stalked by, hundreds abreast, bending their sinuous necks and sticking out their tongues to crop a bit of dry bush from ground which looked absolutely barren. For fully nine hours, till half-past four, the monster procession continued to pass. When the horses of the archæologists were taken to the pool that night, nothing remained except a muddy hollow, trampled by the feet of ten thousand camels. The beasts passed on towards Gilead and Galilee. Passing through southern Hauran, they ate the grainfields to dust, even as they had drunk the

---
[1] *Herodotus*, ii, 18.
[2] The daughter of Kashta, King of Napata *circa* 800 B.C., had the title of " Great Mistress of the Temehu ".

pool to slimy mud. The poor villagers shot at the Arabs, and then ran to their villages for shelter, much as the people of old Edrei probably did when they took refuge in their caves and passageways. Soldiers were sent to stop the Arabs, but in vain." [1]

Nor did the vaulting ambition of Sheshenq I, the founder of the Twenty-second Dynasty stop at the Nile, for we read that :

"In the fifth year of King Rehoboam (933 B.C.), Shishak, King of Egypt, came up against Jerusalem, because they had transgressed against the Lord, with twelve hundred chariots and three score thousand horsemen, and the people without number that came with him out of Egypt ; the Lubim (Libyans), the Sukkim, and the Cushim (Ethiopians)." [2]

The last may have been negro troops or perhaps Beja nomads. At any rate Sheshenq, like the great Muhammad 'Ali after him, realized the importance of Bedouin auxiliaries on a desert campaign.

Camels seem to have been introduced into Africa with the Persians about 525 B.C. and it took several centuries for the African Bedouin to realize and exploit their full military value. Meanwhile the Eastern Desert remained quiet throughout Ptolemaic times. In the pages of Agatharchides, the tutor of Ptolemy X, we may read enough about the Bedouin of his day (c. 170–100 B.C.) to see that in their pastoral lives, the lax morality of their women, their diet of milk and blood, their refusal to let their cattle die normal deaths, and their constant warfare about the grazing, they did not differ greatly from the modern Beja.

The search for gold went on and was supplemented by mining for emeralds. Elephants were found useful in war and expeditions were sent to fetch them from the Sudan coast. To protect and assist the caravans, forts and watering stations were built along the routes by Ptolemy Philadelphus, so that, at certain seasons, the desert became quite thronged with traffic. Owing to the difficulty of beating up the Red Sea against the north wind, ports had to be selected as far south as the roads to them could be guarded. First, Leukos Limen, and then Berenice were felt safe, and this Red Sea trade increased greatly when the discovery of the monsoon, about A.D. 47, enabled fleets from Berenice to trade with India.

All the harbours were connected with civilized Egypt by routes radiating out from the great bend of the Nile where Qena, Qift, and Qus were used in turn as points of departure.

[1] *Palestine and its Transformation*, 301.   [2] *Chronicles*, xii, 2, 3.

THE DESERT IN ANCIENT TIMES

Even in those days, the rainfall along the northern littoral must have been a scanty one, for the Libyans or their Græco-Roman successors cut out an elaborate system of rock-cisterns to conserve it. Thanks to their energy a chain of thriving Greek towns and villages with cultivated fields and vineyards then extended from Alexandria to Cyrene.

These cisterns are now mostly filled with silt, and nothing is left of that civilization above ground, but mounds of potsherds, and some broken pieces of statuary in the Alexandria Museum. But it died hard, and the town of St. Menas, with its great Basilica built by Arcadius, does not seem to have been destroyed till about A.D. 900.

Various arguments have been used to account for the desiccation of this country west of Alexandria since the Ptolemaic period. Slight changes in level have taken place, but these would not affect the water supply in the district away from Lake Mareotis, while I attach even less weight to the theory that the introduction of the camel has de-forested North Africa. The camel certainly came into Egypt before that period, and Alexander the Great employed them to convey his supplies on the march to Siwa. But the goat is a far more dangerous animal to young shoots than the camel; and the goat has always been there. If the rainfall of the district had not always been scanty, the ancients would not have been obliged to construct the elaborate system of cisterns in which they preserved it.

Actual records of rainfall made early in the second century A.D. by Ptolemy the geographer [1] show that the total number

[1] The exact year is unknown, but it probably falls within the period of his astronomical observations which were made A.D. 127–151*.

	Rainy days	ψακάς (mist, drizzle)	Mean at present day †
Jan.	4	1	11
Feb.	3	–	6
Mar.	–	1	5
Apr.	5	3	1
May	3	4	1
June	1	5	–
July	2	–	–
Aug.	–	–	–
Sept.	3	2	–
Oct.	4	–	1
Nov.	3	2	7
Dec.	2	2	10
Totals	30	20	42

The maximum number of rainy days during the period 1889–1922 was 65, the minimum 22.

* G. Hellmann, "Über die ägyptischen Witterungsangaben im Kalender von Claudius Ptolemæus," *Sitzungsber, d. Kgl. Preuss. Akad. d. Wiss.*, 1916, xiii.

† Mahmud Hamed, *The Climate of Alexandria* (Egyptian Physical Dept., Paper 19), Cairo, 1925.

of rainy days was then much the same as at present, but that they were more evenly distributed throughout the year.

This more even rainfall and the more industrious habits of the ancients, who did keep their cisterns in repair, seem to have permitted the settlement of places a good deal farther inland than the present narrow strip along the coast. Such former prosperity is also attested by the large Christian town of Abumina and the church of Qasr el-Qitaji, both sites well inland without permanent water-supply.

Besides the Greeks who founded Cyrene in the seventh century B.C., and thronged into Egypt with Alexander, Jewish colonists seem to have settled along the North African coast from an early date, for we hear of a Jewish revolt in A.D. 116, near Alexandria and at Cyrene, which the Romans put down with their usual iron hand. The destruction of the small temple of Isis in the desert south of Dhab'a may have taken place during this disturbance.[1]

Christian ascetics, led by Amun, began to build monasteries in Nitria (the Wadi Natrun) about A.D. 315, and we are told of a raid on them in 407 by the " Mazices ", whom R. Basset identifies with the Imazighen, a section of the Luwata Berbers.[2]

Little by little a storm was gathering. The tribes began to raid the caravans in the Eastern Desert, and the Romans recruited a camel corps (*ala dromedaria*) to protect them. Finally, just as two thousand years before the Hyksos horsemen had burst into Egypt, the Blemmye camelry came surging up from the south. Had these new invaders had only the native Egyptians to conquer, they might have repeated the success of the Hyksos, but the Romans restricted their inroads to the district south of Thebes and eventually drove the Blemmyes back beyond the First Cataract. There they settled the Nobadæ, whom they had brought in from the Great Oasis, to keep the Blemmyes out. There is a curious cartouche of the period which made M. Revilloud think that some Blemmye chieftain had been so puffed up by a temporary success that he styled himself Emperor of Rome.

The Blemmyes continued to raid both east and west of the Nile ; in the fourth century some of them used a pirated

---

[1] G. W. Murray, " A small Temple in the Western Desert," *JEA*., xvii, 1931.
[2] The Luwata are first mentioned in Justinian's time as " Leuathæ " in the neighbourhood of Leptis. In later days they produced the great traveller Ibn Battuta.

THE DESERT IN ANCIENT TIMES

vessel to raid Tor in the Sinai Peninsula, while in the fifth they dared to ravage the Great Oasis, defeat the Roman garrison, and carry off some of the inhabitants as slaves. In their retreat they were pursued by some of the Western Bedouin, the " Mazices ".

This raid led to a punitive expedition in 453, during which the general Maximinus severely defeated both Blemmyes and Nobadæ and compelled them to conclude peace for a hundred years, restore all Roman captives, pay for the damage they had done, and surrender hostages. On their side they were allowed to visit the temple of Isis at Philæ and borrow her statue at certain seasons. This treaty they promptly broke.

Egypt, however, did have peace for nearly a century, for we do not hear of the Blemmyes again till 545, when Silko, king of the Nobadæ, defeated them and drove them out of Taphis and Talmis. But in 577 the defences of Philæ had once more to be strengthened against them.

The names, but not the tribes, of the Blemmyes now vanish from the desert and soon, after the conquest of Egypt, we find the Arabs disputing the possession of the eastern gold-mines with the Beja, while leaving, for a century or two, the north coast and the oases to be raided by the Luwata from Cyrenaica.

Before proceeding to recount the details of the Arab adventure, we may usefully set down here some of the differences between the two races, Asiatic and African, that now met in conflict.

From the days of Absha there had been Arabs in Egypt. The Greeks named the eastern desert Arabia because it was out of that desert that the Arabs appeared, and villages of Arabs that had exchanged their nomadic life for a sedentary one appear as early as 152 B.C. when two Arabs of a village, Pois in the Memphite nome, got one of the local Greeks to write a letter for them. A century earlier there were Arab herdsmen in the Faiyum. Strabo speaks of Arab miners at the emerald mines and the name of a Nubian tribe of nomads, the Megabari, has a rather Semitic look.[1]

At the death of the Prophet, these Arabs had become both physically and mentally differentiated from the simple African Bedouin. They had abandoned the matriarchal system of their

---
[1] Cf. Mujabara, the name of the modern inhabitants of Aujila.

forefathers by which all inheritance passed through the daughters, which was still in force among the Libyans and the Beja. Such queens as Zenobia, or Candace, or that Kahina who was to rouse the Berbers against them were nevermore to rule over the Arabs. Their women had lost in freedom and gained in morality.

There were other less significant differences, the Arab women pitched tents, the Hamitic ladies built matting huts. The Arab warrior was turbaned, the Beja wore their own hair.

Arabia has always been a great whirlpool of contending tribes, which from time to time vomits flotsam and jetsam, broken fragments of clans on her border. Sinai is full of such. For the true Arabs are the most mobile of people and the vicissitudes of war, pestilence and famine continually break up their strongest confederations and drive the tribes from one end of their peninsula to the other and sometimes out over the borders, as in the great explosion of the Conquest. These out-pourings are very difficult to trace and define—one might as well try to reconstruct the primitive Highland clans from Macdonalds in Canada and Camerons in the Antipodes.

But after the death of Muhammad in 632, the eruption shook the whole civilized world; every wild Bedouin who could followed 'Amr ibn el-'As and Khalid, while only some forty years later Sidi 'Uqba spurred his horse as far as he could into the Atlantic to show he had conquered North Africa.

Civilized Egypt went down before them like a pack of cards, though the fierce Nubians and the Beja resisted them for centuries. In North Africa their easy conquest calls for explanation. Equally armed, the Arab warrior possessed indeed some advantage in his horse, but a much greater one in his new creed. Pagans equipped with nothing better than animal-headed deities and childish beliefs in stocks and stones could not wage successful war against generals like 'Amr and 'Uqba, inspired by the Prophet and driven on by such a Caliph as 'Omar, terrible in his simplicity.

The uncompromising monotheism of Islam, its clear-cut demands in the way of worship, and above all its insistence on the brotherhood of all believers, lit up the religious darkness of North Africa like a lightning flash, so that the Berbers joined as natural allies with the Arabs in the felling of the

THE DESERT IN ANCIENT TIMES

decadent remains of the Græco-Roman civilization. The new faith indeed came to suit these native Africans far better than the somewhat freethinking Arabs who had converted them. To that, the continual religious revivals of North Africa bear witness.

Greed, too, played its part in attracting the invaders, for Egypt was a very tempting prize.

Chapter II

THE ARAB INVASION

"*When, however, fortune still shone on the Muslim arms and the Syrian campaign was more nearly over, 'Amr renewed his proposal to Omar, pointing out the ease with which Egypt could be conquered and the vastness of the prize. There was no country in the world, he said, at once so wealthy and so defenceless.*"—The Arab Conquest of Egypt.—*Butler.*

The Conquest of Egypt—The Yemenites and Ishmaelites—Invasion of North Africa—The Berbers—Warfare with the Beja—The Beni Hilal and Beni Suleim—'Aidhab—The Bedouins in the Middle Ages—Return of the Arabs from the West—Muhammad 'Ali Pasha and the Bedouins—Present-day Conditions.

Such was 'Amr's anxiety to take possession of Egypt, that he set off with only four thousand horsemen, who were reinforced later by twelve thousand under the hero Zubeir ibn el-'Awwam, who led in person the storm of the Roman fortress of Babylon near Cairo.

Egypt fell an easy prey and only four years after he had crossed its frontier, 'Amr was able in 643 to proceed to the conquest of Cyrenaica. Here also there was little or no resistance and he received the formal submission of the Luwata who then occupied most of that country.

Southwards, the Arab invaders reached Aswan, but an expedition which 'Amr sent beyond the Cataract was repulsed with heavy loss by the skilled Nubian archers.

Their prize was so rich that we may conjecture that the conquerors at first paid little attention to the deserts.

Some of the first desert Arabs to enter Egypt were Bedouins of the tribes of Juheina and Billi, sent by the Caliph 'Omar. These claim to be true Arabs, of the elder Qahtanid stock, nominally descended from Qahtan through Qudha'a.[1] Most of them settled in the Nile Valley, but some in the desert, where they soon began to quarrel. Eventually the Billi had to be content with the barren Eastern Desert of Egypt while the Juheina pushed south into the richer territories

---

[1] The Arabs have always divided themselves into '*Arab el-'ariba* or true Arabs, the descendants of Qahtan, whose original home was the Yemen, and '*Arab el-must 'ariba* or naturalized Arabs, the descendants of Ishmael. But Robertson Smith considered the descent of Qudha'a from Qahtan to be forged, and that the Qudha'a were really Ishmaelites. *Kinship*, 9.

THE ARAB INVASION

of the Sudan. The Billi have long abandoned the desert, but their name survives in Wadi Billi, an important valley near the ancient porphyry quarries. Many of them are settled in the Nile Delta near Qaliub. There are Juheina in Upper Egypt near Dishna, and there was formerly another small colony of them on the coast at Bir Quei. Of true Yemenites perhaps the only representatives now in Egypt are offshoots from the Beni 'Uqba, children of Judham, such as the almost extinct Beni Wasil.

Of the Ishmaelites, or *'Arab el-must 'ariba*, the three most famous confederations were the Mudar, the Rabi'a and the Iyadh. The last do not concern us, but from the Mudar sprang the famous tribe of the Qeis 'Ailan,[1] with such branches as the Beni Hilal, the Beni Suleim[2] and the Ghatafan. Other leading Mudari tribes were the Beni Tamim and the Kinana, the noblest of all, since from them sprang the Qureish, the tribe of the Prophet himself. The Rabi'a themselves supplied not only the early conquerors of Nubia, but from their descendants, the modern Beni 'Atiya, nearly all the present Sinai tribes, such as the Tiyaha, Terabin, Laheiwat and Ma'aza, with the great Syrian tribe of 'Anaza, are offshoots.

The Moslem conquest of Egypt was soon followed by an invasion of North Africa, completed after seventy years of struggle by Musa ibn Nuseir. Among his followers the names of many undoubtedly indigenous tribes are included from patriotic motives by Ibn Khaldun. And one may suspect that the invaders themselves were not all quite orthodox, since the use occurs in Morocco at the present day in the *'ashura* ceremony of two figures, male and female, called Yaghussa and Yauka, which can be none other than the pre-Islamic gods Yaghuth and Ya'uq, mentioned in the Koran.[3]

But this early conquest of North Africa by the Moslems was not really a Bedouin affair after all. Ibn Khaldun admits as much. " The Arab armies penetrated the Maghreb and captured all the towns of the country. But they did not establish themselves there as tent-dwellers or nomad tribes ; the necessity for safe-guarding their rule over the country obliged them to remain in the towns." Consequently we do

---

[1] By 750, there were 3,000 Qeis 'Ailan settled near Bilbeis.
[2] All the Western Arabs of Egypt claim descent from Suleim.
[3] *Ency. Brit.*, ed. xiv, i, 305 (Africa).

not find any of the present-day Western Bedouin of Egypt, who are all returned immigrants from the Maghreb, claiming descent from these early conquerors, but from the later Beni Suleim and Beni Hilal invaders of the eleventh century.

Nor were the Luwata Berbers yet dislodged from the west, where they were in possession of Kharga Oasis down to 951, when we read of a Nubian raid upon them there.

Meanwhile, in 854, the wild Beja nomads put to the sword the Arab miners in the emerald mountains and raided Upper Egypt, plundering Isna and Idfu. To reduce them to order, 7,000 soldiers were dispatched from Qus and to aid their transport, seven ships with stores were sent from Suez to Sanga near 'Aidhab. The Beja adopted guerrilla tactics, but were at length forced into a battle to cut the Moslems off from their supply ships. They were completely defeated and their king made peace, and visited the Caliph at Baghdad. The Moslems then advanced as far as " Dongola ".[1]

Towards the end of the ninth century, the rediscovery of the ancient mines led to a sort of gold-rush to the Beja country by the Rabi'a Arabs of Upper Egypt. The emeralds proved worthless and the gold was hard to win, so the Rabi'a quarrelled violently among themselves. Some returned to the Hijaz ; others settled at Aswan and became lost in the Nubian population. Others again commingled with the Beja, marrying the daughters of the chiefs and thereby securing to their children the chieftancy of the Beja clans, since inheritance among the Beja was matrilineal. The present-day 'Ababda must be the result of some such alliance, since this Arab-Beja amalgam has proved hard enough to resist all subsequent Arab invaders, who have been obliged to keep north of the Qift-Quseir road.

In 969 Egypt was conquered from the west by Jauhar, the general of the Fatimid Caliph, Mu'izz, who captured Fustat with an army largely composed of Berber tribes and founded the city of Cairo. For nearly another century the Berber nomads were to remain in undisturbed possession of the North African countryside, as apart from the towns, but in 1049 an Arab invasion of far more ethnic significance than the first Conquest took place.

Hasan el-Yasuri, vizier of the Fatimid Caliph el-Mustansir, sent the two tribes of Beni Hilal and Beni Suleim to re-conquer

---

[1] Not the province of that name, but a harbour, now called Dongonab.

THE ARAB INVASION

Tripoli and Tunis from his rebel Governor Mu'izz ibn Badis. The main invasion took place in 1051, when each man was given the simple equipment of a camel and a gold piece for the campaign. Fierce fighting took place and Qairwan was not recaptured till 1068.

The Beni Hilal passed on westwards, but the Beni Suleim settled in the "Green Mountain" of Cyrenaica, whence their descendants have been drifting back ever since. These Arabs must have left the Luwata Berbers in possession on the north coast of Egypt, for in 1069, Mustansir's commander-in-chief revolted against his master with the help of "40,000" of their horsemen, who overran the Delta. Order was not restored till 1074.

During the Crusades the land route to Mecca through Sinai and Northern Arabia had become unsafe for the Spanish and North African pilgrims, who preferred to ascend the Nile as far as Qus or Aswan, whence roads could be followed through the desert to 'Aidhab, a new harbour on the African coast of the Red Sea opposite Jidda. Maqrizi indeed says that for 215 years from 1058 the Mecca caravans followed this route, and that "it counted formerly among the most important ports of the world, because the ships of India and Yemen disembarked their merchandise there". The Mecca pilgrims were not, however, safe even at 'Aidhab, for in 1182 the Crusader Renaud de Chatillon, among other piratical exploits, sacked the town, massacred an entire caravan, and destroyed sixteen ships in the harbour. For this and other interference with the pilgrim traffic, Renaud, the Lord of Kerak, alone among the Crusaders, was not granted quarter by Saladin after the battle of Hattin five years later. On a flat and waterless mound, in wet weather almost an island, separated by ten miles of flat desert from the majestic wooded peaks of Jebel Elba, lie the ruins of this lost city, nowadays called Suakin el-Qadim (Old Suakin).

'Aidhab was visited in 1326 by Ibn Battuta who started from near Idfu on the Nile, in the company of Arabs of the tribe Dugheim. He says, " Our course was through the desert, in which there were no buildings, for a distance of fifteen days. One of the stages at which we halted was Homeitra, the place in which the grave of El-Wali Abul Hasan esh-Shadli is situated. After this we came to the city of 'Aidhab, the inhabitants of which are the Beja, who are blacks.

Among these people, the daughter never succeeds to the property.[1] At this time two-thirds of the revenue of 'Aidhab went to the king of the Beja, and the remaining third to the king of Egypt."

After the fall of the Latin kingdom of Jerusalem, the Mecca caravans from the west returned gradually to the route through Sinai, so that by 1359 the traffic through 'Aidhab had become restricted to pilgrims from the Sudan. Although thus gradually deserted by the pilgrims, trade with the Far East must have gone on right down to the final destruction of the town, for some of the sherds of blue-and-white China porcelain on the site are definitely Ming in date, that is, later than 1368. The port was known as Zibid, not 'Aidhab, to Leo Africanus, who gives an account, truly African in its horror, of the end of the ill-fated city, which took place in 1426 under the Circassian Mameluke Sultan El-Ashraf Bars Bey.

"They had once a rich towne situate upon the red sea called Zibid, whereunto belonged a commodious haven, being opposite unto the haven of Zidem (Jidda), which is fortie miles distant from Mecca. But a hundred yeeres since it was destroied by the Soldan, because the inhabitants received certaine wares which should have been carried to Mecca, ... whence notwithstanding was gathered a great yeerely tribute. The inhabitants being chased from thence fled unto Dongala (Mersa Dongola or Dongonab) and Suachin, and at length being overcome in battaile by the governor of Suachin, there were in one day slaine of them above fower thousand, and a thousand were carried captive unto Suachin, who were massacred by the women and children of the citie."

No doubt the inhabitants of Suakin, colonists from Hadramaut, were only too glad to help in the destruction of their rival in trade. Down to the present day a tradition lingers among the Bisharin that the " Dawla " (Government) formerly existed there. An occasional fisher may cast a net there now, but the only inhabitants I saw in 1926 were the ubiquitous land crabs.

Just as the Rabi'a Arabs of Aswan merged with in the Nubians, so the Rabi'a of the desert became lost in the Beja. Northwards the poverty of the land exhausted the Billi and they retired to the cultivation.

In 1302, a terrible blow was dealt to the Arab tribes in Upper Egypt, which accounts for the paucity of the Juheina

[1] So the MS. says, but the reverse would have been more correct.

THE ARAB INVASION

and Billi there nowadays, and perhaps for the return of the Sawalha and 'Aleiqat to Sinai. The Bedouin there had thrown off the Sultan Nasir's authority and, a much graver offence, commenced to levy taxes on the *fellahin*. Nasir's army in three divisions " slew mercilessly every Bedouin in the land and carried off their women captive ".[1]

This drastic solution of the Bedouin question removed the pure Arab descendants of the Conquerors from the scene and so enabled the Beja to preserve themselves as an African race practically uninfluenced by Arab blood, while leaving the desert edges of Upper Egypt free for settlement by the Western Bedouin.

The anti-Bedouin policy of the Mamelukes continued and must have greatly encouraged the Arab immigration into the Sudan. In 1382, Sultan Barquq transplanted a colony of the Hawara, a Berber tribe then settled in Lower Egypt, to Girga,[2] where they began to reclaim land from the desert. These Hawara captured Aswan from the Arabs and destroyed it in 1412, and became the dominant power in Upper Egypt south of Asyut. Their power was not broken till 1813, when they suffered a crushing defeat at the hands of Ibrahim Pasha. Of course they had long since called themselves Arabs. The Luwata settled further north in Bahnasa, where they formed the bulk of the population, and also in Giza and Menufiya.

Next, the descendants of the Beni Suleim began to return from the west, their stock much adulterated with Libyan blood. In 1689, there was a notable invasion of these Western Bedouin under a sheikh called Abu Zeid Ibn Wafi. They were repulsed from Beheira, but plundered the oases, and invaded Upper Egypt near Isna. The Hawara were induced to attack them, and they suffered a grievous defeat near Manfalut, losing 1,700 laden camels. Finally they were driven out with much loss.

But the infiltration continued for the next thirty or forty years, and the Hanadi became the principal tribe in the west for nearly a century.

Among the tribes dispossessed by the Hanadi were the Beni 'Una, who allowed themselves to be absorbed by the

---

[1] Sir W. Muir, *The Mameluke or Slave Dynasty*, 57.
[2] Throughout this book, I transliterate the Arabic ج by J, as the Bedouin, unlike the *fellahin*, pronounce it, except in the case of place-names which appear on the Survey of Egypt maps. There, to avoid confusion, I have retained the official spelling, thus : Girga, Giza, Gilf Kebir.

peasantry and left their vassals, the Jumei'at, at the mercy of the Hanadi. The vassals, made of sterner stuff than their masters, continued the struggle and invited the Awlad 'Ali, warlike cousins of the Hanadi, to come over from Cyrenaica and help them. A brisk warfare, which was to last till Muhammad 'Ali's time, broke out between these tribes.

After the landing of Napoleon's troops at Fort Marabout, west of Alexandria, at daybreak on 2nd July, 1789, they were attacked by the Hanadi. The skirmish at once afforded proof of the worthlessness of the Bedouin in regular warfare.

"At five o'clock, the first Bedouins were seen on the flank of the army, and shortly afterwards one saw four or five hundred; it was the tribe of Henady, the fiercest Arabs of these deserts. They were almost naked, swarthy and lean; their horses seemed worn-out hacks; save for the helmet, it was Don Quixote as represented in the engravings. But these hacks moved with the rapidity of lightning; from full gallop, they pulled up dead, the special quality of the horse of this country. Seeing that the army was without cavalry, they grew bold and threw themselves into the intervals and on the rear of the columns. There was a moment of alarm. Communication with the landing place was interrupted. The troops halted to form up. For his part, Desaix (at the landing place) placed outposts and called to arms. If these five hundred Arabs had been Mamelukes, they would have been able to obtain a great success at this first moment, when the soldiers' imaginations were alert and ready to receive any impression, but these Arabs were as cowardly as the Mamelukes, who had charged an hour before, were brave."[1]

Although on 4th July, thirty sheikhs of the Hanadi, the Awlad 'Ali and the Beni 'Una made their peace with the new power, yet "eight thousand" Bedouin horsemen formed the left wing of the Mameluke army at the battle of the Pyramids on 21st July, who, seeing the battle was lost, made off and disappeared in the desert.

After the eviction of the French, the Hanadi found themselves hard pressed by the Awlad 'Ali and offered a hundred thousand "tallari" to the rising star, Muhammad 'Ali, to restore their lands to them. But the Awlad 'Ali proved too strong for this and defeated the Pasha's soldiers and the Hanadi combined in a battle at Hosh 'Isa. Muhammad 'Ali consoled the beaten tribe by granting them land in the Wadi Tumilat.

[1] D. Lacroix, *Bonaparte en Egypte*, 75.

THE ARAB INVASION

In the Eastern Desert, one Bedouin tribe after another welled into Egypt from Sinai and finding itself in a barren land up against the hostile and warlike Beja, while driven on by the tribe coming behind, gave up the struggle and took to the edge of the cultivation. The Beni Wasil, the latest successors of the Billi, had now to make way for clans of the Ma'aza and the 'Atawna, themselves driven out of Arabia by the Haweitat. This remnant of the 'Atawna was soon exterminated by the 'Ababda, but the Ma'aza have persisted down to our day in the Galala mountains.

To maintain himself on the throne and hold the Mamelukes in check, Muhammad 'Ali continued to make use of the Western Bedouin, for at that time there were no troops in Egypt except a small remnant of Turkish soldiers. The sheikhs supplied him with both mounted and dismounted men on the condition that the Government provided these with arms and food and also exempted the Bedouins in general from forced labour such as work on the Nile banks in time of flood and payment of all taxes. These Bedouins were of great service in his Syrian and Arabian expeditions; and eight hundred of their horsemen joined him in 1815 just before the great battle at Bissel, where he broke the Wahabi power. His son Isma'il in his expedition to conquer the Sudan, took with him not only these Maghrabi cavalry, but also seven hundred 'Ababda mounted on dromedaries. But like their descendants, the " Friendlies " of a century later, these latter were of little military value in action.

Later on when Muhammad 'Ali reorganized his army and conscripted the *fellahin*, he exempted all Bedouins from enlistment on account of their former services, but obliged them to undertake the guarding of the desert roads, posts, and the frontiers of Egypt.

Although they have since been relieved of these obligations, their immunity from military service continues. This naturally leads to numbers of the *fellahin* claiming exemption as Bedouins, and terribly complicates the task of the recruiting authorities.[1]

[1] In 1904, the Director of Recruiting reported the following inflated totals of different " Bedouin " tribes :—

        290,095 settled and living in their own farm colonies.
        240,880 living among the *fellahin*.
         70,472 real Bedouins or nomads.

        601,447

Throughout all history, the Arabs of Sinai have heard the invading legions thunder by without being greatly disturbed from their nomadic existence. They have inevitably sooner or later discovered themselves on the winning side, and to this law the Napoleonic adventure and the episodes of the Great War afforded no exceptions. Until quite lately they have always been able to console themselves for any loss their flocks might sustain in war by exploiting in peace the two cross-streams of Christian pilgrims going to Mount Sinai and Moslems on their way to the Holy Cities of Arabia. Ever since the Black Stone fell from heaven, the pilgrims have had to buy their way to Mecca, and a system had sprung up of making each tribal sheikh responsible for his section of the road, and paying him a small subsidy for security.

In Egypt, pilgrimages by land are now things of the past, but the Government has continued these small salaries, and, since none of the tribes is sufficiently independent of civilization to do without grain, it has always possessed this way of exercising pressure upon them. So the sheikhs, the tribal representatives, are always greedy of official recognition, which strengthens their position with the tribe.

An ironic comment on the safety of civilized institutions is afforded by the complete immunity from pillage which the Greek Convent of St. Catherine, alone among Christian monasteries anywhere, has enjoyed ever since the fifth century. But the restraint here exhibited by these savage mountaineers may be due as much to the strong walls of Justinian the founder, as to the skilful diplomacy of the monks inside them.

In the west, a century has seen the once warlike Awlad 'Ali settle into more or less peaceful cultivators of barley and breeders of sheep and camels. Instead of raiding, they traffic in dates with the oases. The partial sacking of Alexandria after the 1882 bombardment broke the monotony, and they were all ready to rise against the Christians at the time of the frontier dispute with Turkey in 1906. But, during the Great War, very few of them joined the invading Bar'asa and 'Ibeidat, who made up the bulk of the Senussi army. Nor, in their late desperate struggle for independence, did those gallant, if mistaken, tribes of Cyrenaica, receive anything but lukewarm sympathy from this side of the frontier. That chapter is now closed, and peace once more reigns both in Egypt and Cyrenaica.

THE ARAB INVASION

To summarize, those of the Egyptian Bedouin who still live in tents may be divided into six separate categories.

1. Remnants, now very scanty, of the Arab tribes who came over at the Conquest or shortly after—Billi, Juheina, and perhaps Beni Wasil. If their genealogy can be believed, these are pure Arabs, *'arab el-'ariba*, of Yemenite origin, but their present physical appearance belies this. They have long left the desert for the edge of the cultivation. We may perhaps include with these a fragment of the Muzeina, a very noble and ancient Arab race, which came over into Sinai from Arabia some time in the Middle Ages.

2. The Rabi'a, the mediæval invaders of Nubia, were Ishmaelite Arabs *'arab el-must'ariba*. These seem to have died out in Egypt, unless the 'Aleiqat *fellahin* between Sebu'a and Korosko be their remnant, while, in that case the 'Aleiqat and Sawalha of Southern Sinai, who are known to have returned from Egypt in early times, must also be included here. A later invasion of the same stock, nearly all sprung from the Beni 'Atiya, has filled North Sinai with nomadic clans like the Laheiwat, Masa'id, Tiyaha, and Terabin. The Ma'aza, driven by the Haweitat from Midian into Egypt, are the latest arrivals of this stock. The Haweitat themselves, an aggressive modern combination of uncertain derivation, have followed them into Egypt and Sinai from the east and may be added here.

3. Outcast Arabs of the class called Hiteim, with whom none of the foregoing will intermarry. They are scattered throughout Sinai and the Nile Valley, but never seem to have wandered further west.

4. Western Arabs, all claiming descent from the Beni Suleim invaders of the eleventh century. These have returned from Cyrenaica with a strong admixture of Libyan blood. They hold the Mediterranean littoral, and have flooded into the Faiyum and Beheira, but are fast losing their romantic habits and becoming cultivators.

5. Almost pure Berber tribes that have drifted in from further west. The Luwata and the Hawara are now lost among the *fellahin*, but the 'Amayim, Jahama, and Tarhuna, more recently arrived from Tripoli, are still on the desert edge in Upper Egypt.

6. Aboriginal Hamites, with the slightest Arab veneer;

the Beja tribes of 'Ababda and Bisharin. These are still true nomads, " following the rains ".

The great extension of the cultivated lands of Egypt, which has taken place during the last century, has been followed and is about to be outstripped by a similar increase in its population. Human beings, like lower forms of life, breed quickly up to their food supply. Circumstances have so brought it about that, among these additional millions added to the Egyptian nation, there is a higher proportion than usual of healthy Bedouin stock, a factor that can do the future race nothing but good. But the problem of overpopulation is about to become pressing in Egypt as elsewhere, and the difficulty of absorbing immigrants from the desert acute.

PART II

Chapter III

THE TRIBE

"*According to the theory of the Arab genealogists, the groups were all patriarchal tribes, formed, by sub-divisions of an original stock, on the system of kinship through male descents.*"—Robertson Smith, *Kinship*.

Composition of a Tribe—Pedigrees—The Food-covenant—Wayfellows (*Rafiq*)—Refugees—Tenants—Vassals—Outcasts—Power of the Sheikh—Inter-tribal Relations—Tribal Brands—Disputes about the Right to Hire Camels.

All the tribes of Egypt and Sinai, with the exception of one artificial combination, the Towara, ought, if taken at their own valuation, strictly to be designated " clans ", since each of them pretends that the society comprised under its title had a common ancestor. In actual fact, none of these tribes is anything like homogeneous, but is made up of the descendants of the tribal " ancestors ", generally a ruling minority ; some remnants of the tribe that possessed the present grazing grounds before them ; and a whole host of fragments of broken tribes that have sought refuge with them since. All the cards in the pack have in fact been dealt and redealt in endless varying combinations.

Superficially the Arabs of Sinai and Midian all look much alike, and the race is undoubtedly a very pure one. But incessant intermarriage, for they always begin by marrying their first cousins, ends by producing a strong family likeness between all the members of each clan. Kennett[1] noticed this among the Jawabis, and Jarvis[2] among the Bayadiyin. In fact the sheikh of the Muzeina says he has only to look at a Sinai Arab to be able to say which tribe he comes from.

I once told a sheikh that, among us, people who lived in wild places, like our Highlanders, were proud of their descent and set great store by pedigrees ; while the townsfolk could hardly tell who their grandfathers were. " I suppose it is because they are too busy," I added. The sheikh dismissed that idea briefly with the remark, " They are too stupid."

The natural desire for a theory which will explain every-

[1] Kennett, 101. [2] Jarvis, 17.

thing has induced the Arab genealogists to invent pedigrees, going back to Ishmael and Qahtan, for every tribe in Arabia. In this way they have erected a framework into which with a little ingenuity almost any clan can be inserted. Naturally in the vicissitudes of Bedouin life, many of the great tribes of the Prophet's time have disappeared, and their elements have re-assembled to form new combinations. These associations, forgetting their former history, sometimes require new pedigrees for the new coalitions. When these pedigrees are only verbal, they are naturally constructed from the best materials to hand ; thus the 'Ababda told Burckhardt that their ancestors were the Beni Hilal, and the Haweitat are well on the way to establishing their descent from the Qureish.[1] All the tribes of the Northern Sudan have ennobled themselves in like manner, and even the Somalis in East Africa are now claiming descent from the Prophet.

Robertson Smith [2] has rightly pointed out the danger to a historian of trusting to the system, and indeed all that can be said for it is, that it does throw some light on the wanderings of certain stems. And in the case of the pedigrees with which all sedentary Arabs have now provided themselves, these can often be trusted for seven or eight, sometimes more, generations to the ancestor who has brought about the separation of the clan from the main stock of the tribe.

For every tribe (*qabila*) is composed of more primitive associations of families, which have a better right to be called clans. Sometimes when the leadership of the tribe passes from one of these sections to another, it results in a change of name. Or there may be a break-away. Such an example in modern days of the start of a tribe is to be seen in the Tahawiya clan of the Hanadi. These are the descendants of Et-Tahawi, a man of such striking personality that it has obscured that of Hind, the tribal ancestress. No doubt when they become sufficiently numerous, the Tahawiya will constitute a separate tribe from the Hanadi. In this case, some of the other sections may well follow the new lead and represent themselves as Tahawiya also. The temptation to do so is of course increased, when the old name is somewhat opprobrious, and so the Beni Kelb " children of the dog " and other ancient tribes have vanished from the desert.

[1] See Burton, *Land of Midian*, 152, for their supposed ancestry.
[2] *Kinship*, chap. i.

THE TRIBE

The Arab names for these clans or sections vary from tribe to tribe. Thus the Awlad 'Ali call their sections by the name of *'eila*, while an 'Abadi refers to the division of the tribe to which his mother belongs as *lahma*, and that of his father as *'usl* or *'usla*. This latter group helps when a sum of blood-money has to be raised, but this is not the case with the *lahma*.

That is to say that nowadays, whatever may have been the case with the pagan Beja, the son is recognized as being of his father's kin. For as Robertson Smith says, the practical test of kinship is that the whole kin is answerable for the life of each of its members.

Five separate generations of a family are liable, in varying degrees according to the closeness of their relationship to the slayer, to contribute towards the payment of blood-money when a member of their family kills the member of another. Conversely they receive a varying amount of the blood-money paid for a loss on their side. This liability certainly acts as a strong incentive to any Arab to study the pedigree of his clan.

Clan-relationship is not always an affair of birth, it may be acquired by complying with various legal fictions. In fact, in the time of the Prophet, the Arabs used to regard the children they adopted as true children, a practice denounced by Muhammad.[1] Honorary membership of a family may be obtained nowadays by making a food-covenant with one of its members. In Jaussen's words :—

> " Two men, married or single, conceive the idea of uniting their efforts in a common life. They call together a certain number of witnesses and in their presence sacrifice a victim called *dabihet er-riwaq* ' victim of the tent '.
>
> " In shedding the blood, they say ' in virtue of this *dabiha*, we are become one family '. After that, all is in common : dwelling, food, work, profit or loss. One looks on them as members of the same *'ahel* ; the verb used to denote this act is *ta'ahal*, ' become one family.' "[2]

Another case is that of the guest who must be protected by his host, so long as the food they have eaten in common remains in his belly. A temporary membership may also be acquired by a stranger who makes a food-covenant with one of the tribe, whose territory he wishes to traverse. They then become way-fellows *rufaqa* (sing. *rafiq*) and are bound

[1] Koran, xxxiii.   [2] Jaussen, 13.

to defend each other on the march. But, as in practice the obligation falls almost entirely on the Bedouin, the latter will expect a fee for his trouble.

The *rafiq* is bound to protect the traveller with his life, and it is thought great shame to him if he does not. The 'Aleiqat still show a place on the Suez–Tor road called *Mahatt el-Mezraq* the "javelin-cast", where two cowardly *rufaqa* deserted an old man and a girl whom they were escorting. Fortunately the old man rose to the occasion and, killing one of the assailants with a javelin, defeated them single-handed.

Nothing more is necessary to make people *rufaqa* or "way-fellows" than the act of eating bread and salt together. This was done ceremonially in 1822 when Sir F. Henniker quitted the convent of St. Catherine. He says :—

> "It is customary, previous to embarking on an expedition of danger, to demand the Arab assurance of fidelity, and I now had an opportunity of witnessing this ceremony. On mentioning the subject to the eldest of the party, he immediately drew his sword, placed some salt upon the blade, and then put a portion of it into his mouth, and desired me to do the same ; and ' Now, cousin ', said he, ' your life is as sacred to me as my own ' ; or, as he expressed himself, ' Son of my uncle, your head is upon my shoulders '." [1]

This legal fiction of "food-brotherhood" is always talked of by the Arabs as if it conferred real *kinship* on the guest or the *rafiq*. But that such a term is only a metaphor may be inferred from the fact that the ignominious blackmail paid by a weak tribe to a strong, to avoid being raided, is also called *khuwa* or "brotherhood". In sober facts the tribes who pay *khuwa*, so far from becoming kinsmen, are reckoned among the Hiteim, a class with whom free Arabs will never intermarry. In Sinai, the term for this tribute was *khafar* "protection". At one time each Christian family in Tor had to pay *khafar* to a Bedouin family, who protected them from the other Arabs.

After a defeat by the Haweitat, the famous old tribe of Beni 'Uqba were treated as follows. I quote Sir Richard Burton.

> "After a time the Beni 'Ukbah returned, and obtained pardon

---

[1] F. Henniker, *Notes during a Visit to Egypt*, 238.

THE TRIBE

from Alayan the Huwayti, who imposed upon them six conditions. Firstly, having lost all right to the land, they became ' brothers ' (i.e. serviles). Secondly, they agreed to give up the privilege of escorting the Hajj-caravan. Thirdly, if a Huwayti were proved to have plundered a pilgrim, his tribe should make good the loss; but if the thief escaped detection, the Beni 'Ukbah should pay the value of the stolen property in coin or kind. Fourthly, they were bound not to receive as guests any tribe (enumerating a score or so) at enmity with the Huwaytat. Fifthly, if a Shaykh of Huwaytat fancied a dromedary belonging to one of the Beni 'Ukbah, the latter must sell it under cost price. And, sixthly, the Beni 'Ukbah were not allowed to wear the 'Aba or Arab cloak." [1]

This is just the situation that Sir Walter Scott describes in the Highlands before 1745.

" Each important clan had some of these Helots attached to them; thus the MacCouls, though tracing their descent from Comhal, the father of Finn or Fingal, were a sort of Gibeonites or hereditary servants to the Stewarts of Appin; the MacBeths, descended from the unhappy monarch of that name, were subject to the Morays and Clan Donnochy or Robertsons of Athole." [2]

In Arabia, the Dhuwi Hasan, a tribe of Ashraf or descendants of the Prophet, who live to the south of Jidda, have made quite a good thing out of transferring the custom of *rafiq* to the sea. In normal times, piracy and the robbing of the few pilgrims that attempt to pass through to Mecca are added to their more ordinary means of gaining a livelihood. But dhows on leaving Jidda could always purchase immunity by taking on board some member of the clan who acted as *rafiq*, or as they say locally *khawi*. This *khawi* would leave the dhow he had protected at Dauqa or Qunfuda, and return perhaps with a north-bound craft. An old friend of mine, a Harbi sheikh, Muhammad 'Arif bin 'Arifan was once either too mean or too optimistic to take a *khawi*, and with three friends moored his boat one evening beside the Turkish fort at Lith, intending on the morrow to run through in a single day to the similar fort at Qunfuda. (With a good wind this is possible, as James Bruce of Abyssinia showed.) But the enterprising Dhuwi Hasan swam off during the night, murdered his three companions, wounded him severely, and threw him into the sea after a stout resistance during which he killed one of the aggressors.

[1] *Land of Midian*, 170.   [2] Waverley.

Blood-feuds there are seldom compounded by a fine, and if a man of Sherifial descent is killed by one of another tribe, four lives are supposed to be exacted for his. So although Muhammad 'Arif had lost his three companions, yet he had committed the sin of killing a Sherif, and so his blood or that of his family is still sought by the Dhuwi Hasan.

A guest who remains beyond the period of three days to which Arab hospitality is limited, becomes a *tanib* or " refugee who has taken hold of a tent peg ". Again, when a family of one tribe feels itself oppressed by their sheikh, they may take refuge with the sheikh of another tribe by pitching their tents beside his, and demand protection against their own sheikh. Such refugees are at first called *tanayib* (pl. of *tanib*). The problem is usually resolved by the sheikh of the foreign tribe making peace for them with their own sheikh, but if not, they later pay a tax for their use of the pastures, and are now called " tenants " (*qusara* sing. *qasir*). After a few generations they become incorporated into the bosom of the other tribe and consider themselves descended from its tribal ancestor.[1]

So after the feud in which 'Aid and Mudakhil each killed the other's father (p. 209), the Hamaida clan of the 'Aleiqat became the tenants of the Muzeina, and are now, fifty years later, in a fair way to become assimilated to that tribe. Conversely, the Faranja have deserted the Muzeina for the 'Aleiqat. Sometimes these fugitives rise to high position in the clan they have adopted. Thus the Jibali family of Samalus origin is now the ruling family of the Harabi tribe in Egypt. The family of the second sheikh of the Sinana division of the Awlad 'Ali came originally from the Qatifa tribe, and the family of the second sheikh of the Awlad Kharuf is Jeridat in origin. The 'Azzami, the ruling family of the Sinaqra, are sprung from Sinqir, a Frankish castaway.

Enough has now been said to show that the clans are the permanent elements of the Bedouin community, while the " tribes " are merely the names under which these clans are gradually from time to time re-assorted.

The process has gone a step further in the Sahara, where the Tuareg have established what amounts to a feudal system.

---

[1] When a *tanib* finds that the clan which has sheltered him has been raided by the clan of his origin, the duty of *qasir* devolves on him, and he is expected to protect or recover the goods of the two tents of his hosts to the right or left of his own.

THE TRIBE

Among them, the Imushagh divide themselves into Ihaggaren and Imghad. " The latter pay tribute of service in various ways and lack certain privileges ; in some cases an ' ignoble ' tribe may not own camels, or, in others, bear arms." Just so, among the Beni 'Amir (Beja) in the south-eastern Sudan, there is a division into " noble " and " vassal ", while the sections possessing camels despise those who have none as " aborigines ".

Among the Western Bedouin of Egypt, the tribes of " Murabitin ", though bearing a famous name,[1] are usually split up into families who pay tribute to the " Sa'adi " tribes among whom they dwell. Thus some of the once famous Hawara are now vassals of the Awlad 'Ali. Other Murabitin, such as the Jumei'at and the Jawabis, formerly vassals, have gained their independence.

Es-Sayed Idris, the Senussi leader, gives it as his opinion that these " Murabitin " are descended from the tribes, mainly Yemenite in origin, who colonized North Africa after the first Moslem invasion and that the " Sa'adi " or " helping " tribes of to-day represent the Beni Suleim nomads of the eleventh century, who never settled on the land but continued to live as Bedouin. They obliged the peaceful and religious " Murabitin " to pay a blackmail known as *sadaqa* or " alms ", while they, the Beni Suleim, dignified themselves with the title of *Mesa'diyin* or " helpers ". I fancy too that the descendants of the original settlers are somewhat despised for having allowed their Arab blood to become contaminated by Berber.

A desert community is of necessity a poor one, and since government, even by consent, costs money or its equivalent, the organization of a Bedouin tribe has only reached a very simple stage. Every sub-section of a tribe has its petty sheikh, and from these is chosen the " Sheikh " proper, to represent the tribe in all its transactions with other tribes, or with the outside world in general.

The power of this Sheikh, exaggerated as a matter of course to strangers, was originally very limited. He was not a law-giver, unless he united with his office that of the judge,[2] still less was he a law-maker. For all the possible complications

---

[1] That of the " Almoravides " who ruled Spain in the Twelfth Century.

[2] The present governor of Sinai has abolished the tribal judges owing to the exorbitance of their fees, and legal cases are now decided by a council of " Sheikhs ".

of a desert existence have already occurred long ago, and the customs dealing with them are already in force. The laws of the tribe are made, and cannot now be modified.

But the effect on a tribe of contact with the outside world is to exalt the power of the Sheikh, since it is through him that the decrees of government are transmitted to the tribesmen, and to increase his wealth, for all the contracts for camel-hire, on which he very naturally levies commission, must pass through his hands.

Among the Hamitic tribes of the 'Ababda and Bisharin, the Sheikhs have accordingly arrogated to themselves almost feudal powers. But the Sinai Arab tribesmen still stand in little awe of their Sheikhs.

Other tribal officials such as the *qadi* or judge, and the *'aqid* or raid-leader, have seen their functions abrogated by contact with the police and law-courts of civilization.

The power of the sheikh in the primitive community therefore depends largely on his wealth, and on his ability to reason with the tribesmen. It was he who used to conduct negotiations for peace or war, though always in consultation with the chief men of the tribe ; he still fixes the spot for new encampments, but not until after the discussion of the reasons for moving camp. Even then,

> "His orders are never obeyed, but his example is generally followed. Thus he strikes his tents and loads his camels, without desiring anyone else to do so ; but when they know that their sheikh is setting out, his Arabs hasten to join him." [1]

The sheikh is expected to maintain the reputation of the tribe for hospitality, and he is enabled to do so by his lawful commissions on camel-contracts, and by less reputable methods (in civilized eyes only) such as a larger share of the blackmail extorted from the peasantry of the neighbouring cultivation, or from the pilgrims to Mecca should they have to pass through the area within which his tribe wanders.

The case does not now arise in Egypt, but whenever the sheikh was permitted a hand in collecting a tax, he seldom failed to enrich himself while so doing. This he naturally regarded as a legitimate return for the expense he had been put to in entertaining.

The office of sheikh, like those of raid-leader and judge,

[1] Notes, 67.

THE TRIBE

passes from father to son. Usually the eldest son inherits, unless the tribe decides that he is altogether unfit to do so.

All the Arab tribes in Sinai are bound together with a series of verbal treaties, though these are not always of the same nature. There is an agreement to abstain from war or raiding called *qild*, and a stronger form, an offensive-defensive alliance called *hilf*.

When two tribes wish to conclude an alliance, each appoints a representative (*hasib*) learned in inter-tribal law, and the two ambassadors with all the sheikhs of both tribes then meet at a camp of some neutral tribe. Then one ambassador puts his hand into the hand of the other, and both swear before Allah that the two tribes will inhabit the same area in peace, that their foes and friends shall be in common, and this shall continue " as long as the sea is the sea and hair does not grow in the palms of their hands (*madama el-bahr bahru wa el-kaffu ma yunbitu sha'ru*) ".

After this, should camels be stolen by one tribe from the other, the owner of the stolen camels complains to the *hasib* of the thief's tribe. The *hasib* is obliged to recover the camels for him, while the thief is dragged before the *ziyadi* (a judge who specializes in cases of camel stealing) and severely punished. The denunciation of a peace treaty (*qild*) is called *naffadh*, and when this is done formally, an envoy (*rasul*) belonging to a third tribe should be sent, and thirty days' notice given to allow the contending parties to gather in their outlying people and camels.

Armistices are called *'atwa*, and peace *sulh*. Peace was concluded by the *hasaba*[1] in council, and the lives lost during a war were not assessed at the usual rates of blood-money but at a flat rate of £5 each.

There is an old *hilf* between the Haweitat, Laheiwat, Terabin, and Towara ; while just before the war a new *hilf* was concluded between the Terabin and the Tiyaha. There is a *qild* between the Suwarka and the 'Ayaida on the one part, and the Terabin on the other. Also the Suwarka have a *qild* with the Tiyaha and another with the Laheiwat.

According to Na'um Bey Shuqeir, the making of these treaties is said to be still influenced by an ancient division of the tribes into two parties, that of Sa'ad and Haram. He was told that the party of Sa'ad was composed of the Tiyaha,

[1] Pl. of *hasib*.

Suwarka, Rumeilat, 'Ayaida, Sam'ana, Akharsa, Awlad 'Ali,[1] and Bayadiyin, while that of Haram included the Towara, Haweitat, Laheiwat, Terabin, and 'Aqliyin.

Not only Sinai, but all Egypt was once so divided, as mentioned by Lane[2] and Antes.[3] The latter states that, after searching many years for the explanation of the schism, he was at length told by an old man that on the day when the Caliph 'Ali was murdered, the " followers of 'Omar " (*sic*) called it a lucky day *Nahar Sa'ad* and their adversaries *Nahar Haram*. The expression has now lost all meaning, and the ex-sheikh of the Towara, Nassir Musa, admitted recently that he had forgotten which of the parties his tribe was supposed to favour.

In ordinary circumstances, a Bedouin is very chary indeed about revealing his identity or the name of his tribe to strangers, for fear of meeting someone who has a blood-feud against them. Raiders, of course, emulate this anonymity for obvious reasons.

But, in the shock of a regular set-to combat, this precaution is thrown to the winds and the excited warriors charge, crying : " I am a Tihi ! " " I am a Terbani ! " etc., etc.

This helps to prevent mistakes, not only by friend or foe, such as the mishap narrated in Chapter IX, when an 'Abadi speared his fellow, but also by Allah, should he wish to intervene on one side or the other. This appears from a story in Na'um Bey Shuqeir, where one of the Tiyaha became furiously angry at being swept away, camel and all, by a sudden spate of the great Wadi el-'Arish, the home wadi of his tribe. He screamed in rage as he struggled in the water " I am a Tihi ! I am a Tihi ! God, if you don't believe me, look at the brand on my camel ! "

This brings us to another subject, that of the tribal brands. Just as each Highland clan has its tartan, so every Arab tribe has its *wasm*, or mark with which it brands its camels and marks its store-houses. The *wasm* too is sometimes scratched in the sand to show who has passed that way. The *wasm*, like the hieroglyph and the nome-standard, is a degenerate and conventionalized picture, and goes by the name of the object it is thought to represent. Thus the brand of the

---

[1] These are not the Awlad 'Ali of the West, but a small Sinai tribe.
[2] *The Modern Egyptians*, 202.
[3] *Observations on the Manners and Customs of the Egyptians*, London, 1800.

THE TRIBE

'Awarma + is called a " spindle ", and that of the 'Aleiqat ⊃ a " fork ", while the Wilad Sa'id have a double sign ☽| " the crescent and the *dafana* (callosity) ".

Twenty years ago, at the start of an expedition in the Sinai Peninsula, it used to seem that nothing was easier than to hire camels, for the custom was that the three tribes of Sawalha, 'Aleiqat and Muzeina took such contracts in turn, so that I would be at once provided with a caravan-leader and a caravan of sorts.

Soon, however, we would become involved in a maze of local politics ; the actual make-up of the caravan would be continually changing, while fresh squabbles about the partition of the loads would break out every morning. For it would now appear that the composition of our party depended also on the district to be visited, so that if it was the Sawalha's turn for a contract, while the area happened to be in 'Aleiqat territory, the first-named would supply the caravan-sheikh and half the camels, while the other half would come from the 'Aleiqat. There would also be some private agreement between them about carrying certain awkward loads in turn, which would be violated at every opportunity, for each individual avoided these loads in his camel's interest as long as possible.

To make an equitable division once for all was far beyond their abilities or desires. Prominent among our desert-lawyers was Sabah Musa, the son of the judge of the Wilad Sa'id [1] and grandson of the Sheikh Nassar, who conducted Sir Richard Burton from Cairo to Suez at the outset of his pilgrimage. This boy had brought with him two very fine and powerful camels belonging to his father, and every morning loaded them with some of the heaviest boxes without fuss. But this done, Sabah's duty to his tribe at once overcame any further inclination he may have felt to serve his employer's interests, and he would rush into the verbal fray, not to hurry things up, but to make full use of the forensic abilities, stentorian in character, which he had inherited from his sire.

Again, one cannot go far in Sinai without crossing some tribal boundary (always in dispute), so in a day or two the Muzeina would be contesting the claims of the 'Aleiqat.

On the last day of each month a series of quarrels would take place over the division of the money, for the sheikh

[1] The Wilad Sa'id are a section of the Sawalha.

always attempted to deduct old debts before paying anyone; while perfect chaos would ensue next day and the whole personnel of the caravan might suffer change. For immutable custom decreed that, on the first day of each month, any man of the tribes concerned had a right to turn up and share in the plunder of the foreigner. Nor were those who had shared already excluded. This last seemed unfair, but I clung to it, as it was the only chance I had of retaining men who knew their work.

So, if there was work for one sheikh and eight camels from the Sawalha, and eight camels from the 'Aleiqat, the impatient traveller might discover that his sheikh was not worrying about him at all, but attempting to solve some such problem as this.

Twenty-three Sawalha, each with his camel, had presented themselves, not wanting to work, yet each entitled to a twenty-third share in the camel-hire for the ensuing month, and seventeen 'Aleiqat in a like predicament.

From these he had to select eight of each, to be paid by the others actually to do the work. In the background might be lurking a mysterious number of Muzeina alleging that he had crossed or was about to cross their tribal boundary while yesterday's participants in the plunder were still grumbling and being dunned by a host of creditors, among a large crowd who had come to do nothing but hear the fun and give advice.

Little survey work could therefore be done either on the last day of the month or the first, while the arithmetical problems involved became acutely distressing to their simple intellects. Suleiman Ghoneim, the Sheikh of the 'Awarma,[1] used to solve his problems much as follows. He would first say to me, " Put all the money in one heap, and take away one day's hire from the lot. They started so late the first day, that I shall tell them you wouldn't pay for it ! " Then having pocketed this, he would continue rather sadly, " Put all the 'Aleiqat half by itself, I can't touch their money," and brightly, " Now make a heap for each of the Sawalha camels." Greedily, " Where is the lame camel ? He owes me a pound. Where is the yellow camel ? He owes me two pounds." Then, tying each amount separately into

---

[1] Another division of the Sawalha. Suleiman was son of Sir Flinders Petrie's old sheikh, Ghoneim.

various corners of his clothing, Suleiman would sally out for an all-night debate with his clan.

On these occasions all would be armed to the teeth with antique swords and guns, all would be screaming and threatening at the top of their voices ; nobody would be killed or injured, and not a word of gross personal abuse would be exchanged. Such is the effect of carrying arms and being in honour bound to use them if insulted. Many a one of the older men had killed his man in cold blood, as the result of careful stalking, but not in an undignified squabble.

Things are duller nowadays. Yet, in 1929, I was shown near Dahab the spot where, five years before, a Haweiti had shot in blood-revenge an 'Aleiqi camel-man belonging to one of our survey parties. The slayer had tracked them for several days and selected a good ambush among rocks from which he shot his man just as the caravan was starting one morning. The unfortunate 'Aleiqi's corpse was buried at Dahab, while the bold Haweiti escaped to Arabia.

Chapter IV

LIFE IN THE TENTS

"*But to speak now of the nomad inhabitants and how they lead their lives.*"—Doughty, *Arabia Deserta*.

Childhood—Young Girls—Status of Women—Relics of "Mother-right"—Slavery—Hospitality—Occupations—Song and Dance—Medicine among the Arabs—Dress—Weapons—The Tent—Its Furniture—The Beja Hut.

An excellent old sheikh of the Harb once said to me, in displaying a boatful of young boys. "You English spend all your lives amassing gold, which your Government will take when you die. Now the wealth of the Arabs is in their children."

This Arab pride of race envisages the future as well as the past, so all the sheikhs are ambitious of having immense families. 'Ali Bey Mustafa, a former Sheikh of the 'Ababda, had at least twelve grown-up sons, as far as possible each from a different wife. One woman disarranged his scheme by giving birth to quadruplets, all of whom survived, though one was an idiot. Old 'Ali considered that no woman was ever intended to have more than two children at a time, and divorced the lady.

The giant Sheikh 'Ilwani of the Jumei'at takes pride not only in the numbers [1] of his children but in their size. "From my experience," said he, "I have found that small people are always thieves."

The Sinai mothers carry their babies on their backs in bags slung from their foreheads—never on their hips as in Southern Arabia, and the Sudan. Their babies are not weaned till they are three years old (by Arab reckoning four). The tiny baby boys and girls alike wear bead necklaces with charms attached, and are dressed quite similarly in cotton shirts. When they are old enough to run about, the children put over their heads a padded shawl, of dark-blue cotton on the outside, heavily stitched over with coarse thread to keep the padding in place. Their clothes are very dirty, torn, and ragged, and their hair always looks unkempt and full of dust and bits of bush.

[1] Of forty sons born to him, 'Ilwani had living with him in his tents twenty-four; while two others were absent on some journey.

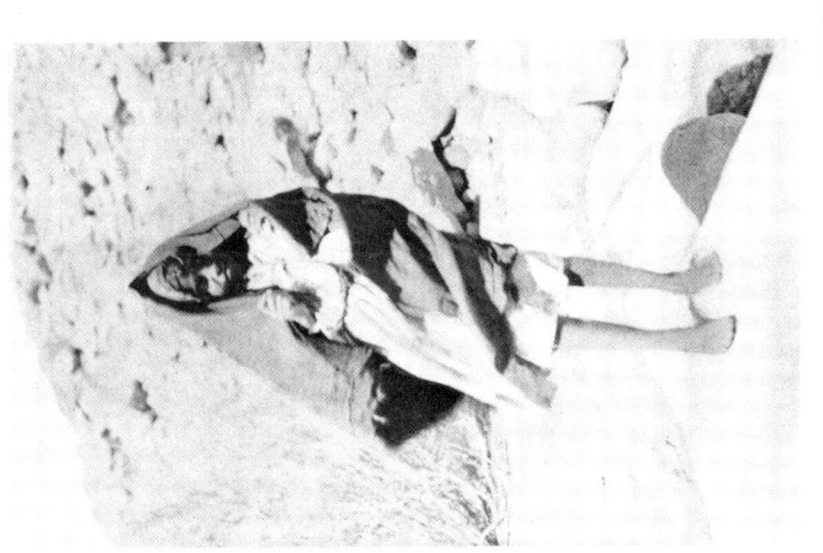

YOUNG SINAI GIRLS

LIFE IN THE TENTS

Until they are old enough to go out with the goats, the Arabs make great pets of their small daughters, but later on they take far more interest in the boys.

At a very early age, these young Sinai maidens and boys are out from dawn to dusk on the hill-sides herding the sheep and goats. During the day they cover a lot of ground, often very rugged and inaccessible country indeed, and must sometimes be content to satisfy their perpetual hunger and thirst with little else than the milk of their charges. But commonly the children who go out to tend the goats carry either a water-skin with them, or a porous earthenware jar which they leave in the shade of a rock at some distance from the tents. They take out food with them, too, and cook it in a hollow in the rocks away from the wind.

When about to return, the girl goes on a bit and cries to her animals Brr ! Brr ! Brr ! Haya ! and waits till they come up, grazing as they go. This has to be repeated many times, for the beasts are seldom anxious to go back, and so their progress homewards needs a lot of patience.

All these girls and children go barefoot. At night they sleep huddled up among their animals for warmth, all in the same tent. They soon become good trackers ; often a sharp small boy is called in to read tracks that have puzzled their elders ; and they acquire some practical botany by discerning which plants the beasts eat and which they avoid. From this servitude to the flocks, the boys are set free when they are circumcised at seven or eight years of age. The girls, however, have to continue in attendance on the goats nearly twice as long till they don the *shibeika*,[1] an ornament which signifies that they are candidates for matrimony. They have then usually not long to wait before some youth releases them from their rather degraded existence.

My wife thus describes a visit to some Arab tents for the purpose of photographing a maiden in her *shibeika*.

" On reaching the little row of black, and fawn-and-black striped tents, I found all quiet. No one was to be seen. But, espying a small scout on top of a rock waiting for my arrival, I realized that the inhabitants had gone into hiding. A scuffling mass of goats round one tent revealed where the girl was, and there I found her crouched on the ground

---

[1] This refers to the girls of the Sawalha and 'Aleiqat only ; the Muzeina maidens do not wear the *shibeika*.

together with her two sisters. As they sat there with their arms full of struggling kids, they barricaded another score or more into the tent ; while outside the full-grown animals fretted at the unaccustomed delay in starting out to their pasture.

"It was not an easy interview, for Hamda was shy and overconscious of eyes and ears in the neighbouring tents. She scarcely dared to move or look up, and only mumbled when I tried to talk to her. Little by little, I coaxed her into speech, showing her the gifts I had brought, and trying to make her unbend. She was determined to maintain her correct attitude towards inquisitive strangers, so long as there were any witnesses who might criticise her and gossip about it afterwards. As fast as I gently unloosened the folds of her mantle behind which she had withdrawn, she again folded it across her face. Her sisters continued the occupation of milking the goats and left us undisturbed.

"After several rebuffs, she permitted me to have fleeting glimpses of her *shibeika*. But I was only allowed to uncover a little bit at a time, and that just for a second or two before she got panicky and retreated again behind her sheltering mantle. The *shibeika* is a deep tight-fitting 'bandeau' which entirely covers the girl's brow and throws a heavy shadow over her eyes. It is made of six densely packed horizontal rows of white shells, ending in a border of large silver coins. These are sewn on to the rim as closely as possible, almost overlapping. The shade is light in weight and is attached in turn to a bonnet of red cotton which covers the front part of the girl's head but not the back. The round top and side pieces of this bonnet are gaily ornamented with shells, chains, and strips of mother-of-pearl. Long metal chains fall to half-way down her bosom, and are there joined together by a clasp. Network curtains of tiny multi-coloured beads fall from the corners of the 'bandeau'. In the presence of a stranger, a girl draws her mantle across the lower half of her face, thus retiring entirely from sight, while leaving the 'bandeau' of shell and coins visible. So the bonnet and bead sidepieces were only visible when I looked under Hamda's mantle. Her married sister, who was not nearly so shy, informed me that Hamda's hair and her own were done in the same way in a horn above their foreheads. But in Hamda's case, the horn was completely covered by the *shibeika*. Hamda laughed when I asked if she removed her *shibeika* at night before going to sleep. She replied emphatically that she *never* took her *shibeika* off, a remark which cast a truthful light on how often she washed her face."

Although the Arabs are strict fathers, not allowing a boy to sit down or eat in his father's presence, yet they teach their sons to be independent at a very early age. When his son Sabah was ten years old Mudakhil, the sheikh of the 'Aleiqat, set him on a camel and told him to go alone by night to some other encampment. Sabah went, but he confessed to being dreadfully frightened. " I clung to the camel till I fell asleep, and when I woke up, I had reached their tents ! "

Again in 1924, I found two 'Ababda boys of about eight or nine years old living all by themselves in the small palm-grove where Wadi Gemal reaches the sea. The dates had been gathered by their elders about a month before our arrival, and the youngsters were now leading an extremely simple life on whatever fish they could catch and the brackish water of El-'Ain, a small seepage *below* high water mark, in the coral reef of the coast.

The hardihood and self reliance of the Bedouin children is amazing. One hot day in June, 1915, two boys, one perhaps seven years of age, the other younger, arrived at the " bridge-head " post of El-Kubri on the Suez Canal, having walked from 'Ain Sudr thirty-six long desert miles without water. They explained that they were orphans, who had been staying with a Bedouin family there, and that when food had run short, they had been turned out and told to " get their food from the English ". Unaware that they had accomplished a feat well beyond the powers of the infantry on the canal at the time, they asked for Birkil Bey,[1] and broke down and wept when they learnt he was not immediately accessible. Fortunately we were able to hand them over to him within an hour.

In 1929, I met in Sinai an old Haweiti, with a small boy about eight years old and six camels, wanting to return to Arabia by way of Nebk. At the head of Wadi Rahaba the urchin was missing, so my wife and I with an Arab corporal rode back to recover him. We found him on the Rutig-Rahaba divide, coming along pretty well, but as soon

---

[1] Colonel Parker, then Governor of Sinai.

as he saw us the boy began to limp and wail. Our corporal took him up on the saddle with him, and we delivered him to his father, who said, " Why did you bother ? He should have been left behind for the dogs to eat." The old man obviously only missed him when he needed help with the camels.

In fact, there is something to be said for the theory of Elie Reclus that woman invented civilization. He ascribes to her the invention of the hut as the outcome of the nests she made to shelter her children and her baggage, while, whatever may have been the origin of fire, women have always been its guardians and preservers. Among all primitive peoples, the hut or tent is looked on as the woman's sphere, and often as her exclusive property. In Munzinger's time, the Beni 'Amir women owned the huts and, if they were divorced, they took them away with them.[1] Even nowadays among the Kababish, the sheikh, who had entertained Professor and Mrs. Seligman in his wife's tent during her absence, was embarrassed at the news of her return, and asked them to change to a smaller tent.[2]

The Sinai women carry all the family treasure on their persons. I have seen Haweitat women with their veils completely covered with silver coins, and though the poorer tribes of the south cannot afford this, yet even there, the women carry a good deal of treasure in the form of silver anklets, bracelets, and numerous necklaces. The herds of small cattle are entrusted to their charge ; in fact they are custodians of all the family property, except the camels. Usually the women and children alone sleep under the tent, while the men are content to lie outside in the shelter of a rock or bush.

A Bedouin woman, though married, never ceases to belong to her father's family and returns to it at once, if she considers herself ill-treated. Then it is for her father or brother, not her husband, to revenge her death or injury. So also her family has to pay for the wounds she inflicts, and receive compensation for any damage she may sustain in her turn.

Thus, Bramly once saw two women having a good set-to beside a well, while the husband of the losing lady stood by without attempting to save his spouse from her trouncing. Common-sense appeared to have entirely ousted romance

---

[1] Munzinger, 320.   [2] *Kababish*, 130.

from his soul, for, on being urged to do what Bramly considered to be his duty, he coolly replied. "Certainly not, it would mix up the settlement. Let her brothers and father come to the rescue, it is their business."

In Sinai, defamations of a woman's honour are heard by the *munshid*, but all other cases in which women are involved must go before a special judge called the '*Uqbi*.

Disputes between husband and wife are not rarer among the Bedouin than elsewhere among mankind. But there is no equality between the sexes in Arab law. Among the 'Aleiqat if a man is struck and injured by his wife, he complains to her father, who ought to pay three times the normal compensation for the damage done, and also build him a white cairn to whiten his face. Yet, if a man strike his wife with the flat of his hand, she can only claim damages to the extent of a piastre for each slap. If she be slightly injured by the blow, he must pay a four-year-old she-goat or £1 in cash. Should the wound be severe, it must go before a judge to be assessed.

Most Bedouin are monogamous only from necessity, and in the case where a sheikh can afford more than one wife he does so. He is then obliged to pass his nights with each in turn. Should a lady be neglected, she may keep a record of these slights by making knots in a cord and finally appeal to her father to take her before the '*Uqbi* who should sentence her errant husband to pay a six-year-old she-camel for each knot in the cord.

An important aspect in the social history of the Bedouins is their gradual evolution from clans which reckoned their descent (and therefore kinship) through their mothers to the ordinary patrilineal organizations of to-day.

The ancient Semites, as Robertson Smith [1] was the first to point out, were originally matrilineal people, whose "matriarchate" endured in Israel down into the historical period, and among the Arabs till the advent of Muhammad.

Relics of it still exist; some tribes, like the Muzeina and the Hanadi, are named after a female ancestor, others use the word *batn* "belly" to denote a clan. In this connection, Robertson Smith remarks "It is safe to say that *batn* can originally have meant nothing else than constituted or propagated by mother-kinship".[2] Thus the Batn

[1] and [2] *Kinship*, 26–34.

el-Monasir in the Sudan reckon their descent from a female ancestor Ghaliya.

Just the same system prevailed among the Beja. Maqrizi writes of them : " Their relationships follow the female line ; every sept has its chief, but there is no ruler over them, nor have they any religion ; they pass the inheritance to the daughter's son or sister's son, to the exclusion of the ' son of the loins '." [1]

The Arabs of the fourteenth century, surprised to find existing among the pagan Beja these customs which their forefathers had abandoned seven centuries earlier, at once took advantage of them, and by marrying the daughters of the Beja sheikhs, thereby obtained the chieftaincies of their tribes.

In ancient Egypt, traces of this earlier matriarchate appear. There too, the line of succession ran through the queens, and it was by marrying them that the succession passed. So when Sheshenq, the Libyan, founded the Twenty-second dynasty, "he married his son to the daughter of Pesibkhenno II, the last of the Tanite kings of the Twenty-first dynasty, and thus gained for him the right to the throne through his wife, as well as unquestionable legitimacy for his son." [2]

The custom must have once been general throughout North Africa. Ibn Battuta, writing of a Tuareg tribe, the Messufa, in Senegal, says :—

> " Their men show no signs of jealousy whatever ; no one claims descent from his father, but on the contrary from his mother's brother. A person's heirs are his sister's sons." [3]

Among true matrilineal peoples, where descent is reckoned solely through the mother, some at least of the following customs usually prevail.

(1) Their marriages are matrilocal, that is on marriage the husband goes to live with his wife and her relations in their camp, and remains with them till the birth of the first child or longer. This is still the custom with the 'Ababda and Bisharin.

(2) The inheritance of property passes from maternal uncle to nephew ; to niece or niece's children ; or from brother and sister to brother and sister. Sometimes it is

---

[1] *Khitat*, i, 194. [2] Breasted, *A History of Egypt*, 528.
[3] Ibn Battuta, 321.

Girl with *Shibeika*

Muzeina Maiden

SINAI MAIDENS

[face p. 54

" office " only that passes from man to man, and the " property " remains vested in the woman. Among the Beni 'Amir, the tent belongs to the woman, and when she is divorced, she walks off with it.[1]

(3) Very often the child pays no particular regard to his father, but treats his mother's brother (whose heir he is) with much greater respect.

(4) Just as when a child he revered his mother, so when a man marries and goes away to stay with his wife's relatives, he must treat his mother-in-law with immense respect, and avoid meeting her. This is the case with the Beja.

So long ago as 1819, Belzoni discovered a custom among the 'Ababda, which pleased him greatly, that men and their mothers-in-law may not exchange a word together.[2] Indeed among all the Beja, a man still avoids his mother-in-law by not speaking to her, touching her, or eating in her presence. Jennings Bramly writes :—

> " At Abu Tabaq in the Sudan, the wadi came down in a spate and caught some of the Mallak section of the 'Aliab. While struggling in the water, one young man bumped into his mother-in-law. No sooner did he see what he had done, than he threw up his hands and disappeared for ever. This was said to be very ' good form ' by the other Bisharin."

A very few avoid this prohibition by paying a fine of about thirty piastres to the mother-in-law. The mother-in-law's sister is not avoided in the same way, nor does a woman avoid her mother-in-law.

The following relatives may not be addressed by name by an 'Abadi : Father's brother, father's sister, father's father, mother's brother, mother's father. Most amazing of all, among the 'Ababda of the hills as among the Beni 'Amir, a wife may not address her husband, nor the husband his wife, by name. Primitive folk the world over believe that a man's name is a part of him, and a very vulnerable part, just like his shadow.

The avoidance of the mother-in-law and the taboo, on names do not occur among the Ma'aza. But Nu'um Bey Shuqeir[3] says of the Sinai Arabs :—

---

[1] The tent to which Isaac brought Rebecca was his mother's (Gen. xxiv, 67), and Sisera sought refuge in the tent of Jael, wife of Heber the Kenite (Judges iv, 17).

[2] Belzoni, *Narrative*, ii, 41. This custom is found not only among all the Beja, but in East and South Africa, and among the Berbers of the oases in Southern Morocco.

[3] Shuqeir, 388 ; also cf. Doughty, 178–9.

"The wife does not eat with her husband out of politeness and shyness. She does not call him by his name, but addresses him by his son's or his daughter's name, saying 'O, father of so-and-so'! Or if they have no issue, by the name of his father, 'Son of so-and-so'!"

The Seligmans hazard the shrewd suggestion that the practice of veiling has obscured relationship avoidance among the Arabs.[1] That is to say that once the women were veiled, there was no longer need for a man to avoid his mother-in-law or she him.

Another avoidance is at the birth of a child among the Beja, when the husband must avoid his wife and child for forty days. Then he kills a sheep and sees his son (or daughter) for the first time.

It is obvious that the inevitable result of the change over to patrilineal institutions is a lowering of the status of women. They tend to be lumped along with the property they formerly controlled, become chattels, and are practically bought and sold. But the Hamitic matriarchate dies hard, and Miss Blackman's remarks about the independence of the *fellahin* women in Upper Egypt[2] agree closely with Munzinger's observations on the Beni 'Amir women.[3] Also in the west, the women of the Awlad 'Ali, possibly as the result of the tribe's contact with the Berbers, have far more freedom than the ladies of Sinai and the Hijaz.

In ancient Arabia, even men of pure Arab blood might be enslaved through the fortune of war, and emancipated at their master's discretion. Such was the double fate of Zaid, the slave of the Prophet. This has long been repugnant to Arab thought, though the enslavement of aliens has always been permitted. As a Sudan *nisba* says "The tribes of the Arabs are seven, and whoever is not included in them may be lawfully enslaved".[4] Once enslaved, the unfortunate African possessed little in the way of rights. *El-'Abd bahim* "a slave is an animal" was once said to me by a very mild 'Abadi, though it does not follow from this that he would have ill-treated either animal or slave. In fact a slave was looked on as a valuable possession. In Sinai, damage done to a slave used to be compensated for as if it had been done to a woman, though if he was slain the *diya* was only two

---

[1] *Kababish*, 129. [2] Blackman, 38.
[3] Munzinger, 326. [4] MacMichael, ii, 21.

PLATE V

'ABABDA TYPES

camels. " So if you hurt a slave, it was cheaper to kill him outright " as was pointed out to me once among the Towara !

At a camp-fire, out in the Qa' plain, I was roused one night by a tumult. A deaf and dumb lad's camel had been stolen, and he and his friends had tracked the suspected thief, a very negroid youth, to our bivouac. High above all the altercation, I heard the voice of the judge's son, Sabah Musa, screaming out his knowledge of the law. " Kill him ! Kill him ! A nigger's only two camels ! " Fortunately extremes were not proceeded to on that occasion.

Slavery is now a thing of the past in Egypt, though quite recently some refugee Arabs from Cyrenaica brought slaves with them into the Faiyum. In the Hijaz it still exists, and at rare intervals a negro is kidnapped from the Sudan and sold into bondage there. Sometimes they escape back ; in 1916, a small boy in a canoe hailed H.M.S. *Venus* off Qadhima, and I was able to restore him safe and sound to his relations near Suakin. In 1919, some Juheina trepanned a negro corporal of the Camel Corps at the mouth of Wadi Gemal in Egypt, and sold him in El-Wijh, whence he was recovered some months later.

Slaves are usually well treated ; so, in 1917, I was surprised to read of the Dhuwi Hasan living south of Jidda that " blacks captured at sea are invariably enslaved and hamstrung to minimize their chance of escape ".[1] But on visiting the district, I was told " that is one of the slanders spread about us by Muhammad 'Arif.[2] Of course if a slave was in the habit of trying to escape, we would hough him."

Under the *shara'*, a slave has the right to claim to be sold, but the Beja did not recognize this, and a cumbrous procedure became necessary. Just as to-day the Awlad 'Ali hand over the beast that kills a man to the deceased's relatives, so the slave of the Bisharin could effect a change of masters by killing somebody else's camel, and getting handed over in exchange for it. Bramly came across an actual case of this. According to Mr. J. W. Miller, the slaves used to take advantage of the Beja custom by which the owner of a house was responsible for what was done outside it. " They would decamp with their masters' camels, kill them outside the house of the man they wished as master, and trust that

---

[1] *Handbook of Asir*, 28.   [2] See p. 39.

he would prefer to repay one camel and gain a slave than kill the slave and suffer dishonour from a broken custom."[1]

In Roman law, an owner was liable for the torts of his slaves, but possessed the privilege of handing over the delinquent's person in full satisfaction of the damages. The parallel is exact, but can hardly be more than a coincidence.

Marriage of a free woman to a slave is rightly looked upon in Sinai as disgraceful; so much so that Suleiman Ghoneim, then Sheikh of the 'Awarma, was once puzzled by Colonel Parker's attitude to the matter, and sought my advice as to the English law upon the subject. He stated his case as follows :—

"Thirty years ago (he spoke in 1910) one of the Qararsha acquired a slave.[2] When this slave grew up, he said to his owner, 'Times have changed, master, I am free!' His master replied 'You can call yourself a king if you like, so long as you stop here and do the work!' So the slave went on growing up, and presently put forward another request, this time to one of my tribe, the 'Awarma, 'Give me your daughter in marriage.' But the 'Armi[3] replied 'You are a negro, and can only marry a negress. If there are no negresses, you will have to do without!' Later on again, after the 'Armi's death, his son, an ignorant youth, bestowed the hand of his sister upon the slave. All my tribe felt very strongly about this, so much so that four young men set upon the slave one day as he was working underground in the turquoise-mines, and cut him to pieces with their hangers.

"We thought this was the end of the case, but 'Birkil' Bey (Colonel Parker) had me arrested and confined at Nekhl till I produced the murderer. (This is the normal procedure.) So after some time, I collected one of the young men as the murderer, and handed him over to 'Birkil'. 'Birkil' sentenced him to *five years imprisonment*! Is that right? In your country do you let the slaves marry the women?"

I appeased Suleiman somewhat by saying that in America they often acted just like his young men. (I speak with a Sinai sense of humour.) The youth after his sentence had been imprisoned at Tor, awaiting removal to Tura prison

---

[1] Letter communicated by Mr. J. W. Crowfoot.
[2] According to Colonel Parker, the Governor, the man was dark-skinned, but not a negro, and came to Sinai via Suakin.
[3] Singular of 'Awarma.

LIFE IN THE TENTS

near Cairo. The jail is not strong, so he at once escaped to the mountains.

The police at Tor, themselves Tiyaha Bedouins, were greatly annoyed, and went to one of their spies, an old woman known familiarly as *Umm el-Bulis* ' mother of the police ', to see if she could arrange his recapture. *Umm el-Bulis* demanded a sheep, which was paid, and went through various incantations. She then said to the police " Go to Wadi Isla, and you will find him there quite silly. My spells have disturbed his brain till he does not know east from west, and you will catch him quite easily ". Obeying their mother, the policeman hastened to Wadi Isla, and caught the poor zany. But then thinking that *Umm el-Bulis* had rather overdone the thing with her spells, and fearing to get into trouble, they demanded that she should restore him to sanity. Amazed at their waywardness, *Umm el-Bulis* gazed on the lunatic, and then spoke sternly to her children. " First you want him mad, and then you want him sane. I don't know whether it can be done. All I know is, it will take a long time, and cost a lot of money ! "

The story ends happily. The spells of *Umm el-Bulis* were not lasting in their effect, and not long after the youth had been imprisoned at Tura (near Cairo), he escaped again to his native land. In those days, escape from Tura Prison was reckoned so difficult that his feat seemed to border on the miraculous. ' Birkil ' Bey himself thought highly of it and said, " I consider that anyone who can escape from Tura deserves his freedom, so, when letters came through from headquarters asking for his recapture—I took no further steps in the matter ! "

In so far as the Arabian Bedouin practise a religion, it is that of hospitality. As they told Doughty, all are God's guests and should share and share alike. Nor is it confined to their tribesfolk, strangers are welcomed everywhere.

Once only have I had a doubtful reception, and that was in war time. Four stranger Arabs and myself, approaching an encampment of Harb near Rabugh in Arabia, were received by a middle-aged butcherly fellow, stripped to the waist, and girt with a large important-looking knife. No words did he return to our greeting, but there was a dull menacing look in his eye as of a bull about to charge. Conventions having failed, I tried the unconventional. " Hullo, old man," I said, "how many have you killed with that knife?" Pleasant memories awoke in his mind, and a delight that even these strangers had heard of his prowess seamed his countenance with a brutal grin. "Two," quoth he, "Juheina," and in a twinkling we were guests.

All people of a Sinai encampment take it in turn to receive guests; but if a guest arrives with a particular claim upon a man, that man has a right to entertain him if he will, in spite of the (pretended) opposition of others. Should a man see a guest from afar, and declare his intention of receiving him, he can receive him out of his turn, except in the case cited above, where the man upon whom the guest has a claim, can take him from him. An animal, usually a sheep, is slaughtered for a guest, and its blood is smeared on the guest's camel's neck. When the meat is given to the guest, he must first of all make a present to the host's wife—this is called *lahm el-ferash*. When the guest has eaten and is washing his hands, if anyone present claims the right to entertain the guest for the next meal, he takes precedence over all, except the man on whom the guest has a claim. It is lawful in case of need to requisition another man's sheep for the purpose of entertaining a guest.

It may be ungallant to say so, but this system of keeping open house has never commended itself to the still matriarchally-minded Beja. Burckhardt reviles them for this.

> "The inhospitable character of the Bisharin would alone prove them to be a true African race, were it not put beyond all doubt by their language."[1]

Yet even they rise to the occasion when necessary, for 'Ali Kheir, my 'Abadi guide, never tires of telling of the kindness shown him, after he had been lost for three days, by some Bisharin.

The male Arab is quite content to pass the day smoking, chatting and drinking coffee. Herding the camels is his only office; all the work of erecting tents, looking after sheep and goats and bringing water he leaves to his women.

The weaving of carpets and rugs became regularly organized into an industry after the War, to rescue the Awlad 'Ali women from the poverty into which the tribe had fallen. The carpets of 'Amriya exhibit different shades

[1] *Nubia*, 372.

of blue and grey; those from Cyrenaica are gaily dyed with crimson, but this colour runs when the carpet gets wet.

Somewhat similar carpets used to be woven by the western Arabs settled in the Nile Valley at Beni 'Adi. But the striped patterns of those carpets went with the weft, whereas the stripes of the 'Amriya (and Hijaz) carpets went with the warp. The Beni 'Adi carpets were also richer in colours. Bright red, deep blue, and orange were seen.

A loom is a rarity in the Eastern Desert, and the place where one has been set up is talked of for years afterwards. I have never seen the weavers there at work, but Crowfoot says of the nomads in the Northern Sudan :—

> "The Arabs did not even introduce the common Bedu methods of spinning and weaving; the Beni Amer women use a spindle without a whorl, and the Hadendawa women weave blankets without a heddle."[1]

Mrs. Theodore Bent thus describes the Bisharin weavers :—

> "The yarn had been wound over two sticks about 20 feet apart, and that stick near which the weaving was begun was tied by two ropes, each a foot long, to pegs in the ground. The other was simply strained against two pegs. At this end a couple of threads had been run to keep the warp in place. There was no attempt to separate the alternate threads so as to raise each in turn. There was a stick raised 4 or 5 inches on two forked sticks to separate the upper and under parts of this endless web of 40 feet. The weaver sat on her goat's hair web, and never could get the shuttle across all the way. It consisted of a thin uneven stick, over a foot long. She had to separate twelve or fifteen threads with her hand, and stick in a pointed peg about 10 inches long, while she put the shuttles through that far; then she beat it firm with this instrument and went on as before."[2]

The Western Desert loom is also very simple. When the length and breadth of the stuff have been decided upon, four pegs are driven into the ground at its corners. Two poles are then put across at either end, and the warp is wound between them in quantity according to the breadth, the warp threads being one next to the other over the whole breadth.

When a plain piece of stuff such as a tent-roof is needed, a flat "shedstick" *minshaz* resembling a broad wooden sword

---
[1] "Christian Nubia," *JEA.*, 1927, viii, 148.　　[2] *Southern Arabia*, 337.

is passed between the warp-threads, the odd threads being evenly brought up and the even threads pressed down. (If the covering is to have a pattern, more or less threads from top and bottom are taken up according to the design required.) When the *minshaz* is in position holding the warp thread apart, the weft carried on a piece of wood is passed through. The *minshaz* then is pulled out and a gazelle horn is generally used to bring up the weft thread into position, and then again the weft is pressed home by the *minshaz* before it is used for a new line of weft. Much practice is required to make the stuff of even texture, even when making a plain cloth. When it comes to weaving in patterns, the Arab woman carries the number of threads to be taken up or missed in her head—and this has been taught her in early childhood when she sat beside her mother weaving.

The Arab patterns are very simple devices of chevrons, lozenges, and triangles combined with stripes, and they prefer patterns going with the warp, while it is unusual for them to make a line at either end as a finish.

The spindle used for making thread is four to twelve inches long with a rough wooden flywheel at one end to help the spinning of the thread. Also the great differences in the qualities of the threads to some extent determine the nature of the stuff to be woven.

Their carpets are woven for home use and rarely come on the market. Curiously enough none of their wearing apparel is woven on these portable looms, for all the shawls in common use are imported from Tripoli or Tunis, except for a few made at Hosh 'Isa by the *fellahin*.

Occasionally, when he is hard up, the Bedouin will attempt manual labour. Thus the young men in Western Sinai, when they wished to earn a bride-price, would work for a little in the turquoise-mines [1] at Maghara, using home-made gunpowder, or, very rarely, lend a hand in the more strenuously organized manganese mines of Umm Bogma. Poverty has made fishers of the Muzeina on the shores of the Gulf of 'Aqaba, and they also sometimes go to sea in the dhows belonging to Tor.

Similarly those sections of the 'Ababda, settled in the Nile Valley, provided most of the labour for Egypt's short-lived gold industry, and still take part with the *fellahin* in

---

[1] Only " mines " by courtesy, their method is mere grubbing.

PLATE VI

Arab playing *Rababa*

Sinai Boys

ARAB TYPES

the phosphate-mines and oilfields. But four months' work in the year is the average miner's limit.

More akin to their Bedouin nature is the barter for camels, sheep and goats, and large flocks of these are driven yearly into Egypt from all directions. The Bedouins are also great charcoal burners, and a lot of charcoal is brought by the 'Ababda into Upper Egypt and by the Towara into Suez. Acacias are the trees usually sacrificed. The tree is dug right out by the roots, chopped up, and burnt for two or three days under a heap of earth. If a supply is wanted at short notice, a few branches are burnt for a few hours. Tamarisk and *tundub* [1] wood they reckon very inferior material.

The Arabs still respect their poets as endowed with magical powers by the *jinn* or by Allah. Just as Balak sent for Balaam to curse Israel, so Feisal's army marched upon El-Wijh equipped with a poet on the right and a poet on the left. In truth they think a good poet, like a diviner or wizard, has something uncanny about him.

They love to record their adventures, particularly in the melancholy course of true love, in ballads which endure for centuries. Richer in imagery than in imagination, these ballads are usually sung to the double-stringed viol, *rababa*. Of the *rababa* which the player rests upon his heel, Doughty says :—

> " The Beduw make the instrument of any box-frame they may have from the towns; a stick is thrust through, and in this they pierce an eye above for the peg; a kid-skin is stretched upon the hollow box; the hoarse string is plucked from the mare's tail; and setting under a bent twig for the bridge, their music is ready." [2]

Besides this viol, the Sinai Arabs have two other musical instruments, a brass flute *shabbaba* with six holes, and a double pipe or reed, *maqrun*. A single pipe they call *ghab*. They buy the yard-long reeds for the pipes in Suez; and cut the holes to make the notes as follows. The last note is cut four fingers breadth from the

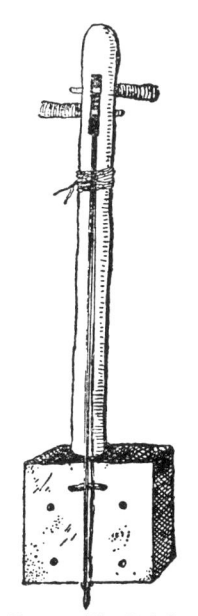

FIG. 2.—The *Rababa*.

[1] *Capparis sodada*.   [2] Doughty, i, 263.

end, and the other five follow at intervals of two fingers breadth apart. The pipe, open at both ends, is played by almost closing the top with the upper lip and conducting the air down the pipe. On this Arab reed, they produce delightfully soft music in quarter-tones within a very limited compass by our notation, and repeat their little wandering tunes over and over again. When heard in the evening from the bed of some ravine, beneath overhanging cliffs, the echo of their harmonics is very beautiful and eerie, resembling a far-off organ played *pianissimo*.[1]

The Bisharin have very long pipes with two holes *ambilhot*, and the 'Ababda four-hosed pipes *zummara*.

Hida' el-bil is singing to camels on the march or while they are watering, and is believed to encourage them greatly. Jacob has suggested that the camel's swing, bending the rider's body double at each stride, taught him to sing rhythmically. The Arab soon noticed that if he hurried the pace of his recitation, the camels would step out with quickened pace. Thus was born the *hida'*, of which every tribe has its own tune and scansion.[2]

The *Dahiya* is the favourite amusement of the Bedouin of North Sinai. In this a row of singers is formed with a poet[3] (or sometimes two) among them. Before them a damsel called " the attendant " [4] starts to dance with a sword in her hand. The singers begin by repeating *Ed-Dahiya* ! *Ed-Dahiya* ! several times, clapping their hands, and inclining their heads. Then the poet begins to improvise, and each time he completes a verse, the others repeat the chorus, still clapping their hands, and bowing their heads and shoulders right and left, advancing towards the " attendant " who retreats before them dancing, until they attain the limit of the playground where they and the " attendant ' all fall on one knee together. Then they sing a little, and then the men retreat backwards gradually with the girl following up face to face with them, till they reach the place where

---

[1] The Arab, shown in Plate IV, accompanied his ballad with the following monotonous tune on the *rababa* above a drone bass, as near as our notation can render it.

[2] *Studien in arabischen Dichterm*, iii, 179.   [3] Called *El-Badda'*, i.e. " improvisatore ".
[4] Called *El-Hashiya*, perhaps best rendered by the French *assistante*.

PLATE VII

BEJA DANCING

LIFE IN THE TENTS

they first stood. They now begin all over again, the poet improvising, and the men chanting the chorus. Should there be more than one poet among them, these take it in turns. There may be also two or three girl-dancers hand in hand. If two, the girl on the right holds the sword; if three, the central dancer. This *dahiya* has only recently been introduced into Sinai from the east, and the Towara Arabs still favour the older dance called *samir*.

The *samir* is of two kinds, *El-Khojar* in which the women improvise, and *Er-Raza'* where the poets are men. In the latter the men form up in two curved lines like a broken crescent, each group with a poet, and a dancing lady with a sword in her hand in front, still called " attendant " or sometimes " camel ". Each poet begins a verse, which his group repeats after him, while all the time both groups clap hands, bow their heads, and advance towards the girl as in the *dahiya*. In a variant called *mashriqiya*, the poets chant longer verses to a rather different tune to that of the *samir*.

In the *khojar*, the women stand between the rows of the men with two female poets, each singing to one group of the men. These never leave their places till the end of the play.[1]

Burckhardt gives a lively description of the *samir*.

" About two or three hours after sunset, either the girls and young women, or the young men, assemble on an open space before or behind the tents and begin to sing there in choruses until the other party joins them. The girls then place themselves either in a group between the men, who range themselves in a line on both sides, or if the number of the females be but small, they occupy a line opposite to that of the men, and at a distance of about thirty paces. One of the men then begins a song (*qasida*) of which only one verse is sung, repeating it many times, always with the same melody. The whole party of men then join in the chorus of the verse, accompanying it with clapping of hands, and various motions of the body. Standing close together, the whole line inclines sometimes towards one side, sometimes towards the other, backwards and forwards, occasionally dropping on one knee, always taking care to keep time by that movement, in measure with the song. While the men do this, two or three of the girls come forth from the group, or line of their companions, and slowly advance towards

[1] This description of the *dahiya*, etc., is abridged from Shuqeir, 344–50.

the men. They are completely veiled, and hold a mellaye or blue cloak, loosely hung over both their outstretched arms. They approach with light steps and slight bows, in time to the songs. Soon the motions of the girls become a little more lively, while they approach within two paces of the men; still dancing (as it is called) continuing to be extremely reserved, strictly decent, and very coy. The men endeavour to animate the girls by loud exclamations, with which they interrupt their song from time to time. They make use for this purpose of exclamations and noises, with which they are accustomed to order their camels to halt, to walk and trot, to drink and eat, to stop, and to lie down. They do not address the girl by her name, which would be a breach of politeness, according to Bedouin manners, but style her 'camel', affecting to suppose that she advances towards them in search of food or water. This fiction is continued during the whole dance. 'Get up, O camel'; 'Walk fast'; 'The poor camel is thirsty'; 'Come and take your evening food'; these, and similar expressions, are used on the occasion, added to the many guttural sounds in which camel-drivers talk to their beasts. To excite the dancer still more, some of the gay young men spread before them upon the ground their own turbans, or headkerchiefs, to represent food for the camel. If the dancing girl approach near enough to snatch away any article of dress, she throws it behind her back to her companions; and when the dance is finished, the owner must redeem it by a small fee paid to the girl. I once released a handkerchief by giving to the girl a string of pretty beads made of mother-of-pearl, observing that it was meant as a halter for the camel; with this she was much pleased and hung it round her neck. After the dance has continued five or ten minutes, the girl sits down, and another takes her place, beginning like the former and accelerating her movements according as she herself feels interested in the dance. If she seems animated and advances close to the men's line, the latter evince their approbation by stretching out their arms as if to receive her; this dance, which continues frequently for five or six hours, and till long after midnight, and the pathetic songs which often accompany it, most powerfully work upon the imagination and feelings of the Arabs, and they never speak of the mesamer but with raptures." [1]

Bramly adds, " I have more than once seen in Sinai a man go down on one knee, and putting both hands together, point a finger (as gun-barrel), and then click a finger and thumb with the other hand in pretence that he was shooting at the girl, who accepted this as a sign that they wanted an other. This is generally done when the dancers reach the edge of the ground."

[1] Burckhardt, *Notes*, 143–5.

LIFE IN THE TENTS

There is never anything improper about these amusements, all is decent and restrained. So far from seclusion of women are they, that the Arabs of the Tih have mixed parties called *khalat*, in which the youths and young women meet at a fixed hour near their camp without the knowledge of their parents. The youths bring with them lambs, flour and water; the girls butter and milk. The sheep are slaughtered, and they eat and pass the time together, and then disperse to their tents. Should a lad be known to have misbehaved during the party, he is obliged to marry the girl, or be killed in default.

By contrast with the fever-stricken inhabitants of the oases, the desert Bedouin generally enjoy robust health, for, on the coast, the influence of the Mediterranean tempers the rigours of heat and cold to the Awlad 'Ali and the Arabs of Northern Sinai, and the animated expressions and shapely bodies of the 'Ababda and Bisharin afford proof of the invigorating nature of the hot dry climate of the Nubian desert. It must be admitted, however, that this cheerfulness vanishes with the first breath of the cold gales they occasionally experience. And, in the high mountains of Sinai, the half-starved poorly-clad mountaineers suffer terribly in winter from chronic bronchitis, and articular rheumatism. On a frosty morning, it seems a long time before the sun thaws out their stiffened limbs.

Conjunctivitis, too, is as common with them, as it is said to be rare in Northern Arabia. Malaria hangs round the palm-groves of Wadi Feiran, and, so far back as 1912, Suleiman Ghoneim told me that it was due to the mosquitoes.

The desert is full of valuable medicinal plants, yet the Bedouin seem to have little faith in them. Castor-oil is used by the Nubian beauties only externally, while, though the 'Ababda bring in both colocynth and senna for sale, I have never actually known them use any. The Sinai Arabs occasionally split a colocynth gourd, scoop out the seeds, and fill the two hollows thus created with milk. After it has stood for some time, the liquid which has absorbed some of the active principle of the plant, is drunk as a purge. Though the colocynth is incredibly bitter, its seeds are sometimes ground and eaten in times of famine.

In 1923, the camel-load (four hundredweight) of dried senna leaves from the Eastern Desert was selling at Idfu at 105 piastres a hundredweight. My guide 'Ali Kheir declared that the medicinal senna *Cassia acutifolia* grew much thicker in his valley than the closely allied *Cassia obovata*, "as the seeds of the latter stay several days in the camel, while the former are voided at once."

In Sinai, a decoction of the white broom *Roetama roetam* is sometimes drunk to relieve pains in the back, and an infusion of *Santolina fragrantissima* for colic. *Hyoscyamus muticus*, "sakaran" is occasionally smoked by would-be drug addicts. The strongly aromatic *Artemisiæ* " shih " and " beithiran " are said to be used by the fellahin to drive vermin out of the bedding, but I cannot imagine a Bedouin fussing over such trifles. 'Ali Kheir fumigated some influenza patients with dried hyrax urine, while sulphur ointment is esteemed by many as a cure for mange in both man and beast.

But their sovereign remedy for all complaints, whether human or bestial, is the cautery. 'Ali's faith in this simple remedy cannot be shaken. "When I was ten years old, I used to help the cook at the Sukari mine. One day a tendon in my breast stuck. I knew what to do. I got a nail. I heated it. I burnt myself. The cook was so sick at the smell of burnt flesh, that he called me a little pagan, and chased me out of the kitchen. That cook was soft. If I had burnt him or stuck a knife only an inch or two into him, he'd have screamed!"

Of smallpox they have a great fear, and stories are told of sufferers from this complaint being abandoned. I lost a camel-driver from smallpox in 1911, though I was able to get a Nubian who had had the disease to attend him. Nowadays most of the Bedouin children have been vaccinated by the Frontiers Administration.

All Bedouin have an almost religious dread of cold water, and strong opposition was offered to my drenching an 'Abadi who had collapsed from heat stroke. His relations all declared he would die, and his sudden recovery startled them for the moment.

Their eyesight is not particularly good; whenever I have asked a Bedouin hunter to focus my field-glasses, the indicator has always registered below normal, yet their faculties of observation are so remarkable, that it is well nigh impossible for mounted men to surprise the Arabs of North Sinai. During the winters of 1914–15 and 1915–16, when I was employed mapping outside our outpost lines on the Suez Canal, I felt perfectly safe from the Turkish cavalry on that account.

Even the loss of sight does not always disable them; I once heard of a blind 'Abadi, who was quite capable of finding his way alone along the ninety waterless miles of desert road that separate Bir Umm Qubur from Kom Ombo in the Nile Valley. " He used to haunt abandoned camp-sites, and fight with his stick against the children for things we left behind." Bedouin leave little behind them when they move camp, so his was a strenuous employment.

Throughout the Sinai Peninsula, the Arab dress is much the same, though the quality of the stuff may be better in the case of a *sheikh* or rich man. The head is covered with a skull-cap of camel-hair, which is knitted by the men themselves. For needle they use a stick cut from the first bush, or a dry twig, which they rub smooth on the earthenware bowl in which the coffee is ground. The women, however, usually spin the wool with thread. A few wear a linen skull-cap over the knitted camel-hair one, and over these again a kerchief which in the south is generally a white piece of linen, cut from the same stuff as the shirt. This they fold so that a straight piece of linen comes over the forehead, while the points hang down one on each side of the head and one at the back. In the north, black and red or red and white kerchiefs from Gaza are sometimes worn over the white one. A rich man may wear a silk one, *kefiya*; these are of many colours, yellow, red, blue, and green, in stripes; sometimes a very rich sheikh has one worked with gold and silver thread with long tassels hanging down, costing from two to three pounds. These are usually worn over a white silk or linen kerchief.

The *kefiya* used to be kept on the head by a black goat's hair cord called a *marira*. *Marirat* from Gaza are made of twisted strands of goat's hair cord about half an inch thick; this they double twice round their heads, and the ends hang down in separate strings, making in general six or eight small cords, which keep the kerchief down over the neck when the wind blows. But it is also the fashion with many to wear these tags at the side. Other woollen *marirat* are simply ropes, with two openings, one at one end, and the other about a foot from the other end. The rope is now passed three times through the end hole, thus holding the three circles together, and then fitted to the head. Such a *marira* is often used as camel-halter as well.

Since the War, the homely *marira* has been replaced nearly

everywhere by the showy *'uqal*,[1] an open skein of either silk twists or camel-hair, with bindings of gold or silver thread about an inch apart. This also has tassels. The ends of the *'uqal* are bound into loops, held together by the cord with which the *'uqal* is either shortened or lengthened to suit the head. It is customary to attach a charm to the tags of the *'uqal*—a verse of the Koran sewn into a small leather pocket, generally triangular in shape. In Wadi Feiran, the Sawalha Arab often wears a turban instead of the *kefiya*.

The common linen shirt *tob* is made from one pattern, differing only from an ordinary night shirt in the cut of the sleeve, which from the elbow down is full and open. Its wide mouth tapers into a long thin strip, which all but touches the ground when the arm is down at the side. These long, tapering ends often act as pockets into which small articles are tied. They are fastened together and passed over the Arab's head round the back of his neck, when he wishes to bare his arms. Many Arabs wear two shirts, one over the other, and reserve the under one, which is generally a shade or so whiter, for exhibition on state occasions.

Every Arab has a leather belt, to which is attached a pouch, made from the skin of an ibex or young camel. In this, if he has no other receptacle, he stows all his property, The pouch of a poor Arab will hold the steel with which he strikes a flint to make fire, a piece of cotton reduced to tinder by being rubbed into a sheep's back after the stuff has been well washed—or some very dry grass, or perhaps the cotton-like parasitic growth of the *shih*, which grows everywhere on the Sinai desert, an old ship's nail sharpened to mend sandals, with a further collection of odds and ends picked up by the way in view of possible future utility.

A richer Arab likes to wear a belt, made if possible from disused machinery belting, with his pouch on the left side. This is supported by a band over the shoulder, and on the right side is a strap passing over the other shoulder. This strap is generally of plaited leather two inches wide, and to it are attached by little brass chains his steel, one or two brass tubes in which powder and small things are carried, and a pair of small iron tweezers for extracting thorns.

---

[1] The same word is used for the rope which ties the camel's legs after it has been "barracked".

Plate VIII

ARAB WITH *KEFIYA* AND *'UQAL*

LIFE IN THE TENTS

A knife, also attached by a chain, lies in a case at the back of the strap.

On the right side, attached to the belt, and worn above the hip there used to be an iron hook (*bersheq*), designed as a serpent, with an attempt at a serpent's head (which looked more like a heart). This was worn to support the butt of the flint-lock, when priming the pan, as a third hand is required to do this. To it also is hung the powder-horn, made of wood but shaped like a horn and sewn over with hide. The widespread introduction of rifles after the Great War meant the disappearance of the flintlock, and with it the *bersheq*.

A Ma'aza sheikh in winter wore a black mantle *'aba*, a blue *jibba*, and a striped *quftan*. Below these he had a striped gown and a white shirt. If his mantle had been woollen, he would have called it *diffiya*. In cold weather, they add a sheepskin jacket, or in Sinai the skin of a gazelle or a leopard. These sheepskin jackets, worn with the wool outside, are cured with alum, and when new are often as stiff as cardboard. Before the War, cheap jackets, covering very little of the person, could be bought for twenty piastres. Good coats went down to the knees, and were ample in cut, but the sleeves never went below the elbow, and there was no means of closing the garment in front. A good coat would be lined outside with blue cotton, with a diamond-shaped patch of coloured cloth sewn in to the centre of the back as ornament.

The Ma'aza and the Towara wear drawers, but the Arabs of North Sinai till recently despised them.

Frequently they go barefoot, but their feet are usually defended by sandals made of sharkskin or dugong-hide,[1] sometimes nowadays of old motor tyres. The Arab sandal, like the ancient Roman, consists of a light leather sole, usually fastened by a thong of hide, which passes between the great toe and the second toe, over the foot, and round the heel. The sole is further connected with this thong by two straps on either side, so that the whole sandal fits almost as tightly to the foot as a shoe.

Most Sinai women wear a black mantle (formerly dark blue), with a black or white girdle which they pass three times

---

[1] The covering of the tabernacle, Exodus xxv, 5, and the sandals of Jerusalem, Ezek. xvi, 10, were made of "seal-skin".

round their waists. Over this they wear a red belt from which tassels hang on the right side to the knee. The Muzeina women wear black dresses, embroidered in red and orange, and their shawls are also black with red borders. Sometimes they don white pieces of cotton instead of these black shawls.

The North Sinai women arrange their hair in two plaits, but the Turi women plait their hair over leather to form a sort of horn over their foreheads, on which they wear a coloured bead to keep away the evil eye. The colour of this bead varies with the fashions ; in Palmer's time it was red, and in Na'um's blue. Nowadays it is often white. Every female, whatever her age, does her hair in this horn ; even the tiny girls have the beginnings of a little horn under the shawls.[1]

The unmarried girl's ornament *shibeika* has been already described. The bridegroom takes this away by force on the wedding night, and it is replaced later by a nose-ring.

A Muzeini virgin does not wear the *shibeika*, but a substitute of her own hair arranged in thick plaits, which cover her forehead down to the eyebrows. The remaining hair hangs in two smaller plaits on either side of her head. Nor does she put up the horn of hair till after her marriage.

Beneath her eyes is her mask, a plain piece of black cloth without ornament of any kind. Under cover of this she wears as many cheap beads as she possesses with a mother-of-pearl amulet. Her feet are bare and her dress is simple and scanty, consisting of a skimpy sleeveless bodice of thin black cloth and a long wide skirt of the same stuff, roughly gathered in at her waist. This has for girdle a thin piece of rope, which is threaded through the material and then knotted in front, leaving an untidy, unhemmed edge of three or four inches' width. The pouch of her bodice, above the knotted rope, forms a handy pocket in which to stow away her treasures. Later on, this is all tucked away neatly under a belt, but unmarried girls do not wear belts.

Beneath her dress, she wears clumsy drawers and a long undergarment of a coarse calico which once was white. Her shawl is black and of the same material as her dress ; but

---

[1] In Arabia, the Billi and Beni 'Atiya women wear this horn of hair and bead. See Doughty, i, 75 and 382. In Lady Hester Stanhope's time, the Druze women wore a horn, made of silver or tinned copper among the richer, of paste board among the poorer. But this is no longer seen. Roundell, *Lady Hester Stanhope*, 55.

PLATE IX

ARAB WOMAN'S MASK (BURQU')

LIFE IN THE TENTS

her mother embroiders a gay border on the edge of it in red and orange stitching.

When away all day with her goats, she slings a small square bag of goat's hair from her head to hang down behind her shoulders.

The married women veil themselves with a peculiar vizor-like mask called *burqu'*. This consists of three parts, (1) The *waqa* or *waqai'a* a bonnet which may be of black cotton with variegated silk thread covering the head and ears and bound under the chin with two strings. Another Muzeina *waqa* was made of chains and shells over red cotton. (2) The *burqu'* proper, a rectangular piece of red, yellow, or white cloth ornamented with rows of small pieces of gold, silver, or copper which covers the face from the nose to the chin, and from this again a chain pendant *razzet el-burqu'* sometimes hangs as low as the belt; and (3) the *jabha*, a piece of the same cloth as the *burqu'* which covers the forehead, with a ring at each side from which hang gold or silver chains, coins or strings of cowry shells.

Over this mask the women wear a black kerchief *quna'a*, with which they cover their faces when meeting the men. The Haweitat women of Midian (Sheikh Abu Tuqeiqa's clan) do not wear the *burqu'* though the Haweitat women of North Sinai do. Indeed the *burqu'* is by no means invariably worn in the Hijaz, where Doughty considered it a sign of Nejd influence.

All the Bedouin women are fond of silver rings which they wear in their noses, on their fingers, round their wrists, and ankles. But although their thumbs are adorned with these rings, their forefingers are left free. On one lady I counted sixteen strings of cowry shells. But they do not pierce their ears like the Egyptian women. Unlike the men who preserve their finery for festivals, the Bedouin ladies have to support the weight of their heavy jewellery all day and every day. Besides all this, on their backs and under the two head-shawls, they carry their babies in a cotton bag slung from the head.

The 'Ababda near the cultivation are hardly to be distinguished from the fellahin of Upper Egypt, except that they never wear black mantles, but the men of the hills go bare-headed with a wonderful frizzed-out coiffure called *dirwa*, nowadays often replaced by a turban. Through this mop boys stick a plain skewer, but the young men often have a three-pronged wooden hair-pin (*holal*). They wear drawers, and above the waist nothing but a long thin strip of calico called *tob*. On their arms and round their neck are many amulets paper charms wrapped up in little square leather cases. Unlike the men, the 'Ababda women always wear dark-coloured cotton stuffs. Two pieces make the complete outfit, one tied at the waist reaches the feet, while the other is laid shawl-fashion about the head and shoulders. Under these garments unmarried girls wear a girdle of leather thongs called *rahat*[1] (which the bridegroom removes), and leave their hands bare.

Klunzinger wrote of the 'Ababda women of his time (1863–1875) :—

> "The women clothe themselves with a white cloth drawn under one or both armpits, so that one or both shoulders and the arms remain free, and over this a large outer wrapper, also generally white, which can conceal the whole form ; in winter, instead of this, a mantle of brown woollen stuff is also worn, as among the female peasantry of the Nile Valley. They plait the hair from the crown down into many rows of plaits, the foremost of which, in front of the ear, has more freedom of movement than the others."[2]

Fig. 3.—The *Holal*.

Their ornaments consist of bead-necklaces, silver rings, and if possible gold, or gilt noserings. Head-gear is unknown to the true Beja, though Bent talks of the Bisharin possessing "tall, conical hats with long streamers used for dances at weddings, entirely covered with cowrie shells in pretty patterns ".[3]

The Awlad 'Ali and other western Arabs wear a red fez with blue tassel, the true fez or skull-cap ; not the cylindrical *tarbush* of Egypt. Besides the usual shirt, drawers and mantle *'aba*, they swathe themselves in a most graceful wrap, the *jird*, a direct descendant of the Roman toga. There are many qualities of *jirds* from the coarse coloured work of Hosh 'Isa in Behcira to the thin wool-and-silk or all-wool *jird*

---

[1] This *rahat* is the sole attire of the very little Nubian girls. Doughty saw a young boy wearing one near Mecca, and " hareem wearing the like over their smocks ". Doughty, ii, 477.
[2] Klunzinger, 253.
[3] *RGS Journal*, 1896, 338.

of Tunis. All the western Arabs are rather particular about the wearing of this garment, and freely criticize those who are slovenly or careless in putting it on. One corner is looped to the edge about a yard and a half from the end ; the right arm and head are then passed through the aperture thus formed, the loop resting on the left shoulder. The long end is next passed under the left elbow, and is then thrown across the right arm and shoulder. This is the usual way of wearing it in towns, but when the Arabs are exposed to the sun or wind, they pass a part of the breadth over the head and bring the end over the left shoulder in front.

The fringed end should fall straight behind, to a height just above the slippers. The knotting of the loop and the length of *jird* that hangs in front, and the amount of freedom given to the arm when the *jird* is flung round it (all difficult points for a European to recognize) constitute differences of appearance equivalent in their eyes to those that we see between a reach-me-down and a suit cut in Savile Row.

It is extraordinary how warm or how cool this garment can be made, by either bringing it tight against the whole body, or piling it upon one shoulder between the wearer and the sun.

The Western Arab wears a leather bag embroidered in many colours, with many pockets in it. This is slung over the right shoulder by a cord of cotton or silk, and is worn over cotton shirt but under the *jird*. It contains a knife, an awl for mending sandals, a packing needle, and a hundred and one other small items, picked up on the chance of being useful. Generally he makes fire with matches. On his feet he wears yellow heel-less slippers. A well made variety comes from Tunis, which have a seal in one, to prevent the right slipper being slipped on the left foot by mistake. In the desert, the western Arab wears a similar roughly made shoe, with a sole of untanned camel-hide.

The western woman wears a black shirt (*khamis*), which is generally embroidered in red and green silk at the opening in front. A red woollen cloth (*wasta*) encircles the waist, and a second shirt (*rumiya*) of rather different cut is worn over the head, or is twisted double and hung from the waist-cloth behind—for the more western Arabs look upon it as immodest to display the form. I have seen a *khamis* so hung, and am told that further west a *jird* is cut, and a piece is hung from the woman's waist-belt. She wears a black veiling round her head, and covers her face with a corner of her garment whenever a stranger approaches. On her feet she wears a kind of boot, generally embroidered all over with red and green silk.

Burckhardt saw a picture in the Convent of St. Catherine depicting the arrival of a sixteenth-century archbishop in which all the Arabs were armed with bows and arrows as well as matchlocks, but he adds his belief that " bows are no longer used as regular weapons by the Bedouins in any part of Arabia ". Nowadays, they have only a vague memory of the use of the bow, though javelins are often mentioned in their tales.

It is hard to understand the non-existence of the bow in the Beja country, for there, even to-day, firearms are few and far between, and one would have expected a hunter to prefer a bow and arrow to a throwing-stick or a wheel-trap to catch his game. But the Beja, unlike the Blemmyes, seem never to have been bowmen. They are of course intensely conservative, and the materials for archery were no doubt hard to obtain away from the Nile.

Even matchlocks were rare in Egypt in Napoleon's day, except among the Libyan Bedouin ; General Andreossy (1798) writes of the Arabs east of the Nile as armed with " pikes and lances four or five metres long ".[1] Such weapons I have not elsewhere heard of, but Burton and Wilkinson (1822) describe the 'Ababda as carrying long lances with which they transfixed even wild sheep. In Southern Palestine a lance (*shelfa*) is still sometimes seen stuck in the ground outside a sheikh's tent as a symbol of his dignity. Swords and daggers are worn pretty generally in Sinai. These are always curved, for the Arab knows the value of a drawing cut. Their sword closely resembles a cutlass and is quite different to that of Egypt and the Sudan. This latter (Fig. 4) has neither pommel nor ordinary guard, but from the cross-guard or *quillon* a small metal spur projects downwards parallel to the blade in which to catch the enemy's sword. Its scabbard is of wood, sewn over with leather, and hangs by a noose of cord over the left shoulder very close to the armpit.

The barbed lances of the Bisharin (Fig. 4*a*) and the more " shovel-headed " spears of the southern Beja were most formidable weapons in actual hand-to-hand encounter,

[1] *Memoirs relative to Egypt*, 298–9.

LIFE IN THE TENTS

and a Highlander has recorded[1] that at the battle of the Atbara in 1898, he found his claymore useless against them.

In ordinary salutation, clasping the hilt with your left hand you extend your right, and touch the stranger's forehead with your own. This is to prevent the stranger, when he puts out his right hand, from seizing your sword, and abruptly

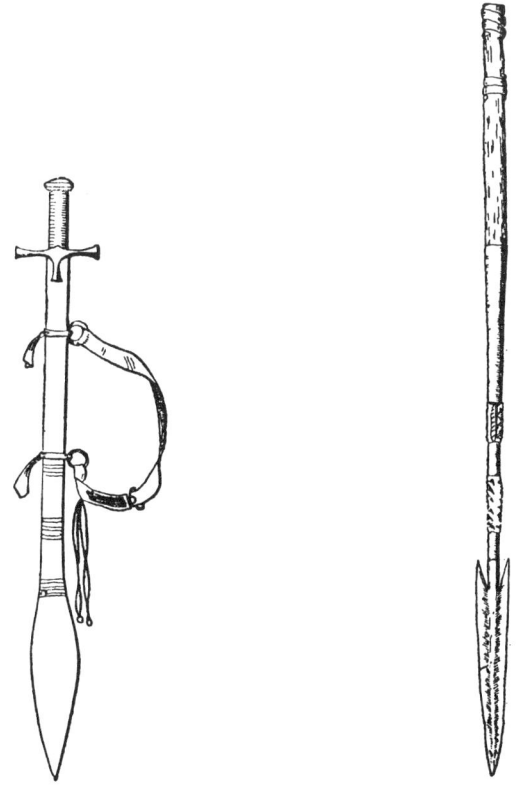

FIG. 4.—Beja Sword and Scabbard.   FIG. 4a.—Bishari Spear.

discontinuing his salutation. It is also a custom, when mounted, never to give the hand to a stranger on foot " for he could easily pull you out of the saddle, if he wanted to ".

The image of a serpent used formerly to be engraved all down a sword, and I once saw it thus beautifully engraved and inlaid with gold on the sword of a Nekhlawi.[2] On the

---

[1] " Reminiscences of a Subaltern," by " J. McN.," *Egyptian Gazette*, 20, ii, 33.
[2] The Nekhlawiya are the descendants of a Moorish garrison left in the castle of Nekhl in Sinai on the old Hajj route. On the abandonment of Nekhl after the war, they were moved to El-'Arish. Doughty met a similar garrison at El-'Ula.

ordinary Bedouin sword it has now become a figure of concentric circles with the merest blotch for the head of the snake—so far has the figure of the snake become conventionalized in our time, that the original device bids fair to be forgotten. Possibly it was to render the bite of the sword poisonous. In the same way, a scorpion appears on most North Sudan weapons.

As to their firearms, modern rifles, stolen from battlefields or issued by the Turks, have now completely ousted the old flintlocks and matchlocks. These were often 5 feet from muzzle to stock and heavily bound with brass. One who has not tried cannot imagine the patience necessary to use a matchlock or a flintlock gun. With the matchlock, the lighting of the home-made tinder, the care with which the gun had to be held, lest the igniting powder be upset, and the indeterminable time before the gun exploded, while all the time the aim had to be shifted upon the slowly grazing animal, all made up a trial that only Bedouin patience could endure. With the flintlock it was much the same, the spark would not take, or there was as like as not a flash in the pan. Yet I never remember an Arab becoming exasperated with his gun, as a civilized man would have been.

The powder for these weapons was sometimes made in the desert, for saltpetre was obtainable from some dark shale hills behind 'Ain Markha, and the charcoal from a bush *gurdi* (*Ochradenus baccatus*), though the sulphur had to be brought from Suez. The Bedouin are also diligent, though far from expert, in refilling old cartridge-cases. They are nowadays usually better shots than their fathers, who used to hold their heads away from the rifle in case it burst, and knock off the backsights as useless.

It may here be noted that the flint-containing limestones do not occur in the Eastern Desert south of lat. 25°—a fact even in our own days of some economic importance. During the War there was at one time a famine of matches in Upper Egypt, so much so that at Aswan small pieces of flint fetched five piastres (1s.) each, and certain 'Ababda of my acquaintance were reduced to twirling a stick of *markh* wood (*Leptadenia pyrotechnica*) in the hole of another piece of the same wood till fire was produced. The 'Ababda do not know, or have forgotten, the " fire-bow ", and say that the wood of any bush which makes good charcoal for gunpowder will

LIFE IN THE TENTS 79

serve equally well for producing fire. Such are *ushr* (*Calotropis procera*) and the *Ochradenus* mentioned above.

In the west, the Awlad 'Ali keep numerous rifles for use, and old silver-mounted guns and horse-pistols for show. There, the most dangerous use to which an Arab puts his shot-gun is firing it off at feasts. Their custom is to put the muzzle close to the ground and fire. The closer it is to the ground, the louder the noise and the greater the glory to the firer. A stout wad of donkey-dung usually replaces the bullet. One day the muzzle gets too close and the gun bursts. But the Arabs are always very careless, so that people often go home with a load of lead in their legs, and spend months recovering from the hearty welcome they received at so-and-so's wedding. Sometimes it happens too that unpopular persons are damaged in this way, through mere exuberance of spirits no doubt.

The 'Ababda and Bisharin are almost unarmed. Here and there a hunter possesses a rifle to shoot gazelles, while straight swords of the "crusader" type and round shields of hippopotamus or giraffe hide are sometimes seen. They usually carry daggers of different types strapped to their left arms above the elbow. With these the boys play a rough game. Two boys sit facing each other; each has a dagger in his right hand, which is grasped by the opponent's left. The stronger boy then pushes his right hand over his opponent's left shoulder and stabs him in the back, thereby scoring one point. Another game is to give a boy a shield and throw stones at him, for this teaches him to become expert in its use.

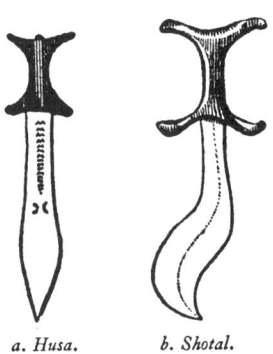

a. Husa.   *b. Shotal.*
FIG. 5.—Beja Daggers.

The Beja all carry heavy curved throwing-sticks with which they knock over hares. The style is of great antiquity, as old as the Aamu (see p. 14), and though the archæologists will refer to them as boomerangs they are never thrown as such.

They were used in warfare, as recently as the second battle of El-Teb, 1884, when "the Arabs also threw their boomerang-like clubs of tough mimosa wood at the horses' legs, thus bringing many of the horses to their knees".[1]

[1] C. Royle, *The Egyptian Campaigns*, 1st ed., ii, 153.

The Awlad ʻAli are so far on the road to becoming fellahin that they carry heavy sticks of olive wood instead of swords and daggers.[1] In Sinai, camel-sticks (*mahjan*) made of almond wood or tamarisk wood and shaped like the ancient Egyptian *uas* are sometimes seen.

The Arab calls his tent *beit shaʻr* " house of hair " or often simply *beit*[2]; never *kheima* which means a canvas tent of European pattern. The covering is composed of strips of coarse cloth woven from black goat's hair. Each strip is about three-quarters of a yard in breadth, and runs the full length of the tent, a very variable distance. So a rich sheikh of the Awlad ʻAli may need strips 10 yards long, a poor Sinai Bedouin only half that amount. Six or eight of these strips are stitched together to form a covering (*shuqqa*), which, when new, keeps out even the torrential winter rains of the Mediterranean Coast.

To make a larger tent, two *shuqqa* are joined together

Fig. 6.—Sinai Camel-Stick.

by a H-piece, of which the actual joining piece forms the gable of the tent while the arms are stitched cross-wise across the *shuqqa* to strengthen them. The tent covering now consists of sixteen strips, eight in front, and eight behind the ridge of the tent, strengthened by the arms running from front to back.

The walls of the tent are called *riwaq*, and the back-wall " the tent's tail " (*deil el-beit*). They generally pitch their tents with these back-walls to the prevailing north-west wind. The *riwaq* consist of one or two strips, always of wool, and a piece of sackcloth *sifla*, which trails on the ground. In Sinai, the back-wall is pinned on by wooden pins (*hilal*). It can thus readily be moved to close the tent-front, if the

---

[1] The Bisharin are fond of making sticks with ornamental striping from the wild olive trees of Jebel Elba.

[2] The Arabic word *beit* is used in both senses of the English word " house ", (1) " dwelling ", (2) " noble family ". Of this usage, Robertson Smith points out, " If the tent was originally the woman's, and not her husband's, the use . . . is itself a confirmation of an old law of female kinship." *Kinship*, 170.

PLATE X

Sinai Tent

Western Desert Tents

ARAB TENTS

LIFE IN THE TENTS

wind changes. Usually nine poles in rows of three support the tent, of which the central gable pole is usually called *wasit*.

Names vary slightly from tribe to tribe for the others. Two schemes are :—

<table><tr><td colspan="3" align="center">MA'AZA.
Front.</td></tr><tr><td>Rigl</td><td>Miqdim</td><td>Rigl</td></tr><tr><td>Jobir</td><td>Wasit</td><td>Jobir</td></tr><tr><td>Rigl</td><td>Miqdim</td><td>Rigl</td></tr></table>

<table><tr><td colspan="3" align="center">SINAI.
Front.</td></tr><tr><td>Yad</td><td>Maqdam</td><td>Yad</td></tr><tr><td>Amir</td><td>Wasit</td><td>Amir</td></tr><tr><td>Rigl</td><td>Zafra</td><td>Rigl</td></tr></table>

A large tent of the Awlad 'Ali had two main poles *jeibir*, and the two poles in the central row, one on each side of the *jeibir* were called *kimm*. The tent pegs were called *mathbat* and the tent-ropes *ramma* ; these latter were secured to the *shuqqa* by a guy, *jeizir*.

The tent was separated into two portions by a partition, the right-hand one, looking out, being for the women, while the left-hand one served as a guest-room.

On a great occasion, a whole tent may be cleared for the reception of visitors. The Awlad 'Ali reserve their newest and best tents for winter, and spend the summer using up their old ones. Some of the North Sinai Bedouins build straw huts *'arish* pl. *'arayish* in summer.

The Beja hut, in colour and shape like a hay-cock, is built of matting woven from the leaves of the dom-palm, *Hyphæna thebaica*.[1] The mats are stretched over long curved sticks, and fastened there with wooden skewers. The hut is invariably set up with its back to the north wind, so the door, only 2 or 3 feet high, is thus on the less steeply-sloping side. It is curtained generally with a piece of sacking. The interior, only about 10 feet square in all, is always divided into two parts by the erection inside the matting hut of a tent of goat's hair cloth entirely closed by a curtain. A small space is left by the door for cooking, and the reception of visitors.

This inner tent contains a plank-bed with a mat laid on it, and perhaps a hard leather pillow, or the elaborate head-rest,

---

[1] The late Lady Clayton showed me a photograph of very similar huts used by the Tebu at Kufara.

just like that of Ancient Egypt, by which their fuzzy coiffures are preserved from contact with the floor. This is made from the root of " ushr " (*Calotropis procera*). They say this head-rest keeps them watchful, as whenever one of them turns his head, it wakes him up.

The hut usually contains also a large water-jar, basketry milk-bowls (woven from the dom-palm leaf), and bottles made from gourds or hollowed out of solid blocks of wood.

The furniture of the Arab tent consists simply of carpets, which the Awlad 'Ali women in the west weave for themselves, saddles (of which something will be said later) and weapons. Their saddlebags are made of wool, ornamented with tassels and generally brightly coloured, green, red, and yellow. They sleep on woollen quilts.

In the women's part are copper cooking pans (unknown to the Beja who prefer stone pots), griddles, sieves, and mortars for pounding corn. The Arabs have also stone handmills, which are often brought from Sinai even across Egypt to the Awlad 'Ali, although the latter have a quarry of their own near Sidi Abd er-Rahman. The Bisharin do not know the mill, but use rubbing-stones (*marhaka*) ; the lower, a flattish plate ; the upper a cylindrical roller of silicified sandstone.

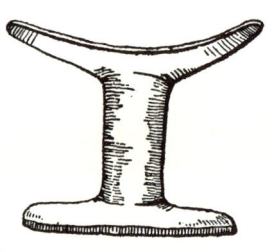

FIG. 7.—Beja Head-rest (*metar'as*).

The Sinai Arabs have all the same coffee service bought in Egypt, a pestle and mortar for pounding the beans and an iron frying pan for roasting them. The mortar is of baked clay, and the pestle is just a thick stick of wood, a yard or more long. The real spoon in which the coffee is roasted is called *tasa* ; it is about 4 inches across, of very thick iron to prevent the beans getting roasted too quickly and becoming burnt. The handle of this spoon has a joint so that it can be folded to go easily into the saddle bag. Attached to the spoon by a small chain is another spoon with a small head which allows the coffee-maker to turn over the coffee grain by grain while it is being roasted.

The frying pan is a novelty which came in at the beginning of the present century. When it is used, the grains are tossed every half-minute instead of being turned over. Their

LIFE IN THE TENTS

coffee-pots are always of copper, and the coffee is served in little cups of thick porcelain without saucers. The cups are served round half-full; the offer of a full cup being considered " bad form ". Sometimes the cups are brought in on a brass tray with wooden handles. The Sinai Arabs have rectangular wooden vessels for milking, but the Awlad 'Ali use round wooden bowls (which come from the Sudan via the oases). The Beja always milk into vessels of closely woven basketry.

Leather waterskins are universal; these are generally tanned with red chips of *Acacia etbaica*; or, if very superior, with the rind of a pomegranate. In making these skins, the hides of goats are always preferred to those of sheep, because they are more porous and keep the water cooler; gazelle-skins are also used. The process has been well described by Sir Samuel Baker :—

"The flaying process for this purpose is a delicate operation, as the knife must be so dexterously used that no false cut should injure the hide. The animal is hung up by the hind legs; an incision is then made along the inside of both thighs to the tail, and with some trouble the skin is drawn off the body towards the head, precisely as a stocking might be drawn from the leg; by this operation the skin forms a seamless bag, open at both ends. To form a girba, the skin must be buried in the earth for about twenty hours[1]: it is then washed in water, and the hair is easily detached. Thus rendered clean, it is tanned by soaking for several days in a mixture of the bark of a mimosa and water; from this it is daily withdrawn, and stretched out with pegs upon the ground; it is then well scrubbed with a rough stone, and fresh mimosa bark well bruised, with water, is rubbed in by the friction. About four days are sufficient to tan the thin skin of a gazelle, which is much valued for its toughness and durability; the aperture of the hind quarters is sewn together, and the opening of the neck is closed, when required, by tying. A good water-skin should be porous, to allow the water to exude sufficiently to moisten the exterior; thus the action of the air upon the exposed surface causes evaporation, and imparts to the water within the skin a delicious coolness. The Arabs usually prepare their tanned skins with an empyreumatical oil made from a variety of substances, the best of which is that from the sésamé grain; this has a powerful smell, and renders the water so disagreeable that few Europeans could drink it. This oil is black, and much resembles tar in appearance; it has the effect of

[1] Two or three days, according to my informant.

preserving the leather, and rendering it perfectly water-tight. In desert travelling each person should have his own private water-skin slung upon his dromedary; for this purpose none is so good as a small-sized gazelle skin that will contain about two gallons."[1]

The Beja distil an oil from colocynth seeds, which is also used for tanning waterskins. They build a miniature "hut" of loose stones with a hole in the roof, over this hole they set a pot (with partially choked mouth) full of colocynth seeds upside down and light a fire round it. When heated, oil drips from the pot through the hole into a bowl placed inside the "hut". This contrivance they call *balanda-b*.

Both the Sinai Arabs and the Beja make stone tobacco-pipes of steatite, but the Sinai Arab embellishes his with a long wooden stem of almond or other wood.[2] A bodkin for cleaning the pipe and a small pair of pincers for picking up the glowing charcoal are attached to his pipe by a chain.

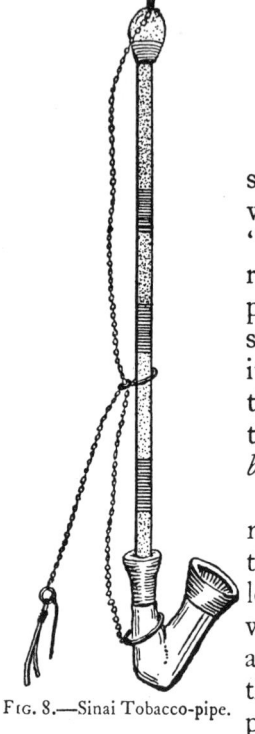

FIG. 8.—Sinai Tobacco-pipe.

[1] Sir Samuel Baker, *The Nile Tributaries of Abyssinia*, 49, 50.
[2] This stem is itself smoked when his tobacco runs out!

Chapter V

FOOD

"*The very first baker of bread that ever lived must have done his work exactly as the Arab does at this day.*"—Kingslake *Eothen*.

Food always eaten in Common—Men and Women feed apart—Baking Bread—Bread from the seed of Wild Plants—Meat—Expedients in Time of Famine—Food Taboos.

The world to early man must have been sharply divided into his pack, the people with whom it was safe to feed, and the others. Our desert Bedouins are separated by many thousands of years (and very little else) from that primitive arrangement. To-day the camelmen of a caravan split up at night into as many messes as there are tribes represented in the party. The hill 'Ababda won't eat with their cousins from the Nile, nor either of these with fellahin or with Arabs if there be any in the party. True, they are all willing to accept hospitality from anyone who may offer it, but the same might be said of any other animals. And food still remains a sacred thing among the Arabs. To this day your guest is safe from you, even though you may have a blood-feud with him, so long as your food is in his belly. The pack still shares alike (no Bedouin eats alone), and the women and children still wait till afterwards for the scraps.

Perhaps the most curious thing about Europeans in Bedouin eyes is that men and women feed together. This is unknown among the Arabs,[1] where only the small male children feed with the *harim*.

The normal Bedouin diet consists of barley (in Sinai and Mariut), maize, wheat, rice, lentils, and dates. Dates grow in abundance in Sinai at Feiran and Qatia, but in the West the Awlad 'Ali are obliged to bring them from the oases of Siwa and Bahariya. The 'Ababda usually obtain them from the Nile, but sometimes a sailing boat from Arabia appears on the coast and is besieged by eager Bedouins seeking *'ajwa*, that is dates crushed together in a paste. Buttermilk is commonly used

[1] Robertson Smith thought this dated back to a time when a man and his wife and family were not usually of one kin, and only kinsmen could eat together.

in their dishes, whereas fresh milk is seldom seen. Every morning the women prepare butter by shaking the milk in skin bags. A favourite dish is *jereisha* " coarsely ground wheat ", well boiled, over which butter-milk has been poured ; *'asida* is a mere paste of flour and water.

Burghul is wheat, coarsely brayed and dried in the sun. This is then reboiled with butter or oil.

A butter made from goat's milk with *shih* [1] in it for seasoning is sometimes brought at the morning meal with bread of the night before. I never once remember newly cooked bread at this morning meal, unless the arrival of guests necessitated it.

Sometimes the Arabs mix the barley meal with that of maize or wheat. They grind the corn with stones (*rahai*), or pound it in a wooden mortar, and bake two sorts of bread, both unleavened ; in one case thin flaps of bread are baked on a griddle (*saj*), in the other the dough is spread on hot stones and buried in glowing ashes. Both these methods are current also in Palestine, and represent no doubt the fusion of two cultures.

The kneading of bread is looked upon by the Sinai Arab as a business of importance. The flour is carried in special bags made by the women, who take some trouble over the ornamental line that they weave into them. These bags have a kind of bottle-neck opening woven in wool to stop the flour from escaping easily, while a lump of rock-salt is sometimes kept inside for mixing the dough. When they knead, they put the flour into a wooden drinking-trough, or into enamelled tin basins which are imported into the desert from Suez. The art lies in putting just enough water into the flour to knead, so that after kneading no dough is left on the fingers or on the dish. The dough must be well kneaded, for real hard work is required to make it rise. Finally it is patted into a flat round cake. The ground must be broken up so that when the fire is lit, it heats the sand right through. Then it will not stick to the dough when the charcoal is brushed aside and the cake is thrown upon the red-hot ashes and sand. The charcoal is then spread on top of the dough, which is left to cook for about a quarter of an hour.

In the Western Desert a griddle is used, and the dough, usually wheaten, is patted into a much thinner and larger

[1] *Artemisia herba alba.*

THE BEJA HUT

cake before it is thrown on the heated iron plate, and turned until cooked through.

The Bisharin do not knead at all, but first prepare a heated round of flat stones by burning a fire over them. Then they mix their flour, generally that of the large millet, and water in a copper pot into a very thick paste. This is poured on to the heated stones. A wisp of grass is lit and held so that the wind blows the flame over the paste. This gives a glaze to the cake, and once the flame is out, the charcoal from the fire is pushed with a stick over the dough and left there till the cake is cooked.

Bread is also baked by the Bedouin women from the seeds of wild plants. Their favourite is *samh*,[1] " a leafless green wort, a hand high, with fleshy stems and branches full of brine-like samphire. At each finger end is an eye, where, the plant drying up in early summer, a grain is ripened."[2] The seeds must lie dormant in dry places for years, for I have seen the dismal clayey waste west of Maghra become suddenly covered with the yellowish-green of this plant after a downpour.

Mrs. Crowfoot describes the mode of collection thus :—

" All among the plants were little round threshing-floors. These were shallow depressions in the sand, and in them a most strange kind of threshing was being practised by the Bedu encamped nearby. Water was first poured into them, and the harvest of dry flower-heads thrown in. Now these seed vessels, as in certain other desert plants, have the property of remaining dry when closed and opening when wet, so after they had lain a time in the threshing pools, they opened and the black seeds fell to the bottom. When the water evaporated, which did not take long in that fierce sun, the women came and collected the seed at their ease. It was then pounded into a hard mass, forming a kind of ' bread ' which is supposed to be very nutritious, but which, our informant said, to his taste, was very nasty."[3]

The 'Ababda also make bread from the seeds of *hudak*, a plant which I have collected but unfortunately have not been able to get identified. It also grows in Sinai, but the Arabs there did not eat it, though they said that the Haweitat of Midian did. I have eaten the 'Ababda bread, it was quite palatable.

---

[1] *Mesembryanthemum forskalii.*   [2] Doughty, i, 313.
[3] *From Cedar to Hyssop*, 48.

The ants of the desert also collect all these seeds into their granaries, and bring the grain out again to dry in the sun, if it gets wetted by a shower. The Bedouin respect them greatly for this wisdom.

The Bisharin pound the husks of the dom-palm nut till they look like cocoa, and eat them mixed with milk.

Meat, that is the flesh of domestic animals, only forms part of the Bedouin diet, when a festival has to be celebrated or a guest welcomed.

All Bedouins observe most faithfully the rite of *halal*, that is, slaying an animal by cutting its throat, and allowing the blood to run. The words *halal, allahu akbar* are pronounced at the moment of sacrifice. The blood is not allowed to lie on the ground, but is at once covered over by a little heap of dust or gravel.[1] When a hunter shoots a gazelle or ibex, he cuts the throat of the dying or dead animal, for even when life is extinct, so long as the blood runs, the *halal* makes it lawful food.

Falls, describing a wedding in the Western Desert, writes:—

"Sheikh Sadaui ... in the name of Allah cut the creature's throat, not quickly, but out of love for the animal slowly, with several cuts. The Awlad 'Ali all regard swift killing as a sign of a hard heart, and the victim's head must never be quite cut off. The animal must lose all blood."[2]

When both host and guests are generally starving, the art of cuisine has little chance to develop and is sometimes disgustingly simple. Robinson wrote of some Arabs feeding:—

"Our Haweity guide had brought along his family, with two or three camels; and to them the offals of the kid were abandoned. I looked in upon this feast; and found the women boiling the stomach and entrails, which they had merely cleaned by stripping them with the hand, without washing; while the head, unskinned and unopened, was roasting underneath in the embers of a fire made chiefly of camels' dung. With such a meal our Tawarah would hardly have been content."[3]

To roast game, a hole is made in the ground and lined with stones, and a fire of desert-wood is kindled over this. When

---

[1] Ezekiel, xxiv, 7, and Doughty, i, 492.
[2] J. C. Falls, *Three Years in the Libyan Desert*, 316.
[3] *Researches in Palestine*, i, 304.

the stones become red-hot, the wood is pushed aside and the oven exposed for use.

Meanwhile the hare has been cut open and cleaned, though the pelt is left on. The charcoal is then pushed in over the carcase, and the whole covered over with earth. When after half an hour the mound is opened, the pelt, reduced to parchment, can be peeled off, since the fat has kept it from sticking to the body, and the meat will be found excellent. Even ibex are sometimes baked in this way.

Ibex-meat is highly esteemed, and is preferable to the ordinary goat's flesh, though I have never found Kashmir sportsmen to believe this.

The Hadendawa sometimes cook mutton by lighting a large fire in a hole in the rocks, and then putting the meat into the heated hole. A great number of sheep were so baked at a grand meeting that Bramly rode to with Slatin Pasha.

At all Bedouin feasts, mutton is the invariable *pièce de resistance*. A lamb, which has been boiled in fat, may be served whole on a gigantic wooden platter, bathed in melted butter and surrounded with rice, on a pile of bread and sometimes vegetables. Despising spoons and forks, the guests wash their hands, and plunge them boldly into the savoury mess. Sometimes the platter is set on a sheepskin coat, and the guests rub the fat from their fingers into the coat to make it waterproof.

When an animal is killed, the Arabs often eat the liver and kidney raw, adding a little salt. Some 'Ababda of my acquaintance killed an ibex, and devoured all the intestines raw, sqeezing the contents of the gall-bladder over them as sauce.

The Arabs reckon the meat of the gazelle excellent eating, though to Europeans it seems almost intolerably dry. Both 'Ababda and Bisharin used to eat the wild ass, when they could get it, and the Western Arabs eat the jerboa, a clean vegetable feeder. So I have seen pious Murabitin annoyed because my terrier would not eat the desert rats he killed ; they thought it waste of good food, since they could not very well eat after him.

Pig's flesh of course is taboo to all good Moslems, so a Muzeini sheikh once surprised me by begging ham outside the Monastery of St. Catherine. I found however it was to be eaten by his camel, not himself, " to restore its sight."

But the Western Arabs, like the fellahin,[1] did not despise the wild-boar, now extinct in Egypt.

Hunger knows no law, the Towara eat vultures, ravens, hyenas and leopards. One modern hunter told me " leopards always make me sick ", though another, who had slain five, found them good eating. It may be an acquired taste ; Bedouins will always eat a cat, which must be very much the same thing.

In time of famine strange expedients are used, locusts and snails are eaten, while in 1915 the Arab women of Qatia boiled the camel-droppings and extracted the few grains of corn therefrom to still their hunger.

The idea of cannibalism must have been as repugnant to the early Arab as to us, for so soon as the idea dawned that the souls of the dead might pass into birds and reptiles, food taboos began to be created. Yet even after death, their ancestors were wary, and seldom, if ever, passed into domestic animals.

In Sinai nowadays there is practically no animal in which a soul could be sure of refuge, though some of Professor Palmer's Arabs would not eat the flesh of the hyrax, and said " he who eats him will never see his father or mother again ". This taboo is no longer observed, at least, I have known many Sinai hunters infringe it. But, in Egypt, Salem Faraj of the Ma'aza said " we don't eat the hyrax, for it has ' understanding ' and is formed too much in human shape ". Salem referred to the likeness of its fore-paws to hands, for they have four toes, while the hind-paws have only three. Superficially the hyrax resembles the Alpine marmot in appearance, size and habits, though with a cleft upper lip, and it inhabits much the same rocky dens. The 'Ababda eat hyrax readily, but I have heard Bisharin jest when eating it, *sanok buwar tumteina* " are you eating the hyrax your brother " ? And they also say of it in Arabic *Muhammad buwar tarad min et-tahar* " Muhammad the hyrax ran away from circumcision ". So, in spite of his orthodox name, the hyrax is regarded as a pagan.

The Prophet Muhammad would not eat the spiny-tailed lizard *dabb*, and tradition says that he gave as his reason for not eating it, that a clan of the Israelites had been transformed into reptiles, and he fancied that the lizard was sprung

[1] See Lane, *Modern Egyptians*, 299.

from them. " This was before it was known that the metamorphosed human beings leave no issue."[1] The Ma'aza won't eat the *dabb* ; they say " it is good, it kills snakes ". Nor will the Beja. Yet an old Arab proverb says " none but those who eat the flesh of the *dabb* can call themselves Arabs ". They eat this lizard in North Sinai, and say it should be larded with clarified butter and its belly opened and filled with this butter to make it taste like mutton. Doughty tells of the Arabian Fuqara and the *dabb* :—

> " The thob ; which they call here pleasantly ' Master Hamed, sheykh of wild beasts ', and say he is human, *zillamy*—this is their elvish smiling and playing—and in proof they hold up his little five-fingered hands. They eat not his palms, nor the seven latter thorny rings of Sheykh Hamed's long tail, which, they say, is ' man's flesh '. His pasture is most of the sweet-smelling Nejd bush, *el-arrafej*. Sprawling wide and flat is the body, ending in a training tail of even length, where I have counted twenty-three rings. The colour is blackish and green-speckled, above the pale yellowish and dull belly ; of his skin the nomads make small herdsmen's milk-bottles. The manikin saurian, with the robust hands, digs his burrow under the hard gravel soil, wherein he lies all the winter, dreaming. The thob-catcher, finding the hole, and putting in his long reed armed with an iron hook, draws Hamed forth. His throat cut, they fling the carcase, whole, upon the coals ; and thus baked they think it a delicate roast."[2]

Taboos on eating fish, birds, and lizards are widespread in North Africa, and may be survivals of an early general Hamitic culture. Gautier found them among the Tuareg, and Oric Bates,[3] citing him, says " The Imushagh explain their abstention from fish, birds and edible lizards on the score that these (totemic) animals are ' their mother's brothers ', a form of expression emphatically matriarchial ". The expression is indubitably matriarchal, yet Bates overstresses the point when he calls it emphatically so.

Just the same phrase is used by the ordinary Cairene when he hails the extremely tame hippopotamus, which has lived for twenty years in the Giza Zoo, as " *Amm Sa'id* ", without meaning more than that it is almost human.

According to Mas'ud,[4] the pagan Arabs believed the

---

[1] Robertson Smith, *Kinship*, 198, quoting Damiri, ii, 88.
[2] Doughty, i, 326.
[3] Bates, 112, quoting E. F. Gautier, *Sahara algérien*, 138.
[4] *Les Prairies d'Or*, iii, 311. See also, Doughty, i, 168.

soul became an owl after death, and the Bisharin still consider it a great scandal, as they did in Burckhardt's time, to eat the flesh of birds. Certainly the 'Ababda will not kill the sand-grouse or the desert partridge, and both tribes are particularly afraid of killing or harming the bearded vulture (*Gypætus barbatus*). Here the objection to eating these birds seems to be that they may be metamorphosed human beings. I once caught Muhammad Buleib, an 'Aliab guide, stoning a bird for prophesying evil to him. Earlier in the winter a croaking raven had warned him of coming evil; and eight days later he had heard of his brother's death.

Fish are eaten by the 'Ababda who live on the coast, but these are despised as not having sprung from the tribal ancestor, and are quite possibly the descendants of the ancient Ichthyophagi. By the 'Ababda and Bisharin of the hills, fish are considered " dirty snakes ", and are taboo. Just so did the ancient Ethiopians abhor fish, while the nobles and chiefs of the Delta were not allowed an audience of their King Piankhi because " they were fish-eaters ". In the west, the Awlad 'Ali also despise fish.

Between Ras Rawaya and Suakin the mediæval traveller Ibn Battuta met a tribe of Beja who would not eat gazelles. Possibly they considered the gazelles metamorphosed human beings, or perhaps there was some local rule protecting them near the tomb of a saint.

I fancy there is a prejudice against drinking anything but " fresh " water; at any rate, a pious old sheikh from the west always declined the bottled products of France or Italy in favour of the extremely saline water of his home in Mariut.

An amusing story of true cannibalism came from the 'Ababda. In talking of famines, I asked if they were not sometimes so hard put to it for food, that men ate one another. They said " Never, but a man once had a black slave so fat, that when the negro died he thought it a pity all that good grease should be wasted. He built a great fire, and set the corpse before it, intending to make ointment for his camels. But the roast slave smelt so good that the hungry 'Abadi tasted him, and the taste was so good, that in the end he ate most of that negro."

Fortunately the custom did not spread, or we might have a complete 'Abadi parallel to the Chinese discovery of roast pork.

Chapter VI
DOMESTIC ANIMALS

"*On the continent of Europe down to comparatively recent times the lower animals were in all respects considered amenable to the laws. Domestic animals were tried in the common criminal courts, and their punishment on conviction was death ; wild animals fell under the jurisdiction of the ecclesiastical courts, and the penalty they suffered was banishment or death by exorcism and excommunication.*"—Frazer, *Folklore in the Old Testament.*

No trace of former Totems—Possible former Belief that Animals contained the Souls of the Dead—Milk Customs—Sheep—Goats—Dogs—Horses—Saddles—Donkeys.

How the first animals came to be tamed is a fascinating problem which has exercised many ingenious minds. Some have painted a pretty picture of a savage woman, possibly childless herself, taking pity on a pair of kids of different sexes and making pets of them. Others, notably Frazer and Salomon Reinach, have poured scorn on this idea, saying the hungry tribe would have eaten the pets long before they grew up, and put forward instead, the theory of an origin from cherished totemic animals. But neither in Australia nor in the whole American continent, both areas where totemic beliefs are rife, did the early explorers find any domesticated animals, with the single exception of the llama in Peru. If another theory is wanted, I would prefer the idea that the dog domesticated itself one evening when it was hungry, and that the possibility of taming other animals was suggested by this.

We find our Bedouins possessed from the very earliest times of the ox, sheep,[1] goat, and dog. The horse did not come into Egypt till the time of the Hyksos, and, though the Asiatic Bedouin were in possession of the camel from a very early period, it was not introduced into Africa till about 500 B.C., possibly on account of the adverse climatic conditions. The beast is now of such importance to the Bedouin that it demands, and will receive, a chapter to itself.

Though regarding the Ancient Egyptians as definitely

[1] The sheep must have come into Africa from the east, because there are no true wild sheep in the Dark Continent.

totemistic, so painstaking an investigator as Professor Seligman failed to find

> "any evidence suggesting that animals were associated with the social organization or with the worship of the pagan Beja, nor have any traces of animal cult been discovered among the Beja of the present time. Sacred animals do exist among the pagan Hamites of Abyssinia, among them are the hyena, the snake, the crocodile, and the owl, though there is no reason to suppose that these are totems." [1]

Yet the primitive Hamites must always have shown a great respect for their animal comrades, for Agatharchides, speaking of the Troglodytes on the African coast, says: "They gave the name of parent to no human being, but only to the ox and cow, the ram and ewe that supplied their nourishment." And he adds "those cattle that grow old or are sick, they knock on the head and eat"—a custom still observed by the 'Ababda, who never allow an animal to die a natural death.

Further, that the cow was personified in ancient times by the Beja is also extremely probable. Meinhof,[2] after drawing attention to the fact that the so-called masculine gender in Hamitic languages is really that of persons, while the feminine is that of things, has the following remarkable passage:—

> "In Bedauye,[3] ša' denotes 'cow' ... yet this animal is grammatically masculine, since it is of such importance in the livelihood of the people that it is reckoned as a person. The same word is used grammatically as feminine when it is meant 'meat', in other words, when it denotes not a person but a thing."

And some people of the past, living where the Bisharin do now, if they did not venerate their cattle, at least buried them in cemeteries with some care.[4] The second declaration required of the deceased Egyptian by his Book of the Dead was "I have not made the cattle to suffer", and something of the same care was exhibited by the early Hebrews, though later the advent of new religions, which promised a heavenly paradise for the soul instead of a living dwelling-place, dissipated their beliefs and customs to the undoubted detriment of the animals. And so in the first century A.D., St. Paul's

---

[1] *Hamites*, 653. The sacred animals mentioned are all wild ones.
[2] Meinhof, *Die Sprachen der Hamiten*, 23.
[3] Or to Bdawi, the Beja language.
[4] G. W. Murray, "Graves of Oxen in the Eastern Desert of Egypt," *JEA.*, xii, 1926.

DOMESTIC ANIMALS

business-like mind rejects the idea that the prohibition " Thou shalt not muzzle the ox when he treadth out the corn " was intended to benefit the cattle ; while, at the present day, many of the Mediterranean race would be better men if their minds still retained some faint trace of the superstition that ancestral spirits might lurk somewhere inside their beasts of burden.

The Sinai children spend the whole of the daylight in herding the goats and sheep, and as they sleep in the same tents with them at night, may fairly be called the comrades of their animals. In fact the nomads' animals have to share their masters' fortunes for good and evil. The kindly Ma'aza tie the placenta or the severed foreskin to a camel's neck to make it prolific or increase its virility, whereas the Hebrew custom of the scapegoat went to the other extreme.

This consideration shown for the cattle has given rise to a peculiar regard for milk, still universal among the Beja, which has led to the establishment of a code. Among the 'Ababda, Bisharin, Amar Ar, Hadendawa and Beni 'Amir, in fact the whole of the Beja, these rules are strictly observed.

(1) Only men may milk. They despise the Arab tribes with whom they are in contact for allowing women to milk.

(2) One may only milk into gourds and basket vessels, especially the latter, though skin vessels may be used. In no circumstances may milk be drawn or put into an earthenware pot, or modern bowl of tin or china.

(3) No man may drink of the milk he has just drawn, until some other has drunk it. When alone on a journey, an 'Abadi will endure thirst for hours rather than break this rule.[1]

The milking referred to is that of camels and sheep, but further south where cattle are met with the same rules obtain.

It has been shown by Sir James Frazer that most pastoral tribes believe in a sympathetic relation between a cow and the milk drawn from her.[2] The cow is supposed to remain in direct physical sympathy with her milk, even after she has parted with it ; so the boiling of milk, the use of earthenware, or metal vessels, the touch of the women are all thought to be dangerous to the cattle. These superstitions, which

---
[1] Compare from a distant part of the world. " Among the Kaitish a Water Clansman when alone may drink ; but if others are with him he may drink only when water is given him by a man of another totem."—Carveth Read, *The Origin of Man*, 294.
[2] Frazer, *Folklore in the Old Testament*, 364. Also cf. Seligman, *Pagan Tribes*, 73.

the Beja share with the Galla, must have come down from the cattle-owning days of the past and been transferred by the northern Beja to their camels, when they came to be possessed of such animals.

In this connection, I would quote Plowden on the Habab, a Beja tribe of Eritrea :—

> "In each small village there is kept a cow of one breed from generation to generation, on which the good fortune of the entire herd depends. This cow (or there may be two) is milked in peculiar vessels, and the milk must be drunk out of those vessels, as it would be sacrilege to drink it out of any other ; those are of earthenware, while the other cows are milked into wicker-work vases. Should this ceremony be omitted or varied, it is supposed that the cows of the tribe would become dry, or die ; and this, amongst a people who feed, it may be said, on milk, would be equivalent to a famine." [1]

And Burckhardt, speaking of the Arab tribes of Ja'afira and Rowaja, settled in the Nile Valley near Isna, says :—

> "If any person of the family die, the women stain their hands and feet blue with indigo ; which demonstration of their grief they suffer to remain for eight days, all that time abstaining from milk, and not allowing any vessel containing it to be brought into the house, for they say the whiteness of the milk but ill accords with the sable gloom of their minds." [2]

But one may suppose that really they feared lest the milk in their cattle might suffer injury.

The 'Ababda sometimes dedicate the milk of a beast to their patron saint, Shadli, and the milk of such beasts is always milked into separate basketwork vessels lest it become mixed with the milk of some other animal.

The twins of the fellahin in Upper Egypt and the Barabra are believed to turn into cats at night. The twins of the 'Ababda are prevented from doing this by being given camel's milk as their first drink in the world. But then their stuttering children are given asses' milk to prevent their stuttering—a procedure which defies rational analysis.

But in the Western Desert, our Bisharin camelmen were disgusted to find the women of the Awlad 'Ali milking, and refused to drink the milk thus obtained.

In Cyrenaica, the custom is, when paying the bride-price, to give the mother of the bride a sum of money as the price of

---

[1] *Travels in Abyssinia*, 14.   [2] *Notes*, 159.

the milk with which she had suckled her daughter. And the sordid Awlad 'Ali refuse full blood-money for damage done to the breasts of an aged woman, as " the *diya* is only for the milk ".

Milk possesses some sanctity among the Arabs of Sinai, because they told Palmer that the leopard had been formerly a man, who, for washing himself with milk, was turned into a beast and became the enemy of mankind.[1] There, as in Arabia, only girls and uncircumcised boys may milk the goats and sheep, and the camels are tended by men.

Milk, like water and salt, loses much of its virtue by being bought and sold. All African and Arabian Bedouin agree about this, and even the town-dwellers used to think its sale shameful. I again quote Sir Richard Burton, " None will at the present day sell this article of consumption even at civilized Mecca, except Egyptians."[2]

Dogs, though now unclean, may have once been sacred, for both Arabs and Beja reckon it *'aib* " shame " to traffic in them, as they do to sell water or milk. The Arabian *jinn* often take the form of dogs, and at night, the Beja will not stone them, for " they don't know who it is ".

Yet the Prophet detested dogs, and was once on the point of issuing orders for the extermination of the species. Accordingly they are reckoned *nijis* " abomination " by all good Moslems, a prejudice which I once turned to useful account when clearing a path through the overcrowded decks of a pilgrim ship. Holding a terrier in front of me, I walked along shouting, " Make way for the *nijis*." The would-be Hajjies laughed and made way.

There are almost as many strains in the dog tribes of Egypt as among the Bedouins, their masters. Indeed if their traditions be true, the stocks must have coalesced ! For the desert 'Ababda all firmly believe in the existence somewhere to the south of them of a race called Beni Kelb, whose males are all dogs but able to talk, while the females are normal women. This fairy tale was told to Doughty in Arabia and Hamilton in North Africa, and is widespread elsewhere as far as China. It probably has its origin in a confusion of the genuine name Beni Kelb, that of a famous tribe in the early days of Islam, with some traveller's tale of the baboons in the mountains of Southern Arabia or Abyssinia.

[1] *Kinship*, 204.   [2] *Pilgrimage*, i, 247.

An ordinary traveller of to-day cannot hope to receive the hospitality of such marvels, but he will certainly meet the Pariah, "the best barker in the world." Not unlike the dingo or Australian wild dog in appearance, these pariahs act as watch-dogs to every tent, and, on the whole, the Arabs do not treat them badly. It is rare to see a dog that is starved, though, like the rest of the family, he is by no means pampered. The dogs go daily with the women, children, and donkeys to the well for water, and for the rest they prefer to hang about the tents on guard, rather than follow their masters about the country. On their return they welcome them with all the affection exhibited by a European dog on such occasions. As a matter of fact, they seem to follow the women in preference to the men, if these by any chance go out to pick herbs or to visit other women at a distance. These dogs fight a good deal among themselves, but should they turn fierce about the tent, the Arabs pull out the eye-teeth to render their bite harmless. Pariahs make quite good sheep-dogs, if brought up when quite young with the herd. The Hanadi, when hunting jackals, always take one or two with them, as the Arab greyhound will not close with a jackal, whereas a good pariah will when the greyhounds have brought it to a standstill.

The Awlad 'Ali watchdogs are big curly-tailed dogs, often with a lot of white on them, which strongly resemble the Tripolitan dog, an ancient breed in the Eastern Mediterranean. I once met one of these dogs far in the desert running quietly along the day-old tracks of a motor car, which he had followed about five miles out of sheer curiosity. When he saw for the first time the strange beast he had been following, he set about returning home quite gravely and sedately.

There is a sheep-dog used by the Awlad 'Ali in the west, which reminds one of the sheep-dogs of the Maremma, the Italian marsh country north of Rome. But it is smaller, and of the chestnut colour so common with the pariah, instead of the ordinary white colour of the Italian dog.

The Soluqi or Saluki of Sinai must be an offshoot from the Persian or Afghan hound. It is white or pale coffee colour with feathering on the tail and ears.

Though Jorrocks justly derided all greyhounds as daft, yet the saluki does still retain some of the intelligence that has been bred out of our racing greyhounds. There is nothing of the cat's paw about the saluki's, but a good splay foot, to meet the sandy ground that he has to run over. The Arabs keep his foot in condition with henna, which tans the pad, and also reduces inflammation caused by cuts and bruises. This hound will kill both hares and foxes, but I have never known one swift enough to run down anything but a very young gazelle, though most Arabs say he can do it. Indeed a hound in Arab hands is not fed sufficiently generously to give it stamina necessary to catch an animal, which saves its life by its speed probably most days of the week. The best salukis are owned by the Arabs near the Palestine frontier.

The Hanadi possess also the Algerian greyhound. This hound has no feathering and looks very much like a diminutive European hound.[1]

The Bisharin have a peculiar greyhound with prick ears and curly tail, which must, I think, be a descendant of the *tesem* of the Ancient Egyptians, itself with a skull very like that of *Canis lupaster*, the largest of the three varieties of Egyptian jackal. In the Etbai,[2] the Bisharin feed their hounds on milk with very little solid food for most of the year, so that few of them are equal to the running down of a good hare alone, though they may do this sometimes when the hare is caught napping in a bush and gets a very bad start, or if more than one hound is in the hunt.

The Sinai Arabs possess a cross between the saluki and the pariah which they call *dirra*.

The fierce Armenti watchdogs of Upper Egypt so closely resemble the Pyrenean sheep-dog, that they are nowadays said to be descended from the dogs brought over by Napoleon's army. This is unlikely, since Wilkinson, writing only thirty years after the French invasion, calls them Hawara dogs, after the well-known Berber tribe of Upper Egypt.

Abd el-Wanis, a youth of the Jumei'at Arabs of Mariut, introduced to our camp a canine initiation-ceremony, which, though entirely novel to me, could hardly have been his own invention. Having come into possession of a dog, which had strayed or perhaps been stolen, from some other encampment, he cut off its ears, minced them, and mixed them with

---

[1] Perhaps the kind seen by Hamilton in Cyrenaica. "There is a race of greyhounds peculiar to this country generally of pale fawn colour, with very short hair and limbs almost as fine as those of the Italian pet greyhound."—Hamilton, *Wanderings in North Africa*, 181.

[2] The Red Sea Hills.

flour. The dog was then induced to eat its own ears, and
" Wanis ", in no way a cruel boy, honestly believed it was
thereby greatly improved. He could, of course, give no
rational explanation of this. Was it a *rite de passage* by which
a stolen dog changed its identity and became his own
property ?

Here and there in the Eastern Desert, the Beja still point
out to the traveller large stones with a " waist " to them, " to
which the Arabs of old tied their horses," but the nomads
are all camel-riders nowadays, and the horse only survives
among the sedentary Arabs of the Mediterranean coast.

The Sinai Arabs have no horses of their own, for they
have nothing to feed them on, but show great interest whenever one crosses the frontier. Even in Southern Palestine,
the Arab steed is a sorry-looking animal, for the Arab cares
very little for the points of a horse and much for his breeding.
He thinks that the offspring of two well-bred horses, however
wretched in appearance, is bound to turn out well, while a
good-looking but badly-bred horse only inspires him with
distrust as to its progeny.

There the Arab usually rides his horse without a bit.
There is a headstall of embroidered homespun, and a chain
like a snaffle is bound about its head to which is attached a
hair or woollen rope. Voice and knee are all the Arab needs
or should need to guide it with.

Some experience is also necessary. One of Bramly's
Laheiwat friends, on his way to Gaza, wished to cut a dash
before a beautiful girl, so he borrowed a horse on which to
ride up to her. But he had never mounted one before, and,
unfortunately, when he made it gallop, he was unable to make
it stop, and it thundered away into the next tribal area. The
Laheiwi was so busy riding that he never saw the lady at all,
and by the time he returned, she was gone. Such is Sinai
horsemanship.

In the old raiding days, horses were always used to fight
from ; being led besides their masters' camels till the actual
moment of attack. The horse was then the real companion
of its master ; it understood much of what he intended, and
when sleeping together in the open desert would wake him
up if it thought danger was approaching. In the tents to-day
it walks in and out undisturbed, with the children playing all
round and under it. Though he cares little whether its back

DOMESTIC ANIMALS

is galled or not, many an Arab would deny himself bread to let his horse have a feed.

Very many Arab horses are " gone " in front, owing to the unnaturally early age at which the Bedouin begin to ride them. The Arabs know this is harmful, but say " It is necessary for their training ". In sandy country the horse goes unshod ; in stony ground, a plate is used instead of a shoe which gives no ventilation to the foot.

The Western Arab rides the Barb, ugly in comparison with the Arab horse, but a strong serviceable hack that generally walks its master to wherever he wants to go. If it is to a wedding, the guest on arrival scrapes the beast with the edge of his square iron stirrups and dashes furiously up and down in front of the wedding tents. At the end of each gallop, the horse is pulled to its haunches as the roof of his mouth feels the prod of the iron spike that forms part of the bit. Altogether the Western horses cannot enjoy a wedding very much.

Bramly rode to a fox-hunt once with ten or twelve Western Bedouins armed with shot-guns. When Reynard was viewed, all the Arabs galloped forwards to head him off, shouting, standing in their stirrups, the reins and the gun-barrel in their left hands, the trigger in their right, crossing one another at top speed, riding into one another, firing anywhere and everywhere. " There was an enthusiasm and enjoyment of what was going on without any regard for their own or anyone else's safety that made it rather fine to watch."

The saddle is called *sarj* (pronounced *sharz* in Sinai) and bears a strong resemblance to the mediæval tilting saddle, in which a chair-back is used to aid the knight with the whole weight of his steed at the moment of impact. The square iron stirrups, with sharp edges which serve as spurs, can be traced back to the Middle Ages, just as the cross-handled swords still used in the Northern Sudan. Altogether the wars of the Crusades have left a distinct mark on the Arab horseman's equipment.

It is curious that the Arab, though a keen horseman, has never adopted any riding costume. He is always obliged to twist the ends of his *quftan* into an uncomfortable knot round his waist, and leave his bare legs to be chafed by the saddle.

The donkey-population of Egypt used to contain a high

proportion of magnificent well-fed beasts, often white in colour, on which the well-to-do perambulated the town. Well-bred and high-spirited, they sometimes called for a horseman's ability to ride them. In the villages, the Omda's stately donkey was sometimes as big as his mule. But now Henry Ford has changed all that, and the donkey-stands of Cairo and Alexandria have been empty for many a long day.

Such fine animals demanded and received far better nourishment than the desert is likely to afford, yet from time to time some sheikh would sally out to visit his tribe on one. The 'Ababda still relate how their Omda, 'Ali Bey Mustafa, mounted his ass at dawn at the Ras el-Jisr, near Qift, with five camelmen in company, and did not halt till he reached Bir el-Beida, 90 miles away; all the camels but one having fallen out on the way.

The ordinary Bedouin donkey is a very small, nimble, mouse-coloured, half-starved beast. It is a general utility animal, which can carry about a hundredweight, and is particularly useful in getting down full waterskins from high rock-pools beyond the ungainly camel's reach. It has to do long marches of sometimes two and three days without water, and in the old Pharaonic days must have been the mainstay of their caravans. A wit might divide the history of desert exploration into three stages; donkeys and determination, camels and comfort, and Fords and freedom.

Chapter VII
THE CAMEL

"The camel they think is a profitable possession, a camel will bring forth the camel, but money is barren good that passes quite away in the using."—Doughty, *Arabia Deserta*.

The Camel unknown in Ancient Egypt—Its Value to the Bedouin—Regarded as almost Human by the Pagan Arabs—Not a Totemic Animal—Points of a good Camel—Its Intelligence—Camels as Draught Animals—Its Dentition—Names applied to it at different Ages—Time it can go without Watering—Racing on Camels—Different Breeds of Camel—Anecdote of the Zareiqa—Camel Saddles.

A Bedouin friend once told me that, in the days of his youth, some small steamship in distress anchored off the mangrove swamp at Mersa Wadi Lahami, where no steamer had ever been known to anchor before. While her engineers repaired the machinery, the crew came ashore and spent the afternoon catching crayfish and making friends with the modern Ichthyophagi of the beach, although neither party had a word of the other's language. After dark, a sort of fish-dinner was in progress, when my informant rode suddenly into their midst on a camel. From their amazement, it was clear that the strangers had never seen one before, or even dreamt that such a creature was possible. They fell to talking excitedly in their outlandish lingo, and feeling the beast all over to make sure it was real. Finally they got into their boat and rowed away, still jabbering and casting glances back at the wonderful monster.

The tale that the Japanese (?) had to tell when they got back to their ship must have been a startling one, based on a fleeting impression caught by the light of the Bedouin fire. Even to myself, grown callous after a quarter of a century on camel-back, the beast appears sufficiently amazing.

The Arabian variety of camel has never been found wild, nor are wild camels told of in history, so that it must have been one of the first animals to be tamed by man. Now, alone of the brute creation, it is so thoroughly domesticated that a superstition has sprung up that it cannot breed unaided and would become extinct in a single generation if left to its own devices. Such is the universal belief in Arabia and Egypt, where the male is always helped in the act. But it is a superstition as Bisharin practice shows.

The beast seems to have been known to the Egyptians from the earliest times,[1] though curiously enough we do not find it in use by them till 500 B.C. ; and I have often cast about in my mind for an explanation of this. Most probably the reason was a material one, the unsuitability of Middle and Lower Egypt for camels. Even at the present day camels cannot exist in the oases of Bahariya and Siwa, and there is a poisonous fly which causes a great mortality among them in Middle Egypt and the Delta. This fly needs stagnant water to breed in, and so, in earlier and marshier times, the impossibility of breeding camels in lower Egypt may have constituted a real bar to the ingress of the camel, an Asiatic animal by origin, into Africa. But Upper Egypt is free from fly, and as soon as the Hamites there, no doubt very conservative people, and the Libyans in the west became accustomed to the strange animal, camels bred by these tribes would find their way over the country generally. Very probably too a hardier breed of animals was evolved as time went on. But Lower Egypt to this day remains so unhealthy, that its camel population requires constant renewal from Upper Egypt or Palestine. There is a small bronze figure of a kneeling camel in the Khartoum Museum from a tomb of 25–15 B.C., which shows that the animal had been introduced into the Sudan before that date. But all the desert transport of the Ancient Egyptians down to the time of the Persians was done by the donkey.

To this ungainly animal the Bedouin owes nearly everything, and he repays this with as much affection as his rather material nature can muster up. They love their camels, and most of the Sinai quarrels are begun about them. An old Arab once said to Bramly. " You cannot imagine my joy at being kept awake all night by the bellowing of my camel-calves ! " and again, " A man of property is he who sitting on the ground, sees his horizon limited in every direction by the bellies of his camels ! "

---

[1] There is a remarkable rock-drawing of a man with a camel on the rocks at the mouth of Wadi Abu Ajaj, near Aswan. This is dated by a hieratic inscription to the Twelfth Dynasty. Schweinfurth, *Zeitschrift fur Ethnologie*, 1912, 627.

Plate XII

Bisharin Camels

Awlad 'Ali Camels Ploughing

CAMELS

THE CAMEL

Everything that the Arab requires, and no tribes in Egypt are completely independent of the cultivation, has to be carried on its back. With its help, he makes long waterless journeys where no other riding animal could survive, and at a pinch it becomes his sole source of support. In 1915 I met two youths of the 'Ayaida, who had been out three weeks with the milch camels of their tribe, neither eating bread, nor drinking water; camels' milk their only sustenance.

An animal of such value was looked upon as almost human by the ancient Arabs.

Camels have indeed appeared on occasion as God's messengers, one such being sent to the pagan Arabs of Thamud, who hamstrung her in spite of a warning from the prophet Salih,[1] while, much more recently, another reproved the Billi for their lack of hospitality.[2]

St. Nilus, writing of the Saracen inhabitants of Sinai in the fourth century A.D., describes a sacrifice in honour of the morning star, to which they offered up the best product of the chase or captive boys of comely appearance, on an altar of unhewn stones. Failing these, they took a fattened white camel without blemish.

Camels are still sacrificed by the Sinai Bedouins on special occasions, such as the 'Id ed-Dahiya, while one used to be slaughtered annually at the turquoise-mines, when its blood was smeared upon the mine-face to ensure a good yield during the coming year.

A piece of evidence, which at first sight would seem to permit the inference of a former sacred aspect of the camel in Sinai, is that among the 'Aleiqat, the blood-money for a camel used to be greater than that for a man. Sabah, a young Aleiqi, on hearing of the murder of a camel by an 'Abadi, exclaimed, " He was let off too lightly, he should have had to pay forty-four camels ! " " Nonsense," I said, " why the blood-money for a man is only forty ! " " That's right," he said in a sort of chant, " Forty camels for a man, forty-four for a camel ! " " Come now, Sabah, you don't mean to tell me anyone ever paid forty-four camels for one ! " " Not like that," he said, " but long ago a man of another tribe murdered one of our camels. We went to law, and were awarded forty-four camels. His tribe handed him over to

[1] Koran, vii, 71–6.   [2] Doughty, i, 426.

us and we killed him, that was forty camels. Then they paid up four, that made forty-four!"

But even this does not necessarily mean the camel was a sacred animal, but only a very valuable one. Eighty years or so ago in Nevada, horse-theft was popularly reckoned a more heinous offence than murder ; and an uncle of my own formed one of an indignant Vigilance Committee that hanged a horse-thief. Yet that is no proof that the horse had acquired totemic status among the cowboys.

One may conclude that, though the pagan Arabs looked upon camels as well-nigh equivalent to human beings, evidence that they considered them as akin to themselves is lacking.

At the present time, about twenty-five thousand camels are annually slaughtered in Egypt for food. Outside Cairo, the chief camel-eating districts are, as might be expected, Sharqiya and Beheira.

A good camel should have nearly the same points of breeding as a horse ; well-shaped ears, intelligent liquid eyes, firm coat; but unlike the horse, small oblong hind-feet. The Sinai Arabs call the fore-foot *yad* " hand ", and regard those who say a camel has four feet as ignorant. One might observe here that the area covered by the camel's padded feet on the sand exceeded the surface gripped by the tyres of a motor car, till " air-wheels " came into fashion.

Though these big feet give the camel a special purchase on the sand, he is otherwise clumsily built for draught ; yet, in days gone by, the mining companies made great use of him in desert traction over the gravelly and sandy surfaces of the Eastern Desert. Awkward single loads up to 800 lb. could be packed on selected strong camels. But when heavy wagons of mining machinery had to be pulled, teams of sometimes twenty camels would be harnessed at once to specially constructed wagons with large wheels and broad iron tyres. Camels have also occasionally been harnessed in pairs to light carts, and fair distances accomplished in the day with them. But the motor car has now killed all such enterprises as dead as the dodo.

The Arabs do not despise the intelligence of the camel, which, however, is seldom employed in the furthering of his master's interests. As a young man engaged in the triangulation of Mariut, I used to ride out daily on a young Bisharin camel, which soon learnt to distinguish the

THE CAMEL

poles marking the main stations of the survey from the ranging rods of the less important points. He left these latter aside unheeding, but would not pass the former without attempting to kneel down. But he hated being ridden; so much so, that, every day, he spent the hour devoted by me to observation, in trying to chew through the rope that confined the joints of his foreleg. The closing of the lid of the theodolite-box was invariably the signal for him to attempt to bolt, and if his efforts to chew through the rope had been crowned with success, he would lead myself and chainmen a merry dance.

A hill camel they value for its hard pads, for a soft-padded animal may be a great nuisance, and may need boots or a patch of raw hide, which the Arabs have to stitch over the sore place to the living pad, without doing the camel any harm. A paste made from henna [1] is a great help if the sore foot is tied in it for a night. Usually the tannic properties of the henna will last about ten days. A mixture of salt and onions pounded together is also commonly used as a substitute for henna.

The stallions are in rut during the coldest time of the year and the mares carry their foals for thirteen months, so that the young camel is generally born in February or March. Then the jackals are a great danger to the newly-born foals, but the mothers can usually guard them. Of one which let her foal be killed in March, 1929, the Awlad 'Ali said, " It was her first, next year she will know how to protect it." That year a foal two days old walked up the 900 ft. ascent of Naqb Abu Dweis, and another was born at the top. I have seen a boy of thirteen carrying a new-born camel-colt to camp with the anxious mother in attendance.

Bramly was alone one night in the hills of Sinai, with his she-camel tied close to him. Her foreleg was strapped up to prevent her straying, and her foal was tucked up by her side. During the night he was roused by the camel rising on three legs, and saw her standing in the moonlight unable to help her foal. A large jackal or wolf (of the sort the Arabs call *Dib Sirhani*) had it by the throat, while its mate stood by, ready to help. All this took place within a few feet of Bramly. He drove them off, but the foal carried the marks of the wolf's teeth on its throat, till he sold it six months later.

[1] Henna (Ar. *khenna*) is prepared by pulverizing the leaves and twigs of the Egyptian privet *Lawsonia inermis*.

Camels do not cut their teeth with the annual regularity of a horse, and their development is also affected by the nature of the grazing. By six months old, the animal's temporary set of twenty-two teeth is complete, and at one year old a pair of molar teeth begins to appear in both upper and lower jaws. At three years, a second pair appears in each jaw, and thereafter there is no great change till the animal is four and a half. Then comes a critical period of about a year, during which its mouth is a wreck as far as its teeth are concerned, for it loses from twelve to fourteen temporary teeth and acquires from twelve to sixteen permanent ones in exchange. At six years, the first pair of permanent incisors " tushes " appear, which the Arabs call *na'b el-awwil*, and six months later tush-like premolar teeth erupt in both upper and lower jaws, and by eight years of age the animal's dentition is complete. Then, but not till then, the name *gamal* " camel " is applied to it by the Arabs ; for the earlier age-periods the following list of names [1] is in use :—

(1) *Huwar* sucking camel (the 'Ababda call it *Beidi* and the Awlad 'Ali *Makhkhad*).
(2) *Mafrud* weaned camel, at about one year of age [2] (some Arabs have an intermediate stage here called *Libni*).
(3) *Marbut* or *Bilabun* ('Ababda and Awlad 'Ali).
(4) *Hiqq* camel of two or three years old.
(5) *Jida'* camel of three or four years old.
(6) *Tany* camel of four and half to five and a half years old, which is getting its second lot of teeth.
(7) *Raba'* camel of five and a half years old, which has lost the *raba'iya* teeth.
(8) *Sadis* at the first appearance of the tushes, at about six years old, and finally
Gamal when its dentition is complete.

The camel attains much the same age as the horse, that is to say, it does not greatly exceed twenty years.

Naqa is a female camel, *bakra* a female after its first foal, *ba'ir* a baggage camel, *qa'ud* any young camel. A riding camel is called *hagin* in Egypt and *delul* in Sinai.

Before the young camel is in possession of its second

---

[1] These names are also applied to sheep, goats, ibex, etc.
[2] By the Arab reckoning, it is now two years old, as it is considered one year old from the date of its birth.

THE CAMEL

lot of teeth, it is necessarily restricted in its diet to the more tender green shoots, so that, except in very good years, its physique develops rather slowly. It is hardly ever able to gain more than a mere subsistence from the tough desert vegetation ; and ought never to be burdened with a full load. But the older camel with its full set of teeth can be relied on to pick up its own living from the rough and thorny plants almost anywhere ; and in consequence its value is double that of the younger animal.

Camels can eat most of the varied flora of the desert, and in their interest the Bedouin becomes a botanist. Most youths are able to name fifty or sixty species, some a hundred and fifty. Dry bushes and plants that might serve as camel-fodder should never be put on a fire ; only a foolish or stupidly careless person would do that. On the Red Sea coast, the camels have to eat fish, and I have seen them knee-deep in the sea, feeding on the mangroves.

The hump (the Arabian camel has only one) is only to be seen in very young camels or in those which have been out to grass for some time. Working camels have no hump to speak of. A large hump makes the Sudan camel very uncomfortable to ride, as it sticks up through the hole in the *makhlufa* saddle. Bramly says that the people of Berber remedy this by making an incision in the hump and removing the fat.

The camel takes his rest while chewing the cud, and only spends a very few minutes every day in real slumber. He sleeps on his haunches with his neck at full stretch and his head on the sand.

So little care does the beast require, that, in the Eastern Desert, they are often left for months to their own resources. Such camels will always return to a well that they know, and if they find no one present to water them, they just sit down to await the next arrival. It is then incumbent upon the next Bedouin to water these camels, whether he knows their owner or not. Working camels require to be watered every four or six days ; and, when time permits, the animals should be watered twice, once in the morning, about 8 or 9 a.m., after the water has got a little warmed up ; and again in the afternoon about 3 or 4 p.m. Meanwhile the camels sit by the side of the well and chew the cud. They drink fifteen to twenty gallons at these double waterings, and should never be ridden beyond walking-pace after such a drink for fear of rupturing their water-laden stomachs. If they are merely grazing they need very little water.

Burckhardt [1] and Doughty [2] are both rather scornful of the possibility of obtaining water from a camel's stomach. Sinai Arabs, who are hardly ever hard put to it for water, also ignore the practice. But some of the refugees driven from Kufara by the Italians in 1931 were forced to this expedient in their attempt to reach Dakhla Oasis, and 'Ali Kheir tells me of a Bisharin who recently saved his life in this way on the Sudan frontier. His camel died under him, so he cut it open, and, straining the contents through his cotton wrap, drank the liquid thus obtained and was thereby enabled to reach Bir Juqub.

In November, 1925, copious rains fell in the Jebel Elba district, and the vegetation that sprang up was kept green by dew and further showers. The camels of my caravan drank near Mersa Sha'b on November 22nd, and did not drink again till March 28th, when they were watered at Bir Umm Bishtit. During the intervening 126 days they had moved my camp 375 miles by very easy stages. Grazing animals would easily go six months in the cool of the year on fresh herbage without any doubt whatever. But in hot weather, it is a very different matter. Ahmed Bey Hasanein's march of 270 miles in ten nights in May from 'Uweinat to Erdi, represents about the best that can be done without either water or grazing. Hunger, as well as thirst, has to be endured by the unfortunate camels imported annually from the Sudan into Egypt. The Hiteim Arabs engaged in the trade buy camels, chiefly aged or immature beasts, very cheaply in Kassala Province and drive them to Berber. Thence they cross the Nubian Desert to Daraw in Egypt in about sixteen days, watering only once at the wells of Ongat or Mashushenai. The camels move in great droves, sometimes hundreds strong, called *diboki*. There is seldom any grazing on this route, so the camels get little or nothing to eat, especially if the men with the *diboki* are only servants and not the owners of the camels. Consequently the camels arrive in a very poor shape at Daraw. Some are sold here, but the cautious 'Ababda regard the purchase of a *diboki* camel as a risky speculation. "When a camel has eaten nothing for fifteen

[1] *Notes*, 260.   [2] i, 459.

days, its stomach is closed up, and it will never eat again." The greater part are driven down the Nile Valley to Isna, and cross there to the west bank of the Nile over the barrage. Thence they undergo a second desert journey to Farshut, cutting off the Qena bend of the river. Here they are sold for the most part to butchers, for perhaps four times their cost as Kassala. This traffic continues throughout all the winter season.

A camel has a wonderful sense of direction—the Arabs say that if it has been once to a well, it can always return there. Once, when some Jawabis were approaching Bahariya Oasis at night, the guide said he was not sure of the right direction of the Naqb el-Ghurabi pass down into the oasis. So a young camel, which had been there two years before, was driven in front, and although it did not change the direction much, it changed it so far that by daybreak they were on the top of the pass. This was possibly not the result of memory, but of following the scent of camels that had passed there before. Camels' eyes are about seven feet above ground, so they can see farther than a man on foot, and when in rut the male can recognize females (by scent ?) at several miles distance.

In 1910, an old rutting stallion ran away from our camp near Jemsa on the Red Sea, and was caught next day near Qena on the Nile 150 miles away. Nor had he hurried on the journey, *ohne Hast ohne Rast*, at six miles an hour he was well on the way to his beloved in the Nile Valley when our harsh postman rounded him up and brought him back to camp. He accomplished this distance without being distressed, but, had he been hurried, would have collapsed, as did the camel which attempted the feat recorded by Burckhardt in the following paragraph [1] :—

"The greatest performance of a hedjein that ever came to my knowledge, satisfactorily ascertained on credible authority, is that of a camel belonging to a Mamelouk Bey of Esne, in Upper Egypt, which he had purchased from a Bisharein chief for one hundred and fifty Spanish dollars. This camel was to go for a wager, in one day between sun-rise and sun-set, from Esne to Genne and back again, the whole distance being equal to a space of one hundred and twenty-five miles. It arrived about four o'clock in the afternoon at a village sixteen miles distant from Esne, where its strength failed, after having travelled about one hundred and fifteen miles in eleven

[1] *Notes*, 262.

hours, and twice passed over the Nile in a ferry-boat, this passage across the river requiring at least twenty minutes."

The true distance from Isna to Qena and back is at least 145 miles, so that, if the story is true, the camel did about 20 miles more than Burckhardt estimates.

Except when rutting, the camel is mild and docile, though, like his master, he makes a great fuss over doing anything like work. Overworked camels in the cultivation may sometimes snap at their brutal drivers, but among the patients thronging to any camp in the desert, cases of camel-bite are remarkably rare. Indeed the camels of the Bedouin are only ill-treated when they undergo firing with a hot iron, the Arab panacea for every sickness of man or beast. In Sinai I have known camels come to their master's call like dogs, and like dogs I have seen two young ones galloping about the landscape in mock fight with each other.

Once I heard of a youth being killed by his camels at Bir Mab'uq near Suez. He had been wearing a newly-killed jackal's skin over his shoulders, and the smell of this so enraged the milch camels that they trampled him to death with their knees. When a camel attacks a man, it comes at him with its head high in the air and tries to knock him down with its head, kneel on him, and maul him. I have also heard of a camel picking an Arab up with its teeth and shaking him in its powerful jaws. A man is safer on its back than on the ground, for it has one very vulnerable spot, the black sweat-glands at the back of the neck, where even a slight blow from a stick will nearly stun it. The camel knows this weak point, so he keeps his head high, when attacking anyone on the ground; and low, if trying to dislodge his rider.

In Egypt and the Sudan, the Bedouin generally ride stallions, though the Bisharin sometimes prefer mares. In Sinai and Arabia, the female is nearly always ridden. Camels do not jump naturally, though they can be taught to do so. The first camel I ever bestrode, the famous Monasiri racer, "Abu Rusas",[1] had been taught to jump over numerous high waterwheel channels in Dongola, and when brought to Egypt cleared the hurdles on the Gezira race-course in good style. I have been on (and stayed on) a grand Bisharin

---

[1] Abu Rusas means "father of lead", and he was called so because he carried a Dervish bullet inside him.

stallion, when, frightened by a snake, he flew over a large bush. A bad rider may be told from a good one at a glance by the violent action of his elbows.

Galloping is reckoned bad form, and camels can only gallop for a few miles at a time. After that they will be passed by a trotting camel. Ten miles have been covered in 42 minutes, and fifty miles in four hours and twenty minutes at races in the Sudan. The load for a desert camel should not be more than 300 lb., but twice and thrice that amount is regularly carried by the large camels of the *fellahin* for short distances.

The Awlad 'Ali have numerous troops of camels, but none fit for riding, so they commonly prefer to ride horses. Their animals are short, sturdy, brown beasts, very slow on the march; and with them they move their camps, and bring away the date crops from the oases of Siwa and Bahariya. But the Western Arabs move very seldom, and their camels spend most of their lives in idle grazing and are chiefly bred for the markets in the Delta. They have no trees to feed on, perhaps this is the reason why they are such dull animals.

The Sinai camels are small active shaggy beasts, whose agility in the mountains is surprising. When chased by horsemen, they can usually make their escape if the country is at all broken. Arabian camels, called from their yellowish-white colour Wudheihan, or Banat Wudheiha, are sometimes imported into Sinai by the Haweitat or into Egypt at the port of Quseir.

The 'Ababda camels are better in speed than the foregoing, but the best camels in Egypt or the Sudan are the beautiful white camels of the Bisharin, especially those of the 'Aliab. The Bisharin themselves attribute the superiority of their camels to their having regularly bred animals to hunt the ostrich, yet a considerable factor in this must be the excellent grazing on the various species of *Acacia* in the Etbai hills, and the magnificent climate there, since Bisharin beasts taken to other parts of Egypt generally deteriorate.

A tall leggy camel from the Sudan, whose erect ears recall those of the Indian variety, is the 'Anafi, on which Slatin Pasha made his famous escape from Omdurman. But they have not the stamina of the Bisharin camel, and are usually very rough to ride. So they are seldom imported into Egypt.

A fine-looking breed from Arabia is the 'Umani,

originally from Êl-'Oman, which Philby calls "the best of all Arabian strains ".[1]

The late Prince Kemal ed-Din had one, and Linant de Bellefonds gives a plate of another in *L'Etbaye*. They are trained to run with their heads low, which the rider keeps down by prodding with a long stick. But they are not fast.

The Sinai tribe of Tiyaha relate that the best of their camels, the Zareiqan,[2] are sprung from a camel mare called Zareiqa in the 'Ababda country which was covered by a magic camel. He sprang out of the sea, married her, divorced her, and disappeared all in a twinkling.

Having heard of this wonderful event, the Tiyaha sent an astute fellow who became a *ra'i* or herdsman to the owner of Zareiqa. When her foal was two years old, this sharp Tihi fixed a needle between its teeth so that it pricked its gums, whenever it went to feed. The unfortunate beast soon became scraggy and very forlorn. The owner poured melted butter down its nose, tried in vain all the other accepted remedies, and finally concluded that the animal must be suffering from the evil eyes of its many admirers. So in despair, he presented it to the Tihi as his annual fee.[3] Whereupon the clever one pulled out the needle and went off with the foal. Both lived happily ever afterwards.

Another legend about the stealing of an 'Abadi camel by the Tiyaha was related by Sabah Mudakhil.

On one of their raids the Tiyaha captured a magnificent camel-mare from the 'Ababda, and kept her with them till a foal was born. Then one day, an aged negro presented himself at their camp, having dropped out of the ranks of the Mecca pilgrims as unable to travel. This poor old man stayed with them a few months, until at some festivity the young men of the Tiyaha had ridden their camels to a stand-still by racing and showing off. Then the Tihi sheikh said in jest to the old negro, "Can't you do something to amuse us?" "Yes, if you let me ride the mare." All laughed to see how clumsily the old man mounted, and then,

---

[1] *G. J.* January, 1933, 3.

[2] *Zareiqan* is the plural of *Zareiqa* "little dark female". The breed called *Tihi* is not bred by the Tiyaha (as Musil asserts) but by the Shararat. For their origin from another mythical wild camel, see Doughty, ii, 239.

[3] The remuneration for a *ra'i* who follows camels at pasture is a weaned colt each year for a group of not less than 50 camels; and for 50 camels downwards, an unweaned one.

THE CAMEL

seeing him disappear rapidly in a cloud of dust, rushed headlong for their tired camels. But the Tiyaha never saw their mare again. Late that night she splashed through the Birket el-Ambaj, the marsh where the Bitter Lakes now roll, and in two days' time (mythical camels must be allowed mythical speed) her owner had brought her safely back to the 'Ababda country.

The Arab camel-saddle *ghabit* has high brass-mounted pommels and "is held on by the double 'cinch', and the straps that fasten the cinch to the saddle are tied exactly as the Canadian ranchman ties his ".[1] This knot must have travelled along North Africa to Spain, thence with the Conquistadores to Mexico, Texas and the States.

Though one can get a certain grip with the knees, and in case of need wind a leg round the pommel, yet the *ghabit* is much more difficult to sit on than the Sudanese *makhlufa*, which has been adopted and improved by the camel corps. On it the driver sits aloft on a sort of rectangular tray, padded

FIG. 9 —Escape from the Tiyaha.
(*After a drawing by G. Bonomi.*)

with a sheepskin and usually rides by balance alone. But if the camel bucks, the legs have a tremendous grip under the flaps of the saddle. Stirrups are never used.

Bramly, who competed twice in the great fifty-mile race in the Sudan, writes "I have been thrown off a bucking

[1] *Researches in Sinai*, 226.

camel with a Hijazi saddle, and seen Arabs dislodged by a side swerve of their mount; but I have never been thrown or felt the least uncomfortable by a bucking camel with a *makhlufa*."

Saddles for baggage camels are called *shaddad*, *withr* or *hawiya*, and are not even girthed up.

It is surprising that the Bedouin who takes so much trouble about his animal has never invented a better saddle. Both the Sudanese *makhlufa* and the Sinai *shaddad* are saddles built on a pair of fore and aft wooden trees. The aftertree rests on the hind rim of the padding, so it depends upon the size of the hump or the amount of padding whether the wooden tree is kept off the sharp rib bones behind the hump. Practically every riding camel bears a circular mark, where the Arab has fired his animal to cure a bad sore resulting from the chafing of the end of the ribs. These sores are difficult to cure, as whenever the camel goes on a long journey, the wound is apt to fester again, when the saddle works down and rubs the old sore.

CHAPTER VIII

THE CHASE

" *And Cush begat Nimrod : he began to be a mighty hunter in the earth.*"—
Genesis, x, 8.

Tracking—Traps—Leopards and Cheetahs—Catching Hyenas—Ibex-hunting with Dogs—Walking down a Gazelle—Wild Sheep—Addax—Ostrich-hunting—Hare-hunting—The Wild Boar—Catching Quail—Falconry.

Although there are no tribes in Egypt, like Doughty's " Solubba ", who have no domestic animals but the ass, and live by hunting alone, yet every Bedouin youth aspires ardently to become a hunter, as the Spanish boy a *torero*.

Among human abilities the most prized by the Bedouin is *athr*, the art of reading footprints or tracks in the sand. Every child learns much of this as a matter of course, and knows all the family footprints, those of neighbours, and all the camels, goats, sheep, etc., in the vicinity. On some soils these are difficult to read, but in sand undisturbed by wind, all the news of the last few days and even weeks can be read at a glance. Youths who are to be successful hunters must perfect themselves in this art, and wonderful tales are told of their skill. They judge the age of the footstep partly by its freshness and partly because by night certain beetles come out and run over the tracks of the day before, and they can distinguish at a glance whether these were made before or after the dew or the recent rain. The freshness of animal droppings lets them judge how near they are to the beast they are pursuing. By the depth of the impressions they know if the camel was heavily or lightly loaded or had nothing on its back. The length of stride gives its pace and also its sex. The track of an animal going to water is direct, coming away from it it deviates.

No Bedouin ever expects to escape the detection of his crime—it is all written there for his enemies to read—it only remains for him to outstrip the inevitable pursuit. I once heard 'Ali Kheir disputing with another 'Abadi about the number of camels in some military patrol that had passed weeks before, and asked him how he knew it was a patrol at all. He replied pityingly, " When camels go straight behind each other, when they are all about the same size, when they are all male camels—it is a patrol ". He might have added, when their droppings are stuffed with millet seed—no Bedouin ever overfed his camels. Smugglers' camels usually go straighter and much faster than the leisurely caravans of the Bedouin traders, who stop at every patch of grazing. In Sinai, Sabah Mudakhil once pointed out to me something entirely beyond my European eye's grasp. " There are last night's tracks looking fresher than this morning's. There was a little dew, and they have ' set '. The breeze has not disturbed them so much as the more recent ones."

A nation interested in tracking must often have wondered what sort of tracks were left by supernatural beings. Just as the Australian Arunta say their high god's feet are like those of an emu, so the Arabs of Sinai and Arabia know that the *ghul* has one leg like a donkey's.

The tracks left by the feet of the fish-eaters along the coast, who spend much of their time walking on the reefs, are of course quite different to those of the mountaineers ; or of course to the tracks of any man who has ever worn boots.

Here I may remark that 'Ali Kheir once said to me, " Wear what boots you like, I will tell your tracks anywhere." This from the fact that I press harder with my right foot and half a dozen less obvious characteristics.

A good tracker rarely does a cast, but just follows the track, ticking off every third or fourth footprint with his stick. One of the signs which he always looks for is the small spurt of sand which is thrown forward by the camel's two toe-nails ; this is an indication that the trail is very fresh. In following a track among pebbles, he keeps his eye open for any break in the glint of the gravel, that shows where pebble have been displaced. For their underside is always duller, except among flints. An axiom with a Bedouin is never to move from a spot till he has made out what he is looking at, and always to follow the track for some distance before giving his opinion. Curiously enough, the Bedouin find great difficulty in discerning from its tyre-marks which way a car has been going, unless of course they know the car and its tyres.

Bramly has found that a wounded gazelle sometimes casts off at a quite different angle when it reaches harder

'Ali Kheir

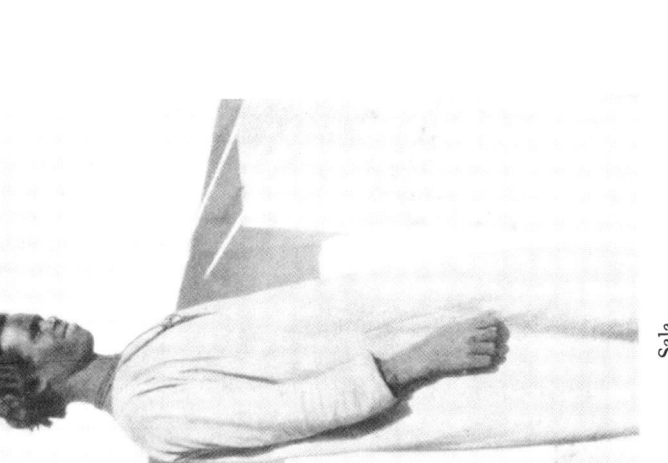

Sala

'ABABDA YOUTHS

[*face p.* 118

ground. They can have little experience of being hunted by a man, and no other animal follows them up by looking at their tracks, so it is rather mysterious. But he has known it happen more than once.

Should an injured gazelle try to rejoin the herd, the others butt it with their horns and drive it away, lest the hunter come after them too.

The true desert naturally contains very little game, but there are a fair amount of ibex on the higher hills, and plenty of gazelle on the steppes south of the Mediterranean littoral and by the Red Sea near the Sudan frontier. These are the Dorcas gazelle. The true ariel *Gazella Soemmeringi* occasionally trespasses over the Sudan frontier into Egypt, and Loder's gazelle *G. leptoceras* (which the Arabs also call "ariel") is sometimes seen in the western desert near Maghra. Both these are large gazelle with white rumps. Like the Arabs, the gazelle follow the rains, and the cheetahs follow the gazelle. Early in 1930 cheetahs were common round Maghra, judging by their tracks. But in dry years they are never seen so far east. Curiously enough the Awlad 'Ali told me that "cheetahs never touch sheep". But they killed a lot of young camels round my camp that winter.

Leopards are only found in the Sinai hills, where they eat ibex, hyrax, and sometimes young camels. In 1929 one killed eleven donkeys near Wadi Hebran. This Sinai leopard has much thicker fur than the Sudan variety, and indeed resembles the Abyssinian leopard in that respect. Arabs frequently offer skins for sale, but I believe that only once has one fallen to the rifle of a European.

Salem Anis, the judge of the Muzeina, lost his right hand through following a wounded leopard into a cave, and the Arabs tell a tale of four men who stole some cubs, and were all murdered by the leopardess that same night. They can be impudent too on occasion, coming down in daylight to tents when the men are away, to steal goats and dogs from the women. But, unless chased or molested, they leave mankind unharmed.

Hyenas are rare visitors to the mountains of Egypt, but are commonly found on the borders of the cultivation. In Sinai, they are widespread, and objects of considerable interest to the Bedouin, who say they teach their young to kill by bringing them a wounded animal just as cats do. And they have the vulpine habit of wounding for woundings' sake. Once under Jebel Umm Rijlein, I found a shepherdess wailing, and saw her flock of sheep all mauled and bleeding. None were dead yet, but nearly all were going to die. Silently they cropped the grass, though some had nothing but trailing entrails to put it in. This heart-rending sight provoked a vigorously-conducted hunt but the murderer was gone.

Near Bir Meisa, in the Etbai, 'Ali Kheir avenged just such a killing this year. The assassin, a fine male hyena "twice as big as those in the Zoo", was sleeping sated under a rock, when a shot from 'Ali broke his back, and the Bisharin finished him off with their swords.

To catch them, the Sinai Arabs build rubble "houses" with a slate "portcullis" supported by a string and a stick. To the latter they tie a piece of meat when a leopard or hyena is expected. The beast lets the gate down behind him, and, thus imprisoned, falls an easy prey to the hunter later.

The Hamada, a subordinate tribe, of the Wadi Zubeir, where hyenas used to abound, were held responsible for the behaviour of their animals by the nobler 'Aleiqat of the adjacent Wadi Lahian. A hyena-trap had to be maintained at the head of Wadi Zubeir, and kept properly baited. If a Hamdi hyena caused depredations in Wadi Lahian, its track was followed back to Wadi Zubeir, an easy matter for a nation of trackers. Then, if the trap was discovered to have been left unbaited, the Hamada were liable to pay damages for the misdeeds of their hyena.

The Haweitat of North Sinai are said to go after a hyena into its den, tie a rope round the cowardly beast, drag him out, and cut its throat in the open. In Egypt, Jennings Bramly actually saw his hunter 'Abdalla do this.

> "His most remarkable feat was to go into a hyena earth, and bring the animal out at Qasr Sagha in the Faiyum. The striped hyena is harmless in the dark—so this man (and he assured me others could do it as well) would crawl at full length down the earth, and feel the hyena all over, which seemed to be petrified with fear—the animal has to be well tied up and is then dragged out, the second it is in the light it fights like a madman, so that it is very important that it should be securely tied before being dragged out."

In Sinai, ibex are caught by the help of a breed of greyhound, *dirra*, which holds them at bay in the rocks till the

PLATE XIV

ETBAI SCENERY

THE CHASE

hunter's arrival. On the flat the ibex is no faster than the ordinary goat, but among precipices he usually gets away from the hounds by a series of daring leaps. Jennings Bramly once saw one fail.

> "Some of these dogs chased an ibex up into difficult rocks to a spot from which it could not get forward, and held it at bay, while Khidr the Laheiwi, all legs and arms, and shaggy hair, scrambled over the most impossible places, and, having got above the ibex, pushed it off into the abyss with a long stick. This return of Khidr with the ibex on his back to his father, a blind old man who loved his first born, recalled to me the return of Esau with the savoury meat that Isaac so loved."

The Arabs say that, when driven into a spot from which he can neither advance nor retreat, an ibex sometimes saves himself by throwing himself down and landing on the curve of his horns. Canon Tristram saw an ibex do this in Moab. "Once I saw him drop and break the force of his fall by lighting on the front of his horns."[1]

The late Prince Kemal ed-Din maintained a sort of ibex reserve at Bir Afandina in the Galala mountains. Here they got very tame and came to drink in large numbers—so large that one of his Arnaut gamekeepers told me that he had to keep order among them with a stick. In Sinai I once met a mixed herd of sheep, goats, and two ibex, all drinking together at Bir Nukhul. But these latter were really tame, having been caught as kids. Unfortunately a leopard killed one, and a European shot the other, so this experiment in domestication was a failure. Major Jarvis[2] says that in Jebel Maghara there is a herd of females, visited annually by males from South Sinai, and I have been asked to believe that there are normally only females at Bir Afandina. Undoubtedly the males do sometimes travel great distances, but there are plenty of both sexes at Bir Afandina as a rule.

The Dorcas gazelle is a much more stupid animal than the ibex, but fortunately for itself, it is very speedy and can run forty or fifty miles an hour for five miles or so. When first startled, it rushes off leaping high in the air, for about a hundred yards, and then foolishly stops and looks round for its pursuer ; a move which has proved fatal to many. But

---

[1] *The Land of Moab*, 292. [2] Jarvis, 208.

once well away it is so much faster than the *saluki* that, as has already been mentioned, only half-grown or injured animals fall victims. The coursing of these beautiful creatures with either hound or motor car is a cruel sport, rightly forbidden, for the unfortunate beasts which escape only too often die a lingering death of thirst afterwards.

Both Arabs and Beja reckon a man superior in perseverance to a gazelle, and bound to catch it, so long as its tracks can be quickly followed. This is best done in soft sand, and in hot weather. For the swift gazelle has but little stamina, since it does not drink, and is consequently soon exhausted. " You should choose a day so hot that it burns its feet, and take a good drink of water before you start ! " said 'Ali Kheir.

Resolution however plays a greater part than endurance in the test. Just as a rabbit, when followed by a stoat, first tries to put the stoat on another rabbit's scent, and then, finding nothing can put off its enemy, tamely surrenders, so too does the gazelle when hunted by a man. Yet the hunter, who aspires to walk a gazelle down, should carry a waterskin on his back and food in his scrip, lest the chase turn out a long one. Indeed, running down gazelle on foot in heavy sand in a shade temperature of over 120° Fahr. is never likely to become a popular sport with Europeans, though I have heard an old Bishari exclaim with delight, " This day is so hot that a man could catch two gazelles ! " Others, not so energetic, prefer to catch their gazelles and even ibex in a remarkable trap, found all over North-East Africa, but not, so far as I am aware, on the other side of the Red Sea.

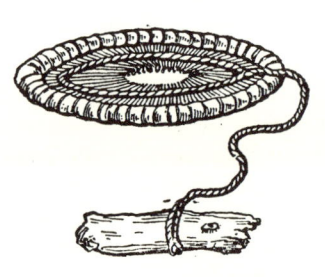

FIG. 10.—The " Wheel-trap ".

This, the " wheel-trap " spoken of above, consists of a hoop made from palm fibre with spikes projecting towards the centre (like a wheel with spokes but no hub) into which the animal can put his foot, but is unable to withdraw it. (The 'Ababda make the hoop from dom-palm fibre, but, near the Pyramids, date-palm fibre is used, and the sharp ends of the date-fronds are used for the spikes.) This is buried in the sand where the gazelle is expected to feed, in the following way. First a ring of plaited palm-leaves is sunk in the ground, making practically a golf-hole. The spiked hoop is put over this and above it again, a noose is laid attached to a stick, or in the case of larger animals a log. Grass is laid so that the " golf-hole " below the spiked hoop is not filled up, everything is buried in sand; and the surface is smoothed over. As a finishing touch, the trapper then makes a false gazelle's track with his fingers over the whole affair to mislead the animal.

As the stick, or log, is not attached to anything else, the gazelle, when caught, walks off towing it about. It may even scratch off the spiked hoop, but in doing so, generally tightens the hemp noose about its leg. It can walk about and feed, but is easily tracked by the trail left by the stick, and if it tries to bolt, it is thrown to the ground by the cord twisting about its legs.

The Arabs usually do not visit their traps more than once in three or four days, so that sometimes they are obliged to follow for a long distance, before coming to the animal that has been caught. This contrivance is known on both sides of the Nile, and as far afield as Dakhla Oasis, though I have not met with it among the Awlad 'Ali. Jebely, a Muzeina Arab from Sinai, expressed surprise and delight on meeting with this trap, which he declared to be unknown to the Arabs. Its use in Egypt dates back to the very earliest dynastic times, and Professor Seligman sees in it a universal ancient Hamitic hunting weapon.[1] Sir Samuel Baker says that animals as large as the rhinoceros used to be caught by its aid.[2]

It might be supposed that if any animal did not know how to swim, it would be this Dorcas gazelle. But I have seen a captive gazelle leap into the sea from the Egyptian lighthouse steamer *Aida* and swim remarkably well, turning away repeatedly from the boat which was sent to save it. They are sometimes seen on the seashore, and a fable relates that they drink salt water. They really go there for the salt, not the water.

---

[1] The spiked wheel-trap ... is, as I know from personal observation, in constant use among the tribes of the Upper Nile to the North of Lake Victoria, the Lango, Acholi, and others as well as farther north among the Nuer. It also occurs among such half-Hamites as the Nandi, Suk, and Turkana. C. G. Seligman, *Egyptian Influence in Negro Africa (Studies presented to F. Ll. Griffith,* 457). [2] *Nile Tributaries of Abyssinia,* 366.

The Barbary sheep still lingers in the Eastern Desert, but it has vanished from the west, except in the remote south-western *massif* of the Gilf Kebir. Here the late Lady Clayton " found a cemetery of mountain sheep. Hundreds of skeletons were piled one on top of the other in a narrow cleft. Whether it is the place where mountain sheep go to die, or a herd was overtaken by some catastrophe, it is difficult to say ".[1]

I think Lady Clayton's memory may perhaps have deceived her as to the numbers, for she told me on her return from the desert that she had seen " seven or eight bodies lying together under some shady rock ". Even that is remarkable, but when uneducated men die of thirst in the desert, they sometimes exhibit the same tendency. For, of some workmen who strayed from the Safaja Mine in 1911, four were soon found dead in the same place. And the herd instinct is much stronger in sheep and gazelles. In 1928, Mr. P. A. Clayton found 23 dead and dying gazelle at the base of a low cliff in the Qattara depression. These he supposed to have been stampeded during the night by a cheetah.

The Barbary sheep's horns are not uncommon in the swamps and cliffs of this depression, so it must once have extended over the whole area.

The " wild cattle ", still remembered by the Western Bedouin and the oasis dwellers, were the addax antelope. Sheikh 'Ilwani saw four near Maghra when a boy, and one was killed near Bir Sheb west of Wadi Halfa in 1930.

The wild boar has only recently become extinct in Egypt. His Highness Prince Omar Toussoun killed one in the Wadi Natrun in the nineties of the last century, while I remember seeing one from the Faiyum in the Cairo Zoo, whose cage bore the legend, " The last wild boar in Egypt." In the past, they were very numerous in the Delta and caused such damage to the crops, that in 1846 a regular campaign was undertaken by the Government to exterminate them in the provinces of Lower Egypt. 832 soldiers under 19 officers were detailed for this, and they shot in Gharbiya and Menufiya 756 wild boars, and 104 in Sharqiya and Daqahliya. But from the correspondence on the subject, the Minister of the Interior remained dissatisfied with the results.[2]

---

[1] In a letter which appeared in *The Times* of 16th September, 1933, after her death.
[2] Prince Omar Toussoun in a letter to the *Egyptian Gazette*, 4th January, 1933.

THE CHASE

Although in European eyes, the wild ass is not a game animal, the 'Ababda consider it " very good eating ". They call it *homr* to distinguish it from the tame one *himar*. I have been shown alleged *homr* frequently in the Eastern Desert, but all these seemed to be merely tame donkeys run wild. Bramly saw the true wild ass in Jebel Shindeib on the Sudan frontier, and further south, they are not uncommon in the Bisharin country. The wild ass stands from 12 to 13 hands high, with remarkably large hoofs for its size. It does not bray, but whinnies like a horse, and, on the sight of man, stands and lets out a tremendous snort. Then it trots off with a high-motioned step that soon out-distances the best riding-camel, though the Bisharin sometimes ride down foals, or when the Atbara falls, catch young asses that have stuck in the mud. They have found it impossible to tame a full-grown one, and those they catch young are never entrusted with the water-skins, as they are inclined to go wild. Many of them are very difficult to approach. In fact, the 'Ababda say of these half-wild asses that, to catch them, one must send out a woman for " they will come to a woman, but not to a man ". The Bisharin occasionally tie up their female donkeys in a ravine which a wild stallion is known to frequent, but the offspring of such a union is also considered untrustworthy, and it is only the grandchildren of the wild ass that really settle down to domestication.

Fragments of ostrich egg shells are found everywhere in the sandy parts of the Egyptian and Sinai deserts, though the bird itself is now extinct. Vansleb (1673) saw troops of them during a journey to the Monastery of St. Antony, while Burckhardt, who saw two in 1816 on the Cairo-Suez road, seems to have been the last European to see them wild in Egypt. Yet they have only just disappeared from the Libyan Desert, where Arabs still living claim to have seen them. South of the Sudan frontier they are still met with, east and west of the Nile. The Bisharin used to chase ostriches on camels, hunting them for days until they were tired out, and then spear them.

For the west, Jennings Bramly writes :—

" The Hawawir of Dongola used to hunt the ostrich once a year. To do so, it was necessary to get their horses into hard condition, and ready to drink camel milk instead of water. This they did by painting white the inside of the vessel, from which the horse is served his daily feed, so that the horse got accustomed to the colour. Then they kept the animal from drinking, and filled the pail with milk. A thirsty horse would drink quite a lot, before he found out that it was not water, and after a little got accustomed to the new drink. For food, they would put a ball of meat down his throat. According to these tribesmen, when they first come up, the ostrich goes off for miles, but then foolishly comes back to see what he has run away from—thus, when he has spent much of his energy, the huntsman rides him down."

There are two species of hare in the Eastern Desert, both very fast indeed.

I have often gone after hares in Jebel Elba with the Bisharin, but never seen one run down by their hounds. For the hare has an annoying habit of always choosing an isolated rock in the middle of sand, and also sleeping with his head towards the direction from which he has come, so that he generally is awakened by the tracker's approach and sees him coming some time before his arrival, and so gets a good start—too good for the hound. But once indeed, I saw Puss bound out from her rock just under my terrier's nose, and the moment after she did so, the dog leapt straight on her back.

In Sinai, Jennings Bramly was once travelling down a wadi with two Arabs of the Laheiwat who asked if he had noticed a hare asleep under some stones above the wadi bed.

"I said not; but if they put it up I would try and shoot it. They said they had a better and surer way, and breaking off four *retem* branches, twisted them round till they looked like handbrooms. They then made a long circle and came very cautiously up to where the hare was sleeping below them. They threw the branches, it seemed to me at his face, and one dived down with his mantle out and a minute after came up with the hare. He explained to me that the hare is afraid of hawks and eagles, and therefore shelters near a place he can get into if attacked by these. The Arab notes where this is and throws the branches which make the sound of a stooping hawk. The hare wakes and rushes into his refuge over which the Arab at the same moment puts his mantle and catches him."

The Arab usually hunts small game by following up their tracks and digging them out, but, in the case of a jerboa, he is obliged to cover the ground with a net. Other rats make holes with various entrances and a multitude of passages from a main run, from one of which they hope to escape if an enemy enters. But the jerboa makes only one hole, which goes down into the ground for about a yard, and then comes up at an angle to very near the surface, without breaking it, so that there is no indication of where he will come out, if pursued into the ground. The Arab therefore puts a large net out, to cover as much ground as possible in the direction he finds the run is taking and soon after he begins to dig the jerboa breaks out of the ground like a jack-in-the-box, only to be caught in the net. The horned viper sometimes takes possession of these holes, but it leaves such distinctive tracks that the Arab boys always know what to expect when they are digging anything out. The Arabs are fond of the jerboa ; because it has a white meat and feeds on vegetation, it tastes therefore much like a rabbit. The ordinary desert rats are eaten everywhere in Mariut.

Birds are not eaten by the Beja, but in Sinai even vultures and ravens are considered edible. Partridges they catch sometimes with grain soaked in spirit. Bustards are said to be caught by riding in circles round them till the bird falls dizzy.

Along the whole northern coast of Egypt from Rafa to Salum, the Arabs anxiously await the autumn migration of the quail, which begins about the second week of September. Curiously enough the birds invariably arrive just before dawn, and are usually so exhausted that they are taken by the thousand in the nets and traps of the Arabs. Immediately they are caught, they are fed and watered, and are then crated in long cages made of palm-sticks, for dispatch to dealers in Port Said and Alexandria. The quail which escape, after a day or two's rest, proceed southwards on another long flight, this time over the desert, and are not seen in the Nile Valley till their return northwards in February and March. On this occasion, the Arabs make no attempt to catch them as they leave the coast. In 1933, after many lean years, the quail appeared in abundance, perhaps as the result of the legislation on their behalf. Falconry has been re-introduced into Egypt from the west, and is only practised by the Awlad 'Ali, and the Hanadi exiles in Sharqiya Province. Lovers of the picturesque will regret that the Arab falconer rides out to his sport nowadays as often in a Ford car as on a stallion " shod with fire ".

The following notes (Wilfred Jennings Bramly's) are

not a general treatise, but a record of some points in which the Arab falconry differs from the European. The object of the Arab falconer is to catch something he can eat by the quickest and most certain method possible, while the European, who is only out for sport, wishes to see as good a flight as possible, and thinks little of the nature of his quarry, often herons, magpies, rooks, or other birds unfit for eating.

"The Arab falconer prefers the saker and lanner to other falcons. He does occasionally use the small peregrine (*shahin*) to take duck, but it is not his favourite, for its rather wild nature in comparison with the lanner's annoys him in its training.

"Passage hawks are usually caught by putting a saddle of horse-hair nooses on the back of a pigeon. This saddle is kept on the pigeon's back by a loop round its neck and a loop on each side through which the wings are passed; while it is also secured to the pigeon's legs by two slip knots. A length of about thirty yards of string is attached to the saddle. When a hawk is seen, the unhappy pigeon in this 'contraption' is allowed to fly off as best he can with the string unwinding out behind him. Generally he manages to cover about a hundred yards, before the string, now full out, catches in a bush and brings him down. When a hawk sees that a bird of the sort that he most cares to feed on is in trouble, he stoops, kills, and feeds on it. Very often one of his claws gets caught in the horse-hair nooses, and the hawk is caught.

"Another way is to take a tiercel (male peregrine) or lanneret (male lanner), and seal its eyes, that is, to pass a thread through the lower lid of each eye and draw these under lids up over the eyes so as to leave the hawk in partial darkness and knot the thread. When its eyes are sealed, a bunch of feathers and horse-hair nooses is attached to the hawk's claws, and he is let fly. The female falcons are much larger than the males, and so, when they see what they think is a male going off with a good meal, they immediately give chase, and 'bind' to the catch. Again the horse-hair noose commonly entangles the wild bird with the male, and both birds come to the ground in a bundle.

"There is a third method; when the falconer sees a hawk on a large kill, such as a bustard or a hare, which the falcon cannot carry, the Arab scares her off and buries himself, half on the ground and half under uprooted bushes as quickly

THE CHASE

as he can. Then, with his hand under the kill, he waits for the hawk to return and catches it by closing his hand on its foot while it is feeding. This must seem merely a 'tale' to those who have not gone in for the sport, but it is quite extraordinary with what persistence a falcon will return to her kill in face of every danger.

"I have myself found a kill, and driven off the hawk, then attached a cord to the kill and, hiding in a bush, drawn both the hawk and the kill very gradually into my other hand, which I had kept out ready for it, and so taken the bird, a peregrine.

"The sparrow hawk is very rarely used, and then only by the Arabs in the cultivation. It is caught in an ordinary fisherman's net, dyed blue. When the sun is well up, and the hawks resting in the shade of the trees, the falconer proceeds to a lemon garden. When he sees a bird that he wants, the falconer's sagacity and knowledge enable him to select the line between the trees that the hawk, if startled, will most probably take to gain the open country. Then, having found a gap in this line, he hangs his net to close the opening from only two leaves, which he tears to make the net hang more lightly. The net is not attached below to anything. The falconer returns to the spot from which he proposes to frighten the bird, and then claps his hands. He quite often gets the hawk, which flies into the net, thus lightly held aloft, and falls in a bundle of netting to the ground. In this way I have seen a falconer catch three good hawks and discard a fourth in a morning.

"The hawk's furniture in the desert is necessarily very rough in comparison to that made in Europe. The Arab is not a good maker of a hood, for he uses soft leather and rarely shapes it well. He calls the hood *kimma*, and the wooden shape upon which, when wet, it is pressed a *galib*. These hoods are inclined to give the hawks sores about the cere, and often give them sore eyes. The jesses are often two little pieces of leather round the leg, the rest of cord with two knots at the end, and as sometimes the Arab uses no swivels, these are just noosed with a slip knot in a piece of thin rope, and attached as often as not to the glove, which he fills with sand for the hawk to sit on as a block.

"A few of the richer Arabs in Sharqiya have blocks, but usually the hawk is tied to anything convenient, and comes to less harm than might be supposed, since even if he flies against the sides of the tent these will cause him no damage. No bell is used by the Arab, and none is necessary, since there are no trees in which the hawk can be hidden. The glove is a very rough affair in most cases.

"The Arabs do not use a needle for imping (the mending of a broken feather). They take the same feather, if they have it, and bind the new feather with cotton to the stump of the other. This never makes as clean a join as the European method of using a needle, and although some of their falconers can make a fairly neat job, there is always a break in the webbing of the feather where the join is made.

"When the passage falcon is first caught, her eyes are sealed as mentioned above and her training then proceeds in the ordinary way. But the Arab never teaches his bird to 'wait on', that is, accompany him flying over his head; nor does he take much trouble to teach his bird *not* to 'carry', since his object is the biggest game that he can catch, hare or bustard, and not things that his hawk can fly away with.

"A tribesman of the Awlad 'Ali will start off on foot in the early morning with his bird, often an eyas lanner, that is, a nestling which he has brought up. His nondescript dog is by no means a pure *saluki*, but nine parts pariah with a little greyhound in it somewhere. Its breeding is of small account, for against the combination of man, dog, and bird, the hare has little chance.

"If the hare knows his Arab, the Arab certainly knows his hare. Very soon from under one of the small bushes that grow everywhere on the pebbly surface on the north-western desert, a hare will spring up and away. Away goes the hawk, away goes the hound, and away goes the man. The hare may buck or jump or jink, but soon the hawk has struck and struck again, and once puss fails a bit, the hawk binds to head or stern. Then up runs the dog, and the hawk, seeing him arrive, stands aside and leaves the rest to him. Then up comes the man and all is ended.

"Bustards are not hunted except by the richer Arabs who do so for sport. This is done on horseback (or nowadays from a car) and without hounds. The Arab rides with his hawk in country, where he knows there are bustard, and every now and then will unhood his hawk to see if she can see the game. If her eagerness to be away betrays that she has seen a bustard, the falconer will put his hand out flat across the falcon's beak. Then if the bird bends down to see, the falconer undoes the jesses from the leash, and lets the bird fly off. But if the bird stretches itself to see over the hand before its beak, the falconer rehoods her and rides on, as probably the bustard is still a mile or so away, so keen is the falcon's sight. Generally the bustard crouches upon the ground, hoping to be unobserved or intending to squirt out a fluid upon the hawk when it attacks, its peculiar method of protection. But should he take to flight at any distance from the hawk, the falconer will be lucky if he is caught under five or six miles. On one occasion, the bustard got completely away from a peregrine by flying dead into the teeth of a strong wind.[1]

"The gazelle is only hawked after by very rich Arabs, who use sakers for the purpose. In nature the saker never touches even a half grown gazelle, so the trainer therefore has to impose upon his falcon's wit. He stuffs a gazelle-skin out with straw, and hangs it by cords so that its legs dangle. A lump of meat is tied behind the horns, and here the falcon learns to feed. When feeding freely, the hawk is taken to a greater distance every day, until no matter how far the bird is taken from this lure, she flies to it at once for food. The skin behind the head of the gazelle is then cut open and a piece of meat put under, so that it is visible. At last the meat is completely hidden under the lap of the skin, but now the hawk flies at the gazelle's head whether she sees meat or not. Next a half grown gazelle is taken and the hawk flown at it— the hawk binds to the gazelle's head, the gazelle is killed and the hawk fed on it. The bird is now ready for the desert. When gazelle are found, the falconer chooses an animal that stands watching its advancing enemies—the party of riders stop, the hawks are flown, and generally two hounds are loosed. The riders stand until the hawk stoops at the gazelle, which is not alarmed, since the hawk is not its natural enemy. The hawk binds to the gazelle's head searching for the meat that it expects, while the gazelle dances round trying to get rid of the unwelcome bird. The hawk, to keep its balance, flaps its wings, and so prevents the gazelle from seeing the approaching hounds, who throw themselves upon it. The

---

[1] The bustards seen in Egypt are McQueen's bustard, and are noticeably more common when there is a severe winter in the Lebanon. They are found all along the north coast, and occasionally in the oases.

horsemen now race at the gallop to the spot and finish the business.

"To a European, who finds his sport in watching the chase, there is no great attraction in this kind of hunting; a survival of the time when hawking was a means of getting food, and nothing more.

"The sparrow hawk is never hooded in the east, nor is the bird carried on the fist. The falconer puts a cotton glove on his right hand, and grasps the bird round the middle of its body, with its legs, tail and wings behind, and the head and chest of the bird projecting from the grip of his hand. In this way the bird cannot move, and the cotton glove prevents the feathers being damped by the hand or dirtied. The falconer then passes his left hand continually over the hawk, smoothing down all its feathers, and after it has recovered from its first fright, it seems to like this attention. The ordinary process of training is now gone through, only that when the hawk is sent to the lure, it is thrown without a jerk, so as to help it in the direction it is taking. A thin string is tied on its leg with a piece of white cotton-wool at the end. The object of this is to show where a hawk is, which has gone down with a quail into clover, for the white cotton-wool stands out above the growth. My falconer Gharib has thus taken fourteen quail as they rose, his hawk binding almost at once to its quarry. In other matters of training, and feeding, the Arab and European falconers follow the same system.

"Once, in the Wadi 'Amur in the Sudan, I was interested to watch what seemed a real alliance between man and bird for the benefit of both. I came upon the scene just as a shepherd was running up to a hare which had been killed by a Bonelli's Eagle, or another of the lesser eagles. The shepherd told me that as his flock advanced in a long line, it beat up before it any hares that were in hiding in the bushes, and that the eagles —two generally—attended his flock in the morning and came down on any hare that it put up. When the birds had killed, the shepherd picked up the game, and leaving a portion for the birds, took the rest for himself. The partners seemed perfectly to understand each other, as the eagles came down almost at once upon what was left. The shepherd said the birds were not out every day, but two or three times in the week, and had been with him for about a month."

Chapter IX
RAIDING AND WARFARE

"'*And ye hae the tae half of the population employed and maintained in a sort of fashion, but I wad be glad to ken what the other five hundred are to do?*' '*In the name of God!*' *said I, 'what do they do, Mr. Jarvie? It makes me shudder to think of their situation.*' '*Sir,*' *replied the Bailie, 'ye wad maybe shudder mair if ye were living nearhand them.*'"—Rob Roy.

The Bedouin Arabs a Nation—Organization of a Raid—Office of the 'Aqid—Antiquity of Raiding—Raid of the Blemmyes on Tor—Warfare of the Towara and the Ma'aza—Raid of the 'Ababda on the Beni Wasil—Raid of the 'Atawna on the 'Ababda—Battles of Meisa and Murrat—Battle of Tor—Raid of the Haweitat on the Muzeina.

This chapter makes cheerful reading but melancholy writing for anyone of Bedouin spirit, for it tells of deeds about to be forgotten, and battles long ago. Law and order have settled in like a blight on Sinai and Palestine, nor is Transjordania in much better case. To get the fright of one's life, one has to cross the Arabian border, as my young friend Salem Jebely did in June, 1933, to help the rebel Haweitat and Billi against Ibn Sa'ud. Get it he did, for the affair turned out not a Prestonpans, but a Culloden, and after the battle, according to the victor's own account, " the head of the rebel Ibn Rifada was given to the village boys of Dhiba to play football with." Several other Sinai Arabs crossed the frontier hoping for loot, but I am credibly informed that Salem was the only one who reached the actual battlefield.

Left to themselves, the Arabs are chivalrous; women and children are never touched (except it be in revenge for another woman's injury), and prisoners are usually let go when the excitement has died down. In fact, in their wars with each other, they never fight " to the death ", as Doughty says,

" It is contrary to Arab conscience to extinguish a Kabila ... The danger past, they can think of the defeated foeman with kindness; having compassion of an Arab lineage of common ancestry with themselves." [1]

That is to say there is a true national sense among all the Arabian Bedouin.

[1] Doughty, i, 335.

Nor did the Egyptian Awlad 'Ali object to share their grazing with the tribes driven from Cyrenaica by the Italians. In fact they resisted the Government's efforts to move these refugees on, saying it was contrary to the rules of Arab hospitality.

But they certainly do not reckon the townspeople as beings of the same flesh and blood.

One day, in June 1916, a wild-looking 'Aleiqi, Suleiman Selmi, just escaped from El-'Arish, then in the hands of the Turks, related the following tale of his adventures, admirable in its brevity, to the Intelligence Office at Suez.

" I was walking about El-'Arish with this woollen helmet on my head, when the Turks arrested me as a British spy. They put me in jail, and gave me nothing to eat and drink. After three days, aeroplanes came and bombed the town. Everyone ran away. I ran away. Here I am ! " He was immediately asked, " Was anyone hurt when the aeroplanes bombed the town ? " " Nobody." The tale of destruction at El-'Arish by the British sea-planes had been so circumstantial, that even his sheikh, who was present, was startled by this laconic reply, and asked again, " What, nobody ? " " Well only 'Araishiya (local people) ! " replied Suleiman naïvely. So long as no Bedouin were killed, *impavidum ferient ruinæ*.

Later in the same year the Arabians did really make common cause against the Turks, so that, in November, Lawrence, the Arab Garibaldi, was able to describe to me with enthusiasm the way in which the various sections of Harb and Juheina were fighting side by side. But I have wandered over the frontier again, and must get back.

Camels are quite commonly lifted nowadays by families who think themselves wronged, especially as *withaqa*,[1] but the organized raid (*ghazu* = Fr. razzia) by one tribe on another is a thing of the past on Egyptian territory. A great blow at this sort of adventure was dealt by the cutting of the Suez Canal, which limited the activities of the very enterprising Sinai tribes in the direction of Africa.

In the other direction the Tiyaha used to organize an annual raid on the 'Anaza living near Tadmor, about four hundred miles away. Such expeditions required careful preparation, spies were sent out long ahead, and the stars

[1] See p. 238.

RAIDING AND WARFARE

consulted to ensure that the raid left and arrived on a propitious day. When the time came, all those selected were given a rendezvous at a known well and the name of the *'aqid* or leader. The raiding party (*qom*) would leave as secretly as possible and travel mostly by night. In the first forty-eight hours they would attempt to cover at least a hundred and twenty miles in order to get ahead of the news of their coming. If the tribe owned horses, these would be led behind the camels in reserve for the delivery of the actual raid itself. Each man would carry his own food, of the simplest kind, in one of his camel-bags, and the animal's corn in the other. On arrival in the enemy's territory, a guard would be left on the camels, and scouts sent out. So soon as these reported a camp worth plundering, the raiders would deliver a sudden and usually bloodless attack, loot the camp, and secure as many camels as possible. Goats and sheep were seldom taken, as these are slow on the march, and so cannot he hustled off quickly. No one would be killed if they could possibly help it, since a life has to be paid for sooner or later; and the women and children would be left unharmed. Sometimes of course, when the raiders were careless of pursuit, a completely successful raid would leave nothing behind but a lot of noisy women and children wailing in the desert. But usually the *qom* would put the captured beasts to their utmost speed and ride homewards " hell for leather ", hoping that they had not been recognized or that the victims were not well enough organized or mounted to pursue.

In this ordinary raiding, bloodshed is avoided as a general principle, but should two parties meet, honour demands that they shall fight, as happened in March 1921, when a *qom* of the Laheiwat met some 'Imran Haweitat from Transjordania on Sinai soil. Three or four lives were lost on each side in consequence. Of course if there is " blood " between the tribes, every opportunity is taken in such affairs to get ahead with the blood-feud.

In the confusion of a raid, cattle are occasionally carried off, which belong to tribes in alliance with the raiders. These can be reclaimed, and the burden of satisfying such claims falls not to the sheikh or *qadi*, but to the *'aqid* whose duty is to divide the spoil.

The office of *'aqid* is hereditary in a certain family from father to son, but is seldom united with that of the sheikh in the same person. If the sheikh accompanied the raiders, he came for the time being under the 'aqid's orders, and did not resume his authority till the return of the expedition.

All the members of the tribe were at perfect liberty to accompany the 'aqid on an expedition or not, as they thought fit, but during the operations, he had dictatorial powers, and could punish disobedient persons by withholding from them any share of the booty.

Not uncommonly, when a celebrated 'aqid was known to be contemplating an expedition, enterprising youths of a neighbouring tribe would join him. In these affairs the booty was sometimes divided equally among all who took part, and in such cases, the 'aqid received two, or sometimes three, ordinary shares for himself. But on other occasions, every man fended for himself, though there was an almost universal custom by which the best animal taken was reserved for the 'aqid himself.

The 'aqid sometimes shared in the misfortune too, for the 'Aleiqat relate that many years ago, after a successful raid into North Sinai, some of their raiders asked permission of the 'aqid to return by a route, which proved waterless. Disaster followed. " Fifteen of them died, *and* the people who rode them." (My informant was thinking in camels.) When the leader was arraigned later before a council of elders, he attempted to excuse himself on the plea of deafness, saying he had not fully understood what the ill-fated party wanted to do. Upon this the court-martial came to the conclusion that, as his ears did not seem to do much good, they had better come off. Off they came accordingly, and " he did look funny without his ears ".

There may have once been a golden age without war, before the earth became filled with mankind, but a short inspection of our pre-human ancestors in their forests, or in the Zoo, will show that raiding is an institution of disrespectable antiquity. Job suffered from the Chaldeans, and the early Christian hermits from the Saracens.[1] Sometimes the raiders seized shipping and became pirates. I abridge the following picturesque account of a fourth century skirmish from Miss Eckenstein.

"Forty-three hermits dwelt near Raithou[2] to which place the news was brought that the Blemmyes had seized an Egyptian

---

[1] Saraceni = Sharqiyin, i.e. Arabs from the east.   [2] The ancient name of Tor.

PLATE XV

ARAB OF THE 'ALEIQAT

RAIDING AND WARFARE

boat which was bound for Clysma, and were coming across the sea. The men of Raithou at once collected their camels, their women and children, while the hermits sought refuge in the church. The barbarians spent the night on the shore, and then bound the sailors to the boat which they left in charge of one of themselves, and came across the mountain to the springs where they were met by the men of Raithou. But the invaders were the more skilled archers, and killed 140 men, the rest fled. Then they seized the women and children, and rushed to the tower or church, expecting to find treasures, and went round it screaming and uttering threats in a barbarous language, while the hermits inside prayed and lamented . . .

"In the meantime the barbarians, encountering no resistance, heaped tree-trunks against the wall from outside, broke open the door of the church, and rushed in, sword in hand. They seized Jeremiah, who was sitting on the doorsill, and commanded him through one who acted as interpreter, to point out the superior. When he refused, they bound him hand and foot, and tearing off his clothes, used him as a target. 'He was the first to gain the crown' (of martyrdom). Then the superior Paul came forward declaring his identity, and they bade him reveal his treasures. In his usual gentle voice he replied: 'Forsooth, children, I own nothing but this old hair-cloth garment that I am wearing.' And he held it out, displaying it. But the barbarians hurled stones at him, shouting: 'Out with your treasures,' and, after ill-using him, cleft his head in twain with a sword. 'Then I, miserable sinner,' continued Psoes, 'seeing the slaughter and the blood and the viscera on the ground, bethought me of a hiding place. A heap of palm branches lay in the left-hand corner of the church. Unnoticed by the barbarians, I ran to it, saying to myself, if they find me, they can but kill me, which they are sure to do, if I do not hide.' From his hiding place he saw the barbarians cut down the hermits who were in the church. He saw them seize the youth Sergius, whom they would have dragged away with them, but he snatched a sword from a barbarian and hit him across the shoulder, whereupon he was cut down himself. The barbarians after killing the hermits, searched for treasures not knowing that the saints own nothing here on earth, their hope being of the world to come. Finally they rushed off intending to embark. But the man who was left in charge of the boat, being a Christian, had cut the rope, so that the boat ran ashore and foundered, he himself escaped to the mountain. The barbarians, who were at a loss what to do, murdered the women and children, and then lit a fire and cut down and burnt nearly all the palm trees of the place.

"In the meantime the Ishmaelites from Pharan,[1] some six

---

[1] A town, now ruined and deserted, in the Wadi Feiran.

hundred in number and all of them expert archers, drew near at dawn and attacked the barbarians, who, seeing no chance of escape, met them bravely and perished to a man. Of the men of Pharan, eighty-four were killed, others were wounded. The hermits were all dead except Andrew, who was wounded and recovered, Domnus, who died of his wounds, and Psoes, who was left to tell the tale. The men of Pharan left the dead enemies to the beasts of the earth and the fowls of the air. They burned their own dead at the foot of the mountain above the springs, and made a great wailing. Then, led by the Sheykh Obedianus, they brought costly garments, in which, with the help of Psoes and Andrew they buried the saints. Psoes himself left Raithou, which was deserted, for the Bush, where he begged to be allowed to stay with Doulas, a request which was readily granted." [1]

At the beginning of the nineteenth century, there was a continual guerilla warfare between the Towara and the Ma'aza of Egypt.

Robinson in 1841 wrote of these raids :—

" About thirty years ago, during a war between the Tawarah and the Ma'azeh inhabiting the mountains West of the Red Sea, a party of the former of about forty tents were encamped in Wady Sudr. The Ma'azeh made up an expedition of two hundred dromedaries, nine horsemen, and a company of fifty Mughreby horsemen, to plunder this encampment. Passing Suez in the night, they found the Tawarah had removed to Wady Wardan, and fell upon them as the day dawned. Most of the men escaped ; the women, as in the Bedawin custom, were left untouched ; and only two men, including the sheikh, were killed. The sheikh, an old man, seeing escape impossible, sat down by the fire ; when the leader of the Ma'azeh came up, and cried to him to throw down his turban and his life should be spared. The spirited sheikh, rather than do what, according to Bedawin notions, would have stained his reputation ever after, exclaimed : ' I shall not uncover my head before my enemies ' ; and was immediately killed by the thrust of a lance." [2]

Burckhardt has a grim story of one of these same skirmishes.

" In a skirmish between the Maazy Arabs and those of Sinai, in 1813, the former by chance wounded a woman of the latter, who,

[1] *A History of Sinai*, 102–104.
[2] Robinson, i, 206–207.

RAIDING AND WARFARE

however, soon recovered. In the year following, the Sinai Arabs made an incursion into the Maazy territory, surprised an encampment near Cosseir, killed eight or ten men, and were going to retire, when one of them recollected the wound that had been inflicted on a female in the preceding year; he therefore turned on the Maazy women, who were sitting weeping before their tents, and with his sabre wounded one of them, to avenge the blood of his country-woman. His companions, although they applauded what he had done, acknowledged they should not like to imitate his example." [1]

On the occasion of another of these Ma'aza raids into Sinai, the invaders are supposed to have sent an old woman ahead to spy out the herds and flocks of the Towara. To guide her tribesmen to the spot, the old lady is related to have kindled a fire on the summit of Qurein 'Atut, a hill of the shape and size of the Great Pyramid, in the plain behind Tor. This beacon failed in its purpose through excess of visibility, for the marauders caught sight of it as they topped the rise out of the Wadi Feiran 50 miles away. For the rest of the night the Ma'aza galloped their horses to get there, and by daybreak they were still a long way off, and all the beasts were foundered. When the raiders at last reached Qurein 'Atut, the flocks had long since been driven off by the Towara, who before leaving had cast the old spy into the bonfire she had kindled.

Robinson also relates that the Towara used to cross the Gulf of Suez in boats and steal camels from the 'Ababda, while the Tiyaha raided them by land for the same purpose. A cairn in the great plain west of the 'Esh-Mellaha range marks the grave of one Abu 'Amiri killed in these encounters. It was in the old bad days of the salt-monopoly, and Abu 'Amiri was smuggling salt from the lagoon north of Ras Shukheir to Qena. He was accompanied by two boys and an Egyptian from the Nile Valley. When they saw the *qom* approaching, the two lads ran off, but Abu 'Amiri was made of sterner stuff, and shot one of the raiders with a pistol. He was immediately put to death, and the Tiyaha carried off the camels and the effendi. They had at first some idea of holding the latter to ransom, but since he talked so much during the whole of the next day about complaining to the police at Suez, they decided to rid themselves of his presence.

[1] *Notes*, 173.

So that evening, they cut his throat "just like a sheep" at the foot of a little hill now called from the incident Tarbul el-Fellah.

Vansleb, travelling in 1673 to the Monastery of St. Antony, witnessed a brisk little raid by the 'Ababda upon the Beni Wasil.

"Since the Arabs who inhabit the frontiers of Egypt belong to different families and have different interests, they preserve usually such a great hatred, and are so embittered against each other that they hardly ever meet without quarrelling. Such a slaughter took place the third day after my arrival. For the summer caravan, composed of fifty-five camels laden with provisions for the Monastery, and escorted by thirteen horsemen, all Arabs called Benevasel, were to arrive that day. They were spied upon by the Arabs called Ababde, who are their enemies. And as it was the season when the dates begin to ripen on the trees, there were many of them, who, after leaving their loads, did not wish to return the same day with the others to their villages and huts, but wished to stay at the Monastery and spend some days there. The following night, while these were camped outside the Monastery and sleeping without fear among their beasts, they were surprised at midnight by a troop of sixty of the Arabs called Ababde, who plundered them of fifteen camels, seven horses and everything that they possessed; they killed three of them and wounded five, one of whom died three days afterwards; and another was lost without anyone being able to find out what had become of him, for they found his horse riderless four days afterwards in the desert.

"Having made this slaughter, their fury did not stop at that, for they pursued with the same ardour the men who had brought me to the Monastery; of whom they were only able to catch four; they took away from them their four camels, all their gear, the money which they had got from me, and wounded three of them so dangerously that these wretches were unable in this miserable state to continue their journey to their huts; they came back next day to the Monastery quite naked and in the most pitiable state in the world; and what annoyed them was that they were afraid to appear before me, because having broken, contrary to their law, the contract they had made with me, in making me pay twenty-five *meidins* more than we had agreed upon, their conscience reproached them for this treachery, by telling them that this misfortune had 'happened to them to punish their perfidy'." [1]

The tradition still lingers of a return raid, made about a hundred years ago by the 'Atawna on the 'Ababda. They

[1] Vansleb, *Voyage fait en Egypte*, 314–16.

RAIDING AND WARFARE

penetrated about 150 miles into the 'Ababda territory as far as Jebel Hamata, and, finding the country rich and the people few and ill-armed, ravaged happily there for some weeks. This greed proved their undoing, for word came of them to the Nile, and the numerous 'Ababda settled on the edge of the cultivation rallied to the support of their weaker brethren. A force of fifty camels, each bearing two men, was collected and set out from near Qift, while three scouts were sent to ride ahead along the Quseir road to see if the 'Atawna had passed northwards.

The first rode twenty miles to the wells of Laqeita and returned without news, and so did the second who rode fifty to that of Fowakhir; but the third who was to have ridden the whole hundred to Quseir if necessary, came across the *qom* about sunset crossing the road in the Wadi Abu Ziran. Their great drove of captured camels, sheep, and goats took two hours to pass, and then the raiders, some forty strong, camped, killed two young camels and cooked them in great copper pots to the amazement of the scout and a friend. On making their way back, these latter came upon the main body of the 'Ababda quite close behind them. An attack was instantly delivered in the darkness upon the sleeping 'Atawna, who perished to a man below the dark cliffs of Jebel Mitiq. One Arab alone escaped, but was tracked and caught next morning by a rock-pool on the mountain. His life was spared by the 'Ababda *'aqid*, who contemptuously let him go to tell the rest of his clan of the fate of his comrades.

At this time all the 'Ababda still wore the shockhead of hair like the Hadendawa and the other Beja, and a young 'Abadi who had killed an Arab with a fine kerchief and headrope mockingly donned the spoil. While he was admiring his appearance in the novel head-gear, he was run through with a spear by another 'Abadi who had only just come up. The unfortunate jester, unable to speak, tore off the kerchief and the late-comer stood aghast that he had slain a comrade. The 'Ababda followed up their victory by a raid in which they cleared the country of their enemies as far as Suez.

The 'Ababda remember a former bad time when the 'Atawna possessed firearms and they did not. But later, when the 'Ababda obtained guns, it was the turn of the Bisharin and the Amar Ar to suffer. A 'Abadi hero of those days possessed an invulnerable coat of mail, but this was lost when the flower of the ʻAbabda nation perished in an ambush laid by the Amar Ar many years ago.

Another battle of which the ʻAbabda are very proud was the skirmish fought about 1889 at Bir Meisa against a Dervish raiding party.[1]

In 1888, after Bishir Bey, the Sheikh of the ʻAshabab ʻAbabda, had dislodged the Dervishes from the wells of Ongat and Haimur in the Wadi ʻAlaqi, Wad Hajj Saʻad, a disloyal ʻAbadi of the Fuqara, led an invasion of 150 men to Bir Aqwamtra, below Jebel Elba. They were recruited from the Kababish, Jaʼalin, and Shaiqia with a strong leavening of Baqqara.

They had heard that the Hamedorab Bisharin had grown rich from levying taxes on the coasting dhows, but were defenceless through lack of guns. When they arrived, they killed two of the family of ʻAli Tiut, the ruling sheikh of the Hamedorab, built a sort of barrack at Aqwamtra, and for a time did as they pleased. " They killed women and tossed up babies to catch them on their spears." News of all this was sent to Bishir at Aswan by his outpost of 15 men at Haimur. He dispatched Qarabawi, a son of the famous Sheikh ʻAbdalla ed-Dirazi, with 50 men with new rifles, plenty of cartridges, and two good wizards. Of these the Qadi ʻAbdalla Husein was good, but Saʻid ʻAli of the Anqarab was better.

Spies were sent to tell Wad Hajj Saʻad that the ʻAbabda at Meisa were 10 strong with bags of fine flour and fat camels. Hoping to get some loot, the Dervishes came on about 120 strong, leaving a detachment at Aqwamtra. Meanwhile the ʻAbabda had constructed a *geiger* (rubble breastwork) on a hill commanding the well at Meisa, which they only finished the day before the Baqqara arrived. The only Dervish to take any precautions was a Hijazi Arab, who climbed a hill to spy out the foe, but he was killed by two scouts, whom Qarabawi dispatched to deal with him. His gun missed fire, as did usually those of the other Dervishes, owing to the spells of Saʻid Ali. This chief wizard did not attend the battle in person, but after issuing his instructions, went to sleep on the baggage. He told Qarabawi to fire the first

---

[1] My informants about this were various Bisharin and ʻAbabda, including an old man Saʻadalla, who had carried a water-skin and acted as Gunga Din to the victorious ʻAbabda army.

shot himself, and to say if he missed " Sa'id ", but if he hit, " Sa'id, Naharak Sa'id ! " [1]

The hill commands the Wadi Meisa for perhaps 300 or 400 yards both up and down, and Qarabawi allowed the Dervishes to pass him. Their leaders were almost at the well. " Owing to our terror, the Wadi seemed full of them in their jibbas. They had few guns, many spears, and outlandish square shields." Their standard-bearer fell to Qarabawi's first shot (*Sa'id, Naharak Sa'id*), and another and another caught it up, " for their luck was in it." Many were killed thus, " for their luck was bad luck," owing to the malevolent influence of the wizard. Safe in the *geiger* the 'Ababda mowed them down at 200 yards range till they broke and fled. " Their bullets banged on the rocks, but not a man was hit." One hid behind a tree to shoot Qarabawi, but an 'Abadi bullet went through the trunk and killed the Dervish behind it. This tree was shown for many a long year. " The wadi ran red with their blood." Actually 27 dead were left unburied on the field,[2] and a few bones could still be seen there in 1926. The survivors fled to Aqwamtra and spread panic there. Stragglers deserted by twos and threes, and were mostly killed by the Bisharin. The main body by a great detour reached Abu Hamed, many dying of thirst by the way.

Two prisoners were taken at Meisa, whom Qarabawi let go again, many weapons, but no camels. Thanks to the wizards, there were no 'Ababda casualties. *Sa'id! Naharak Sa'id* !

At a similar raid by the Dervishes on Murrat Wells, they came on blowing horns made of elephant tusks. Sala Bey Khalifa, who commanded the Meleikab 'Ababda in the *geiger*, had his stomach cut open by a bullet early in the fight, but he held his entrails in with one hand and fought and encouraged his men all day. In the evening the Dervishes retired and the valiant Sala Bey died.

In the early part of 1915, the following events took place in the Sinai peninsula. The first to join the Turks were the Government policemen at Tor. These were all Tiyaha Arabs from Northern Sinai, who naturally followed the lead given by their tribe. They first cut Tor off from the outside world by severing the telegraph line to Suez. The Egyptian

---
[1] " Fortunate, may your day be fortunate ! "
[2] The enemy's dead are never buried by the Bedouins. See p. 193 and Doughty, ii, 41.

Mamur, not knowing who had done this, went in a fishing boat across the Gulf to Jemsa, to wire to headquarters that he was cut off and get instructions. On returning to Tor, he found that all his policemen, about 30, had deserted with their rifles. This took place immediately after they had drawn their pay on the 1st of January.

Sabah Agha, their bash-shawish or colour sergeant, then attended a conference in the Wadi Feiran, at which were present a Turkish officer, Sheikh Nassir of the Qararsha, Sheikh Khidr of the Muzeina, Sheikh Suleiman Ghoneim of the 'Awarma, and a very wily old man the Hajj Hamdan Abu Zeit, the lame judge of the Qararsha, Nassir's own tribe. The Turk told them they would be continued in their offices if they joined the Turks, but if they joined the English, the Turks would make war upon them. All thereupon made suitable non-committal answers, and departed to take such action as seemed good to them severally. Khidr, who was young and timid, returned to Tor, where a company of Egyptian troops with British officers had come down from Suez. Nassir remained with the Turks, while the foxy *qadi* retired to his tent to wait for Nassir's job. Suleiman Ghoneim, with an ex-driller from the oilfields called Gondos, went to loot and burn at Abu Zenima. At the end of January, some fifty Turks accompanied by perhaps a couple of hundred Arabs advanced on Tor. They contented themselves with blockading the Egyptians and skirmishing with them in the palmgroves of El-Wadi. Their main camp was in a dry water-course at the back of Jebel Hammam Saidna Musa, and was divided into two by a dry waterfall. Here they awaited events. Immediately after the repulse of the main Turkish attack on the Canal on 2nd February, Colonel Parker came down by night in H.M.S. *Minerva*, and brought 500 of the 10th Gurkhas with him. They were landed at night secretly north of Jebel Hammam Saidna Musa and came down on the Turkish camp from the north. Zeidan, Mudakhil's eldest son, guided the Gurkhas. At the same time the Egyptian troops in Tor advanced on their enemy from the south. The Turkish camp was rushed at dawn. The surprise was complete, their sentries having been killed before any alarm was given. About eighty killed and eighty prisoners represented almost the whole of the enemy force, as some of the Bedouins had gone home, and others had gone

PLATE XVI

SHEIKH ZEIDAN MUDAKHIL

[face p. 144

RAIDING AND WARFARE

with Sheikh Suleiman Ghoneim to Abu Zenima. Here fell Husein, of the 'Awarma, the Sheikh ed-Deir, or the representative of his tribe in its dealings with the Convent. He had been my caravan sheikh in 1911, and was a good old man. Sixteen reputable Arabs met an untimely end. 'Aid, who had slain Mudakhil's father, and lost his own father in exchange ; Salama, the eldest son of the Hajj 'Awda ez-Zumeili, Mudakhil's rival ; Sabah Agha the faithless *bash-shawish* ; and Sheikh Khidr's own brother all paid the penalty for being caught in such an indefensible situation.

The hero of this action, in Sinai eyes, was one of the Sawalha. This worthy, who had been stunned, woke up and perceived some Gurkhas dispatching the severely wounded with their kukris. And his own turn was rapidly approaching. So he removed from an already disembowelled comrade a sufficient heap of entrails, and bestowed them about his person to such effect that the Gurkhas passed him over as a corpse. Whereupon he, thinking absence of body an even greater safeguard than presence of mind, decamped across the Qa' plain as rapidly as he could.

The Hajj Hamdan, the lame judge of the Qararsha, continued loyal to the Egyptian Government for some time. But the Turks, who by that time had discovered Nassir Musa to be a fool, let him know that, instead of waiting for Nassir's job, he could have it at once by joining them. This seduced Hamdan from his allegiance, and he joined them to become Sheikh. In the absence of a better candidate he has retained the office ever since.

The contemporary burning of Abu Zenima I give from the narrative of Hamdan Himeid, 14 years of age, who was present :—

"I was asleep with the watchmen at Abu Zenima, when Suleiman Ghoneim came with the German (Gondos) and nineteen Turks on foot and six Arabs on camels. Suleiman boxed my ears, which woke me up, and then told me to carry his gun. He said to the watchman, ' O 'Aleiqat, your fathers are here ! ' and added, ' If " Abu Dagn " (Mr. Westmacott) were here, I would cut off his head with this sword ! ' Early in the morning, Suleiman and a soldier got up and lit the fire in a locomotive. Then he brought two trucks and fastened them to the locomotive, and filled them with blankets and other loot. Then the Government steamer *Managem* came in sight, and they abandoned everything, and fled up Wadi Matalla. (She had on board Colonel Parker, returning from the battle of Tor.)

" I took some dates and native butter, and fled up Wadi Tayiba. Then they fired at the *Managem* without effect and it went away northwards. When it had passed, they came back and I came back too. Many Arabs joined them, when they heard that looting was going on.

"Then they opened the store-room, and found nothing important except four boxes of gelignite which they threw into the sea. They tried to get the locomotive to start, but they couldn't. They broke up all the locomotives as far as possible with hammers and set fire to the houses. They poured oil on the (stationary) engines and set fire to them too. They took everything away on camels and stayed four days at the railhead. Then they stayed two days in the mouth of Wadi Baba and bought three sheep. Then news came of the fight at Tor, when they left the sheep and fled. Suleiman and the 'Awarma went over Naqb Budra to their own country in Wadi Sidri. The Turks and Gondos went up Wadi Nukhul and over Naqb el-Reikna to Nekhl. Fateih and 'Amadi (two local thieves) stole the three sheep."

In 1915, during the Turkish occupation of Sinai, Muhammad Abu Rumeil, the *'aqid* of the Zuweida (a clan of Haweitat, living east of Petra), conducted a raiding party of about twenty-five camelmen into Sinai, intending to plunder the Muzeina. They came on a party of four Arabs, and in the ensuing conflict one of these, a Terbani, was wounded, and 10 camels and 60 sheep were carried off into Arabia by the raiders. Jebely 'Aid, a Muzeini who had married into the Terabin, and through his local influence with that tribe had been made " Mamur " by the Turks of the district between Nuweiba and 'Aqaba, was one of the four attacked.

Although the Terabin themselves seemed content to sit down under their losses, Jebely, taking a *rafiq*, followed the raiders to their home, where representing himself as a Terbani, he claimed the return of the booty from Muhammad Abu Rumeil, as lifted from the Terabin, a tribe for the moment in alliance with the Zuweida. Muhammad acceded to his claim, and Jebely returned with 10 camels and 60 sheep, the amount stolen. Where a sheep had been eaten, it was made good.

According to Jebely, from whom I had this story, the Zuweida would probably have been less generous if they

had not been in great fear of the Turkish commandant at
'Aqaba at that time. What they might have done, if they
had known that the impudent Jebely, instead of being a
Terbani as he pretended, was really one of the Muzeina,
the tribe at which they had meant to strike, can only be
surmised.

PART III

Chapter X

BELIEFS

"*Pay all respect to spiritual beings, but keep them at a distance.*"—Confucius.

Allah—Welis and Sanctuaries—Jinn—Umm el-Gheith—Sacred Stones—Relics of a Serpent Cult—Sacred Trees—Divination—The Bedouin Calendar—Lucky and Unlucky Days—Names of Stars—Vestiges of Christianity among the Beja.

Allah to the Sinai Bedouin is no more than the sheikh of the next world. These Arabs are still in the state of the Israelites before Saul—the idea of a real kingship has not yet entered into their heads—so God is not thought of as a king but rather as a sheikh. Yet Islam, the most democratic of religions, though it originated in such a community, has hardly reached these Sinai Arabs yet.[1] To speak more correctly, it has flown over their heads. Indeed their conception of God and the next world, like that of the ancient Egyptians,[2] is purely a material one. A Sharari, asked by Palgrave, what they would do after death, replied, " We will go up to God and salute him, and if he proves hospitable, we will stay with him, if otherwise, we will mount our horses and ride off."[3] In fact their nature is utterly impatient of all control, whether human or divine.

Jaussen tells how another famished Sharari vowed half of whatever game he might shoot to God. Presently he shot a hare, and, cutting it into two, left God's part on a rock. Then he went on his way. But presently, still hungry, he crawled back, stealthily lest God should see him, and successfully stole God's share. " Allah was unable to keep what belonged to him ; I have eaten his half as well as mine ! " It is fair to add that this tale was told of the Shararat who are reckoned Hiteim.[4] The idea, however, is truly Bedouin.

---

[1] " As to the amount of knowledge that the Bedouins of Sinai have got of the Muhammadan Religion, I can say that there are only very few of them who know the five rules of Islam." Ahmed Shafik Pasha, *Notes on a Visit to Sinai Monastery*. Cairo, 1926.

[2] Reisner says, " The other world in which lived the spirits of the dead was filled with the spirits or ghosts of all things and animals. The other, the unseen, was a duplicate of this world." *Egyptian Conception of Immortality*, 14.

[3] Palgrave, *Journey through Central and Eastern Arabia*, 33.

[4] Jaussen, 288.

Allah is the punisher of evil-doers. Once a valuable riding-camel, belonging to Suleiman Ghoneim, Sheikh of the 'Awarma, backed, with myself in the saddle, over a bank into the sea. Rider and beast escaped unhurt, and Suleiman was loud in his congratulations. " You must be a very good man, or Allah would have seized his opportunity. You must be a very good man indeed, or Allah would certainly have killed the camel ! "

This Suleiman criticized the Wahabis for their irreverence towards saints, and declared that God should be properly approached through a *weli*.[1] " If I wanted to see the Khedive, I would begin by giving a dollar to his door-keeper ! "

But even Wahabis (I speak of Bedouins) sometimes find God a convenient peg to hang responsibility on. " I won't deny I have often pointed my gun at people, and fired," quoth an outlaw of that faith, whom I met in Sinai. " But what happens after that, is from God ! "

Both in Egypt and the Sudan, fanaticism is never a quality of the Arabs, but of the population they conquered and converted. Indeed the Western Arabs are divided into the " free " Arabs and the " bound " (Murabitin = Covenanters), these latter being the pious descendants of former religious communities, mostly founded by converted Berbers.

It must also be confessed that the Sinai Arabs are terribly materialistic. On my inquiring if their dead walked, I was told that there was a rumour of this sort about a man buried near Ras Muhammad, but an Arab to whom the deceased owed money got to hear of it and sat up three nights over the grave with a gun, yet got nothing. Young Sabah Mudakhil, on his first visit to Egypt, condemned the inhabitants of Quseir with a fine scorn as altogether too superstitious. " There is a grave of a formerly prolific lady in the European cemetery. On this tomb those women, who desire offspring, go and break bottles, and they think it does them good. Also those who wish to be married, go before an old man and pay him a good round sum for writing their names in a book. And they think *that* does them good." Very few civilized institutions could withstand this sort of criticism.

---

[1] A *weli* (pl. *awliya*) is the spirit of a man, who during his lifetime was holy, and is now in a position to intervene for you with God.

BELIEFS

The *awliya* are more highly regarded in Egypt than they are in Sinai, where the Arabs fear their dead saints so little that they will cheerfully take false oaths on their tombs. Indeed I found in Wadi Feiran a very material *mubasha'* plying his red-hot spoon, almost within the shadow of the tomb of Sheikh Shebib, who in Professor Palmer's day was a famous punisher of false swearers. Migration from the tombs of their Arabian ancestors may be in part the reason for this irreverent attitude.

A tribal ancestor is sometimes promoted to be a *weli*, but dead saints, like living judges and other consultants, have to make their way in public esteem, and as against the present power of obtaining results, the past rank or holiness of a *weli* counts for little.

To the 'Ababda, their great *weli* is not 'Abad, the tribal ancestor, but Sheikh Shadli, the traditional inventor of coffee. After all, the qualities necessary to found a tribe are not necessarily holy, and perhaps 'Abad's ability to represent the tribe to the outside world, visible and invisible, passed away with his lifetime.

A good *weli* not only intercedes successfully for you with God, and punishes those who swear falsely by his tomb; but also protects objects deposited at his tomb for safe keeping.

The barley-patches of the Awlad 'Ali are often very scattered, so, after ploughing, they are in the habit of depositing their ploughs till the next year with a *weli* in a central position. The protected area sometimes extends for some little distance round. Near Sheikh Hashshash in Wadi Sahu in Sinai, there is a mountain on which the ibex are invulnerable; while, in Egypt, Sheikh Banas, whose head floated ashore at Ras Banas, protects all the animals and plants on that peninsula, and harm will at once befall anyone who destroys them. My favourite hunter 'Ali Kheir, who shot a gazelle in this sanctuary, knowing well such a deed was wrong, was almost immediately arrested by a police patrol for having no gun licence, and carried off by them to Bir Shalatein, where he spent weeks shooting gazelles for them, before going 200 miles to Quseir to be tried.

A saint, though dead, retains many of his living characteristics. Thus some *awliya* are fools and will vouchsafe protection or intercede for you without any proper sacrifice being made to them. The Bisharin possess such a one in Wadi

O Sir Eirab. To obtain his favour it is sufficient to take a sheep there, make the usual little pile of stones to cover the blood, notify the saint that the sheep has been slain in his honour, *and take the animal away again*. Naturally such a saint is very popular, and the immense number of these little piles of stones drew my attention to the spot, and elicited the foregoing story which I heard there in 1926.

Sidi 'Abd er-Rahman, the Libyan Saint Gengulphus, some ninety miles west of Alexandria, used to be visited by pilgrims on foot from the Beheira. But since the Khedive Abbas built him a mosque, and King Fuad repaired it, this *weli* has become a snob, and will do nothing for poor men. So the local people say, and they ought to know.

This Sidi 'Abd er-Rahman was the richest of seven traders from the west, poor men of the tribe Hadahid, who decided to murder him. This they performed by cutting off his head, which they duly buried. Passing the scene of their crime some years later, his treacherous comrades marvelled to see a magnificent water-melon growing there. So luscious did it look, that they plucked it and took it away with them in a bag for presentation to the " Basha ". Unfortunately for them, the bag, when opened, proved to contain the still bleeding head of 'Abd er-Rahman, so the " Basha " ordered them for immediate execution. The triumphant Sidi 'Abd er-Rahman then embarked on a long career of miracle-working, from which the gifts of the sovereigns mentioned above have only recently tended to entice him.

Some *awliya* are invisible, one such called El-'Amri haunts an empty house in the Wadi Feiran, where the women of the Sawalha pay him visits. Another, 'Ali, brother of Abu Talib, whose tomb is in the Wadi Biyar lil 'Ain, can hardly be a good Muslim, for he rings a bell.

Others have lost their virtue, and the Bedouin curse and pelt their graves with stones.[1] Among them are Musabbah of the Darb el-Hajj at Wadi Mishiti, and another 'Amri at the head of Wadi el-'Obeiyid, ten miles from the ruins of El-'Auja, on the road to Gaza.

When the Arabs visit a *weli*, they sacrifice a sheep or goat, and in Sinai, lamps are lighted in his honour. At the

---

[1] In Palestine, *awliya* are sometimes irritated and their tombs defiled to make them show their power. *JPOS.*, vi, 5.

PLATE XVII

Sheikh Shadli

Nebi Sala

TOMBS OF SAINTS

BELIEFS

shrines of great sheikhs, camels are sacrificed at the 'Id, e.g. the Muzeina are then supposed to slaughter three camels on three successive days, one at Sheikh Faranja, the second at Nebi Sala, the third at Nebi Harun near the Monastery, and on the day of the 'Id, a sheep on the very summit of the *Moneijat en-Nebi Musa*, the " hill where the prophet Moses conversed (with God) ".

These camels must be female camels, and all those who contribute to the expense of providing a beast tie white ribbons to its neck, and as many as possible sit upon it " to keep it down " while it is being slaughtered. At the 'Id, when the 'Ababda kill a sheep, as many as possible pretend to ride on it, calling it *markab* " the mount that will take them to Mecca ". But, in practice, it often happens that sufficient subscribers cannot be found ; as in June 1929, when my caravan met in Wadi Zaghra a Muzeini looking for the camel that was to be sacrificed next day at Nebi Harun. He told us that the Muzeina were sacrificing that day at Nebi Sala, so our hungry caravan making a forced march of nine hours instead of its usual six, arrived disgusted at Nebi Sala to find nobody there and nothing doing. Nor was their appetite for camel-meat to be appeased that day, for the Muzeini returned saying " the camel could not be found ", and so the sacrifice did not take place. The real reason was that their Sheikh Musa Sofaran could not get enough people to share the expense with him.

Although they venerate these prophets, no Sinai Bedouin has now any idea of their origin. This is probably because the present Arab inhabitants are relatively recent immigrants, and moreover the fact that oaths on their tombs are seldom taken in vital matters shows that they are not respected in the same way that *awliya* of one's own tribe would be.

The spirit of Moses is still powerful on Mount Sinai, more particularly as the Arabs believe the rainfall of the peninsula to be more or less under his control.[1] Indeed the excessive flood of 1867, which drowned forty of the Wilad Sa'id in Wadi Solaf, is nowadays ascribed to overpraying for rain on Jebel Musa by the celebrated Sheikh Musa Nassir.

The prophet is supposed to have told his namesake on that occasion that the rain would no longer be withheld ; in fact, Musa Nassir was given to understand that he had better get

---

[1] In Burckhardt's day, Moses was thought to have delegated this power to the monks. See his *Syria*, 567–8.

home quick and warn his people. But the Sheikh's riding camel was by no means swift enough to outrun the Divine (but sudden) generosity.

This tale I had from the venerable Hajj Hamdan (about a man we had both known in our youth), and he also recommended the pilgrimage to Jebel Musa to any lady who desired more offspring, as he had found from the experience of his own family that it was particularly efficacious.

The Arabs erect a wooden cage covered with a coloured cloth over the tomb of a *weli*, and over this they build a hut, or for an important saint a dome. Sometimes a second hut is erected, in which the visitors find a copper pan, a coffee pot, a water pitcher, a basin for flour and another for serving food.

The dead of a tribe are usually buried beside the tomb of a *weli*, and the site for these cemeteries is almost always near a water-source.

Among both Bisharin and 'Ababda a curious belief is held about animals sacrificed at the tomb of a *weli*. Such animals turn into gazelles or ibex, and any attempt to shoot such animals is severely punished by the *weli*. Usually the rifle used will not shoot straight for some considerable time, and the hunter is often personally afflicted. Recently a hunter wounded one of such animals, a gazelle, in Wadi Kharit. Immediately a voice was heard saying, " You have wounded my goat ! " and the hunter was afflicted with madness ; an old man cured him, but wisely forbade him to go hunting again. A Bishari, who killed an ibex of this nature, was less fortunate. The beast was found to have its teats tied up with silk (to wean its kids). He died, and his gun was never any more good. Yet another, who killed a gazelle that was grazing near a tomb, got his face smashed in with a stone while he was cutting it up. He lives to tell the tale, and to be thankful that the spirit did not hit him from behind : " If I hadn't looked up when I heard it whizz, I would certainly have been killed ! "[1]

Among the Bisharin, the four leg-bones of the goat killed at the naming of a boy are hung from a branch stuck in the ground inside the hut for a year. This ceremony is called

---

[1] Musil tells of a *weli* in Moab, who was nourished for seven years before his death by gazelles. They visit his grave and repose there. If anyone tries to shoot them, blood drips from his gun, or it bursts, or won't go off. *Arabia Petræa*, 329.

BELIEFS

'*Alaq*, i.e. "hanging", and is not confined to the occasion of naming, for the 'Ababda hang the bones from the right hind-leg of the sheep they kill at the '*Id* from branches set up in the hut. Also if either 'Ababda or Bisharin kill a camel, the lower jaw must be hung in a tree. When naming girls, a goat is killed, but there is no " fantasia " or '*alaq*. When sacrificing, a piece of the victim's right ear is reserved for Sheikh Shadli or some other well-known saint, and hung on the tentpole.

Among the Arabs it is wrong to kill wild animals within the precinct of the *weli*. The Haram of Mecca is a similar sanctuary, which in pagan times contained troops of sacred gazelles. Muhammad, confirming old usage, forbade the cutting of fodder therein, the felling of trees, and the hunting of game. But the raven, kite, rat, scorpion, and the hyena were exempt from this prohibition ; and serpents also could be killed within it.

The Koran indeed extends this protection and forbids any killing of game on land while on pilgrimage, though fishing in the sea is permitted. The pilgrim who kills game intentionally is to make reparation in sheep which are to be offered at the Ka'ba or to be given to the poor.

To the superstitious Bedouin, the earth is crowded with spirits, *jinn*, who may do them harm unless appeased. When their tents are set up in a new place, a sacrifice is usually made for the " lord of the place " (*sahib el-mahal*), or at least at the first meal some of the salt is spilt upon the ground in his honour.[1]

These *jinn* are invisible except in dreams, and nightmares are usually ascribed to their influence. Sometimes they enter into and permanently possess the soul of some unfortunate, who is thenceforth known as *majnun* " possessed "—a word much overworked by the European in Egypt.

Although they cannot be seen, the *jinn* can be heard ; any unusual sound in the desert—the singing of the sands, the detonation when a heated rock splits with the cold, the unearthly howl of the wind, all these are the voice of the *jinn*. Sometimes they call to you from behind a rock—he who answers this call will die within a year. They can call only once or twice ; if you are called thrice, it is a real person who calls.

---

[1] A formula among the pagan Arabs was, " I seek refuge in the lord of this valley from the foolish among his people." Palmer, *Koran*, 503 f.

An 'Abadi told me that he was once travelling alone up a long and winding wadi, when he saw from fresh foot-prints that a large party was just ahead of him. Moreover the sound of music came faintly to his ears on the wind. Yet hurry as he might, he could never overtake them; they were always just round the next bend. The whole afternoon this ghostly band tantalized his ears with their music, but, as he afterwards realized, he was fortunate enough not to overtake them.

But on the whole, they are not very much afraid of their *jinn*. The Ma'aza sheikh, Salem Faraj, said: "The *jinn* abound in our mountains, but nobody but a *fellah* would fear them. Now, wolves are really dangerous!"

A special form of *jinn* actually appears, sometimes as a beast, sometimes as a hairy and bestial caricature of human form. These are called "ghouls" (*ghul*), and may often be found in caverns near wells. One of these haunted a cave in the Jebel Raha near Suez, and was only got rid of by kindling a large fire therein and making the place too hot to hold her. Jennings Bramly was told that a ghoul has one leg like a donkey's, and silver bullets kill them.

The Muzeina of Eastern Sinai possess a moribund rain-goddess called *Umm el-Gheith*. During a drought, on those tantalizing days when clouds promise rain, but do not fulfil their promise, the women go about carrying a dry waterskin on a stick and singing to their patroness :—

> *Ya Umm el-Gheith, gheithina !*
> *Wu billil shinnina, rayina !*
> "O mother of rain, rain on us !
> And moisten our ' drippers ', satisfy our thirst !"

Here "drippers" means "waterskins". Jaussen and Musil recount similar invocations by the Arab women of Moab and Palestine.

In North Sinai, the sea is still worshipped, for Na'um Bey Shuqeir relates how :—

> "The Suwarka, Bayadiyin and Akharsa tribes of North Sinai make annual pilgrimage to the sea every autumn accompanied by their horses, camels and sheep. They wash their flocks and herds in the sea, and sacrifice sheep, throwing the heads, legs and skins of the victims into the sea saying, ' This is your dinner, O sea !'
>
> "The Suwarka may kill their sheep anywhere on the coast between Rafa and El-'Arish, and perform this visit and sacrifice

BELIEFS

without any special ceremony in one day (sunset to next morning). But the Bayadiyin and Akharsa go in state to Mahamdiya and observe a three days' festival with horse and camel races and every kind of rejoicing."[1]

The Bisharin have still a few sacred rocks and cliffs, to which ceremonial visits are performed and sheep sacrificed. Such a place is Kanjar Aweib, " the runaway stone," in Wadi Kajuj, a tributary of Wadi Ibib. Of this stone, the Bisharin relate that it fell from the mountain into Wadi Kajuj during or after a great storm of rain. Everyone was away at the time, and when they returned, they found the valley green with rich grazing, and this marvellous stone lying in the middle of it. Ever since its appearance it has afforded the occasion for an annual sacrifice.

In the Eastern Desert, there is a remarkable dyke of blood-red felsite, which can be traced from Wadi Khashir on the coast for thirty-five miles over the watershed to the wide plains at the head of the Wadi Kharit. Here it appears as a chain of innumerable little red hills, all very much alike. The 'Ababda call these " hills of the demons " (*Araf es-Sul*), and believe that they are constantly altering in number and appearance. Such places are to be avoided after dark. 'Ali Kheir refused to break off a sample of this red rock for fear of the demons.

Anything fallen from the sky must have seemed sacred and full of magical properties to a star-worshipping people like the early Arabs. The Black Stone in the Ka'ba at Mecca is reputed to be of this celestial origin, and, to the present day, the Bedouin believe that swords made from a meteorite, like the mythical sabre of 'Antar, will kill everything they touch. Any metallic meteorites that fall are thus likely to be carried off at once for magical use.

Fire is pretty generally used to drive out evil spirits. When Burckhardt set out from Daraw for Berber on 1st March, 1813, and his camels were about to be loaded :—

> " The 'Ababda women appeared with earthen vessels in their hands filled with burning coals. They set them before the several loads, and threw salt upon them. At the rising of the bluish flame, produced by the burning of the salt, they exclaimed, 'May you be blessed in going and in coming.' The devil and every evil genius are thus, they say, removed."[2]

[1] Shuqeir, 345. [2] *Nubia*, 169.

Later on, when the caravan had to cross the Wadi 'Alaqi :—

"Our guides in approaching the Wady saluted it with great solemnity, and thanked Heaven for having permitted them to arrive so far in safety. In crossing the valley, which is about one hundred and fifty yards across, each person took a handful of dhourra and threw it on the ground, a kind of pious offering to the good genius who is supposed to preside over the Wady." [1]

At Bir Ranga on the Red Sea Coast, among the Qireijab, perhaps the descendants of Pliny's Ichthyophagi, I came across a vestige of a serpent cult. The Qireijab, in appearance indistinguishable from the other 'Ababda, are looked down upon as fish-eaters, and as not descended from the tribal ancestor. "Their ancestor drifted across from Arabia on a plank." The neighbourhood is notorious for the size of its snakes, and one of my men was terrified by a fine specimen he met among some tamarisks. He reported it as "thick as his thigh", and wishing to verify this, I conducted a search. We did not discover the snake, but we found what seemed to be a little shrine of three flat stones set on edge, though there was no direct evidence to connect this with the serpent. The animal appeared to be well known, and gossip said "It was a *weli*". Pretending to be shocked, I ordered it to be produced, through one of the sons of the Sheikh of the 'Ababda, who was attached to my caravan. The locals, after much pressure, produced a very inferior thin animal, which was obviously a surrogate, and no research on our part, though we burned down all the tamarisks, could evoke the *weli*. Afterwards I heard that the people had removed it, fearing it would be harmed. The habit in snakes of frequenting the rubble rings round tombs has no doubt often led to their being connected with the souls of the dead in native belief. But in this case there was no tomb in question.

The 'Ababda regard it as a point of honour not to pass a horned viper without attempting to kill it, and when this has been done, they bury its corpse in the sand with seven camel droppings beside it.[2] Unless they do this, God has to send an angel to guard the grave (to prevent its coming to life again ?) for an uncertain period.[3]

---

[1] *Nubia*, 184.

[2] The Sinai Arabs do the same, lest its relatives follow to avenge it. The seven droppings represent the *diya* or blood-money.

[3] "Near Thebes there are sacred snakes, harmless to men, small in size, and bearing two horns on the top of their heads. These, when they die, are buried in the temple of Zeus, to whom they are said to be sacred." *Herodotus*, ii, 74. Presumably the Egyptians regarded these dangerous asps as "harmless", only so long as they were sacred.

BELIEFS

A sheikh of El-Azhar, the Moslem University in Cairo, who had lost many of his children through the evil influence of the *Qarina*,[1] wrote to 'Awda, an old Muzeini, to kill two horned vipers and lay them out on the ground. 'Awda had then to behead a third, and, holding the head in his hand, walk straight between the corpses of the others. This he performed, and then brought the head to El-Azhar, where the sheikh performed various other incantations over it. The sheikh was blessed next year with a fine boy, who was named Muhammad, and the year after that with a girl-child.

I have heard of a viper being eaten in Sinai as medicine; the reptile was said to be nailed down at the head-end, and eaten alive by the patient who began at the tail. Presumably the head with the poison-fangs did not form part of this potent and strange repast. Altogether snakes are looked on as powerful beings with mysterious but not supernatural powers. The Bedouin knows the dangerous varieties, and has not that silly fear of any and every form of serpent which characterizes the *fellah*, and only too often the civilized European.

Earlier in the book we have inferred a past belief that the souls of the dead passed into animals, and a magical formula used at funerals by the Towara seems to imply that even at the present day the dead are metamorphosed into plants. They address the deceased, saying among other things, "The *Zizyphus*-tree is thy mother, the palm-tree thy sister and the fig-tree thy grandmother".[2] Such a suggestion to the dead man probably implies that in future he should keep himself, if not to himself, at least within his new family circle, and an enthusiast for mother-right might consider it of extreme antiquity, since only the names of female relations are mentioned. Another ancient form of oath, "By the fig and by the olive, and by Mount Sinai, and by this sanctuary" is quoted by the Prophet.[3]

Haynes who visited Sinai in 1882 has the following note:—

"Notwithstanding the little reverence shown by the Bedouin to their few remaining trees, there is one exception to this in the 'shik' tree, one of which is generally to be seen in each wadi, and is sacred to the memory of some great man now passed away. This tree is preserved from damage or destruction; and round it the people assemble on certain days to dance the *tawaf*, and perform their rites. It is interesting to observe that the *tawaf* (a sort of walk-round)

---

[1] See p. 169.   [2] See p. 192 for a fuller formula.   [3] *Koran*, xcv.

is performed with the left hands towards the tree; so that the dancers go round in a contrary direction to the sun."[1]

Half an hour south of Rafa stand two *Zizyphus* trees side by side called *El-Maqruntein* " the united pair ". Each is individually called *El-Faqira* " the poor one ". The western one has a bough bending to the ground with a cavity in which coins, nails, beads, and lentil seeds are placed. From the branches of both trees hang oil-lamps. On inquiry, Na'um Bey was told that the Bedouin women attribute great sanctity to these two trees and make vows at them. When they visit the trees, the women deposit offerings and light lamps as the Sinai Bedouin generally do when visiting a saint.

Half an hour from El-'Arish on the way to Lahfan is a small wood of tamarisks also called *El-Faqira*, which the Arabs visit to obtain blessing (*baraka*), and where they put lights, and deposit their ropes and other possessions. In the garden at Nekhl Fort (now deserted) was a very old *Zizyphus*-tree which the inhabitants believed to be a *weli*, and on which they hung lights.[2]

According to Bramly, the terebinths of Wadi Butum in central Sinai are held sacred by the Laheiwat. Leaves may be taken by travellers, but the branches must not be cut for fuel or charcoal. This rule was made because an Arab, in attempting to make charcoal therefrom, observed that the branches squirmed in the fire. Bramly remarks that the turmoil was probably due to the large content of resin held by the wood, and even by the flowers of the male tree. According to the Laheiwat, the trees were planted in pagan times, and cannot now be propagated from seed or raised from cuttings.

Though trees must have provided much more permanent residences for the soul than short-lived animals, yet the Beja views on potent plants partake rather of animism than of ancestor-worship. The Bisharin consider that certain trees and bushes, especially a variety of frankincense with aromatic gum, must not be cut down, or evil will befall the camels. (No wonder they objected to Schweinfurth prying about in the Elba mountains). Sprigs of others are of great virtue as charms. One Karait declared that in a quarrel with an angry husband who possessed such an amulet, he cut him twice on the

---

[1] A. E. Haynes, *Manhunting in the Desert*, 190.   [2] Shuqeir, 354.

BELIEFS

leg as hard as he could with his sword; but his opponent was uninjured, and Karait was glad when friends came to separate them. The guide, 'Ali Kheir, when employed to collect plants, was afraid of a rare species of *Cleome*, and would not gather anything that even looked like it, for when uprooted " it would exude blood like that of a human being. It is good to give your wife to make her love you; but, in pulling it out of the ground by the roots, a donkey or dog ought to be employed. A negro will do, or a man without any property, but these will expect something for their trouble ".[1]

Though it provides good charcoal, the Beja think it very wrong to use "higlig" (*Balanites ægyptiaca*) for any such purpose.

Even a materially minded Sinai Arab recognizes that there are more things in heaven and earth than are dreamt of in his philosophy. But though ability to influence the invisible forces which seem to work generally to his disadvantage, while presenting somebody in the next tribe with an undeserved windfall, *would* be extremely advantageous; yet his practical nature, suspicious rather than superstitious, distrusts any casual charlatan who may pretend to control them. Wizards are about as rare as hermits in Sinai.

Yet in all communities, there are liaison officers with the unseen, and the Sinai *mubasha'* who detects the guilty with a red-hot spoon is one of them. Moslems declare that he owes his virtue (*baraka*) to being in closer connection with Allah than the rest of mankind. He is *mrabit* bound by a covenant, like the priest-judges of Israel.[2] But for ordinary sorcerers one must search in Africa.

Wizards called *khawwat*[3] are highly esteemed among the Beja, though even in the Northern Sudan, a materialistic outlook does sometimes occur. One old fellow, by profession a maker of amulets, said to his son, when I explained the nature of an eclipse. " I told you, Khalil, there was an explanation for everything, if you could only find it out ! " It must be admitted also that, just as a prophet lacks honour in his own country, the best wizards usually come from the

[1] Cf. Josephus, *Wars of the Jews*, vii, 6, 4.
[2] See Chapter XIV for an account of his activities.
[3] From *khawwata* divination by lines in the sand, a childish science like the English children's " this year, next year, sometime, never " with fruit-stones.

next tribe but one ; in the case of the 'Ababda, from the Amar Ar. And there, as elsewhere, there is a strong professional rivalry among these quasi-scientific men. Each of two old practitioners, who were being gradually overwhelmed by ailments peculiar to old age, ascribed his growing misfortunes to the other's black magic. Naturally each also did his best by spell and rite not only to counteract the evil influence, but also to take reprisals. In the end, the victor, struck blind and deaf, was consoled on his deathbed by the tidings that his rival was even in worse plight. " Musa's arms and legs are drawn up to his sides, and he is now so completely paralysed that he lies on his back. When he makes water, it flies up in the air and comes down on his face ! " On learning of this rather belated triumph over his rival, the old sorcerer died happy.

Their male wizards can only pass their knowledge successfully on to the female, and conversely a witch must impart her lore to a male. If wizards of the same sex try to exchange recipes, these will fail.

Besides these professional exponents, any 'Abadi may practise white magic on his own. One way of getting rid of things is to point at them. When 'Ali Kheir saw a crocodile for the first time, he pointed at it just as the Dynasty V man does in the pictured tomb of Ti at Saqqara. On another occasion, he reproved an ignorant hobbledehoy for pointing at an approaching rainstorm " lest he drive it away ".

If a number of 'Ababda are suspected of using the evil eye, the culprit may be detected by putting a stone for each man in a fire of donkey dung. Next morning, when the stones should be cool, they are put into water one by one. The guilty one's stone cannot refrain from uttering a shrill piercing sound ! [1]

Na'um Bey gives a Sinai method of detecting guilt formerly practised by Sheikh Abu Khalaifa of the Suwarka.[2] In this the diviner applied his mind to the consideration of who was the criminal, and then read something (what, is not stated), and went to sleep. The identity of the culprit was revealed in his dream, and immediately on waking, he gave a decision against him. Lord Cromer scoffed at this in one of his reports, and suggested that

[1] Cf. the method of choosing the Shilluk kings. Seligman, *Pagan Tribes*, 93.
[2] Shuqeir, 399.

BELIEFS 163

for the future the diviner ought to confine himself to the consideration of the evidence he heard in his waking moments.[1]

Yet this is a very ancient mode of obtaining information, which the Romans called " incubation ". Petrie thought he had discovered traces of it at the shrine of Sarabit el-Khadim, where a number of dormitory cells appeared to be provided for the devotees who hoped that the goddess would advise them during their sleep.

Hasan 'Ali Mustafa, the present Sheikh of the 'Ababda, often communes with his ancestors in this fashion. Once his predecessors appeared to him. Hasan, the son of Jubran, was taller than men are nowadays, and wore the Beja mop of hair, abandoned by his civilized descendants. After him, the brother of 'Abdalla ed-Dirazi appeared. These were silent. Another time he saw his uncle Bishir Bey and Lord Kitchener walking together on an island in the Nile. They invited him to join them, but he told them politely to mind their own business. His father 'Ali appears to him once or twice a month, whenever he is vexed or troubled about anything. Père Jaussen heard the same from the Arabs of Moab :—

" Pursued by religious thoughts which disturb or grieve him, the Bedouin during his sleep, often sees a *weli* coming to demand a victim in honour or satisfaction, for he is irritated ; one knows not why. On waking, the nomad, still under the influence of fear, hastens to offer the desired sacrifice." [2]

Any aspect of time, beyond the instant with which it is in contact, is hardly considered by the Bedouin mind. The almost tenseless Arabic verb affords a proof of this, if any were wanted, and to their philosophy the future is as beyond control as the past. So why worry about time ? The Arab looks on his desert much as the mathematician looks on his space-time continuum, though ideas of measurement occur only to the few.

A rough division of the summer was given me by my hunter 'Ali Kheir, who apologized for its imperfections, saying, " The people who know the stars are the fish-eaters of the coast. We only think in weeks ; their mode of living obliges them to think in days ! " Nevertheless he told me sufficient to show that their calendar was

[1] *Annual Report on Egypt and the Sudan*, 1906.
[2] Jaussen, 357.

a stellar and not a lunar one, and derived from the ancient Arab division of the year in twenty-seven periods of thirteen days each plus one of fourteen.[1]

'Ali called his thirteen-day periods *simum*, which means "hot spell", and based his chronology, as did the ancient Egyptians, on the observation of heliacal risings of stars, commonly near the ecliptic. The year he allowed to start with the heliacal setting of the Pleiades, which he called *Wuqqa'* or *Diffun et-Turaiya*, the "fall" or "burial" of the Pleiades, which is observed annually about 5th May.[2]

Two "simooms" later, the Pleiades reappear in the east about 4th June, and the *Simum et-Turaiya* begins. The camels are believed to perceive this heliacal rising before it becomes visible to human eyes, and not to lie down with their heads in any other direction but easterly at the beginning of June. The second half of the month is called *Simum et-Tueiba* or *Simum el-Baqar*, which starts with the heliacal rising of the Hyades (Taurus) about 17th June, and is followed by *Simum el-Jauzi* (or *Simum el-Qurun*), when the horns or foremost stars of Orion rise about the beginning of July. Then comes *Simum el-Luwab*, or simoom of Procyon (?), and about 1st August, the heliacal rising of the Dogstar, so important to the ancients, which the 'Ababda reckon to usher in *Simum Mirzim*. Canopus (*Suhail*) rises next, but no "simoom" is named after him; they prefer to call the latter half of August *Simum el-Kilab* after ϵ and δ Canis Majoris. A "simoom" for which I could not get the name followed, and then *Simum Banat Na'sh* named after the three stars in the tail of the Great Bear, which the 'Ababda call the daughters of *Na'sh*. Yet they do not call the rest of the constellation *Na'sh*, "bier" or "litter", as the ancient Arabs used to, but *El-Karab*. By this time the drought has forced the ibex down to the waterholes, where they fall easy victims to the hunters. So they say, *Ya Simum Banat Na'sh, Tiwarid el-Wahash!* "O Simoom of Banat Na'sh, you make the wild animals drink!"

For the thirteen-day periods of the winter, 'Ali could not give me the names.

---

[1] An article by Mr. J. W. Crowfoot in *Sudan Notes and Records*, iii, 4, gives the names of these, and calls them "The Mansions of the Moon".

[2] The forty days following this event are called by the Arab sailors *arba'inet es-seif*, and are characterized by calms and hot south winds corresponding to the *khamasin* of the Nile Valley. Klunzinger, *Upper Egypt*, 301. The Fellata calendar, quoted by Mr. Crowfoot, starts with the Menzil en-Nath on 8th May.

BELIEFS

Na'um Bey Shuqeir[1] was told the secret of lucky and unlucky days by the Sinai Arabs. They establish a constellation of the Scorpion, far larger than our Scorpio, since it stretches over a quarter of the firmament, and divide it into seven stages. From west to east they name them: firstly, *Et-Tarbi'a* " the squaring ", next *El-Yadein* " the two hands ", thirdly, *Khashm el-'Aqrab* " the mouth of the scorpion ", fourthly, *El Qalb* the red star Antares, which is the heart of Scorpio. Fifthly comes *Esh-Shaula* " the left-handed " (λ Scorpii), the star above the curve in the Scorpion's tail, sixthly,[2] *Dheil el-'Aqrab* " the tail of the scorpion ", and lastly, the hook at the end of the tail, *Sa'd ed-Dabih* " Sa'd the slaughterer ", which we call αβ Capricornis.

During the revolution of the Moon in its orbit, it takes seven nights of each month to pass through this Arab constellation of the Scorpion; that is, it comes into each of the above stages for one night successively. Its passage through each stage is called a conjunction, *qiran* or *iqtiran*. In the first night it comes into *Tarbi'a*, the second night into *El-Yadein*, the third into *Khashm el-'Aqrab*, the fourth night into *El-Qalb*, the fifth into *Esh-Shaula*, the sixth into *Dheil el-'Aqrab*, and the seventh into *Sa'd ed-Dabih*, and then there will be no further *qiran* until the next month when it again begins to come into *Tarbi'a* and so on.

During these seven nights of conjunction in each month the Bedouin do not travel, nor start raids, and in fact do nothing whatever new, unless forced to do so, as they believe these nights to be evil ones, especially the fifth night when the moon enters *Esh-Shaula*. During the beginning of autumn, at the (heliacal) rising of Canopus, the moon enters the Scorpion, *'Aqrab*, when it is one night old, and so the conjunction is called *qurayin leila*. In the next month, it falls into it when it is three nights old, *ibn thalath*, and is therefore called *qurayin thalath*, in the third month it falls into it when it is five nights old and is called *qurayin khams*, in the fourth month it falls into Scorpion when it is seven nights old and is called *qurayin saba'*. It is then the beginning of the winter. In the fifth month it falls into it when it is nine nights old and is called *qurayin tisa'*, in the sixth month when it is twelve nights old it is called *qurayin itnashar*. In the

---
[1] Shuqeir, 356.
[2] In his book, Na'um Bey erroneously reverses these last two in order.

seventh month it returns to its starting point and entering the Scorpion, when it is one night old, is called *qurayin leila* again.

The stars themselves here only appear as milestones on the path of the moon, and do not appear to exert any influence on the fate of mankind. But in the past they were more powerful. Just as one may infer from a new servant's behaviour something of his old master's habits, so too the prohibitions of a new religion give some idea of the belief that it superseded. So the rule nowadays that animals may only be killed by day suggests a former killing by night in honour of some nocturnal deity. Star-worship was one of the heathenish practices to which the ancient Hebrews were prone, and Isaiah and the other prophets declaim vigorously against it. There is an allusion in 2 Kings, xxiii, 5, to those who burned incense " to the sun, moon, *mazzaloth*, and to all the host of heaven ". Schiaparelli has shown that *mazzaloth* here and elsewhere in the Bible means Venus.[1] In later days, the fourth-century Arabs of Sinai worshipped the morning star, and actually sacrificed captives to it.

The advent of Islam extinguished these practices, but at all times and places the Bedouins, both Arab and Beja, have taken a lively interest in the heavenly host. The names of the principal constellations vary but little from tribe to tribe. I have heard the following names :—

	'Aleiqat (Sinai).	'Ababda.
Polaris	Er-Rukn	El-Jidi (the usual Arab name)
Pleiades	Thuraiya	Turaiya
Aldebaran	Nujeida	Tueiba
Capella	En-Naja	Er-Rajib
Orion	El-Jauzi	El-Jauzi
Rigel	Aiyuq	. . . . . .
Canopus	Suhail	Suhail (the usual Arab name)
Procyon	El-Barbara	Luwab
Sirius	Mirzim	Mirzim
ε Canis Majoris	El-Ismakin	Kalb Raqad
δ ,, ,,		Kalb Umm Jurra
η ,, ,,		Kalb el-'Araj
αβγδ Ursa Majoris	Banat Na'sh [2]	El-Karab
ε ,, ,,		El-Fatah ⎫ Banat Na'sh
λ ,, ,,		Umm Genai ⎭
η ,, ,,		El Hamil or Makwart
Arcturus	El-Atum	
Venus	Esh Sha'ala	Fishasha

[1] *Astronomy in the Old Testament*, 83.
[2] Some call these " the followers of the sticks ", *suwaq el-asi*, meaning " the mourners after a corpse ".

BELIEFS

The 'Ababda call the Milky Way "the trail of the ram", *Mujirr el-Kabsh*, meaning the ram which, they say, the hyena brought to Abraham when he was about to sacrifice Isaac.

The Arabs divide their day into the periods of *al-fejr* "the dawn", *es-sabah* "the sunrise", *ed-daha* "the morning", *el-qaila* "noon-day", *el-'asr* "mid-afternoon", *ghraibat-esh-shems* "the setting of the sun", and finally *el-'ashiya* "supper-time".

Chapter XI

RITES AND CEREMONIES

"*To every nation have we appointed rites.*"—Koran, xxii, 35.

Rites de Passage—Pregnancy—Birth—Naming—Circumcision—Hair and Hair Sacrifices—Marriage—Burial—Cairns.

The anthropologist Van Gennep has given the name *rites de passage* to ceremonials invented to protect the individual during the highly dangerous state, often exhibiting itself as an emotional crisis, of passing from one stage of life to another.

The danger that affects people at such crises is diagnosed by the nomads of the Eastern Desert and Northern Sudan as *mushahira*, an illness caused by the moon, which affects boys at circumcision, young people of both sexes at marriage, and women in labour. The sovereign antidote is gold; he who suffers from or fears *mushahira* must take a gold ornament, and show this to the next new moon by holding it up in the air. *Mushahira* takes the form of weakness, and is not particularly dangerous as a rule. A severe attack can, however, only be cured by a pilgrimage to the sea at a time of new moon. Incense is burned in a pot on the beach, and the patient steps over it two or three times, and afterwards bathes in the sea. The moon is naturally confused with the sea because of its influence on the tides.

Mushahira is sometimes caused by the glance of a woman with a cheap gold nose-ring. If her nose-ring has not cost at least a guinea, the child at whom she looks may be affected. Young brides therefore take good care that their husbands do not put them off with cheap articles worth only sixty or seventy piastres.

This superstition is widely believed throughout Egypt and the Sudan, where *mushahira* is often spread by unclean persons of both sexes who have not bathed after sexual intercourse. The antidote is always gold. So the 'Ababda boys, when they are about to be circumcised, are decked in

PLATE XVIII

[Photo. by Mrs. G. W. Murray]

JEBELIYA WOMAN UNVEILED

[face p. 168

the ornaments of their female relatives " to show to the moon ".

People passing from one stage to another also seem to be regarded as in peculiar danger of contagion from the earth. With the 'Ababda, the newly born child is kept wrapped in a calico wrap, and is not allowed to touch earth for 40 days.

In Sinai, boys about to be circumcised may not let their feet touch the bare ground till the operation is completed, and during the ceremony they are seated on flat stones for the same reason. So too women must always ride or be carried to the marriage ceremony ; among the Hadendawa, the bride arrives riding upon the shoulders of a woman. On entering a tent, the guest doffs his sandals or slippers to prevent the earth being brought in from outside. Particular precautions are taken at burials lest earth come into contact with the corpse. This last practice probably provides a clue to the riddle ; there would seem to have been a danger that the soul might become resident in the earth so that special efforts had to be made not only to prevent this, but also to keep the spirits already in the soil from getting out. I have been reminded that the orthodox should consider that it is the earth which is in danger from the people. But this view necessitates a supposition that these precautions have been borrowed in an unreasoning way from the *fellahin*. And of that there is as yet no evidence.

Sand, as distinct from earth, seems to possess no evil influence, since, failing water, Moslem ablutions may be performed with it.

When a Bisharin woman is far advanced in pregnancy, it is the custom to promise her child gifts, a sword or a share in a camel if a boy, or jewellery if a girl, " to ease her labour." Yet whatever such a woman fancies, she must be humoured in and not thwarted, " or marks will appear on the child."

A belief in a spiritual counterpart of the opposite sex,[1] which is born with every human being, a remnant perhaps of the ancient Ka-belief of the Egyptians, persists to-day not only among the *fellahin*, but also among the 'Ababda. The male counterpart *qarin* which accompanies women seems to be beneficent or at least harmless, but the female *qarina* gives a lot of trouble. When you get married, she becomes terribly

---

[1] But Miss Blackman speaking of the *fellahin* of Middle and Upper Egypt says that there a man is always born with a male, and a woman with a female, counterpart. Blackman, 69–70.

jealous, and it is due to her evil influence that so many young children perish in Egypt.

Klunzinger wrote :—

> "When the child dies of spasms or the like while receiving suck from its mother, it is generally the *qarina* that kills it. Even in the official registers of deaths kept by the physicians, the *qarina* was till lately a regular variety of disease corresponding to our convulsions."[1]

'Ali Kheir said that some people pay money to magicians who pretend to kill the *qarina* with a charm. But he didn't believe in them himself; he thought the *qarina* was invulnerable.

To the Sinai Bedouin, the *qarina* is no companion, but merely a female demon, who can be exorcised by a proper use of horned vipers. In Moab, a cock is sacrificed and buried under the threshold to keep the *qarina* away.[2] My Nubian cook got rid of his troublesome *qarina* by being tattooed on his cheeks and his chin, doubtless with some appropriate incantation.

The late Mr. Kennett wrote to Professor Seligman :—

> "The idea prevails in the Western Desert among the Bedouin that if a woman eats camel meat when she is pregnant her delivery is delayed and she will carry the child a whole year. Consequently, if a woman knows that she is pregnant, she does not touch camel meat. If she has already eaten it, and does not wish to prolong the period of her burden, she crawls between the legs under the belly of a she-camel seven times, and this is supposed to neutralize the effect of the camel meat, and induce her delivery at the time ordained by nature."

And in a private letter to me, Jennings Bramly repeats Kennett's view.

This belief that eating camel-meat retards delivery is generally held in the Nile Valley,[3] and the passing seven times under a camel is supposed to accelerate it. Prejudices against women eating camel-meat are still found among the Towara of Sinai (though not among the Ma'aza) and can be traced back to pagan Arab times. Palmer says :—

> "Bahirah was the name given to a she-camel which had ten young ones; her ear was then slit and she was turned loose

---

[1] *Upper Egypt*, 383.   [2] Jaussen, 30.   [3] Cf. Blackman, 66.

RITES AND CEREMONIES

to feed. When she died, her flesh was eaten by the men only, the women being forbidden to touch it. There were, however, cases in which any she-camel was so called and treated."[1]

The taboo seems to be a purely Arab one, for none of my Bisharin or 'Ababda friends knew anything about it.

But there is another reason why a woman should creep seven times under a camel. In 1907, I observed a woman do this at Bahig in Mariut. She did not pass between its hind-legs, but from side to side and selected the finest *male* camel in the district, a magnificent Bisharin racing-camel for her purpose. Long ago Sir Samuel Baker observed this crawling under a camel at Gedaref on the southern limit of the Beja country. He was told correctly :—

> "Should a woman be in an interesting condition, she will creep under the body of a strong camel, believing that the act of passing between the fore and the hind legs will endow her child with the strength of the animal."[2]

That this is right is confirmed by a story which the late Mr. G. H. Morgan, an old colleague of mine in the Survey, used to tell of the arrival of the first train at Girga in Upper Egypt. The occupants, who remained in the train all night, were unable to sleep, owing to the incessant row made by the *fellahin* women creeping all night under the engine.

When the Towara Arabs of Sinai expect a birth, a fire is kept burning for three days and nights outside the tent,[3] and when the child is born, the mother places it at first in a hole dug in the ground.[4] Later it is washed with salt water and sheep's urine, and bandaged from the knees to the loins with cloth. Palmer goes on to say :—

> "Then it is slipped into a special bag, and its eyes and eyebrows are ornamented with *kohl*. Its head is then pressed into proper shape and tightly bandaged up, a piece of perfumed gum placed in its hand, and bracelets of beads, and of small copper coins called *nuss* fastened upon its arms and legs, complete the infant's toilette which is renewed night and morning only."

After childbirth, the mother remains seven days in the tent, and the Muzeina even prolong this period to 40 days.

---

[1] E. H. Palmer, *Koran*, 100 footnote.   [2] *Nile Tributaries of Abyssinia*, 274.
[3] The Amar Ar (Beja) also light a fire for seven days at a birth.
[4] The ancient Arabs used to place a newly-born child under a cauldron till the morning light. W. R. S., *Kinship*, 154.

During the whole of this period, the father is not allowed to see it. On the seventh day, her clothes are scrupulously washed, and, if the child be a boy, a feast is made in its honour, though for a female child no festivities are observed. Jennings Bramly writes :—

> "Before it has tasted its mother's milk, a newly-born child must swallow a finely chopped feather of the long-eared or little owl mixed in milk. This is to make it lucky. To make it scorpion-proof, it is given the ashes of a burnt scorpion in milk."

This last remedy is homeopathic, and some give the baby powdered hornet in similar fashion. The Muzeina also make the child swallow a little dried vulture's flesh pounded up as a prophylactic against snake-bite.

The Ma'aza of Egypt place the newly-born child in a sieve [1] instead of in a hole in the ground, and after 40 days, it goes into a sort of leather cradle called *mazfar*, which hangs from the main tent-pole. In their case the father ties the placenta to a camel. Seligman, who considered that in Ancient Egypt the placenta was regarded as the double, physical and spiritual, of the infant it had nourished, says of the Beja :—

> "The coastal Bisharin hold that it is important for the future welfare of the child that the after-birth should not be eaten by dogs and birds, it is therefore thrown into the sea or placed in a tree and watched for some days. Probably they ensure its safety by some such method as that employed by the Hadendoa, who enclose it in a basket and tie it in the branches of a tree if they cannot throw it into the stream." [2]

The 'Ababda of the Nile Valley bury it, but without taking note of the spot.

Ewald Falls says of the Awlad 'Ali :—

> "We also had a birth in the city of Menas. The mother went about her hard work the same day. If it had been a boy, shots of joy would have been fired. Oil plays a great part at birth, and the mother remains standing, for fear she would die if she lay down. According to the assertions of the people miscarriages are very few. The child is wrapped in rugs, and the name, which is often hereditary in the family, decided on immediately. Some who come to congratulate bring a few pence as a present, 'milk-money'

---

[1] A *fellah* custom. Harding King, *Mysteries of the Libyan Desert*, 249–50.
[2] *Hamites*, 658.

RITES AND CEREMONIES

for the child. For the first three days salt and bread are placed beside the infant as a protection against the devil and evil spirits."[1]

A poet might conjecture that this salt and bread is intended to provide the child with a *rafiq* in the unseen world.

With the 'Ababda, the newly-born child is given a drop of chewed date " to keep it a strong man ". After seven days there is some rejoicing and the child is named, but the chief festival is after forty days, when the husband, who up to that time has not been allowed to see either his wife or child for fear of bringing misfortune, sacrifices a sheep and sees his son (or daughter) for the first time.

The state of religion among the Bedouins is reflected in the names they give their sons. The Sinai Arabs, who, in so far as law and belief are concerned, live happily in a state of " Ignorance " (that is, Paganism), still cling to good old pre-Islamic names such as 'Amr, 'Awda, Salama, Selman, and their diminutives 'Aweimir, 'Aweid, Selim, Suleiman. Other of their names are hardly more than nicknames, Muteir, fem. Muteira (" shower "), Khidr fem. Khudra (" green "), because the babies concerned were born during or after rain. On the other hand, the more recently converted 'Ababda exhibit an enthusiasm for the great names of the Faith, such as Muhammad, 'Ali, Hasan, and Husein, and to a lesser degree for their saint Shadli. An occasional superfluity of children does sometimes lead them to exert their ingenuity further when names like Karrar, Bishir and Mursi are preferred.

Among the Bisharin, really pagan names appear such as Karai (" hyena "), Fajaro (" youth in the pride of his strength "), Onkeir (" rejecter ", because he bit his mother when a baby), Tuweitai (" horned viper "), Hadab (" lion "), etc.

These last recall the Arab custom mentioned by Doughty " that if a child be sickly, of infirm understanding, or his brethren have died before, they will put on him a wild beast's name, especially wolf, leopard, wolverine—that their human fragility may take on as it were a temper of the kind of those animals ".[2] It would therefore be rash in the extreme to prop up any theory of the former existence of totemism on such animal names as are common to-day.

[1] *Three Years in the Libyan Desert*, 319.   [2] Doughty, i, 329.

In the west, the Awlad 'Ali name their children much as Moslem Arabs do elsewhere with such names as 'Omar, 'Ali, Ibrahim, Mirtah, Yadim, etc. Their pious Murabitin are particularly fond of that class of names which commences with 'Abd ("servant") and continues with one of the ninety-nine names of God, such as 'Abd el-Qadir, 'Abd el-Malik, 'Abd el-Wanis.

Negroes from the Sudan still enjoy fanciful names like Murjan ("Coral"), Bakhit ("Fortunate"), Nessim ("Zephyr"), Kheiralla ("Bounty of God") reminiscent of the pet names of slavery.

It is reckoned '*aib* " shame " to give the name of a human being to a dog or camel, yet Sa'id, Zaid, and Merzuq are given indifferently to dog and man among the Awlad 'Ali.

Circumcision, a gift to all the Egyptian Bedouin from their earliest known ancestors, Hamitic or Semitic, was originally a rite practised on those who had reached the age of puberty, and it seems to have been performed in one simultaneous operation on all the youths of the tribe who had reached a certain age, as is still the case among the Dhuwi Hasan Ashraf near Mecca.[1] There each clan of the tribe annually circumcise a number of youths of about 18 years of age, and the ordeal is made a severe test of the lads' courage and endurance. Muhammad is said to have forbidden this form of the rite, which, ironically enough, lingers among his own people. The analogy with the Masai custom is clear, and the Masai form of circumcision seems to have been practised in the deserts of Ancient Egypt.[2] Altogether, we may take circumcision to be a very ancient rite indeed, practised by all the peoples of our area.

Nowadays the rite usually takes place when the child is six or eight years of age, and consists of simple circumcision. It still entitles him to one of the privileges of manhood, in that he can be killed in a blood-feud.

Among the Towara the rite may take place at any time of the Moslem year later than the '*ashura* ceremony, and three or four boys of from six to nine years old are usually operated on together. On the eve of the appointed day, a tent is decorated and carpeted for the morrow's ceremony. When the morning comes, all who can afford it bring a lamb or some

---

[1] G. W. Murray, *Circumcision Festivals in Arabia and East Africa*, Man, 1924, No. 39.
[2] Seligman, *Annals of Archæology and Anthropology*, Liverpool, vii, 43 ff.

RITES AND CEREMONIES

other contribution to the feast, and the proceedings commence with a public breakfast.

Each boy is then decked out in his mother's beads and ornaments, and holds a knife or sword in one hand. Palmer adds " a wooden cross decorated with coloured rags " in the other.[1] At noon, a sheep called the *'aqira* (" houghed ") is sacrificed for each lad, after the tendons of its right hind-leg have been cut by the boy with his sword. They are next ceremoniously washed by their male relations, and set on a camel, which, followed by a procession of men holding pans of burning incense, firing guns, and beating sticks together, circles round the tent three times.

The mothers, before leaving the tent, proceed to wash their feet in the large bowl previously made use of for their children, each holding a hand-mill balanced on her head all the time, after which they join the procession.

When the boys are brought on men's shoulders to the circumcision tent, they are set down on ordinary flat stones (lest they touch the ground ?) and the *muzayyin* appears and starts the operation. All the men gather at the door of the tent with the women behind them. Every mother, whose son is being circumcised, bears a hand-mill on her head, and holds a sword in her hand. During the operation, the boy cries to his parents, saying, *Aleik ya abuyi, aleik ya ummi, irmi er-rahai* ! " " It is on you, father ; on you mother ! Throw away the millstone ! " The father replies, " There is a camel for you."[2] Whereupon the mother trills the *zagharit*, and beats the tent several times with the back of the sword to drive away the evil spirits.

Na'um Bey says, " If the boy's paternal uncle be present," the boy cries, " By your eyes, uncle ! " Whereupon if the uncle has a daughter, he is given to understand that his nephew is asking for the hand of his cousin, and he replies, " So-and-so (giving the girl's name) welcomes you ; she is granted to you as a present ! " But if the uncle has no suitable girl to give to the boy, he only says, " Welcome to you, you will have the camel (naming it) or a sheep or a goat as present ! "[3]

According to Musil, among the Haweitat, the boys are brought into the tent and seated on millstones. The women

---
[1] Palmer, *Ordnance Survey of the Peninsula of Sinai*, 56.
[2] " Camel " here evidently means " girl " as in the *samir*, p. 66.   [3] Shuqeir, 393.

remain outside luluing and beating the tent. The blood flows out on the millstones, the women drag the boys thrice round the tent on the stones, and then carry the stones away on their heads.[1]

Professor Palmer adds that, among the Towara, the lad's severed foreskin used to be placed on one of his sister's toes where the girl carried it till it was worn out. (A similar custom used to hold good among the Bisharin, except that in their case it was the mother who wore it.)

But among the Ma'aza of Egypt, the foreskin is one of the circumciser's perquisites, and he ties it on to a female camel's neck "to make it prolific". (The same thing is done with the placenta.) The Ma'aza mother holds a sword "that the boy may be strong" and trills while he is being circumised. Her sister holds a palmstick, and no millstone plays a part in the ceremony. The day's festivities conclude with a grand *fantasia*, and a goat's head is generally set up for the young men to shoot at.

The Hijaz Arabs similarly shoot at a sheep's skull after a circumcision.[2]

Jennings Bramly says that, among the Arabs of North Sinai, the boys are looked after by their mothers for a week after the operation.

As to the Western Arabs, according to Falls, the boys of the Awlad 'Ali are not circumcised till they are fourteen or fifteen years of age, and girls are not excised.[3] Among their vassals, the Jumei'at, the boys are now circumcised at three or four years of age at the 'Id el-Kebir. There does not seem to be any ceremonial attached.

In the Eastern Desert, among the 'Ababda, a circumcision festival may be combined with that of a marriage. They call both festivals indifferently '*irs*, the ordinary Arabic name for a wedding. In this case, the hut, which is later to be inhabited by the newly-wed couple, is pitched for both the groom and the boys about to be circumcised.

Nowadays, owing to the fear of *mushahira*, Beja boys are usually circumcised within a few days of birth, and a festival held some years later, but until recently the following custom prevailed.

Ten or twelve boys, of seven or eight years of age, were

---
[1] Musil, *Arabia Petræa*, 222–23.
[2] Doughty, i, 340.
[3] *Three Years in the Libyan Desert*, 319.

RITES AND CEREMONIES

circumcised together on the first day of a festival lasting four or five days. They were dressed in new clothing, the finest procurable, and in the case of Bisharin boys wore silver bracelets and gold earrings, borrowed from the *harim*. This may be done to emphasize that the boy is still one of the *harim*, practically a girl, yet, and so deceive bad spirits. (Similarly Masai youths dress as girls at a circumcision.[1]) After the circumcision, the small tufts of hair on the boy's head are cut off.[2]

Tradition has it among the Bisharin that the boy, immediately after circumcision, " to show his manhood," was obliged to throw three throwing sticks at a man who defended himself with a shield.

After the operation, the boys lived together in a special matting-hut erected for them, together with the sheikh who had performed the operation. He seems merely to have attended to their material welfare, not to have imparted any particular instruction. At the end of this period a sheep was killed for each boy, and a great feast made. At the next new moon, the 'Ababda boys, who have not yet worn ornaments, borrow a piece of gold from their female relations, " to show to the moon " and so avoid *mushahira*. Both tribes infibulate their girls, but there is no festivity or ceremonial attached to this custom.

Among the Hadendawa, only those who have their parents and grandparents alive may circumcise boys. So among the Ancient Romans only *patrimi* and *matrimi*, boys and girls whose parents both lived, might be acolytes. There appears here a fear that death may be contagious.[3]

The Arab youths generally wear their hair long ; at puberty this hair is cut by their father or uncle (among the Kababish of the Sudan the father may not do this,[4]) and carefully buried or hidden, to prevent any evilly disposed person getting hold of it. This belief that a man's strength resides in his hair is almost universal among primitive peoples, and its antiquity in this region is confirmed by the story of Samson and Delilah.

Nowadays, when a Ma'aza boy is two or three years old,

---
[1] Hollis, *The Masai*, 298.
[2] Fig. 23 of *Desert and Water Gardens of the Red Sea*, by Cyril Crossland, shows on the left a boy who has just been circumcised with shaven head, and strings of amulets, while the middle boy's *zatur* indicate an uncircumcised youth.
[3] Cf. Crawley, *The Mystic Rose*, 94. [4] Seligman, *The Kababish*, 147.

his hair is cut for the first time by the tribal circumciser, the *muzayyin*, who receives a dollar or two for his trouble. The hair is thrown away, or put in a green tree (Muzeina). In Burckhardt's time, there seems to have been a later adolescent hair-cutting among the Ma'aza.

> " It is an established and remarkable custom, that those young men only are allowed to shave the hair of the head, who have brought home some booty from an enemy. It becomes then a festival in the family, whenever one of the sons for the first time has his head shaved ; while young men are sometimes met among them whose hair still covers their heads." [1]

Nowadays a young Arab wears pendent lovelocks to show that he is unmarried.

A circumstance that clearly distinguishes the 'Ababda from the turbaned Arabs is that the desert sections of that tribe still wear the shock head-dress of hair (*dirwa*) with a large wooden hair-pin, plentifully besmeared with mutton-fat, as do all the other Beja.

The young boy's hair (*'uqqet el-jahil* " the ignorant's first hair ") is generally shaved, leaving little square tufts, and the result of this first shaving deposited with some *weli*. 'Ali Kheir says that his hair was first cut when he was two years old, and it was put for safe-keeping in the tomb of the female saint 'Amira in Wadi Romit. But as to later cuttings, he throws his hair away. When asked if he were not afraid that some wizard might get his hair, he replied, " Our wizards can bewitch you from your footsteps. You can't hide footsteps, why trouble about hair ! " The Bisharin, however, always bury cut hair.

On arriving at puberty, the tufts are shaved, and the youth now grows a mop of hair called *honkwil*. When he becomes a man, he is allowed to let plaited love-locks descend from round the *honkwil*, and this constitutes the full *dirwa* (Bisharin *shekenab*).

The dressing of the hair may be done by the man's *harim* or by a male friend. The hair is frizzed out with combs, the shape of which varies slightly with the tribes, and mutton-fat in the form of white gruel poured over it. The smell from this is, after a day or two, rather overpowering to strangers ; but passes unnoticed by the Beja.

[1] Burckhardt, *Notes*, 133.

Young men renew this magnificence as often as a sheep is killed, old men get indifferent and leave their hair alone for months.

The *dirwa* seems to have excited great curiosity among the Arab raiders. It is told that Rueishid, a famous '*aqid* of the Ma'aza, was once accosted by one of his wives. " Bring me an 'Abadi's head when next you go raiding ! I want to see the *dirwa*." " I will do better than that," he replied, " I will bring you a live one ! Fifty of their spears will not pierce my coat of mail." Pierce it they did, however, for the giant Rueishid was slain by 'Ajib and 'Ibeid, two lion-like men of the Hareinab, and lies buried by the beautiful spring that bears his name beneath the highest mountain in Egypt.

Another *rite de passage* from adolescence to manhood was witnessed by Penfield, a former United States Consul-General in Egypt. He describes what he calls a " courage-dance ", seen at Aswan about 1896. Eight unmarried youths danced round a " sheikh from the Red Sea " armed with a hide whip. With this he lashed any youth whose attention he caught wandering. This continued till all the boys were well thrashed, when eight fresh victims took their places. Any youth flinching was held to be disgraced, and unable to marry at the next '*Id el-Kebir*. Penfield mentions one case of this.[1]

Sabah, a Sinai Arab of the 'Aleiqat tribe, declared that he had seen a similar custom among the Juheina near El-Wijh where the youths applauded a girl-dancer armed with a sword. She laid on with the flat or the edge as she felt inclined, and some of them got hurt. Musil also describes a similar dance at a circumcision festival among the Ruala.[2]

Among the Arabs, every youth has the right to marry his *bint 'amm*,[3] that is, the daughter of his father's brother. The right is absolute, and if her father wishes to dispose of the girl otherwise, he must first obtain (and pay for) his nephew's consent. The vast majority of first marriages (every Bedouin marries several times) are of this nature, and consequently a high proportion of the population are the

---

[1] Penfield, F. C., *Present Day Egypt* (New York, 1912), 351–57.
[2] *Rwala*, 244–45.
[3] In a list of proverbs in Burton's *Unexplored Syria* occurs the phrase, " He who marries my mother becomes my '*amm*." He goes on to explain that " '*amm* means the paternal uncle, the step-father, or the father-in-law ". I have not heard the word in the last meaning ; does the proverb recall an earlier levirate ?

offspring of first cousins. So also an 'Abadi or Bishari usually marries his *bint 'amm*, but the Hadendawa are not so patrilineal and when choosing a bride give no special preference to that lady.[1]

The intending bridegroom with a few companions calls upon the father of the girl he wishes to marry and some haggling takes place between them about the bride-price. In Sinai, the father begins by asking an absurd price, reminiscent of the exaggerated awards made by their judges, and the bystanders help to beat the price down saying " let him off ten guineas for the sake of so-and-so ", and sometimes in the case of the Jebeliya " let him off so much for the sake of the Convent ", until at last a very moderate sum is arrived at, perhaps one to five camels (or a cash equivalent) for a virgin, or half that for a widow or divorced woman.

A Ma'aza bride-price is often 400 piastres. The money should be handed over to the girl's brother to help him purchase a bride ; in the absence of relatives it becomes the perquisite of her guardian. From the bride-price the brother gives his sister a goat or two, and some more at the end of the first year of marriage. When the bargain is concluded there is a show of rejoicing, but the girl herself is supposed to be kept in ignorance of the affair.

The girl's father (we are still speaking of Sinai) now hands the bridegroom the *qassala*, a green twig of any bush, which is to be wrapped in his turban and worn for three days. (The *qassala* is only worn when a virgin is to be married.) This constitutes the legal part of the ceremony ; I have repeatedly heard Sinai women say to my wife. " We are married by *qassala*, and you are married by book." The maiden is supposed to be ignorant of all this, and when she returns in the evening from tending the goats she is met by her betrothed and a couple of men told off *by her father* to assist him.[2] They carry her off by force to her father's tent in spite of her struggles to escape them. Tradition prescribes that these should be very violent, for " the more she struggles, bites, kicks, cries and strikes, the more she is applauded ever after by her companions ".[3] The young men are sometimes

---

[1] J. W. Crowfoot (Personal Communication). It is remarkable too that in the Bedauye language, the same word *dura*, gen. *dira-ta* is used for both paternal and maternal uncles (and aunts).

[2] This is contrary to the " Marriage by capture " theory.

[3] *Notes*, 150.

RITES AND CEREMONIES

damaged, but claim no compensation, though in that case the bride will be soundly beaten by her ungallant swain.

This part of the ceremony is sometimes dispensed with, and she is directly surprised in the women's apartment of her father's tent by one of the bridegroom's relations,[1] who suddenly throws a man's mantle over her, exclaiming, " In the name of God, the Compassionate, the Merciful, none shall cover thee (*ghatik*) but 'Awda." (Or whatever the bridegroom's name may happen to be.) This seems to constitute the actual marriage. The women now gather round, screaming the above words, and uttering the shrill cry called *zagharit*.

Next her mother and female relations dress her in the new clothes provided by the bridegroom, while outside a special tent called *birza* is being erected for her. To this she is led in procession, mounted on as fairly decked a camel as the groom can provide, and circles round it three times, still sobbing bitterly. When she dismounts, the bridegroom sprinkles her with the blood of the sheep which he has sacrificed for the occasion. She is then left in the *birza* with one female attendant, while the other women sing the praises of the newly wedded pair outside. A banquet is now begun, for several sheep have been killed, and everyone feasts heartily on bread and meat.[2]

Later the same night, when the festal rejoicings have died down, the groom enters the *birza*, leaving his sandals outside to show he is within. He tears the ornament called *shibeika* from the screaming girl's face, and the marriage is consummated despite her protests. The bride remains in the *birza* three days [3] during which time only her female relations may visit her. If however she is totally averse to the marriage, she may take refuge on the day after the wedding in her father's tent, or more usually in her uncle's.

On the morning after the wedding, every father in the camp brings a goat as a present to the bride. Two or three of these are killed, and another feast concludes the entertainment.

---

[1] This man is called *khatib* " betrother ", which Palmer mistranslates " the public notary " of the tribe, an impossibility in a peninsula where to-day hardly three Bedouins know how to read and write.

[2] Burckhardt says of the bread, " this is a circumstance absolutely necessary on such nuptial occasions."

[3] In North Sinai, a week.

At the termination of the three days in the *birza*, the bride is conducted by a procession of women to a neighbouring spring, and, after performing her ablutions, is led to her husband's tent, where further sacrifices and rejoicings take place. The neighbours and the women who have taken part in the fête then usually receive some trifling presents from the bride's father.

Van Gennep contesting the idea of " marriage by capture " analyses Burckhardt's account of these Sinai marriage ceremonies as follows :—

> "(1) The young man and two other people seize the young girl in the mountains and drag her to the tent of her own father; (2) The more she defends herself, the more she is applauded by her companions; (3) The young people place her by force in the women's apartment; (4) A relation of her intended covers her with a cloth, and cries, ' None shall cover thee but so-and-so,' meaning the intended; (5) The girl's mother and her relations dress her ceremonially; (6) They put her on a camel, but she continues to struggle while her fiancé's friends hold her; (7) Then they go three times round the tent while her companions mourn her; (8) Then they take her to the apartment for women in the fiancé's tent; (9) If this tent is far away, she weeps during the whole journey. It is plain that we have to do here with a separation of the girl from a group formed by the girls in her place of origin, and if it were a survival of ' rape ', all the family and all the tribe of the girl would resist the capturing by the tribe, family and companions of the young man. Instead of that there are only two age-classes represented in the struggle." [1]

Van Gennep is probably right about this, for in the Beja marriages about to be described, the bridegroom has actually to fight with the *harim* and to carry his bride off from them.

Another interesting point is that the *birza* and the Beja wedding-hut must both be pitched at night, just as at the archaic festival of the heliacal rising of Venus the sacrifice had to be eaten before the sun rose. Was the sun avoided as the malignant enemy of the heavenly host they worshipped, or did some star goddess preside formerly over the marriage ceremony?

Among the Muzeina of Sinai and the Ma'aza of Egypt, it is the custom for the bride to escape when she is placed in the *birza* and seek refuge in the neighbouring mountains. The bridegroom goes in search of her next morning and is

---

[1] Van Gennep, *Les Rites de Passage*, Paris, 1909, p. 1.

PLATE XIX

Honkwil

Dirwa

COIFFURE OF THE BEJA

[face p. 182

obliged to track her by her footsteps, for nobody will give him any information about her. If she likes him, she will soon allow herself to be captured. But she may remain away " for a year " if she likes and can. When he catches her, the marriage is consummated in the open air, and he then leads her home to her tent. According to Burckhardt, she sometimes repeats these flights several times, and among the Shararat of Arabia, she runs away for seven nights in succession. If for any reason she does not run away, she is looked down upon by the other women as a " shirker ".

The Beni Sakhr of Transjordania have the same custom. In Egypt, it is dying out among the Ma'aza, but the Sinai Muzeina still observe it faithfully. The 'Aleiqat and the Sawalha do not, saying, " If our girls run away, we should never catch them." Terabin brides also do not run away.

A real " marriage by capture " exists among the Sinai tribes of Tiyaha, Terabin, Haweitat, Laheiwat, and also among the Ma'aza and 'Ababda of Egypt. There, when a man wishes to marry a girl, and her first cousin has refused his consent, the lover sometimes goes with a friend and steals her. They then deposit her, just as they would a stolen camel, in the tent of some neutral party, who is bound to hold her till the dispute is settled. The lover then repairs with a band of fifteen men or so to her father's camp, and bargains with him and her cousin for her hand. He had better be a rich man for the price asked is bound to be very high, perhaps a double *mahr*, or a *mahr* plus five camels. This is called *nahiba* (from *nahab* to plunder).

A Sinai Arab rarely marries outside his own tribe, and then he usually lives for some time with his new wife's people ; as did Jebely 'Aid, a Muzeini, when he married a Terbaniya. Marriages of this kind are not popular with the Arab women, and, if a Moab youth dares to bring a foreign wife home, she is attacked by all the women of the camp.

> " When the procession approaches the encampment, a really curious scene occurs. The women of the camp assemble, screaming, picking up stones, throwing them at the fiancée. They make her camel kneel, pull her off and set to beating her. Blood flows, but the men soon put an end to this feminine combat. This scene, is renewed, they say, every time the procession has to pass a camp before reaching that belonging to the bridegroom." [1]

[1] Jaussen, 53.

Most Bedouin are monogamous, partly on account of their poverty, and partly because there is very little object in having more than one wife when divorce is so easy. But rich sheikhs, to whom expense is no object, and who glory in the number of their progeny, sometimes maintain the full establishment of four legal wives permitted by the *shara'*.

Where property descended in the female line, there must have been a strong inducement for the son to marry his sisters in order to inherit. This was common in Ancient Egypt, and a man could then marry his full sister, though no doubt half-sisters were more usually married. Even down to the days of Muhammad half-sisters could be married in Arabia, a relic this no doubt of an earlier system of matrilineal descent. But the Prophet forbade all marriages between relatives nearer than cousins on either side. Isolated instances of men disobeying this rule and marrying their half-sisters occur even in modern times. Seetzen gives an instance from Arabia, and Munzinger says " the Beni Amer conform to Moslem law, but children of the same parent often marry each other ".[1] Henniker observed a case in Nubia in 1823.[2]

All these marriages with sisters violate the " law " of exogamy, which does not seem ever to have existed among the Hamito-Semitic race. In fact the tendency seems to be all the other way, for the Sinai Bedouin told Jennings Bramly that they married their first cousins to prevent the animals that constituted the bride-price from going out of the family.

To marry two wives who are sisters is utterly forbidden, yet if a wife dies, the widower can marry her sister at a reduced price.

However, among the 'Ababda the deceased wife's sister is seldom married and then the full *mahr* must be paid.

My wife thus describes a wedding of 'Ilwani Suleiman, a sheikh of the Jumei'at :—

" The bridegroom was a wealthy man and immensely popular, so visions of a gigantic feast hovered before the delighted eyes of our Arabs. When the great day arrived, a hilarious party, shining with soap and conscious virtue wended its way to the sheikh's tents. Bristling with armament, the Fords arrived in such a blaze and thunder of glory that we could hardly hear the words of welcome from our host. From

---

[1] Munzinger, 319.   [2] *A Visit to Egypt, Nubia, etc.*, London, 1823, 165.

SHEIKH 'ILWANI'S *HARIM*

[*face p.* 184

RITES AND CEREMONIES

all quarters the guests were streaming in, on foot, on camel or on donkey; the cars too had picked up as many pedestrians as could be squeezed into their groaning bodies. The two elder sons of the sheikh received us in the absence of their father, who had departed to some neighbouring tents till the ceremony was well under way. The bridegroom already possessed twenty-five sons of all ages, from about forty years to those of a few months, the latter evidently being brought up side by side with his grandchildren. His daughters were uncertain in number and obviously of little consequence. All the little boys were clad alike in pink striped calico, and an enormous brood of pink brats, puppies, and fowls tumbled about the tents, while goats and donkeys strayed among the ropes, so that there were incessant sorties with sticks and loud yells to chase the lot away.

"The camp consisted of a dozen tents with low square roofs; and the main guest tent was a splendid sight. Its roof and walls were covered with brilliantly striped blankets, and the floor with thick carpets of goats' and camels' hair, dyed in strips of different colours, and sewn together with wool embroidery and many hanging tassels of gay hues. The tents and carpets were entirely the work of the women, who shear the flocks, and weave the wool into attractive carpets and camel saddle bags, using such simple dyes as they possess. The tent cloths are made of undyed goats' hair, usually blackish-grey in appearance, and so designed that one side can quickly be adjusted to suit the weather. Since the day was hot, the back-cloth had been folded up to allow the breeze to play through the midst of the large guest tent which held 60 people comfortably. Camel saddles, covered with sheep-skins, made back-rests for the honoured guests, while bustle in the other tents and a coming and going of large platters showed that the women were preparing the wedding lunch.

"As soon as the bridegroom was reported to be in sight, we hastened out to greet him with a salute of all our weapons. Riding an Arab stallion and accompanied by friends on camels, the sheikh made an imposing central figure for the day's ceremony. He was clad in a bright blue mantle with gold embroidery, and carried an ancient pistol with heavy silver mountings, with a sword of modern origin. Both robe and sword, of which he was very proud, were presents from the

King. Sixty-two years old ; in height, width and thickness 'Ilwani dwarfed every other man present. We drank coffee and banana syrup while we chatted, to the accompaniment of spasmodic bursts of firing off stage through which sounded the piercing *zagharit* of the women and the children's excited clamour. Games and songs began, the young men accompanying each other with rhythmical clapping of hands. They also vied with each other in horsemanship, giving displays of galloping and curvetting, doubtless well aware of the admiring audience hidden from us in the other tents. The *harim* too had guests, for the damsels of the neighbouring tents had come to dance. Next the entry of great heaped-up basins of mutton proclaimed that the serious business of the day was about to begin. The mutton, already cut into convenient chunks, was flanked by bowls of succulent stews, liver, rice, and even spaghetti. A basin was placed between each pair of guests, along with two or three flat loaves of Arab bread. The two elder sons waited on us, since they could not sit down to eat with the guests in the presence of their father.

" Then ensued an interval of rest and lazy talk, while the remainder of the guests and relations had their share of the feast in an adjoining tent. When they were satisfied, the remnants were gathered up for the *harim*, but until then the women had to wait.

" It seemed strange to my eyes that even the youngest male child had prior claim and place. This upbringing leads to a free and easy manner of the rising male generation which I noticed with amazement, for no European mother or elder sister, would submit to being bossed by small boys of twelve years of age. Later on, when I was with the women in their own quarters, I was much amused at the important airs of several young scamps. As the afternoon wore on, the young men shook off their heaviness and lethargy, and, with the advent of two amateur dancing girls, things began to hum. Both girls were so veiled and muffled in clothing, that they were little more than shapeless bundles while their arms were covered from wrist to elbows in heavy silver bangles which jingled as they moved.

" To-day's bride had been one of them at the last *'Id*, a fact which no doubt inspired them to future hopes and greater efforts. A *jird*, the plaid of the Libyan Bedouin, in which he rolls himself up in winter for protection against the bitter winds, was each dancer's costume and it was fastened in clumsy folds at the waist with bright red and yellow shawls. Their forms were hardly sylph-like in this distorted get-up. The young men stood in half-circles to sing and clap for them. Most popular was a guessing game, in which the lady made great play over her choice, tapping one of the candidates lightly with her wand. The selected one fell on his knees to beg for mercy ; if she relented, the dance went on, if not, he had to pay a forfeit.

"In the distance a tremendous uproar began, and the dancers and their swains melted away. The second son whispered to me that the bride was being brought out ; would I like to go with the women to welcome her ?

"We hurried out to join the little procession, which was making a grand tour of the tents, after which the bride was to circle her own future abode seven times.[1] The bride, who up till now had been hidden away in the eldest son's tent, rode behind him on a white camel ; nothing could be seen of her features for thick veils.

"The younger boys of the household, also mounted, tore about firing off guns in all directions, but usually at the lady's head. The din was indescribable. Before and behind the bride's camel streamed the women and children, screeching like mad. This was the harim's hour and they filled the air with their piercing *zagharit*, mingled with the sustained singing of a high note during which the mouth was repeatedly tapped with the fingers of one hand. The combined effect of a score of women hard at work was simply overwhelming, and I felt sorry for the sheikh who has to endure this every

---

[1] Falls describes the fetching of the bride to another Mariut wedding as follows :—

"After the meat is cut up . . . the caravan is prepared which is to fetch the bride. The tents of her tribe were in the desert, a journey of a couple of hours. All available horses and camels were decorated. An especially fine camel bore on its back the *karmût* made out of tent-poles, over which hung rugs, like a pretty miniature tent. There the bride would take her place. Women relatives, on this occasion entirely veiled, sat on the other camels, which were draped with gay-coloured rugs. At short intervals they uttered the chant of joy, louder when the men fired their guns, only ceasing when the bride entered the tent of her future husband. Accompanied by Bedouins on horse-back and on foot, the procession marched to the desert to the tent of the bride's father. Without any ceremony the bride in her attire was taken to the *karmût*, and an elderly relative sat beside her on the camel. The procession then went through the neighbouring desert from tent to tent to receive wedding gifts. At last, after an absence of six hours, the caravan again approached the city of Menas. The youths and boys who had stayed behind clapped hands and danced in front of the bridegroom's tent, and amid *sarlûl* and shouts of joy the bride went seven times round the tent. Then the camel knelt down, the girl entered the tent with her relatives." From J. C. Ewald Falls, *Three Years in the Libyan Desert*, 315–18.

time his *harim* gets emotional ! The boys rode closer and closer, and the circles went on, the salutes becoming wilder and more extravagant each time. A Bedouin girl would think shame to flinch when a young man singes her hair, as he is singling her out for honour ; but the imps roared with laughter when they turned their weapons on me. The journey ended, the bride was taken into her tent by her stepson, who would have been a more suitable husband in age for her than his father, and there after ceremonially menacing her with a whip, left her to the women. They gave her a warm, friendly welcome as the household was a prosperous and happy one. She sat, still closely veiled, in a corner behind a curtained partition crying aloud and sobbing. Their kind advances met with little response, but custom among them demands this doleful behaviour from brides and to appear otherwise would be condemned as immodesty.

"Babies were everywhere ; if not in their mothers' arms, they were crawling on the ground or asleep on a pile of garments. One young pleasant-faced woman stood apart, looking sad and lonely. She had been married some years, and as yet had no children ; the poor soul obviously felt uncertain of her tenure in the household and, as far as an outsider could see, her status was very low. She joined in none of the chatter, as if in disgrace, and when I pressed some sweets on her, she declined hurriedly, saying ' Later, later '. To be childless here must be sheer tragedy.

"The principal wife, a strikingly fine-featured woman with beautiful dark eyes, was the mother of many good-looking sons. She wore a most becoming head-dress, embroidered in gay colours.

"After we had all drunk coffee together, the bride appeared quieter and her sobs had dwindled to mournful sighs. She actually smiled at my attempts at the *zagharit*, while the rest of the *harim* was convulsed, and I had to give it up. It should be done by rapid vibration of the tongue, keeping the mouth well open like an ' O '. The new arrival was about eighteen years old, and to me it seemed all wrong that the bridegroom was more than two score years her senior. Yet his *harim* was without any doubt a contented one, and a few months later when I saw her again, she had settled down happily in their midst. By then she was the possessor of a large, ornamental gold nose ring which she exhibited

RITES AND CEREMONIES

to me with proper pride, the token of a bride of the Jumei'at."

Beja marriages used to be arranged when both children were still in their infancy. After a preliminary discussion between the mothers, the boy's father made an official demand for the girl, accompanied by presents. Thereafter, if he could afford it, he sacrificed a sheep annually on the girl's birthday, till the prospective pair arrived at marriageable age.

But nowadays Bisharin girls get married later in life than they used to be, for their parents spend a lot of time looking for good matches for them. So an old friend in the tribe informs me.

The parents of both fix the date of the wedding and warn the mother of the bride some months beforehand so that she can make her preparations.

The bride-price is divided by the Bisharin equally between the father, the mother, and the father's brother (*khal*) of the girl. Bisharin grooms must give a camel and a sheep (or a guinea) to each of these, and perhaps two camels for his bride's other male relatives to eat. Among the 'Ababda the *khal* gets very little.

A Bisharin rarely marries the widow of his deceased brother. It sometimes happens, but there is a prejudice against it.

A special hut is prepared for the couple about to be married, for which the matting is supplied by the groom, but the tentpole must come from the bride's parents.[1]

When the hut with its furniture and the food for the bridal pair have been packed on a camel, an old woman of the bride's family mounts it, carrying on her head the new dresses and in her hand an object called *sinkwab* made of the young leaves of the dom palm.[2] The camel is first led seven times round the bride's mother's hut, followed by the women singing and trilling. It is then made to kneel a short way off, and the tent is pitched about fifty or sixty yards from the hut where the bride-to-be is living with her mother. The hut must be pitched after the sun has set ('Ababda), or about sunset (Bisharin). The *sinkwab* is fastened to the pole at the front of the entrance, where it remains till the first child is born.

---
[1] So too with the Hadendawa, but among the Amar Ar the groom supplies the tent-poles.
[2] The *sinkwab* occurs among the Bisharin, Amar Ar and Hadendawa, but not the 'Ababda. The wedding guests used to attend the bridegroom on the morning of the festival, and present him with the crown of a date-palm.

The groom stays outside ('Ababda) or inside (Bisharin) till the *harim* bring the bride, and circle the hut seven times widdershins with her. Then they go inside. The bride's arms have been tied to her side with a strong goat's-hair cord, which the groom now essays to break, and a sort of scuffle with definite rules takes place in the dark within the hut. If the groom cannot break the cord, the bride is taken back to her mother, and he has to try again on the ensuing night. If the cord is broken, but the *harim* get away with it, he has to ransom it from them with a sheep. When the cord is broken, the women take the bride back to her mother. The cord, to which they gave no special name, is later hung on the curved rafter which supports the roof.

Next day, should the festival include a circumcision, the boys are circumcised, and they and the bridegroom dwell in the hut for five or seven days. When the festivities are over, and the boys have departed, the hut is moved, it may be only a few feet.[1] After the move, the groom lives in the hut for forty days (in the case of the 'Aliab Bisharin, a year) and the bride visits him under cover of darkness. During these forty days the bridegroom may not milk, slay an animal, prepare food, or leave the camp. His food is cooked for him by the bride's mother, whom of course, he must avoid. Nor must he ever eat from the same dish as the bride's father. For the first five days or so he covers his mop of hair with his cloth wrap (*shuqqa*). Then a sheep is killed for him, and he anoints his hair with the grease. The *serir*, or bed, made by the bride's people, is not presented to the young couple for some months, or it may be a year.

One may observe that the disability to milk or slay is a feminine attribute, as is the covering-up of the hair. It would seem as though the manhood of the youth at circumcision and the man at marriage had to be concealed from the evil spirits by disguising himself as a girl. The sun, too, seems to be avoided. The hut must be pitched after sunset, it is circled widdershins ; the bride must only see the groom at night. There is a general resemblance in the ceremonies to those prevalent throughout the Northern Sudan, but the 'Ababda are alone in sometimes combining wedding and circumcision ceremonies. Both are *rites de passage*, celebrating

---

[1] This corresponds to the building of the Kababish *hegil* in place of the temporary tent. C. G. and B. Z. Seligman, *The Kababish*, 134.

RITES AND CEREMONIES

the commencement of a new existence. And what does the breaking of the cord by men symbolize? Certainly the deliverance from some inhibition which has prevented the enjoyment of the new life. Such customs are beginning to be looked down upon by the more orthodox Moslems among them as '*ada-t Fanor*, i.e. " customs of Pharaoh ".

When a death occurs in an encampment, the women of the family at once go outside the tents, and, taking off their headdresses, commence a loud and impassioned wailing, which they continue throughout the day. Falls describes the scene among the Awlad 'Ali :—

> "We often heard in the neighbourhood the terrible Bedouin death-wail when one of their loved ones died. They begin it before death has actually occurred. It reaches its climax after death and during burial, and is sounded for a week every night in memory of the dead person. After death the relatives wash the body and stop up all the openings with camel's or sheep's wool, rags, or even grass. The corpse is then wrapped in cloths, and the wealthier Bedouins sometimes possess a green shroud, in which it is rolled up like a mummy. The funeral follows the day of death, and if possible the corpse is buried where its ancestors lie, and that is often on a hill on the caravan route. The corpse, borne on an improvised bier, is accompanied by all the tent companions and friends to the monotonous sound of ' La ilâha ill' Allah, we Mohammed er rasul 'Allah '. Friends are the bearers, then come the men, and lastly the women, who swing their black transparent head-cloths towards the bier and utter their wailing chant. The grave is not deep, and the face of the dead must look towards the east. The grave is covered with earth and the low mound with the heaviest stones possible, on account of the hyenas and jackals. After the burial, all who had come in contact with the dead man perform ablutions, for they had become unclean. Then the funeral feast takes place, which consists of the usual rice, *mashrûta*, and mutton. At twilight the women form a semicircle in front of the dead person's tent— if a man with two wives, in front of the two tents—set up wailing, and between whiles praise the virtues of the dead. On the seventh evening the ceremonies are concluded by another funeral banquet."[1]

There seems to have been in former times a custom by which the female relatives of the dead man performed a sort of war dance. Burckhardt says : " I have seen amongst ancient Arab tribes in Upper Egypt the female relations of a deceased man dance before his house with sticks and lances

[1] *Three Years in the Libyan Desert*, 320–1.

in their hands and behaving like furious soldiers."[1] Lane speaking of the peasants in Upper Egypt says these dances went on during the first three days after the funeral.[2]

This dance was not confined to the Nile Valley, Munzinger met with it among the Beni 'Amir.

> "When Ukut, Hamed's son died, a brother of Muhammad's, whom we have mentioned above, so many camels, cows and sheep were slaughtered that they could not be eaten, and the air was poisoned. They counted several hundred cows. The women at this festival made a sort of dance of death, in which the widow with her head shaved, and all the relations, took part. One of the sisters of the dead man frizzed out her hair like a man's, and paraded with sword and shield; later the praises of the dead were sung. These 'wakes' often last several weeks."[3]

Although the Awlad 'Ali bury their dead on the tops of the low ridges of the Western Desert, the graves of the Sinai Peninsula and the Eastern Desert are usually located near wells, perhaps for the convenience of washing the corpse, or, as the Arabs told Bramly, to save the dead the trouble of fetching water. The tombs of saints are generally found in such a place, with the humbler dead grouped round them.

Palmer describes the Sinai burial custom as follows:—

> "When a Bedawi dies, the corpse is immediately taken out of the tent to a convenient place, washed with soap and water, and shrouded.[4] A bag containing a little corn (called a *shehadeh*) is placed beside it, and it is immediately buried. As soon as it is placed in the grave, the friends of the deceased beat upon the ground with a stick, recite the *Fatihah*, and cry out 'Oh, thou most compassionate One have mercy upon us, oh, Gracious God'. They then tap with a small pickaxe at the head of the grave, and address the deceased in these words: 'When the twain green angels shall question and examine thee, say, "The feaster makes merry, the wolf prowls, and man's lot is still the same. But I have done with all these things." The *sidr* tree is thy aunt and the palm tree is thy mother.' Each one then throws a little earth into the grave, exclaiming as he does so, 'God have mercy upon thee,' and the party adjourns to a feast in the tents of the deceased. Another entertainment is given in honour of his memory after the lapse of four months."[5]

---

[1] *Notes*, 159.   [2] *Modern Egyptians*, 533.   [3] *Ostafrikanische Studien*, 327.
[4] Winding sheets are much esteemed by the Bedouin and sometimes given as presents. See Lady Anne Blunt, *A Pilgrimage to Nejd*, i, 164.
[5] *Desert of the Exodus*, i, 94.

RITES AND CEREMONIES

The 'Ababda and Bisharin wash the corpse on an oblong rubble platform with a praying place just beside it. This ceremony is called *mitla er-ruh*, or " passage of the soul ". They dig graves six feet deep, and then excavate a niche at one side of the corpse, so that the earth and stones with which they fill the shaft do not come into contact with the body. This is a practice of Upper Egypt, and goes back to Middle Empire times. An earlier custom still followed in Sinai, is to make a rectangular excavation, place the body in it, and roof the whole over with flat stones. This practice may possibly have originated through some idea of protecting the ground from the contagion of the corpse. Just so the Masai abandon their dead to hyenas, because, as they say, the body would poison the soil. But I prefer to think (see p. 169) that the real fear was lest the soul become resident in the earth. A more materialistic friend conjectures however that the original idea was merely to make the dead man comfortable in the new home and prevent all his pots and weapons from breakage.

I have only once observed an article left on the grave for the use of the dead man. Then it was a freshly filled stone pipe on the grave of an 'Abadi who had been a great smoker, in Wadi Salib el-Azraq. Affection, not fear of the dead, was here the obvious motive.

In Bedouin warfare, the enemy dead are always left unburied, and there seems to be some reason for this beyond mere laziness. Jaussen indeed gives a case where the Ruala buried two of the Sukhur whom they had killed, but his instance rather goes to strengthen the idea that the enemy killed are looked on as some sort of sacrifice. For " they took the corpses near a road and buried them, one to the right, the other to the left ".[1] Doughty also says " the fallen of the loser's side remain without burial ".[2]

Certainly after the Meisa skirmish, the Dervish dead lay for many a long year on the battle-field, and those killed at Tor in 1915 were similarly abandoned.

There were in ancient Arabia, annual sacrifices called *'atair* in which the victims were left lying by the altar to be devoured by wild beasts, and Wellhausen quotes various poetical comparisons in which the slain are said to be left lying on the battle-field like *'atair*.[3]

[1] Jaussen, 103.   [2] Doughty, ii, 41.
[3] *Reste Arabischen Heidentums*, Berlin, 1897, 115.

Jaussen says the Arabs despoil the corpses of the slain, but do not mutilate or insult them. The Haweitat, however, mutilated the corpses of some yeomanry whom they killed in a skirmish in Wadi Sudr in 1916.

Na'um Bey gives an instance of mutilation :—

" About 1855, a quarrel took place between Sarrar Abu Sherif of the Suwarka and some of his relatives who despised and persecuted him. He fled to their foes the Terabin, and so the Suwarka and Rumeilat gathered and attacked the Terabin in the land of Qarara by day, and drove the Terabin to Khan Yunis, killing many of them. They captured their relative Sarrar and killed him ; opening his belly and stuffing it with sand with the pretence that he committed treachery to them." [1]

On the completion of an arduous line of levelling from the Mediterranean to the Qattara depression, one of my 'Ababda, Mursi 'Abdu of Idfu, squatted down on the verge of the 700-foot cliff overlooking the swamp and the Sahara, and fashioned a neat little grave with Moslem headstones at its head and foot to dramatize the fact that his disagreeable task was now dead and done with.

A less meticulous boy than Mursi might have built a cairn. For, if Professor Westermarck is right, many of the cairns that a Bedouin, particularly a Western Bedouin, erects to mark the spot where he has made a vow or cursed his enemy, are symbolical tombs. He says to the unseen power he is invoking : " Do so and so, well and good, I will reward you with a sheep. Otherwise * * * ! " Here the asterisks represent the stones of a grave, or perhaps of a lapidation, under which he hopes the recalcitrant *weli* will perish.

The cairn that Jacob and Laban erected as the " heap of witness " of their covenant [2] may very well have been a monument of this kind, but by no means do all the cairns of the Bedouin imply such a sinister threat. On pilgrim routes myriads of small heaps are generally seen wherever any definite landmark, like the sea or the cliffs of the Nile Valley, come into view. These commemorate the prayers and thanksgiving which have been offered on the spot.

A remarkable conical cairn stands in the Wadi Iqna in Sinai where the Sawalha Arabs celebrate the annual festival of the Prophet's birthday. Seven feet high, this cairn is

---

[1] Shuqeir, 582.   [2] Genesis xxxi, 44–8.

RITES AND CEREMONIES

encircled halfway up by a row of niches in which incense is burned and candles lighted.

To recall any event worthy of remembrance, such as a conflict, a murder, a good shot at a wild animal, or even a long jump, the Sinai Arabs erect a small cairn of stones. To "whiten the face" of someone who has been insulted, the judge will order the guilty defendant not only to pay him compensation, but also to build a white cairn in his honour. White cairns are also sometimes put up spontaneously by a man who wishes to honour a benefactor. But our survey cairns on mountain-tops are looked on with suspicion, since there is a feeling that they keep away the rain.

Other cairns commemorate breaches of etiquette, as when a man at night defecates accidentally in the middle of a desert highway. Naturally the Arabs are reluctant to supply any name or explanation for one of these. They say, as they do of any name with an obscene meaning, "*Tayibt ism*, may its name be improved."[1] So mountains and valleys are continually being recorded on the maps of Arabia, Egypt, and Cyrenaica with this name, Tayibt Ism, and doubtless it is as well that they should so appear.

Other large cairns are found on caravan routes, all signification of which has been lost. The 'Ababda call such *tiheiw*. On removing the one seen in Plate XXI, nothing was found below it.

Heavy stones, awkward to handle, are sometimes found by the roadside, by which a youth is tested. If he can lift it, he is a man : if he can't, he isn't. There is one such called *El-Maraza*, south of 'Ayun Musa ; and another about a day's journey north of Qena on the road to the porphyry quarries.

There are two cairns, still cursed by the passers-by on the Suez–Tor road, which marked in Palmer's day the leap of Abu Zena's horse. The present-day story is that they conceal the corpses of Abu Zena's donkey and her foal, which had become ghouls and ate people and so were ambushed and destroyed by the Arabs on this spot. Some fire guns at the principal cairn, some spit upon it or defile it otherwise ;

[1] The large town of Dilingat in the Beheira province is known to all its inhabitants and neighbours by this euphemism.
Compare here, from an article in *The Times*, 1st August, 1934, on the customs of the Danakil by Wilfred Thesiger : Sometimes one passes a large heap of stones by the roadside, and the Dankalis with you will let you cast a stone, crying out "Hess Hess", which means "Preserve us from this". It is where an unmarried girl has had a child or, in one famous case, where a brother and sister having committed incest the child was born.

all should throw stones and repeat a rhyme which begins, " Shame upon you, you castrated one ! " and continues with two lines of obscene abuse.[1]

I have spoken in the previous chapter of the spirits latent in the earth, rocks, trees, and animals, but magical force called *baraka*, " a blessing from God," is sometimes also conveyed through such media as blood, salt, and saliva. Rain, too, is a notable instance of *baraka*. To re-invigorate this force, various rites have to be performed.

Thus the Kurbeilab Bisharin sacrifice a she-camel regularly at each of the wells of Abu Hodeid, Shinai, Qidmib, and Madi and allow the victim's blood to flow over the sides of the well " to ensure a good supply of water ". Madigan noticed " goats and sheep had recently been killed at the mouths of the wells (of Ti Kureitra) so that the blood ran down the sides and into the wells ".[2] I am told the blood should not run *into* the water, so perhaps Madigan was mistaken, or as Ti Kureitra is very salt, an exception to the rule may have been made for its benefit.

Pacts of " blood-brotherhood " do not seem to occur nowadays, but of their former existence, there can be no doubt whatever. The classic example is that of Cambyses, who took most elaborate precautions to obtain safe conduct from a sheikh of North Sinai.

> " He sent messengers to the Arabian, and asked and obtained safe conduct, giving and receiving from him pledges. There are no men who respect pledges more than the Arabians. This is the manner of their giving them : a man stands between the two parties who would give security, and cuts with a sharp stone the palms of the hands of the parties, by the second finger ; then he takes a piece of wool from the cloak of each and smears with the blood seven stones that lie between them, calling the while on Dionysus and Heavenly Aphrodite ; and when he has fully done this, he that gives the security commends to his friends the stranger (or his countryman, if the party be such), and his friends hold themselves bound to honour the pledge." [3]

The above is interesting in several ways ; the seven stones were no doubt sacred stones, the *masseboth* which were set up at various sanctuaries in Palestine. In some of these holes have been found cut, perhaps to receive offerings of oil or blood.

---
[1] Palmer's version of the story will be found in his *Desert of the Exodus*, 42.
[2] *Sudan Notes and Records*, v, 2, 81. [3] Herodotus, iii, 8.

RITES AND CEREMONIES

The taking of a piece of wool from the cloak of each recalls the formalities gone through when a Bedouin appoints a *wasy* or guardian for his children.

Food, not blood, is used to seal the covenant between fellow-travellers nowadays, and between the host and his guests. Such pacts cannot be broken for three and a third days, the period that the food is supposed to stay inside them. The same period was allowed to elapse between a quarrel and the commencement of hostilities between the two divisions of the town of Siwa, where no risk was taken of disturbing the magical influence of any food they might have eaten in common.[1]

Bread and salt were used in the food-covenant entered into by Sir F. Henniker and his *rafiq*, and a sword was used in the establishment of their relationship.[2] Bramly saw a sword used to convey healing power from the image of a scorpion engraved on it to the arm of one suffering from snake-bite, while, also speaking of the Sinai Arabs, Na'um Bey says, " Heroism is much esteemed, and young children are given to lick the saliva of a hero from the edge of a sword, or direct from mouth to mouth." [3]

Hamilton, on a visit in 1801 to the fugitive Mameluke Bey's camp near Aswan, was told by some Bisharin that they liked drinking blood drawn from the living veins of camels and sheep. This custom is very widespread both in space and time, for Agatharchides tells of the Troglodytes, that they fed upon blood and milk mingled together and boiled for a little time, while nowadays such tribes as the Masai and the Turkana regularly drink the blood of their living animals, and the Abyssinians even cut pieces of flesh from them.

The custom existed on both sides of the Gulf of Suez ; for somewhere about A.D. 420 the pagan Arabs met by St. Nilus sacrificed a camel thus at the rising of the morning star. It was made to kneel, and they circled it three times chanting. Their leader then pierced the animal's neck, whereupon everyone drank hastily of the blood that gushed out. Next all the band fell upon the victim, and each one hacked off and devoured a piece of the beast's flesh and skin. The whole carcase of the victim, bones, blood, and entrails had to vanish before the sun appeared above the horizon.

[1] MS. *History of Siwa*.   [2] See p. 38.   [3] Shuqeir, 369.

That some of the ancient Hebrews also drank the blood of animals and ate the living flesh seems probable, because of the frequent reiteration in the Bible of the prohibition against it.[1]

To the disciples of Yahweh, all such practices were as abhorrent as the standing stones on which the blood of the ancient sacrifices were smeared. Blood as the "life" and "soul"[2] of the victim in their eyes belonged to the deity, it was therefore a prohibited food, and had to be poured on the ground in his honour.[3] And so it is throughout all the countries where Semitic influences have penetrated.

Possibly the abandonment of the former blood-covenant, and its replacement by a food-covenant, was influenced by this new idea that blood belongs to God.

Yet even at the present day, the blood is not all poured on the ground. The Arabs in Sinai, after killing a sheep for a guest, smear the neck of his riding-camel with some of the fresh blood. The bride too is sprinkled with the blood of a sheep at the marriage ceremony.

Burckhardt was told in 1813 of the Beja tribe Halenga :—

"A horrible custom is said to attend the revenge of blood; when the slayer has been seized by the relatives of the deceased, a family feast is proclaimed, at which the murderer is brought into the midst of them, bound upon an angareyg, and while his throat is slowly cut with a razor, the blood is caught in a bowl, and handed round among the guests, everyone of whom is bound to drink of it, at the moment the victim breathes his last. I cannot vouch for the truth of this, although several persons asserted it to be a fact, and I heard no one contradict it." [4]

Yet this may once have been a common practice of the Beja. Taha, an old sheikh of the 'Ababda, speaking of his ancestors, said, "Jubran had three sons : Hasan, who succeeded him, Husein, and 'Omar. Of these 'Omar was killed by the 'Atawna, and his death revenged by Husein. He decoyed the sheikh to his tent by means of a girl, murdered him, and drank his blood." Another 'Ababda sheikh said that in old times a revenge was not complete till you could say, "I have killed him and drunk his blood."

---

[1] "But the flesh with the life thereof, which is the blood thereof, shall ye not eat." Gen. ix, 4.
[2] The pagan Arabs also thought the blood was the soul. Mas'udi, *Les Prairies d'Or*, iii, 309
[3] Exodus, xxix, 12.
[4] *Nubia*, 396 ; and cf. Herodotus, iii, 11.

PLATE XXI

Tiheiw

Cairn in Wadi Igna

CAIRNS

[*face p.* 198

RITES AND CEREMONIES

Some of the ancient Arabs used to drink the blood of their enemies, and Doughty was told strange tales of the modern Qahtan. Jaussen too mentions a case of an enemy being devoted " to the face of God ".[1]

When an 'Abadi is wounded, he must drink his own blood " to avoid fainting ". This seems merely to save the precious liquid.

The use of bells was anathema to the Prophet as savouring of Christian devotion, and he instituted the office of muezzin to replace them. Yet small bells are used by the Bisharin at festivals, and are also tied to the camel-litters in which women are carried. This may be a pagan practice, to drive off evil spirits, for they still call them " Pharaoh's bells ". But there are other practices which strongly suggest the former existence of Christianity among the Beja. For instance, according to the late Muhammad Katul of the Kurbeilab, a bell had to be rung very early in the morning of each 'Id in every hut, a practice that is now given up.

When their women and children put *kohl* on their eyes, they make a cross on their foreheads, and call it quite wrongly " Solomon's Seal ". Also a cross of palm-leaves is made and stuck in the hair to " cause one who is far away to return ". Some of the southern Beja, e.g. the Habab, were admittedly once Christian, and such practices may have been borrowed from them.

The imprint of one's right hand has always been thought lucky in North Africa. When Sheikh 'Ilwani of the Jumei'at cleared a cistern near Dhab'a and built a house beside it, his son 'Abd El-Hamid printed his hand in green on the white-wash of the guest-chamber.

So too did Isalas the plasterer sign his hand when he finished plastering a cistern near Paraetonium in A.D. 6— nineteen hundred and twenty-nine years ago in the twenty-second year of Augustus.

[1] Jaussen, 361. Cf. also *Rwala*, 528, where 'Awda Abu Tai is said to have " drunk the blood and eaten the heart of an enemy." I suspect this only means that Musil's informant thought that a hero like 'Awda should have done so.

Chapter XII

THE LAW OF BLOOD-VENGEANCE

"*As to what you have told us of prayer and almsgiving, that is easy; but when you say, ' He that kills shall be killed, and he that steals shall have his hand cut off, and he that commits adultery shall be flogged or stoned,' that is an ordinance which we will not lay upon ourselves. Begone elsewhere!*"—Answer of the Lamtuna Tuareg to the Moslem missionary 'Abdalla.

Preliminary Remarks—Their Law only a Civil Code—Individuals not recognized—Blood Revenge usually a Private Affair—The *Diya* or Bloodwit—A Sinai Blood-revenge—Surrender of the Homicide to the Dead Man's Relations.

Exasperated by the innate irresponsibility of their tribesmen, various leaders among the Semites have attempted at one time or another to hammer into them a stricter discipline, and, under the disguise of religious brotherhoods, forge nations out of clans. Indeed the Wahhabi King 'Abdalla Ibn Sa'ud is engaged on such an experiment at the present time. But true nomads are essentially irreligious, and the strict law of Islam has always seemed as repugnant to the Bedouins as that of Moses did to the children of Israel before they settled down.

Before the British occupation of Egypt in 1882 Sinai was administered by a Governor at El-'Arish. There were subordinate officials at Nekhl, important as a castle and watering station, halfway between Suez and 'Aqaba, on the pilgrimage route to Mecca, and Tor, a fishing village and palm-grove on the Gulf of Suez, which about 1875 replaced El-Wijh as chief quarantine station for pilgrims returning by sea. In those days the officials concerned themselves merely with safeguarding the through traffic between Egypt and Palestine or Egypt and the Hijaz and left it to the tribes to settle their own disputes.

Interest in native affairs began to be taken in 1906, when Lord Cromer appointed Wilfrid Jennings Bramly as Inspector, and since then there has been a succession of English Governors; before the War at Nekhl, and after it at El-'Arish.

Until quite lately, the Bedouin judges (*qadi*) were recognized and allowed to hear minor disputes, though their

THE LAW OF BLOOD-VENGEANCE 201

fees were limited to a maximum of £10, while important quarrels were decided by the Governor and a council of sheikhs either at El-'Arish or Tor, where the Governor or one of his magistrates sat in court to ensure that the decisions were equitable. But the peninsula is now so poverty-stricken that it cannot afford its judges, and the present governor has had to abolish the office, so that all cases are now decided by the council of sheikhs. The sheikhs, who receive a small salary from Government, also act as assessors (*qassas*) and are allowed to retain 10 per cent of the fines as their fees.

Since the Arabs' institutions are so rapidly vanishing, I have set down in this and the succeeding chapter as much information as I have been able to collect about their own code from the judges who used to administer it.

In Sinai and Arabia [1] the basis of the law is the simple code of their fathers. Transmitted orally by each judge to his son, it of course varies slightly from tribe to tribe, but is nevertheless so unchanging that the Bedouin have bestowed upon it the epithet of *'urfi* or " sanctified by custom ". The passage of centuries has polished it to so high a state of efficiency that little or no change in it can be traced within historical memory, and it is only now that, faced with altered circumstances, it no longer appears adequate.

To begin with, the point must be stressed that recourse to the law used to be entirely optional—that is to say, before the effective occupation of the peninsula by the Egyptian Government, there was no obligation on any Bedouin to submit themselves to the law at all. Parties, that is families not individuals, only had recourse to a *qadi*, selected by mutual consent from the various practitioners, in order to settle disputes generally of long standing, whose continuance had become intolerable. Here was the weakness of the system ; for powerful families, when discontented with a judge's award, were in the habit of ignoring it completely.

The *'urfi* law is still in the state where individual rights and wrongs are kept strictly within the family circle ; so all that the Bedouin *qadi* has to decide is a dispute in which one family seeks compensation from another. Into this purely civil code the idea of a crime against the community enters

---

[1] Beja customs will be cited when they differ. In the west, where the mass of the population is Libyan with only an Arab veneer, all trace of their primitive law has disappeared, and in its place one finds a code based largely on the *shara'* or Moslem ecclesiastical law. This will be treated of in an appendix.

only as a violation of the honour of the tribe. So it comes about that a Sinai father may kill his daughter without having to answer to the tribe for her life, and when, in 1904, a son killed his father, he was merely " sent to Coventry " by his tribe for the murder. As they said, " Everyone spat at him and refused to speak to him. So he pined away and died."

This absence of a criminal law has prevented the elevation of law itself into a sort of religion where the Judge becomes a priest of Justice. The Bedouin *qadi* is not an official, but a professional practitioner skilled in settling disputes, and the code he invokes to help him is a set of rules of thumb which have worked well in the past and will work again in the future. And the Bedouin judge's responsibility is greatly decreased by his being permitted no discretion at all in the nature of his sentences. The full compensation decreed by the law must always be awarded, to be later whittled down by the good sense of the community. For should the penalty appear to those in court severe, and it generally does, since the law has been framed to meet extreme cases, all the prominent people present beseech the successful litigant, saying, " Let him off one camel for my sake, let him off two for mine." So unless the plaintiff is a regular Shylock, the imposing award made by the *qadi* soon dwindles down to a very modest sum indeed. This is of course just the converse of our system where the jury finds the man guilty and the judge sentences him. At every turn one finds this principle that disputes should always be settled by the interposition of third parties, a murderer finds refuge in a neutral's tent, disputed property is stolen and deposited in a neutral's tent, so that even a lover may take advantage of this and abduct his mistress without damage to her reputation.

There must formerly no doubt have existed a *lex talionis*, but the Bedouin laws have now abandoned the stupidly literal equations of the Mosaic age, " life for life, eye for eye, tooth for tooth " ; in fact the avaricious mind of the Arab has awakened to the fact that two wrongs do not make a right, and the idea that pecuniary gain to the community may outweigh the loss of an individual or part of an individual has allowed the establishment of a system of compensation by fines.

The schoolmasterly ideas of Crime and Punishment are quite foreign to their free Bedouin minds. No *qadi* pretends

THE LAW OF BLOOD-VENGEANCE

that " it hurts me more than it does you ". Their sanctions are never corporal, though occasionally after some heinous offence an individual is made to suffer as well as his family by being chased with a sword, or made to ride a camel smeared with pitch. Expulsion from the community does not seem to occur nowadays.[1] Nor does custom, any more than law, recognize the individual as distinct from his family. So that their system of revenge for the shedding of blood, which ensures that vengeance will fall, if not on the murderer, at least on one of his relations, acts as a powerful deterrent from crimes of violence. A hothead who thinks he has been wronged, and talks of " taking the law into his own hands " to the extent of blood-letting, is likely to be dissuaded by his family from an act so obviously to their disadvantage.

Of course in this respect a family is at the mercy of any excitable member prone to violence, yet such cases are rare. The Arab is cold-blooded (though the Hamite is not), and whatever crime he commits is usually found to have been carefully thought out beforehand.

When tribes are at war with one another, any member of the other tribe may be chosen as a subject for vengeance, and a sort of balance-sheet is struck at the termination of hostilities. But tribal warfare is now a thing of the past in Egypt.

The unit of compensation in cases of major importance is the *diya* or bloodwit for a man, which varies slightly from tribe to tribe, but always contains forty camels, one riding camel, and a *ghurra*.

Nowadays the *ghurra* is a special fine of five camels over and above the blood-wit. But not so long ago the *ghurra* was one of the murderer's female relatives, usually a sister or daughter, who was given to one of the relatives of the murdered person without payment. She remained as his wife until she had given birth to a male child, and not until he was old enough to be able to walk into the encampment holding a sword, would she return to her people. If she continued with him after that he had to pay the bride-price. Girls did not like the custom for they considered themselves disgraced by being given in marriage without a bride-price, and usually preferred to redeem themselves by paying five camels.

According to Bramly, among the Tiyaha or the Laheiwat,

[1] Except among the sedentary Awlad 'Ali of the west.

the murderer used to be sentenced to have his wife handed over as the *ghurra*, and he had to ransom her by payment of six riding-camels. But I have no corroboration of this.

Various tribal scales of blood-money are as follows :—

1. Among the Terabin, forty camels and two hundred sheep or goats. Of these forty camels, there must be eight of each age from 2 to 6 years old.

2. Among the Tiyaha, forty camels of which :

    5 must be *marbut*
    5 ,, ,, *hiqq*
    5 ,, ,, *ruba'*
   10 ,, ,, *jida'*
   10 ,, ,, aged camels
    5 may be any age the defendant may choose.

As the age and condition of each beast are the subject of animated controversy, both tribes are generally pretty hoarse by the time the final payment is effected.

3. Among the 'Aleiqat, the *diya* should consist of forty camels, and a female riding-camel *tulba*. Among the forty there should be :

   1 riding camel (*dhalul*)
   1 milch camel (*dahur*)
 12 *hiqq* camels
 12 *jida'* camels
 14 *ruba'* camels (including the *jira* already handed over). If no *tulba* is obtainable, 50 mejidies may be paid instead. Besides the camels, a virgin *ghurra* should be handed over.

4. Among the Laheiwat, forty camels, one riding camel, and the *ghurra*.

The diya of forty-one camels, reduced by bargaining to perhaps four, is divided among the whole tribe of the murdered man, but the *ghurra*, which is seldom whittled down, remains the perquisite of the victim's family. All the relations who took part in the hunt for the murderer can claim a share. But the full *diya*, though always awarded by the judge, is never paid. Even in 1812 Burckhardt's guide, Hamd, who killed one of the 'Imran who were trying to rob them, got off with a fine of two camels (paid by the sheikhs of the Towara), and twenty dollars paid by Burckhardt.[1]

[1] *Travels in Syria*, 540.

THE LAW OF BLOOD-VENGEANCE

Among tribes living in peace, the blood-vengeance may fall on the members of five generations called collectively the *khomsa*. These generations are :—

I. The grandfather of the murderer.

II. All the male children of the grandfather, that is to say, the father and paternal uncles of the murderer.

III. All the male children of the grandfather's eldest son, and of the murderer's own father. But the sons of the murderer's other paternal uncles can exempt themselves by paying the "sleep-camel" (see below).

IV. Any male children of the grandfather's eldest grandson and the murderer's own sons.

V. The murderer's male grandchildren.

But relations of classes I and V being two generations removed from the murderer may buy themselves off with a "sleep-camel" *ba'ir en-nom* and sleep safely in their beds. So in the table below, if Muteir kills anyone, all those whose names are in ordinary type must go into exile, or run the risk of being killed by the avengers of blood. Hamed and Hasan may buy themselves off, while Himeid and Husein are quite free :—

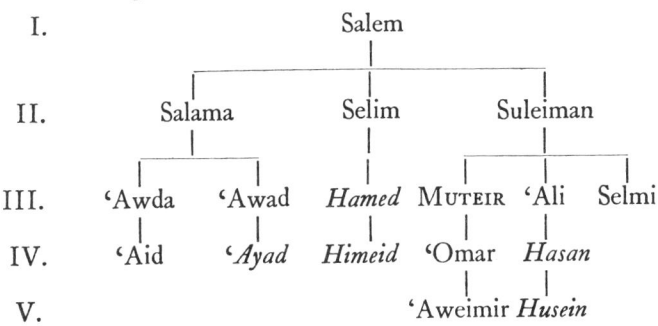

```
I.                        Salem
                            |
             ┌──────────────┼──────────────┐
II.        Salama          Selim        Suleiman
           ┌──┴──┐           |          ┌───┴───┐
III.    'Awda  'Awad      Hamed  MUTEIR 'Ali  Selmi
           |     |          |      |     |     |
IV.      'Aid  'Ayad      Himeid 'Omar  Hasan
                                   |     |
V.                             'Aweimir Husein
```

The 'Ababda are not so bloodthirsty, and only kill the murderer ; or his brother ; or his cousin ; or his grown son ; or his father, if young. Very old and very young men ought not to be killed.

For three days after the discovery of the crime the relations of the victim search for the murderer or any of his family within the degrees of relationship just specified. If his tent is found, it is burnt, his animals slain, even his women and uncircumcised children may fall victims to their unbridled fury. Custom forbids the taking of his property, which must be either destroyed or left alone.[1] However, it rarely happens that the angry relatives find anyone or anything to wreak their vengeance on. Almost inevitably the murderer and all his family have fled to a distance and sought refuge as *dakhil* in the tents of some other tribe, where an act of vengeance would expose the perpetrators to the penalties for breaking " the law of the tent ", a more heinous crime than that of murder. After the three days allotted for indiscriminate vengeance have expired, the nearest relations may commence a careful dogging of the murderer's family, with a view to catching one of them, preferably the murderer himself, off his guard. (But the late sheikh of the 'Aleiqat, Mudakhil, was thus enabled to revenge the murder of his father, Suleiman, not on 'Aid, the actual criminal, but on 'Aid's father.)

Nowadays the family usually await overtures for the payment of blood-money (*diya*) from the relations of the murderer. If peace is agreed upon, these relatives first offer them the *jira* (a six-year old camel) and appoint a representative *kafil wafa'* to pay the money, and obtaining in return a *kafil dafa'* to receive it. A time and place, usually the tent of a well-known sheikh, are then agreed upon for the handing over of the blood-money.

In accordance with the *shara'*, this is assessed in Egypt at " one hundred camels " for a man and half that for a woman. This is compounded for in cash at varying rates.

Thus, in Egypt, the Awlad 'Ali pay the *diya* in cash £300 (women half-price) ; while the Jawabis insist on an extra £100, perhaps in lieu of the *ghurra*.[2] Murder among the Ma'aza is cheaper, costing only £200, and it costs even less among the Bisharin, only twenty she-camels or £100.

There is a general principle in Sinai law that the aggravation of a crime renders the criminal liable to pay fourfold " blood-wit ". So if a man be found murdered treacherously and stealthily in a place where no tracks lie, and his murderer deny the crime, but be subsequently found out, the

---

[1] This destruction recalls the Hebrew custom of *herem* by which the captives and the spoil of war were destroyed as sacrifices to the tribal deity. The spoil of Ai was thus destroyed, while on another occasion Samuel claimed Agag for slaughter as Yahweh's property. But S. Reinach considered that the reason for this was because these spoils of war were infected with a magic power of evil. *Cults, Myths and Religions*, p. 67.
[2] So Kennett thought, but I do not. *Kennett*, 55–6.

THE LAW OF BLOOD-VENGEANCE 207

compensation should be four *diya*. So also for the murder (by a man) of a woman or an uncircumcised child, four, (some say eight) *diya* and the *ghurra* ought to be awarded. Of course if woman kills woman there is no aggravation, and a single *diya* only is due.

The western Arabs seem to have lost some of this chivalry with their conversion to Islam or with their entrance into Africa, for among them an intentional killing is only one-quarter more serious than an accidental one, and the Awlad 'Ali women may be murdered for half-price.

If a woman, who had married into a different tribe, were killed, her husband was only entitled to receive from the fourfold *diya* the bride-price he paid for her. Her father's family took the rest, including the *ghurra*, who remained with them until she had borne a child to replace the slaughtered woman. Kennett adds :—

> "If a woman kill her girl cousin (i.e. her uncle's daughter), the father of the dead girl has the right to take the murderess and marry her to one of his sons. If he declines this option, a special schedule of blood-money in camels is substituted." [1]

One fine day in 1913, I was walking in the Wadi Sidri, when I came across a skeleton lying under an overhanging rock, partially hidden by a tumble-down wall. " The corpse of Sallam," I was told, " who was shot here by the Qararsha." While we were burying him in a proper grave, Sabah, a son of the Mudakhil already mentioned, related the following story.

Sallam was one of the Faranja, a lawless sept of the Muzeina, who had temporarily broken away from their own tribe and were regarded as squatters in 'Aleiqat territory. He and Masri, a Qararshi, worked as partners in the turquoise mines, and afterwards went together to 'Ayun Musa, then a haunt of dealers from Suez, to dispose of their gems. When they failed to sell them to advantage there, Sallam remained behind, while his partner went on to Cairo and got a good price for the turquoises. On his return, Masri informed Sallam that the stones had turned out valueless, and handed him a single guinea as his share of the profits of the transaction. A bitter and futile recrimination followed. Finally Sallam rode out of 'Ayun Musa alone, burning for revenge on the rascal who had cheated him.

[1] Kennett, 55.

He did not go far; about two miles southwards there are some convenient mounds, and there he waited two days for his enemy. Then, as soon as Masri arrived within convenient range, he fired at him and missed! A second shot from Sallam's old pistol tumbled Masri out of his saddle dead. Sallam searched the corpse for the money and took his half-share. He dragged the corpse off the road, and put a blanket over its face to protect it from the ravens, hobbled his victim's camel out of sight of the road, and decamped for Palestine.

Two days later, some passing Arabs heard the camel roaring and discovered the crime. The Qararsha live some sixty miles from the scene of the murder, and by the time they assembled to take vengeance, Sallam was over the hills and far away. So the angry Qararsha, fifty strong, proceeded to the tent of Mudakhil, the Sheikh of the 'Aleiqat, and demanded reparation. The Faranja, who trembled for their skins, asked for a forty days respite after which they promised to produce the murderer. They were as good as their word. By some artifice or treachery Sallam was kidnapped in Palestine, and handed over "all tied up with ropes" to the delighted Qararsha.

Not wishing however to kill him in 'Aleiqat territory, they made off with their captive to Naqb Budra, a pass on the boundary between the two tribes. Here they put him against a rock, and attempted to shoot him. This was found to be impossible, nine successive shots missed. All tribal boundaries are rather nebulous, and the Qararsha now moved Sallam down to the junction of Wadi Budra with Wadi Sidri, to be entirely out of the sphere of any pro-'Aleiqat influence, and again commenced their gruesome target-practice.[1] They were now successful, and leaving his body lying where I found it, went home rejoicing. "But God was angry with them," said Sabah, "and all of them came to violent ends!"

In spite of Sabah's views, this slaying of Sallam (and of Masri for that matter) is always referred to in conversation among the Towara as a *maktal*, that is, a "killing" to which no moral blame need be attached. But the murder of Professor Palmer is stigmatized as *dabiha*, the term used for sacrificing sheep, because he should have been protected by his *rafiq* from the Laheiwat. (This is interesting, as it seems to indicate that a sacrifice is or was regarded to some extent as a crime.)

---

[1] Cf. "Their gods are the gods of the hills, therefore they were stronger than we; but let us fight against them in the plain, and surely we shall be stronger than they." 1 Kings, xx, 23.

Plate XXII

SHEIKH MUDAKHIL SULEIMAN

Sabah's own father Mudakhil, when a youth, had to revenge the slaying of his father Suleiman, upon the Hamaida section of the 'Aleiqat. 'Aid, the actual murderer, had discreetly fled, but the Hajj 'Awda ez-Zumeili, then a friend of the family, discovered the whereabouts of the Hamaida in Wadi Isla, and brought Mudakhil upon them. The youth rather diffidently put 'Aid's father to death; then, emboldened by the deed, wished to continue killing the Hamaida. But the prudent 'Awda restrained his ardour, and saved the life of my informant, a very old man, who gave me coffee almost on the scene of the killing last April. The affair was now balanced, the excitement died down, and 'Aid and Mudakhil, each having killed the other's father, lived in peace though not in friendship. But when Hajj 'Awda was deposed, and Mudakhil became Sheikh of the 'Aleiqat, the Hamaida section thought it better to quit the tribe, and became *qusara* with the Muzeina, where they still remain.

In the case where a family receive the blood-money and still revenge themselves by killing the murderer or one of his relatives, a fourfold *diya* is due for an " aggravated " crime. On the contrary, a slaying by misadventure is only punished by the fine of half a *diya*.

Among the 'Ababda, if people kill one another while playing with swords or knives without malice aforethought, there is nothing to be paid.

A feeling that the homicide should purge his offence by surrendering voluntarily to the dead man's relations appears in modern Beja practice.

Speaking of the 'Aliab Bisharin, Jennings Bramly writes:—

" The murderer escapes, and his friends then set about seeing if the family of the murdered man will accept the *diya*. If they will, a day is fixed, and the murderer and his friends go into a tent, where the assembled friends of the murdered man await them. The murderer is allowed no arms whatever, in fact, he appears stark naked. A discussion begins, and, to show that their regard for their relative who has gone is more than their greed for money, someone starts a quarrel (this is all for good form's sake) and a free fight with sticks ensues. Every now and then it happens that a weapon is used, and the murderer or someone else is killed. Usually, however, after a deal of row, the money is accepted, which of course was in view all the time. On one occasion in the Alaqi I watched the meeting from the hillside—very soon the matted tent began to sway, and for a second seemed more like an immense tortoise—then out of the side shot a naked man, the murderer, and a tremendous scurry of friends and enemies after him—but, except for some very respectable blows, the murderer and his family were allowed to buy off."

Something of the same sort was heard of by Burckhardt among the Awlad 'Ali :—

" The Oulad Aly, a powerful Libyan tribe of Bedouins, inhabiting the Desert between Fayoum and Alexandria, make it a rule never to receive the price of blood, unless the homicide, or one of his nearest kindred, should brave the danger of introducing himself into the tent of the person slain, and then say to the relations, ' Here I am, kill me, or accept the ransom.' The nearest relation may do as he pleases, without incurring any blame ; for the stranger has voluntarily renounced the right of *dakheil*, which all the Libyan Bedouins hold as sacred as the Arabian. A man who gives himself up in this manner is called *mestatheneb*. If the enemy should meet him before he reaches the tent, an attack is almost always the result. If he enters the tent, a ransom is most commonly accepted ; but instances to the contrary sometimes happen."

This may be all hearsay ; at any rate I could hear nothing of this in making inquiries among the modern Awlad 'Ali.

Not the least interesting point about the *'Urfi* law is that the severest penalties are prescribed not for wilful homicide, but for a violation of the laws of honour. For an ordinary offence against them, the judge who specializes in such cases (*munshid*) must impose a penalty greater than the ordinary *diya* or " blood-money " of forty camels ; for, in addition, a negro riding on a white male camel, a negress riding on a white she-camel, and the building of a white cairn used all to be required to " whiten the face " of the aggrieved party. When the crime was more flagrant, as in the case of adultery, the penalties were even more severe.

Such huge fines are invariably lessened by third parties, who use their influence with the plaintiff to be merciful. Na'um Bey gives a case (1904) where a man was sentenced to pay for an insult, a male and female camel and two pounds in cash. (The money no doubt as a " token payment " in lieu of the black slaves.)

Had the blackening been witnessed by two respectable elders, the forty camels would have been added to the fine.

THE LAW OF BLOOD-VENGEANCE

One of the people present asked that the two pounds be waived, while the Governor got the plaintiff to remit the female camel. Ultimately the male camel alone was found sufficient to whiten the injured party's face.[1]

Should the fine imposed prove too heavy for the defendant and his tribe to pay, he pays what he can ; and then, collecting his women and those of his neighbours, he goes and camps beside the man he has injured. A sheep is then killed, and the plaintiff asked to the feast. If he refuses to come, he is held to be a regular Shylock.

A man may also interpose his " face " between the two parties to a quarrel, saying " I throw my face between you ". If one of them continues the combat after that, he has blackened the mediator's face, and become nominally liable to the full penalty. Should he refuse to go before a judge, the mediator will declare his default before witnesses, and may then " steal " his camels (*withaqa*) to oblige him to appear in court. (The 'Ababda call this *'uqal.*)

[1] Shuqeir, 409.

Chapter XIII

LAWS OF THE TENT AND OF WOMEN

" *Originally the tent belonged to the wife and her children, just as it did among the Saracens.*"—Robertson Smith, *Kinship*.

The Law of the Tent—The *Dakhil*—The Tent as Sanctuary—Possible Origin of this—Refusal to enter a Tent an Insult—The story of the *Marqub*—Rape—Abduction—Adultery—Divorce.

There is a higher law than that of blood-revenge. As in the Highlands of Scotland, even a murderer is safe *as a guest* in the tents where he seeks refuge. In 1820, some Ma'aza raiders killed a Laheiwi, Suleiman ibn Eleiwiya, and then took refuge with 'Eid ibn Husein of the same section, the Najmat. 'Eid asked the rest of the Najmat to defer their vengeance till the Ma'aza had left his tents, killed a sheep, lit a fire, and gave the general impression that the raiders would spend the night. At the same time he recommended his guests to leave one by one under cover of darkness. They all escaped successfully, and to this day the Ma'aza recognize their obligation to the descendants of 'Eid ibn Husein.[1]

At the present day any person, whether a member of the tribe or not, has a right to enter a tent, and demand protection of its owner, either from some oppressor or from the avengers of blood. In the first case, his demand for aid is called *dakhlet el-haqq*, in the second his seeking refuge is called *dakhlet ed-damm*.

His entry is usually literal, and he eats and sleeps in his protector's tent, though sometimes he merely pitches his own tent in the vicinity.

Whole clans sometimes take refuge with larger and stronger ones in this fashion. Among the Awlad 'Ali, it commonly happens that the whole family of a murderer seek refuge with another section of the tribe. This is called *nazala*.

The right of entry is néver refused, and in civil cases the protector is bound to further the interests of his *dakhil* as well as he can. He will visit the alleged oppressor, and in the majority of cases manage to get the affair settled without

[1] Shuqeir, 574.

LAWS OF TENT AND OF WOMEN

the expensive proceeding of a recourse to the judge. To deliver up a *dakhil* to his pursuers, or to harm him in any way, is rightly looked upon as a vile form of treachery.

Jennings Bramly once saw a lark take refuge in a tent from a sparrow hawk. Whereupon the owner forbade his children to catch it, since " it had claimed hospitality ".

One of the worst of all crimes in Arab eyes is to " blacken a man's face " by breaking the Law of the Tent, *haqq el-beit*, by killing or injuring someone who has sought protection in it. The perpetrator of such a crime has not only to answer to the murdered man's relatives for the injury done, but in addition an exemplary compensation must be awarded by the special judge who decides these affairs of honour, to the owner of the tent.

Formerly, a black slave riding a white male camel, a negress riding a white she-camel, and the building of a white cairn, as well as the *diya* of forty ordinary camels, were all necessary to whiten the face of the injured party. In these days the slaves are necessarily omitted from the fine.

Should it have happened that there was nobody in the tent at the time to protect the refugee, the penalties would have been even more severe. According to Sheikh Zeidan of the 'Aleiqat, the murderer in such a case would be sentenced not only to pay the *diya* or blood-wit to the relatives of the victim, but also to satisfy the owner of the tent according to the following scheme. Beyond the usual negro and negress, a camel had to be paid for each of the tent-ropes, usually nine in number. Further, a strong man was to throw the stick used for stirring coffee out of the door, and using the distance thus obtained as radius, stride in a circle round the tent. For every step he took, a male and female camel were due.

Of course, such a penalty was never exacted in full, but the whole would be awarded by the judge, and later whittled down to something more like equity by the intercession of those present at the court. Such is the invariable Bedouin custom.

After the coffee-stick was thrown and the bargaining was over, a further ceremony, the event of the day to the spectators, now took place. The unarmed murderer mounted on his riding-camel was chased by the armed owner of the tent mounted on his. Three free sword-cuts were allowed, and if the murderer died, no blood-money need be paid.

Arab law as a rule does not recognize anything less than a family, but in this case the crime was reckoned so heinous, that their Bedouin minds must have considered that the individual should in some degree pay the penalty himself.

Had there been someone in the tent to protect the refugee, the judge would have held that the owner of the tent " might cut the murderer's tongue with three cuts, or take from his property whatever he wished ".

If the refugee (who is called *dakhil*[1]) chances to seek refuge with folk too weak to protect him, they are obliged to accompany him and put him in safety with someone powerful enough to afford him shelter.

So long as his protector's food is in his belly, he is safe and therefore the rights of the *dakhil* are supposed to continue for three days and a third of a day after he has left the tent, and not only for his person but also for his goods and cattle. Consequently if he is robbed within that period, the owner of the tent within which he has been protected, is bound to insist upon the restoration of the stolen property.

Similarly if the avengers slew or wounded one running towards a tent to " enter " it as *dakhil*, the refugee was considered by some tribes to have " entered " if his corpse lay within two javelin-casts, but by others he must actually have taken hold of the tent-ropes to qualify as " *dakhil* ".[2] In such a case, the avengers are held to have violated the " law of the tent ".

Jaussen gives an instance where Hasan, a sheikh of the Rashaida, struck one of the Tiyaha, in the guest-tent of his tribe. Hasan pleaded that the tent belonged to him. But the judge held that it was the common property of the Rashaida tribe, whose honour was thus involved. Hasan was condemned to restore the camel he had stolen from the Tihi, to pay eighty camels, 800 piastres for the wound, and to have his hand cut off or to redeem it with a horse. Further he was to give the judge a riding-camel.[3]

The tent also protects the owner, for it is contrary to custom to shoot a man in his tent. To avoid any such

---

[1] From the verb *dakhal* " he entered ".

[2] Compare Strabo's account of the Temple of Ephesus : " The temple was formerly, and is at present, a place of refuge but the limits of sanctity of this asylum have been frequently altered. . . . Mithridates discharged an arrow from the angle of the roof, and supposed it fell a little beyond the distance of a stadium. Antonius doubled this distance." Strabo, xiv, 23.

[3] Jaussen, 203.

LAWS OF TENT AND OF WOMEN

calamity, the Bedouins always leave their weapons outside a tent, and only take their camel-sticks inside with them.

How does it come about that the tent possesses such sanctity ? It must have been customary and natural at some period of the past, when the matriarchate was still in force, for those in bodily peril to seek refuge with the women of a tribe. Among the pagan Arabs, a refugee was considered protected if a woman threw her cloak over him[1] ; and Linant de Bellefonds relates a tale, in which the women of the Bisharin, touched by a young enemy's fortitude, protect him from the warriors till his wounds are healed, and then allow him to escape.[2] Sisera too sought refuge with Jael, though in that case his confidence was misplaced. Further, in Dr. Jensen's story of the *marqub*,[3] the 'Abadi sheikh actually hides the young refugee in his *harim*, an action almost incredible among true Arabs of to-day.

We may quote here Agatharchides' account of the African Troglodytes, from which one sees the moderating influence of the elder members of the *harim*.

> "In the beginning of their Fights they make their Onsets with throwing of Stones ; after some Wounds given on both Sides they fall to with their Bows and Arrows, whereupon great Numbers are slain in a short time. For by long Experience they become good Marksmen, and being all naked are expos'd to every Shot. At length their old Women by their Intreaties put an end to their Conflicts (whom they greatly reverence, for it's unlawful to do them the least Harm) and therefore as soon as they see them come towards them, they cease casting their Darts immediately, and all are quiet."

The right to protect strangers may have passed (this is merely a guess) from the *harim* to the male owner of the tent through the chief of the tribe. A possible clue to this is also given by Agatharchides, when he relates that among these " Troglodytes " their ruler alone among the males possessed a wife of his own ; and, since, right down to our times, among their descendants the hut has always been the property of the wife, it should follow that in antiquity the chief alone had a private habitation. Should we go further and assume a somewhat similar state of things in ancient Arabia— and Strabo gives a vivid account of polyandry among the tribesmen of Arabia Felix—a step would be taken on our

[1] Aghani, xviii, 137. [2] L'Etbaye, 61-5. [3] See p. 217.

road towards understanding the unusual sanctity that still appertains to a tent among the Bedouins. For in old days, the tent of the chief's wife and its vicinity must have been a sacred precinct forbidden (*haram*) except to his guests, and his women " forbidden ones " (*harim*).

Clients flying to him for protection would seek refuge there, and occasionally when he had been unusually powerful, this ability to protect them would be transferred on his death to his tomb, when he would become a *weli*, with a sanctuary. Robertson Smith conjectures that his right as chief to women of his own came about through the right, which the leader of a raid still possesses, to a greater share in the booty. And as every Bedouin thinks himself as good as his chief, so when polyandry gave way later to individual marriage, each tribesman would not only claim " a damsel or twain " to himself, and a tent or two, but would also assert the privilege of protecting his guests.

Things are different among the Beja. Among the 'Ababda, the refugee is called *hasib*. He is unable to " enter " literally into his protector's tent, for they have only basket-work huts reserved for the *harim*, though he may be concealed there temporarily. And the penalty for killing a *hasib* within the protection of an 'Abadi is only a quarter of a *diya* to the owner of the tent over and above the *diya* paid to his relations. But the views of the hospitable Amar Ar greatly extend the principle of protection, for there the owner of the tent is expected to pay the refugee's fine for him. Naturally this privilege is often abused. Mr. J. W. Miller, writing to Mr. J. W. Crowfoot, says :—

> " You are held responsible for what happens outside your house. That is to say, if A kills B in sight of your house, you must help A against B's people. And B's people will claim the *diya* from you. The same applies to camels. I have a quarrel with A ; a good move on my part is to steal A's camel and kill it outside your house. It is then up to you to repay A, not to me. This annoying custom frequently crops up in cases and I have tried to get an explanation without much success. The most that I can get is that Beirak, the reputed founder of the Hadendawa is supposed to have made his position in that way. A set of camel thieves came to his house, and while they were inside, the owners arrived and demanded the men. Beirak refused to hand them over, and to make sure that the thieves' quarrels were his quarrels, he slew the animals one by one

LAWS OF TENT AND OF WOMEN

before his door and the eyes of the owners. The thieves then acknowledged his power and the custom has come down in its present form."

It follows of course that to decline to enter a Bedouin tent may be construed as an insult, which a formal refusal certainly is. Indeed such a refusal can only be justified in some such circumstances as Bramly describes below.

" Long ago beyond Qusaima in Turkish territory, I asked one Sa'ad Abu Sulb, to show me Ain el-Quds, a well which Professor Palmer thought might be the place where Moses struck the rock. Well knowing the spring was only a few hundred yards from his tents, Sa'ad offered to take me there for £2. To this I agreed. I spent the night in his tents, and went down to the well next morning. During the night he had contrived to take all my money from my pouch, and when I came to pay him, I found I had nothing. I looked up and caught him smiling, and there was no doubt he knew there was nothing in my bag. So I looked very hard at Sa'ad and said, ' I would rather be the man who lost it than the man who took it.' Two or three of those present guessed from this what had happened, and Sa'ad didn't like it. In the evening, when we were to have returned to his tent, I refused absolutely. I told him I would send him the two pounds by one Suleiman who was with me at the time, and then went away about 200 yards and sat with Suleiman on the ground. Sa'ad then came and begged me to go to his tent, which I had dishonoured by sitting just outside, but I again refused. Suleiman said that, after this, we must sit up all night with arms in our hands and not go to sleep. This we did, but nothing happened."

The wild chivalry of the Beja is well displayed in the following story of a blood-revenge.[1]

" Once upon a time a young Beja came to the house of an old well-to-do 'Abadi, and said, ' I claim the right of a guest.' When night fell, the sheikh asked his guest ' What reason have you for this journey ? ' The young man replied ' I have killed a man, and am become *marqub*[2] (fugitive) '. The sheikh asked, ' Whom have you killed ? ' The *marqub* said, ' I have killed so-and-so.' The sheikh heard the name and knew it to be that of his brother's son. The sheikh said to himself, ' This *marqub* is my guest.' But he did not tell the fugitive that he was the dead man's uncle.

---

[1] Abridged from Frobenius, *Afrique* (ed. Cahiers d'Art), 53–4.
[2] Lit. " one who is sought for."

"The sheikh saw the men of his own family approaching. The sheikh said to the *marqub*, 'The dead man's family are pursuing you. I will hide you.' The sheikh did not lead the fugitive into the men's rooms but took him into his own *harim*. He hid him among the women. The men arrived at the sheikh's house and cried to him, 'A man has killed your brother's son and fled. We have discovered the fugitive's tracks and pursued him up to here. He has entered your house. He must be in your house. We want to look for him.' The sheikh replied, 'I have nothing in the house that I can hand over to you.' The men said, 'Can we search the house?' The sheikh said, 'Certainly you can search the house, but you must not enter the *harim*.' The men entered the house, went through every room, looked everywhere. They did not find the *marqub*. They respected the *harim*. They went away.

"For two days the *marqub* remained in the hiding place that the sheikh had arranged for him. Then the sheikh brought him out. The sheikh said, 'You must fly from here, and follow such and such a road. Avoid various places. Go from this well to that one. Take care at certain forks.' He gave the fugitive his best camel and provided him with provisions, water, and money. He said farewell to the fugitive. The *marqub* followed the prescribed route. At the end of one day he arrived at a wadi, where many sheep, goats, and cattle were grazing. Near the cattle was an old slave in charge of the beasts. The *marqub* sat down beside the old slave, saluted her, and asked, 'What is the news?' The old slave told him. 'Great things have happened. My master, to whom all these beasts belong, is Sheikh So-and-so. He had a brother, who had a son. Then a young stranger came from afar. He killed the nephew of the sheikh, my master. The sheikh received the *marqub*. He fed him. When the family came to claim the handing over of the man who had slain his nephew, the sheikh hid the murderer in his *harim*. For the murderer was his guest. The sheikh then provided the murderer with all that he needed and sent him to his family.' The fugitive listened to all this and said to himself, 'So the sheikh who received me was the uncle of the man I killed. He has done too much for me.' The fugitive said to the slave, 'Thank you, for telling me all this.'

"The *marqub* remounted his camel, turned its head round, and returned by the same way he had come. He arrived again before the house of the sheikh. The *marqub* entered the house. He laid down all his arms. The sheikh came and saw him. The sheikh cried, ' You have come back. What do you want ? Have I neglected anything ? ' The fugitive said, ' On my road, I met an old slave who was in charge of a large herd. I asked her what had been happening, and she told me that a man had been killed, that the murderer had fled to the brother of the dead man's father, that he was first received by that man, then hidden, and finally provided with all the advice he needed and all the means of escape. This old woman taught me that you, the sheikh, are the uncle of the man I killed. My mind cannot fathom the greatness of your heart, and that is why I ask you to kill me.' The sheikh said, ' Thank you for coming back. I am going to put an end to this affair.' The sheikh reconducted the fugitive to the *harim*. Then he invited all the men of his family to a banquet.

" The sheikh had four fat camels killed and prepared a rich repast. The guests arrived. The festival lasted a long time, and when it was over, the sheikh and his guests took coffee. Finally the sheikh had a new white winding-sheet brought, put it on his arm and said, ' I have a little affair to manage. Excuse my leaving you. I will be back at once.' He then went into the *harim*. He found the *marqub* and said to him, ' The moment of expiation has come. Put this shroud on your head and follow me closely. Put your hands on my shoulders.' The *marqub* walked behind the sheikh and followed him into the *diwan*. There all the men of the dead man's family were seated.

" The sheikh addressed the men and said to them. ' O my nearest relatives and faithful friends, I am come here bringing you the man who has killed my brother's son. At the time that you sought him in my house, he was my guest and as such under my protection. But since then I have penetrated his heart and measured the depth of his sentiments. That is why he is to-day for me something more than a guest. I have made of him a *hasib*, so that he is completely under my protection. He cannot be killed till myself and my son have fallen in his defence. But I have also to think of the means of freeing your souls from the heavy burden of responsibility and of reconciling your minds to him. First of all I, instead of the *marqub* who is now my *hasib*, am about to pay the *diya*, that is a hundred female camels (the usual amount). And further I am going to ask you not to take part in this affair as if it were an ordinary business transaction, but I insist on you asking yourselves whether you will not find pleasure also in taking him for *hasib*.'

"The family of the deceased rose and saluted the sheikh. They said, ' Out of sorrow comes forth joy. A son was taken from us, but a friend has been given.' The *marqub* became their guest and went from one man's house to another. The sheikh was to him as a father."

So much for the " Law of the Tent " ; actual offences against women are punished with commendable severity, for the punishment for rape is the same as that for murder, while for adultery, an " aggravated " crime, it is four times as great.

Jennings Bramly, speaking of twenty-five years ago, writes that " if a man rapes a girl in the forenoon, her family may, during the three days following the assault, kill anyone of the violator's family without paying *diya* for those killed. The presumption is that before noon, the man must have been lying in wait for the girl, and the crime therefore a premeditated one. But should the assault take place between noon and midafternoon, her relatives are only allowed to kill for one day free of charge, since there are known places with shade in the middle of the day, where the man and the girl might well meet without any evil intention on the man's part.". The feeling is, that in the impossibility of proving premeditation, the penalty should be reduced. At night, the girl's family have no redress, as all the tents are usually pitched close together, and it is presumed that the girl, if she wanted, could have called out and been rescued ". Formerly in such cases, if a girl was discovered to have been seduced, she was usually put to death by her family.

Jarvis says, " the fine for rape is £100 if the assault occurs during the daytime, but only half that amount if it occurs at night." [1]

Na'um Bey gives a much milder scale of penalties, no doubt those actually imposed after the judge's award had been somewhat whittled down in the usual way. He says :—

"When a virgin is raped, the girl should complain to some neighbour other than her relatives, and the news should then come

[1] Jarvis, 53.

from them to her father. Some peace-maker will then probably interpose his 'face' between the families to prevent bloodshed. The fine for the rape of a virgin of another tribe is eight camels, of one's own tribe, six. When the woman is not a virgin, the fines are reduced to four and two respectively. If the woman does not complain forthwith, the fine will be a small camel only."[1]

As I have stated above, the Bedouin youth's first marriage is usually to his paternal uncle's daughter, *bint 'amm*, and, in any case, it is very unusual for a lad to ask to be married to a girl from another tribe. But love occasionally laughs at tribal custom, and some young Lochinvar elopes with a willing sweetheart.

Among those tribes, where the custom of *nahiba* (see p. 183) prevails, she is lawful plunder and the boy pays the usual *mahr* and a fine of five camels. But otherwise, the girl's relatives may accept a camel as *jira* from the boy's family, while some elder " throws his face " between the two parties to prevent bloodshed. If the two are caught, the *munshid* will fine the youth five to fifteen camels and the girl's family will have the option of marrying the girl to the youth on payment by him of the *mahr* or not, just as they like. If she becomes pregnant by him, they will naturally choose the former course. If the lovers belong to the same tribe, the fine imposed on the youth is very small, usually one camel.

Kennett gives a case where a Western Desert Bedouin called Lamlûm eloped with a distant female relative, but was shot at while doing so. For this he impudently claimed damages, which were very properly not awarded. But to avoid further family discord, the Court allowed him to keep the girl and fined him a sheep for the insult to the lady's family.[2]

A youth of course posseses the right to kidnap his first cousin, if he finds her about to be married to another man. Bramly found the course of true love running very far from smoothly in a case of this kind which he had to listen to among the Amar Ar.[3]

Fatma of that tribe was a good-looking girl who loved one Okeil, an excellent match, for he was a rich young man ; but unfortunately he did not belong to her family. A marriage was arranged between them, although the just claim to her

---

[1] Shuqeir, 417.
[2] Kennett, 126–27.
[3] A Beja tribe of the Northern Sudan.

hand belonged to her cousin Hamdan who, though poor, was the hero of the section. Upon the wedding day as the bride-to-be was being taken to the ceremony, she was captured by a strong party under Hamdan, who treated her with very little ceremony. They tied her up in a bundle, slung her over a camel, and rode away over hill and dale. (At the trial which followed, Fatma was very voluble indeed about the bumping she had undergone during this part of the proceedings.)

Okeil meantime mustered his friends and rode hard in pursuit. After a day or two, Hamdan was overtaken and saw his party much outnumbered. There was no time to undo his captive, so Hamdan flung the beautiful Fatma, now a crumpled bundle, on the ground and galloped off. The impetuous Okeil gathered her up, and, without stopping to undo her, commenced to gallop back with her in the opposite direction. (More howls from Fatma to make the court understand the second lot of misery she had undergone). This rescue did not last long, for Hamdan soon reached reinforcements and, turning back after Okeil, chased him so hotly, that he in turn had no time to undo the lady, and for a second time the bundle called Fatma descended with a bump on the side of the road. In recounting this misfortune, the crowd got so excited, and Fatma let out such a piercing yell to indicate the crisis of her woes, that Bramly could bear no more. " I seized the camp table and, raising it up as a method of clearing the room, knocked the matting off its sticks, and the company left through the walls disdaining the door ! " This ended the case for one day.

Next day, seated among the debris of the District Office, four mats and a few sticks, Bramly reheard the tale, again punctuated by Fatma's squeals. In the end the beauty married Okeil and lived happily ever afterwards.

The more spirited of the Sinai Bedouin, like those of Moab, try to revenge adultery with death, the seducer being shot by the husband or by one of the wife's family, which is held to be the one dishonoured. (But since they usually marry their first cousins, this is commonly the same as the husband's). And should a married woman be discovered *in flagrante delictu* with a lover, her injured spouse is justified, in Bedouin opinion, in killing them both on the spot. Even when his wife has fled with the adulterer, he may give chase

LAWS OF TENT AND OF WOMEN

and kill them if he can catch them. But should they succeed in taking refuge with a neutral family, a remarkable state of things prevails for seven days. During this period, the aggrieved family are at liberty to kill any four men, within the five degrees of relationship, of the adulterer's family, and confiscate as many of its camels as they can lay hands on. To avoid this violence, the offending family make all haste to hand over a she-camel, called *jira*, a token payment that they are willing to settle the case legally. Any violence or plundering that these latter may have committed before they accept the *jira* is not counted in the final reckoning.

According to Kennett :—

> "The plaintiff family is allowed to confiscate twenty camels every morning for a week; and if four men from the defendant family be not killed, the blood-money for four men must be exacted in lieu thereof. Thus the plaintiff family is entitled to one hundred and forty camels (twenty a day for seven days) in addition to one hundred and sixty-four camels as blood-money for the four men, while the husband is also allowed to claim the camel or horse on which the guilty pair escaped, the sword, gun, or pistol carried by the seducer, as well as the marriage-money originally paid for the woman." [1]

This, of course, is purely academic; such an award may have been made, but certainly it was never paid in full. Bramly, also writing of North Sinai, says :—

> "A man convicted of adultery would (be sentenced to) pay the price of four men, and ride a camel smeared with pitch round the circumference of four territories." [2]

Of an actual case in 1816, Burckhardt says :—

> "A Tyaha Arab had eloped with a married woman of that tribe; he was overtaken in his flight by the injured husband's brother, and severely wounded; yet he recovered, and the affair was settled by arbitration among the contending parties; and it was decided that the seducer should pay sixty camels, one male and one female slave, one free girl instead of her who had eloped; which girl the husband might marry without paying her price, a fine poniard, and the dromedary upon which the guilty pair had fled." [3]

---

[1] Kennett, 134-5.
[2] P.E.F. *Quarterly Statement*, 1905, 214.
[3] *Notes*, 158.

And no doubt this award was considerably reduced by the intercession of third parties.

The above penalties indicate that the law considers the injured husband should not only be fully compensated for the loss of his wife, but also have his " face whitened ".

Na'um Bey says the sentence given by the *'Uqbi*[1] should include " *Arba'in gamal wuquf, wala ghulam maktuf* ". " Forty camels standing up, or a pinioned youth." The " pinioned youth " means the abductor tied up for slaughter, as Salam was when the Faranja handed him over to the Qararsha. However, the people present would mediate, and the fine would probably be reduced to about ten camels. These penalties which, even when whittled down, remain usually pretty severe, render abduction of a wife a very rare offence.

In an actual case, which happened thirty years ago, 'Ali, the son of a sheikh of the Laheiwat, who abducted a woman and took her to 'Aqaba, was hunted out of Sinai, and had to take refuge in Palestine with a tribe there. One of the woman's family followed, at some risk, since his hosts were by custom bound to protect 'Ali for a twelvemonth. One evening, as 'Ali was sitting before a tent, a man rode up on horseback with his kerchief over his mouth, showing only his nose and eyes (this is not unusual), and his rifle resting across the saddle before him. 'Ali greeted him *Salam aleikum*, to which the stranger replied *Aleikum es salam rahmat allahi wu barakat*.[2] Then, depressing his rifle, he fired at random from the saddle. The avenger instantly fled for his life, for he was in the middle of tents all friendly to 'Ali. 'Ali was wounded in the thigh, but recovered, and peace was not made till a large sum had been paid by his family.

In January, 1916, Sabah Mudakhil and I, riding out one evening to the east of the Canal, found hiding in the bushes of Wadi Murr, a Bedouin lady and child, who were walking in from Ain Sumar. This was Sa'ida, wife of Selim Abu Radi, who had run away from her husband, the headman of the petty sept of Faranja. She gave us some useful information about the Turkish outpost at Ain Sudr, and was handed over to the Intelligence Office at Suez. Later on, Sabah, who was greatly smitten with the fair Sa'ida, persuaded her

---

[1] Judge who specializes in the law affecting women.
[2] " Upon you be peace, the mercy of God, and His blessing ! " (This blasphemy was considered very bad form.)

PLATE XXIII

SINAI WOMEN

LAWS OF TENT AND OF WOMEN

to marry him. Selim Abu Radi at first threatened to murder Sabah, but thinking better of it, shot his camel at Abu Zenima one night in 1917. The affair was not finally settled till after the War by the Governor and a council of sheikhs at El 'Arish. The camel shot by Selim was allowed to the Faranja, so was a second one which he had stolen, while old Mudakhil was obliged to pay a further £16 for Sabah's escapade.

Among the Beja, things are very different; I have not personally met with a case of adultery among the 'Ababda, but the penalty is said to be only five female camels, and the Bisharin allow their women unusual freedom, as do the rest of the Beja.[1] Thus Plowden says of the Habab in Eritrea[2]: "The unmarried girls are preserved from early irregularity by strict precautions, but they indemnify themselves after marriage for all restraint. What distinguishes this tribe from almost all others is the absence of jealousy in the husband, insomuch as he permits his wife a perfect liberty, taking only her gains." So, too, Crossland,[3] of the Amar Ar: "A woman is the more valued by her husband if she gives proof of her attractiveness to other men, even by adultery; he has no resentment against his wife, his honour being satisfied by an attack with his dagger on the first meeting with his rival." According to Karait Batran, their sheikh, things are exactly the same with the Hamedorab Bisharin.

Divorce is very common among the Bedouins, for a variety of reasons; if the woman is sterile, or only bears girls, or simply because the married pair cannot get on together. Very frequently a Bedouin takes an oath, "If I don't do this, or if this is not true, I will divorce my wife." And since Bedouin oaths are very fragile, plenty of wives are divorced on this account.

When an Arab wife is divorced in the ordinary way, the husband takes her to a friend and says to her in his presence "you are divorced and this man is the witness of your divorce". The words "you are divorced" can be pronounced by the man alone. Her husband is then obliged to forfeit the bride-price and to give her in addition seven lengths of cloth, seven goats, and a black donkey. She may also carry away

---

[1] Agatharchides wrote of their ancestors, the Troglodytes, that "they enjoyed their wives and children in common except only the wife of the king. Yet if any of them lie with her, he is only fined by the king in a certain number of sheep".
[2] W. C. Plowden, *Travels in Abyssinia*, 14.
[3] C. Crossland, *Desert and Water Gardens of the Red Sea*, 26.

a coffee pot, a cooking pot, a dish, and a drinking cup. Among the Beja tribes of 'Ababda and Bisharin, the whole tent and its furniture are the wife's property, and she takes them all away when she is divorced. The far-sighted Ma'aza husband only pays two-thirds of the bride-price on marriage, and reserves the remaining third to be paid when he divorces his wife. If the woman desire divorce, she runs away to her father's tent (Na'um Bey says " to one of her relatives, not her father "), and an attempt is usually made by means of the '*Uqbi* to arrange the matter. Perhaps the husband may have to pay some ewes, a donkey, a cooking pan, a grindstone, or a sieve to appease her; and he may have to erect her tent between two of her relatives' tents. But if the woman continues to demand separation, the husband rarely refuses to divorce her. In such a case, he is not obliged to return the bride-price. Na'um Bey says " the '*Uqbi* can pass a decree of separation ".[1]

The custom in the west when recording the bride-price is usually to agree to, say £10, and write down £100 to flatter the girl's vanity. But should the case come into court, the real amount is whispered to the judge, whatever has been set down in the deed. It is a question of manners.

If she become pregnant during the ninety days following the divorce, she may not re-marry till she has given birth to and weaned her child. The husband is obliged to maintain her till the child is weaned. All the children remain with the father unless very young, when the mother looks after them for some time.

A Bedouin can re-marry his wife after the first divorce on payment of a small bride-price, unless she is divorced with " triple divorce ", when in accordance with the usual Moslem custom, he cannot marry her till she has been the wife of another man.

In Sinai, the 'Aleiqat, unlike the Sawalha, do not ever re-marry the wife they have divorced. The worst of all sins, they say, is to divorce one wife, marry and divorce a second, and then re-marry your original wife.

[1] Shuqeir, 418.

Chapter XIV
LEGAL PROCEDURE

"*And it came to pass, when Samuel was old, that he made his sons judges over Israel.*"—1 Samuel, 8, i.

The Judge a Consultant—Rules of Evidence—The Oath—The *Mubasha'*—Judgment—Assessment of Wounds—The Guardian—Inheritance—Recovery of Debt—Taking Camels without leave—Flotsam and Jetsam.

Every Sinai tribe has its *qadi* or judge, before whom such disputes as could not be settled by mutual consent till lately used to be brought. Such a judge was always the son of a judge, often a younger son who had assisted his father in the practice, when the elder sons had departed to work for their own living. There was, however, no obligation to resort to the tribal judge, or indeed to any at all.

Nowadays, the Arabs prefer to refer the affair to the sheikh or council of sheikhs whose fees may be lighter and their sentence less severe. In any case, resort to law takes place only by mutual consent.

Parties did not sue direct, but through some respectable relative, called a *kafil*, who guaranteed the family's abilities to pay whatever fine might be imposed on them. The plaintiff's guarantor was called *kafil dafa*, the defendant's *kafil wafa*. In the very frequent cases where the litigants belonged to different tribes, both parties usually agreed through their *kufala*[1] that the case be heard by the judge of some neutral tribe, renowned for his equitable decisions.

In cases of serious bloodshed or of offences against women, when the defendants dared not appear personally in court the following expedient was sometimes resorted to in order to secure an impartial judge. Each party nominated a *qadi* and these two met and co-opted a third. This judge of appeal, called *dhureibi*, had to be of the Haweitat tribe. The custom then was for the first two judges to retire and leave the case to be tried by the third.

As in other primitive communities, the law, (entirely an unwritten code, which, however, varies but slightly from

[1] Plural of *Kafil*.

tribe to tribe), takes account rather of families than of individuals. And as the family never dies, responsibility for a debt or injury involving compensation is passed on from one generation to another.

The first care of the judge was to exact from the litigants a pledge, often a sword, of payment of whatever fee it was customary for him to demand. This amount varied with the importance of the case at issue. In Sinai, the maximum fee that a judge could exact, used to be limited by the governor to £10, and the minimum to £5. (Nowadays, the cases are heard by the sheikhs at much less expense to the litigants.) In earlier days the fee might vary from an ewe to eight camels, the highest fees being paid in cases connected with crime against women, or " injuries to the face ".

The payment of the judge's fee usually falls on the party against whom the verdict goes, but in some tribes, the accusing party have to pay it. Among the Muzeina, in a case of wounding, the striker pays the fee ; in a case of theft, the winning party pays one-third and the losers two-thirds of the judge's fee.

The judge then proceeds to hear the case, and both sides produce their witnesses. It should be made clear, that although he has to decide the case on the evidence, the idea of a truthful and impartial witness never enters the *qadi*'s mind—all he has to do is to strike a balance between the parties. And in all their quarrels, there is usually a counter-charge in reply to the charge, so that in summing up, the judge commonly finds both parties guilty, and imposes upon them the maximum penalties prescribed by the law. Nothing less will serve, lest he lay himself open to the charge of favouritism.

The final result, therefore, may be, after the whittling down is over, that Hamdan's family has to pay thirteen camels to 'Awda's, and that 'Awda's has to pay nine to Hamdan's. The balance is accordingly adjusted by Hamdan handing four camels over to 'Awda. The penalties however must always be paid in camels or the equivalent—sentences involving death or flogging cannot be imposed. In fact, the person is always respected, except that in a case where obscene gestures have been employed to insult someone, the offender may be adjudged by the judge to lose his hand or have his tongue plucked out. Such sentences, however, are not in practice put into effect—but the guilty one has to ransom his hand or tongue at a pretty stiff price from the one he has insulted.

LEGAL PROCEDURE 229

Occasionally also in certain very heinous offences against honour, the offender may be exposed to public derision, or chased out of camp.

Bedouin law is still in that primitive condition, where all offences are regarded as " torts " or matters which can be settled by payment of compensation to the injured party. Crimes, or offences against the community, are not recognized. These consultant judges go by different titles according to the type of case they try. Simple affairs are dealt with by a court of " elders ", a judge who tries affairs of honour is a *munshid* ; cases of wounding go before an assessor *qassas* ; and here an interesting point reveals some capacity for national organization, for the titles denote the tribes from which they come ; thus divorce, rapes, abductions, and other litigation affecting women are tried by an *'uqbi* from Beni 'Uqba, the analogous expert in camel affairs is a *ziyadi* from the Ziyud section of the Suwarka, while disputes about date-palms go before a *masa'udi* from the Masa'id. Again a *dhureibi* or judge of appeal must come from the Haweitat. Just as the southern tribes have agreed to share in the supply of camels to the Convent, so, at some time in the past, the tribal judges of Sinai must have agreed to specialize to avoid undue competition. (Nowadays, owing to the Beni 'Uqba being well-nigh extinct, it is possible to meet an *'uqbi* who does not belong to that tribe.)

Should the two parties not be content with the judgment of a single *qadi*, the case may be referred to a second, even to a third. But as soon as two judges agree in a decision, the case goes no further.

Arab law divides witnesses into two classes ; (1) those present at the dispute who were called upon *at the time* by one of the principals to give evidence, and (2) those also present who have only subsequently volunteered or been induced to give their testimony. The former are entitled to a fee for their services, and are called *shahidin* (witnesses), and their evidence, though usually biased in favour of the principal who has summoned them, is usually preferred to that of the *hadirin* or " bystanders ". In fact the *qadi* of the Wilad Sa'id in Southern Sinai will not admit the testimony of *hadirin* at all.[1]

The Bedouin point of view is that a witness who has not

---
[1] I am not sure that any Sinai judge would allow the *hadirin* to be witnesses. They can give evidence in Moab.

been paid is not obliged to speak the truth, since he has not covenanted to do so by accepting a fee. This is the exact reverse of our conception of the duty of witnesses, but it is not illogical and it certainly accords with the Scriptural idea that the labourer is worthy of his hire.

Perhaps this may seem unfair to European eyes, but one should always remember that the business of the Bedouin *qadi* is not to do abstract justice, an idea foreign and possibly repellent to their primitive minds, but to effect as lasting a settlement as possible between two contending parties, and this he is obliged to do on the evidence supplied. Testimonies of third parties, however impartial, tend to confuse this issue. Again people ready to bear false witness are by no means unknown in the East, and may even offer their services to either side at a price. The *shahidin*, or witnesses asked at the time of the dispute to attend the court, are bound in honour to present themselves even if encamped at a two days' journey away. As we have said above, they are entitled to a fee from their caller for their attendance. But the " bystanders " are not obliged to appear in court, and the judge may have to visit them in their tents to hear their evidence.

The evidence of notorious thieves, cowards, drunkards, liars, and women who have not yet borne children [1] is altogether inadmissible, and indeed the evidence of women is everywhere regarded as inferior to that of men. In fact, one Sinai tribe, the Wilad Sa'id, will not admit it at all. To decide a case, the evidence of one good witness is sufficient, provided there be no opposition. After hearing the evidence, the *qadi* immediately gives his sentence, which must be the maximum prescribed by law (any variation of this might reflect on his impartiality). But if no witnesses are forthcoming, he orders the accused party to swear a solemn oath professing his innocence; and if this is done, he is considered as acquitted.

In the absence of any evidence at all, the Bedouins, like the old Hebrews,[2] rely upon a solemn oath to establish the truth, or rather a working approximation to it. But whereas the Jews swore by the Lord, the Bedouins prefer the oath

---

[1] Except, of course, when they are parties to the action.
[2] " If a man deliver unto his neighbour an ass, or an ox, or a sheep, or any beast to keep, and it die, or be hurt, or driven away, no man seeing it, the oath of the Lord shall be between them both whether he hath not put his hand unto his neighbour's goods; and the owner thereof shall accept it, and he shall not make restitution." Exodus, xxii, 10, 11.

to be taken on the tomb of a *weli*. Particularly is this the case among the Libyan Bedouin, who do as did their forerunners the Nasamonians.[1] Their oaths are many and varied, but from a practical point of view, the wording of these is usually only of academic interest, for " one cannot bind them to their disadvantage ". Still, except in Sinai, such is the Bedouin fear of certain saints that men, suspected of theft, will often refuse the oath and so tacitly admit their guilt.

Such was the case at my camp in Wadi Gemal in the Eastern Desert, in December, 1923. Three 'Ababda, Qarabawi, Ibrahim, and Shadli had " stolen by finding " six sovereigns in the debris of a hut, washed away by a recent spate. The indignant owner tracked their footsteps for seven or eight miles to my camp and duly identified them the same evening. The culprits of course protested their innocence, but, when asked to take an oath on the tomb of the powerful Sheikh Baghdadi, on the coast near by, they refused and so forfeited such reputation as they possessed for honesty.

In such a case, the plaintiff has the right to dictate the form of oath, to choose the members of the defendant's family who are to swear with him, and to select the sheikh's tomb on which the oath is to be taken.

But the onus of swearing may in certain cases fall upon the plaintiff, e.g. when his witnesses are successfully challenged by the defence and he cannot support his charge with evidence. Or the defendant may elect to accept liability provided that the plaintiff takes an oath that the charge is true. Sometimes this bluff succeeds, for oaths are always taken with reluctance by innocent persons. Any Bedouin has a natural horror of putting himself in the power of a dead saint, who may try to get back on him for some misdeed in the past hardly connected with the present case. Among the Awlad 'Ali, the oath of the defendant alone is sufficient to clear him in unimportant cases, but if a sheep of the value of two pounds is concerned, he must find a relation to swear with him, and in the case of a camel, perhaps four other co-swearers will be necessary to get him off.

In blood-money cases, the number of men necessary to back the defendant's word is usually fifty-four, but some

---

[1] " As for their manner of swearing and divination they lay their hands on the graves of the men reputed most just and good among them and by these men they swear." *Herodotus*, v, 172.

sections of the tribe are content with fifty. In a case where blood-money is demanded for a woman, only half a *diya* is involved (for ladies are rated half-price), so only half the number of hard swearers is necessary.

It often happens that the clan concerned cannot raise fifty-five men (counting the defendant), and in such an event, the whole must take the oath and a sufficient number must swear a second time to make up fifty-five oaths in all, thus giving the unseen powers who punish false swearers another chance, and also preventing the establishment of a precedent for allowing a lesser number to swear.

Should the defendant or anyone of his backers refuse to swear, the case falls to the ground and the verdict goes in favour of the plaintiff.[1]

There are several forms of oath of purgation in Sinai, where the plaintiff may oblige the defendant to swear by his head or by his belt. The Suwarka used to swear by the sleeve of Sheikh Jureir, a living *weli* renowned for his piety. Before the assessor, people swear : " *Wa hayat haza el-'ud wa er-rabb el-ma'bud, wa man akhdarhu wa yabsahu,*" that is, " By the life of this twig, and the worshipped God, and he who made it green, and dried it up." Some swear by the coffee pot, and others take an oath by a well.

Burckhardt gives a form of oath called *yemin el-kheit*. In this the plaintiff led the defendant away from the camp (lest the powers invoked harmed innocent people), and drew on the sand a circle with many cross lines. Both plaintiff and defendant then put their right feet inside the circle and the defendant, facing the Ka'ba, had to swear that he was innocent. Formerly a handful of corn (*shimla*) and an ant (*nimla*) were sometimes put inside the circle, and the oath thus taken was called the " oath of the corn and the ant ", *yemin esh-shimla wa en-nimla*. This latter custom seems to be now extinct in Sinai, but Jaussen records it from Moab.[2]

In Sinai, where there is little superstition and saints are not feared, a more material ordeal used to await the false swearer. The accused had to present himself before a diviner called the *mubasha'* (lit. " Bogey-man "), who kindled a fire, and produced a long iron spoon used in roasting coffee. After

---

[1] In ancient times, a man could buy himself out of taking such an oath, and avoid the consequences of perjury by paying two camels ! *Kinship*, 53.
[2] Jaussen, 188.

the *mubashaʻ* had rubbed this on his arm to clean it, he made it white-hot, and then licked it himself with his tongue to prove that the ordeal was not harmful to the innocent. The accused was then allowed to rinse out his mouth with water, whereupon the *mubashaʻ* touched his tongue three times, pressing the spoon well down upon it. If he escaped unharmed, he was held innocent, but if he suffered injury, he was obviously guilty and lost the case.

Although the *mubashaʻ* is officially discouraged, he sometimes practises privately even now. Thus in June, 1929, one of the Tabana, a tribe who cultivate the gardens in the Wadi Feiran, was accused of stealing from a store-house. He denied the charge, and in turn accused one of the Wilad Saʻid. The Tabana are not reckoned pure Arabs, so such an accusation, made by an outcast, rendered the Wilad Saʻid furious. Although the tomb of Sheikh Abu Shebib, famous in Palmer's time as an enemy to false swearers, was near at hand, yet this would not do for the Wilad Saʻid who, led by their judge, the aged Musa Nassar, constrained the wretched Tabani by threats of violence to consent to the ordeal of the red-hot spoon.

A *mubashaʻ*, a negro immigrant from Muweila in Arabia, was fetched from Tor, and the outcome was unfortunate in the extreme for the Tabani. His tongue was badly burnt, and he lost the case, having to pay the *mubashaʻ*'s fee of £5 and a lesser amount to the *qâdi*. The penalty for the theft was three and a half metres of muslin, and the building of two white cairns to commemorate the event. My tents were pitched beside those of Musa at the time, and we were awakened by the ululations of his women, rejoicing that the character of the noble Wilad Saʻid had been cleared by the conviction of the low Tabani. Later in the morning, we saw the penalty completed by the building of the white cairns. All the Arabs present believed implicitly in the fairness and genuineness of the test. It is remarkable that in all three cases witnessed by Europeans, Kennett,[1] Jarvis, and Bramly, the accused escaped with slight redness of the tongue and were considered innocent. Jarvis[2] says of the North Sinai tribes that the *mubashaʻ*'s fee is £10 ; and that if the accused person is burnt, he has to pay fourfold the usual penalty. Bramly writes :—

[1] Kennett, 112.   [2] *Yesterday and To-day in Sinai*, 45.

"About 1906, two lads fired by mistake on a party approaching Qusaima, thinking them raiders. A man was killed, and since both boys had fired at once, the *mubasha'* was called in to decide which was guilty. The weaker lad paid £5 to the other to undergo the ordeal, and he stood the test successfully. So the weakling's people had to pay the *diya*—a good deal mitigated by the circumstances."

The Arabs say that the guilty man's mouth becomes dry with fear, so that he is burnt at once; while the mouth of the innocent, who *knows* he will not be burnt, retains its usual saliva. Perfect faith is therefore necessary to undergo the ordeal successfully. To a religious Egyptian onlooker, the *mubasha'*'s powers appeared supernatural and derived from God.

Unrecognized by Government, there is a *mubasha'* in North Sinai, Sheikh 'Amir 'Ayyad, who has inherited his position from his father 'Ayyad and his uncle (father's brother) 'Aweimir. Sometimes the Haweitat of Egypt resort to him for the solution of a problem, but the Ma'aza, though relatively recent immigrants from Arabia, do not. Elsewhere in Egypt, the custom is unknown.

In Arabia, the 'Anaza and the tribes of Midian have *mubasha'*, and Thomas has recorded the practice among the tribes of the far south-eastern corner of the Arabian peninsula.[1]

Recourse is not always had to the red-hot spoon. Besides, the method cited by Na'um Bey,[2] bread is sometimes used. Not long ago, a stray suckling camel was found and claimed by two parties; one of the Sawalha and the old judge, Musa Nassar. The *mubasha'* preferred a piece of bread "with something written on it", and the claimant from the Sawalha was bidden to swallow it first. He declined, whereupon the bold Musa essayed the ordeal, and "the camel is in our family now!" as his son informed me.

Woundings are assessed by a *qassas*, a judge who specializes in the assessment of injuries resulting from violence. Like the other judges, his office is hereditary. After a quarrel in which both parties have received damage, they usually agree to present themselves before a *qassas* to strike a balance sheet, as it were, of the situation. The assessor after obtaining the usual guarantee, that the litigants will pay his fee and whatever fine he may inflict upon them, proceeds to examine the

---

[1] *Arabia Felix*, 86. [2] See p. 162.

LEGAL PROCEDURE

wounds. He then pronounces judgment in accordance with a fixed scale, which, in Sinai, runs something like this :—

(1) For the loss of both eyes, both hands, or both legs, the penalty to be paid is the full *diya* or blood-money for a man, that is forty camels, or about £200 in cash at present rates. For one eye, half that rate.[1] (Among the 'Ababda, only a quarter blood-money is paid for a lost eye). In the case where total blindness results from an injury, a slave or the equivalent (£10 in cash) is further awarded " to lead the blind man about ".

(2) Half a *diya* (i.e. £100) is paid for the loss of an arm or hand, and three-eighths (£75) for that of a leg. For the loss of a foot, compensation is given at the rate of a quarter of the full blood-money. Kennett[2] says £10 in cash is also awarded, the value of a slave, who in former days was provided to help the injured man about, and so compensate for the loss of his limb. But my information is that the slave was only awarded to the blind. In Moab half the blood-money is paid, without the sum in cash.[3]

(3) In the case of broken bones, a year is usually allowed to elapse between the date of the blow and the assessment of damages. The damage is paid for in camels.

(4) Wounds on the face. An actual wound on the face is not usually looked upon so seriously as a metaphorical one,[4] but it is always felt that a permanent scar inflicted by someone else makes the unfortunate victim a laughing-stock. Consequently these wounds are assessed more heavily than others. They proceed as follows. The assessor lays a piece of transparent gauze over the plaintiff's face. He then steps a pace backwards from the victim, and calls " *Tulba !* " (a full-grown camel). If he can still see the scar through the gauze he takes another step backward, calling " *Raba' !* " (the name of the second age of camel). If by this time the assessor can no longer see the wound, he orders the aggressor to pay the to victim one full-grown camel and one of the age *raba'*. If he can still see the scar, he continues stepping backward enumerating with each step one of the six age-grades of the camels [5]

---

[1] Jarvis (p. 41) gives £120 for an eye.
[2] Kennett, 117.
[3] Jaussen, 186.
[4] But see Jaussen, p. 40, where at Kerak, 200 *mejidies*, a negress, a negro, a horse, and 200 sheep were awarded (and 30 *mejidies* actually paid) for a broken tooth.
[5] *Tulba, raba', jida', hiqq, marbut, mafrud*, i.e. in inverse order to the list on p. 108.

until the scar becomes invisible. The number of camels enumerated according to these classes will then be paid as damages, the assessor himself receiving as his fee one-tenth of the award as usual.

(5) Wounds *not* on face. Serious flesh wounds which have been sewn up with needle and thread, are assessed by counting the number of stitches, and awarding one camel for each stitch, again according to the same age-grades. Provided that no ligaments have been torn, or bones broken (injuries which come under the second heading of this chapter), the damages awarded are usually priced at from £2 to £10 in money. When a wound has healed by itself without stitches, and is unaccompanied by broken bones, torn muscles, or other complications, the assessor lays his hand across the scar, and measures off the wound by the top-joint of his thumb, each breadth of this representing a camel. If the wound be on the fore-arm, and, besides other damage to the arm, a finger be paralysed, then the full damages for the wound on the arm and its stitches is awarded, but only half the value of the finger is added.

In any of the above cases, if the victim is rendered unconscious by the blow, and has to be revived with water, a further camel must be added to whatever compensation is awarded. But when it is only a flesh wound, sums varying from £2 to £10 in money will be awarded.

In Sinai, according to the judge of the Wilad Sa'id, the fore-finger and thumb are assessed at five camels, the second finger four, the third finger three and the little finger at two camels.[1] The fee of the *qassas* is generally one-tenth of the damages awarded.

Should someone fire a gun at another without hitting him, he will be condemned by the " elders " to lose his gun to the plaintiff and pay a fine, or alternatively to take an oath that he did not aim at that particular man.

For a blow that causes no injury, a fine of one to two hundred piastres is awarded. But should the striker use the palm of his hand, or a small stick, or a pipe, or a coffee pot, a heavier fine will be imposed, since the plaintiff is considered dishonoured by such blows. Formerly the fine for a blow

[1] Kennett, p. 119, gives for North Sinai five camels for the fore-finger and thumb *of the right hand*, and a camel for any other finger. Dumreicher, p. 108, gives a case where a Bishari was sentenced to pay four pounds for each of three fingers and eight pounds for a thumb.

from the palm of the hand was a weaned camel-calf (*mafrud*) but in most cases, an Arab would refuse to accept the judgment of an assessor in such an affair, and summon the culprit before the special judge who tries affairs of honour.

The consolidation of a Bedouin tribe is greatly strengthened by the institution of the guardian or *wasy*. When an Arab father is about to die, he usually leaves his children to the care of his brother, or other near male relative without any formality. But he can, however, even during his lifetime, transfer them by taking an oath before witnesses to the charge of anyone he pleases, even to someone outside the tribe, though this latter case must be most exceptional. The guardian thus appointed is called *wasy*, and he possesses the authority of a father over them till his death. He is bound to protect them against all oppression, and a Bedouin woman, ill-treated by her husband, calls on her *wasy* to help her, if she possesses no male relation.

Burckhardt says of an Arab wishing to appoint a *wasy*.

> "He should present himself, leading a she-camel, before his friend; then he ties one of the hanging corners of the *keffie* or kerchief of his friend into a knot, and leading the camel over to him, says, 'I constitute you WASY for my children, and your children for my children, and your grandchildren for my grandchildren.' If the friend accepts the camel (and it is seldom refused), he and his whole family become the hereditary protection of the other's descendants. . . . Almost every Arab has his *wasy* in some other family, and is at the same time *wasy* to a third; even the greatest sheikh is not without his guardian."[1]

The tying of the knot on the end of the *wasy's* kerchief is a symbolic sign of the engagement that the witnesses are called on to prove. Among the Ma'aza, the *fatha* is repeated when the knot is tied in the *kefiya*, and no gift is necessary from the client to the *wasy*. In the Hijaz the recipient gets a fragment of the fringe of the shawl to keep as his token of the transaction.[2]

According to Jaussen, in extremity, the father may select an absentee as a guardian. The witnesses inform the guardian of his having been chosen, and it becomes a point of honour for him to behave as if he had been formally appointed as laid down above.[3]

---

[1] *Notes*, 130. The camel should be of the class *ruba'iya*.
[2] *Religion of the Semites*, 335.   [3] Jaussen, 198.

On a Sinai Bedouin's death, his property is assessed by his brother or *wasy*, and one-eighth is assigned to his daughters. Often the sheikh or some elder has to be called in to see that these latter get their rights. The remaining seven-eighths is divided equally among the sons.

If the dying man makes a death-bed present of his riding-camel or his sword to his eldest son, his wish will be respected, but it is thought bad form on the eldest son's part to take any such gift without some allowance being made for it when the estate comes to be divided. Nowadays an 'Abadi father, if plagued by having to pay for the too frequent misdeeds of an unruly son, can disinherit him by a formal declaration in writing to that effect before the Omda (sheikh of the tribe) or before a magistrate.

The Sinai Bedouin have a curious custom by which a creditor is allowed to steal camels from a recalcitrant debtor. But he must first declare openly before witnesses on four separate and consecutive occasions that so-and-so owes him so much and refuses to pay. To ensure publicity these declarations must be made by daylight, except during Ramadan, when they can only be made by night. He should summon five witnesses and call them over twice, saying to each in turn ; you are the first *shahid*, you are the second *shahid*, you are the third *shahid*, etc., etc. Then he is absolved from the penalties for taing camels without leave (see below) and may confiscate his debtor's camels, and deposit them with a third party till the debt is paid. The camels thus confiscated are known as *withaqa*. If the debtor catches the creditor with the *withaqa* before he reaches the third party's tents, a fight usually takes place. Riding camels may be taken as *withaqa* only when there are no other camels available.

A snake-bitten man, a thirsty man, or one fleeing from danger may ride away without penalty on any camel he finds but otherwise if a man unfastens another's camels without reason, the case is tried by nine assessors *ziyud* (sing. *ziyadi*) and the maximum penalties amount to :—

(1) 50 mejidies for kneeling down to it (a mejidy = about P.T. 14)
(2) 50 mejidies for putting his hand over the camel
(3) 50 mejidies for unfastening it
(4) 1 mejidy for every step the camel takes
(5) 1 mejidy for every step he takes after it

LEGAL PROCEDURE

(6) 10 mejidies for every time he makes it turn
(7) 10 mejidies for every times he makes it kneel
(8) 10 mejidies for every time he makes it get up,
and all subsequent fastenings and unfastenings like the first.

His *kafil* is responsible that these fines are paid.

(In a similar way, he who steals from a storehouse pays for each stride within it.)

It is permissible in urgent cases, to take another man's goat or sheep without leave to entertain a guest, but for no other reason. The penalty otherwise is very severe. He may have to pay, *Arba'in wa el-qidr wa es-sekkin* that is "forty (goats) and the pot and the knife" which he used to kill and cook the animal with. One may note that the rigid Mosaic code only condemned the thief to pay "four sheep for a sheep" (Exod. xxii, 2).

Anything cast up, on the western shore of Sinai, north of Tor, ought to be divided equally between the Sawalha and the 'Aleiqat, as it formerly was between the Hamada and Beni Wasil. And, to avoid conflict in the division of these windfalls, those Arabs who carried off the spoil were supposed to share out equally with any late-comers they met, so long as the wreck was still in sight. I suspect that the rigid carrying out of this enactment, must have given rise to innumerable complicated lawsuits, dear to the litigious hearts of the Sinai Arabs.

But the power of the Government is nowadays exerted to spoil sport in this matter, and to assert the rights of the shipowner, hitherto ignored entirely.

In 1911, a dhow bound from Suez to Tor, with a cargo of groceries for the Monastery of St. Catherine, went ashore on the reef at Ras Abu Rudeis. Many of the two tribes went down to the beach, and among them the youthful Sabah, son of the Sheikh of the 'Aleiqat was the first to board the wreck. Pushing through the throng, he waded through the surf to the stranded vessel, and at once discovered that she was not likely to get off. So, pointing out his companions to the affrighted skipper, Sabah harangued him somewhat as follows ; " There," said he, " are the fellows who have come to cut your throats. But fear nothing ! I am here to protect you, and if you will put yourselves in my hands as the representative of government, no harm will come to you ! "

When the trembling mariner inquired what he should further do to be saved, Sabah recommended him warmly to change clothes with himself. "For then," he said, "the Bedouins will take you, if not for me, at any rate, for one of the clan!" The *reis* was soon out of his fashionable Suez garments, and into the dirty wet rags of the Bedouin, but before Sabah could carry out any other scheme of self-aggrandizement, his jealous associates arrived on board, who without more ado, carried everything that could be carried on shore. All this was then shared out; indeed Sabah declared later that the captain of his own free will opened the boxes and gave the goods away. Without inquiring too closely into Sabah's idea of free will, we may believe there was little left on the beach when they had done, except some wine and cognac, which to them had no appeal.

The captain and crew then walked fifty miles to Tor, without any food or water beyond what they took with them, and laid an information about the business.

On the police turning up, which they did in time to catch one old ruffian struggling to reload two great sacks of grain which had fallen from his camel, they sternly interrogated Sabah as to the meaning of this scandalous affair. "What could I do?" replied that astute personage, "you are Bedouins yourselves, and know how impossible it is to do anything with Arabs at a wreck! Yet I did what I could; here is a list of all who were there, and how much each got away with!" In this list his own name did not appear, and indeed, as he explained to me privately, "I was careful to take only a few tins of fruit, which were soon out of the way." Some of the elder men were sentenced to six weeks imprisonment, a light penalty for Bedouin, who have no objection to regular meals with nothing to do. These bore Sabah no grudge, and his reputation began to spread as a coming man and a worthy son of Mudakhil.

The Ma'aza of Egypt hold it wrong to take anything from a wreck, or even from abandoned properties such as mine-buildings. Such trove is called *maksar* and if you take it, your camel will fall ill, and you will never prosper. So says one of their sheikhs, Salem Faraj, but most of the other Ma'aza I have met would be quite prepared to accept the *maksar*, and any risk that might be attached to it. Yet in south Sinai, a wooden hut, abandoned in 1893 by the German naturalist

AN OLD MA'AZA

Kaiser, was still unplundered in 1921, and the wooden buildings at the Samra Mine, deserted in 1904, were still standing in 1929. This, in a cold country (at least in winter), with a notorious scarcity of fuel, seems sufficiently remarkable, and speaks well for the honesty of the Muzeina, who were the tribe concerned.

Once, riding along the unfrequented sea-side of Jebel Zeit, we found the beach littered with cocoa-nuts jettisoned from some tramp. The young 'Ababda of the party began to crack and eat them, but our old guide 'Atalla refused. " If I were to eat it, I might not like it, and I should be sorry I had eaten it. Or else I might like it, and wish for more. And as I couldn't get more, I should be sorry I had eaten it ! "

The appeal to his spirit of adventure having failed, I fell back on his politeness. " Sheikh 'Atalla, if I eat some, will you eat some ? " The old man fell and nibbled.

PART IV

Chapter XV
ARABS OF SINAI AND THE EASTERN DESERT

"*And God was with the lad and he grew ; and he dwelt in the wilderness, and became an archer. And he dwelt in the wilderness of Paran ; and his mother took him a wife out of the land of Egypt.*—Genesis, xxi, 20, 21.

'Ayaida—Badara—Haweitat—Laheiwat—Masa'id—Arabs of Qattia—Suwarka—Terabin—Tiyaha—Towara—The Jebeliya or Serfs of the Monastery—The Ma'aza of Egypt—Hiteim.

The Arabs of North Sinai, with the exception of the Haweitat, are nearly all nominal descendants of Wa'il, the ancestor of the Beni 'Atiya of Arabia and the Ma'aza of Egypt.

Historically they are fairly recent immigrants from El-Hijaz, as slender in build and as hooknosed as their Arabian cousins. The Haweitat are even more recent immigrants than the rest, and seem swarthier, this perhaps is due to a negro admixture. In the palm-groves of the north, among the sedentary Arabs of Qatia are found a number of *fellahin* from Egypt and Syria and perhaps also some relics of an earlier population.

In the mountains of the south, the 'Aleiqat and the Sawalha are Arab tribes returned from Egypt not long after the Conquest, while the Muzeina are a noble tribe from El-Hijaz. Not uncommonly in the south one sees coffin-shaped heads and blunter features recalling some pre-Arab race of the past. They are all conservative to a degree, incurably greedy, incurably generous, incurably romantic, and incurably lazy. Their contempt for the accumulation of worldly possessions and their chivalry are their best points, their love of litigation their most tiresome.

Though the plains whence the Tiyaha sallied "sixty years since" to raid Tadmor have now become the happy hunting ground of the Levantine motorist, though the present-day governor can find nothing larger than locusts to wage war upon, though the monks of St. Catherine are fast turning the Monastery into a hotel, vanity and pride of race have kept romance alive in minds where hunger and poverty have never allowed religion to find a footing. When I was young times were certainly more exciting, each of the older sheikhs had " killed his man ", and 'Awda Abu Tai was, even before the War, a living inspiration to the younger men. Now Sinai is in the condition of the Highlands a generation after Prince Charles's rebellion; a situation that demands an Arabian Walter Scott.

'Ayaida.—The 'Ayaida of Sinai are a small tribe of perhaps 300 souls inhabiting a large area due east of Ismailia, while a larger portion of the tribe lives west of the Suez Canal in Sharqiya Province. Burckhardt[1] says that 200 years ago they formed a tribe of 600 horsemen, but in his time (1816) they were, as they are to-day, a poor tribe of about a hundred tents, more or less allied to the Haweitat, sometimes drifting south after rain into the northern Galala mountains, but found usually on the low ground north of the Cairo–Suez road.

During February, 1915, the milch camels of their Sinai section wandered over some rich grazing just east of the Suez Canal battle-field, whence on one occasion I rounded them all up with the help of three or four troopers of the Bikanir Camel Corps, and brought them into the Serapeum bridge-head post, in case the Governor of Sinai wanted to put pressure on the tribe. But he did not, and they were all let go again to the disgust of the Indians who thought they had captured " wild camels ", *jungly oont*. The 'Ayaida boys with the herd had been three weeks without water feeding on camel-milk alone. Next year the herd was captured again, this time by some Australians, who complacently boasted the capture of " a hundred Turkish baggage camels ".

Their sub-divisions are :—

'Ayaida	} Under Musallam ibn Saba, the Chief Sheikh
Salatna	
Fawa'ida	Sheikh Selim Abu Fuda
Jerab'a	Sheikh 'Aid Abu Rish
Qawa'ila	Sheikh 'Aweimer ibn 'Ayad ('Amir 'Ayyad, the *mubasha'*, comes from this section).

Their chief wells are Abul 'Oruq, Maqeibra, and Murra.

At some former period, they owned gardens in southern Sinai in Wadi Feiran and Wadi Solaf.

[1] *Notes*, 224.

Badara.—A small tribe of about twenty tents living in Jebel 'Ejma. Na'um Bey considers this mountain to be called 'Ejma because they were 'Ajam, that is non-Arab. Their omda is Salam Hamdan Abu Arbid.

In Na'um Bey's day they were affiliated to the Laheiwat, but have now returned to the Tiyaha, their former protectors.

Haweitat.—Tribal fortunes rise and sink like those of families, the coalitions of the present seem pushful upstarts, while the great tribes of the past are fading into genteel obscurity.

The modern Haweitat are an aggressive race, continually increasing at the expense of their neighbours. According to the philosophy of Suleiman Ibn Jad, one of their most important sheikhs, the human race was divided at the beginning into three classes ; the tent-makers, the agriculturists, and the Haweitat.[1] No doubt in his opinion the first two classes were created exclusively for the support of the third.

Not content with their triumph over the Beni 'Uqba,[2] the Haweitat have been continually pushing westwards for more than a century, and now find themselves in possession of a considerable area in North Sinai. In Egypt, they have occupied the country south of the Cairo–Suez road as far as the northern Galala hills. Others have settled in the provinces of Sharqiya and Qaliubiya and are now indistinguishable from the *fellahin.* These Egyptian Haweitat numbered in Burckhardt's time about 600 tents. They all recognize as their sheikh the family of Isma'il Bey Shedid of the Ghanamiyin living near Bilbeis.

The true Haweitat live east of the Jordan, where rove the famous raiding clans of Ibn Ghazi and Abu Tai. 'Awda, the late *'aqid* of the latter used to boast of having raided as far north as Aleppo and as far south as Mecca, and is well-known to readers of *Revolt in the Desert.* Their tribal ancestor is Haweit ibn Ham, and from one of his descendants called 'Alayan all the Haweitat in Midian are descended.

The Haweitat of Egypt and Sinai are offshoots from these 'Alayan Haweitat. I again quote Sir Richard Burton :—

> " According to their own oral genealogists, their first forefather was a lad called 'Alayan, who, travelling in company with certain Shurafa (' descendants of the Apostle '), and *ergo* held by his

[1] Jaussen, 109.   [2] See p. 38.

descendants to have been also a Sherif, fell sick on the way. At El 'Akabah he was taken in charge by 'Atiyyah, Shaykh of the then powerful Ma'azah tribe, who owned the land upon which the fort stands. A 'clerk' able to read and write, he served his adopted father by superintending the accounts of stores and provisions supplied to the Hajj. The Arabs, who before that time embezzled at discretion, called him El-Huwayti ('the Man of the Little Wall') because his learning was 'a fence against his frauds'. He was sent for by his Egyptian friends; these, however, were satisfied by a false report of his death; he married his benefactor's daughter; he became Shaykh after the demise of his father-in-law; he drove the Ma'azah from El-'Akabah, and he left four sons, the progenitors and *eponymi* of the Midianite Huwaytat." [1]

The pedigree is :—

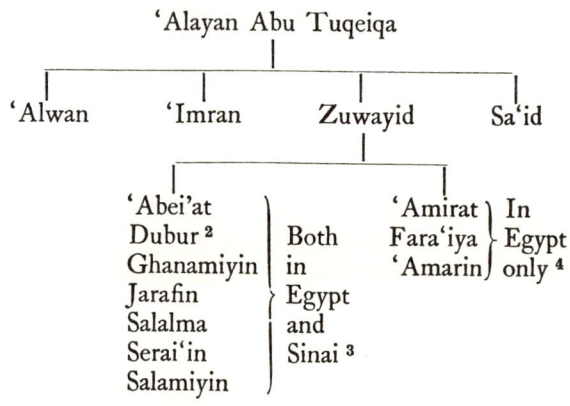

```
                    'Alayan Abu Tuqeiqa
        ┌──────────────┼──────────────┬──────────┐
      'Alwan        'Imran         Zuwayid      Sa'id
                       │              │
                  'Abei'at        'Amirat ⎫  In
                  Dubur [2]       Fara'iya⎬ Egypt
                  Ghanamiyin ⎫    'Amarin ⎭ only [4]
                  Jarafin    ⎬ Both in
                  Salalma    ⎬ Egypt and
                  Serai'in   ⎬ Sinai [3]
                  Salamiyin  ⎭
```

The Haweitat of North Sinai (255 souls) used to be reported savage and treacherous, and furnished some of the murderers of Professor Palmer in 1882. They wander widely towards Egypt and Syria, but their recognized headquarters are in the Jebel Raha, south-east and south of Suez. They claim the rights of watering at Gharandel and Mab'uq (as do also the 'Aleiqat), also Hajiya, El-Jidi, and Maqeira. Their sanctuaries (burying grounds) are El-Jidi, Mab'uq, Maqeibra, and El-Elu.

[1] *The Land of Midian*, 162–3.

[2] The Dubur were once an independent tribe. Scattered sections are found with the Palestine Tiyaha and Laheiwat.

[3] According to Sir R. F. Burton, some of the same sectional names occur among the Haweitat of Midian.

      'Amirat   occupy the Shifa
      Jarafin   in the Jebel Sharr
      Ghanamiyin south of the Sharr
      Salalma   near Jebel el-Jimm, the needle of Jebel Dibbagh.

[4] Other Egyptian sections are Risha, Mawadi, and Kilalba.

ARABS OF SINAI

Before and during the War their chief was Sa'ad Abu Nar, who was detained in Suez until he had effected the arrest of a famous smuggler and spy, Shablaq, of his tribe, who had been acting as a Turkish agent. During the War, the Turks

ARAB TRIBES OF SINAI

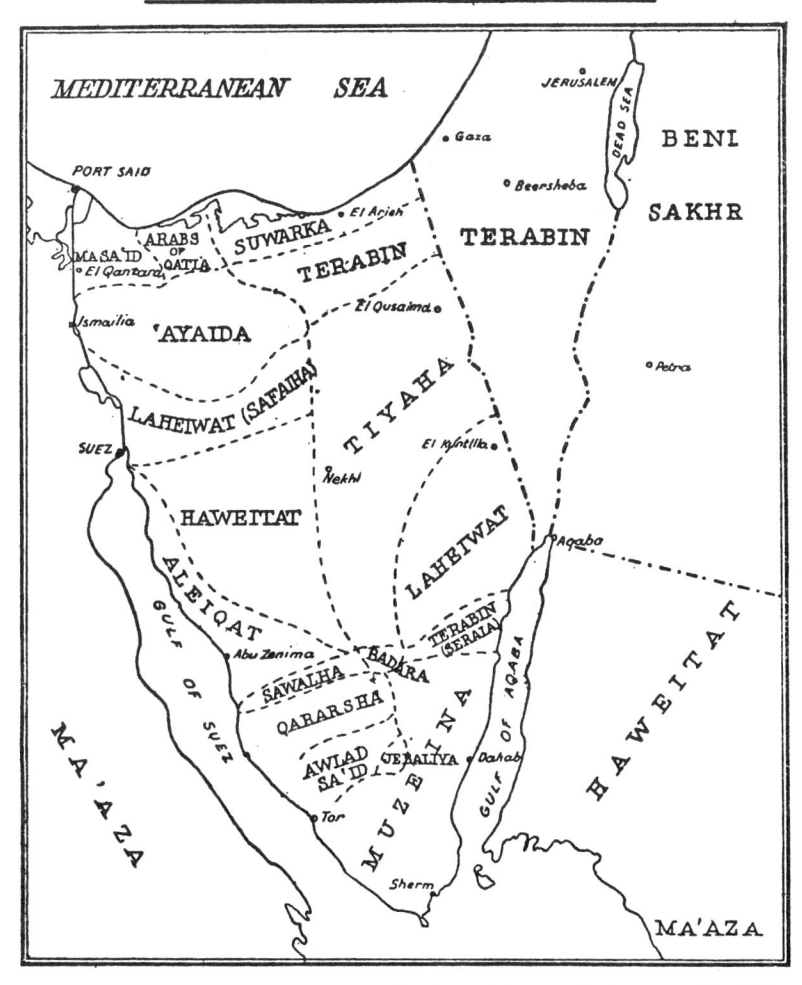

appointed 'Aid esh-Shilh, of the Ghanamiyin as Sheikh, but on their evacuation of Sinai, Sa'ad Abu Nar resumed his office.

Previous to the War there were four or five families of 'Alayan Haweitat from Midian settled in South Sinai. During and after the War, their numbers have been considerably increased by families of Fahamin and Qara'n, who have come across the gulf of 'Aqaba to escape famine there.

This has produced a lot of friction between them and the Towara, more especially as they were accused of bringing in a disease which killed many camels and goats in 1928. The rightful sheikh of these 'Alayan Haweitat was Shadli 'Alayan, but his position was usurped more than twenty years ago by Ahmed Abu Tuqeiqa. These Haweitat and Billi have recently been in revolt against Ibn Sa'ud, and were heavily defeated by him in July, 1932, near Jebel Sharr, when the heads of both the Abu Tuqeiqa and Ibn Rifada families were killed.

The children of the second son 'Imran have been a vigorous independent tribe on the eastern shores of the Gulf of 'Aqaba for over a century, and an annual exchange of raids between them and the Sinai Laheiwat was only put a stop to in 1925, when the Transjordanian gendarmerie occupied 'Aqaba.

Burckhardt wrote of these 'Imran :

> " At the time when Muhammad 'Ali, Pasha of Egypt, had reduced all other Bedouins on the Egyptian hadj road to complete subjection, the Omran still proved obstinate. In the year 1814 they attacked and plundered a detachment of Turkish cavalry near Akaba, and in 1815 they pillaged the whole advance corps of the Syrian pilgrim caravan from Medina to Damascus." [1]

In 1811, the Egyptian Haweitat under Sheikh Abu Shedid of the Ghanamiyin assisted Muhammad 'Ali's army against the Wahabis in Arabia, while seventy-two years later, one of his descendants organized for Sir Charles Warren the expedition which searched for Professor Palmer's murderers in Northern Sinai. Isma'il Bey Shedid is the present sheikh. Some of the Jarafin have settled in the Nile Valley, and become cultivators near Qaliub.

Laheiwat.—The Laheiwat are a section, which has broken away from the Masa'id division of the Beni 'Atiya, and now forms a tribe of its own, famous for its enterprise and ferocity. Of their past, they say that the Masa'id and Beni 'Uqba departed together from Nejd and came to Wadi el-'Araba. At that time the Masa'id had a clan of Muteir living

[1] *Notes*, 221–2.

PLATE XXV

YOUNG ARAB OF THE TOWARA

[face p. 248

among them, who had to pay tribute to them. The Muteir considered this oppressive, and appealed to the Beni 'Uqba to help them. This led up to a violent quarrel about a beautiful daughter of the sheikh of the Muteir, whom the Masa'id captured from the Beni 'Uqba at a battle in Wadi el-'Araba. The sheikh of the Masa'id wished to marry this beautiful Muteiriya, but his mother abandoned his tent, saying she could not live under the same roof as a woman of Hiteim, whereupon the sheikh changed his mind and drove the captive and her people away. In the Wadi el-'Araba, there are still shown the graves of those who fell in the " battle of the Muteiriya ".

After the battle, the Masa'id departed to the neighbourhood of Gaza, and later separated into three division, one of whom, the Awlad Suleiman, went to Egypt, leaving a section at Qatia still called Masa'id, another lot of Awlad Suleiman to the Hauran, while from the third are descended the Laheiwat.

The main body of the tribe ranges from Nekhl down to 'Aqaba ; in fact the Khaleifa live beyond the frontier in Wadi el-'Araba. The ruling section, the Najmat, say that Najm ibn Salama ibn Ghanim was the first to receive payment from the Egyptian Government for the protection of the pilgrim route from Nekhl down to 'Aqaba itself. But the Haweitat of 'Aqaba used to claim to take over the Mahmal at Ras en-Naqb, saying that they had acquired that right from the Terabin who inhabited 'Aqaba before them.

In 1856, the Laheiwat assisted the Terabin in their war with the Suwarka when the latter were defeated and chased into El-'Arish. The Laheiwat claim the wells of Kontilla, Heisi, Themed, Ghadian (in Wadi el-'Araba), and in the west 'Ain Sudr and Jifjaffa.

Continual raids also used to take place between the Laheiwat and the Dhullam (Tiyaha living in Southern Palestine), and the Ma'aza and the 'Imran Haweitat from Transjordania.

Burckhardt says of their feuds with the latter :

" The tribes of Omran and Heywat act upon a rule, which forms an exception to the general Bedouin system of blood-revenge remaining within the ' khomse '. When one of their people is killed by an unknown tribe, they think themselves justified in retaliating upon any individual of that tribe, either innocent or guilty ; and if the affair be compromised, the whole tribe contribute to make up the dye, or fine, in proportion to the respective property of each tent. For this reason, the Arabs say, that ' The Omran and Heywat strike sideways '—a practice which is much dreaded by their neighbours."

Their ancestor was Sa'ad Sadiq el Wa'd. From his three sons, Shufan, Hamad and Suweilim, the tribe descends:

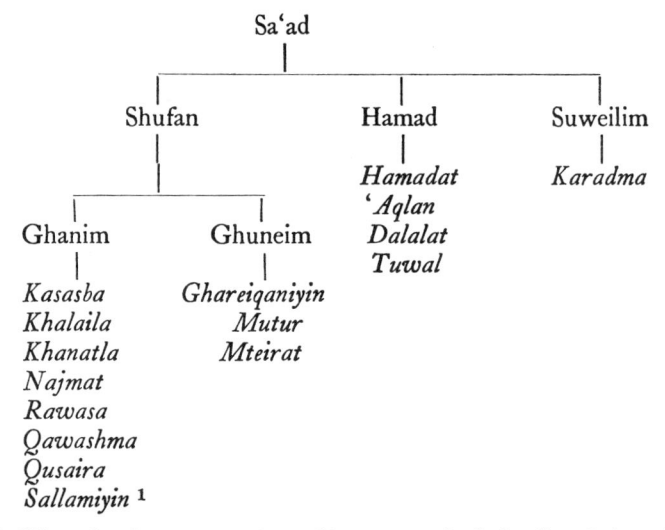

```
                        Sa'ad
          |               |              |
        Shufan          Hamad         Suweilim
          |               |              |
     |         |       Hamadat        Karadma
   Ghanim   Ghuneim     'Aqlan
     |        |         Dalalat
  Kasasba  Ghareiqaniyin Tuwal
  Khalaila   Mutur
  Khanatla   Mteirat
  Najmat
  Rawasa
  Qawashma
  Qusaira
  Sallamiyin [1]
```

Affiliated clans are the Khawatra (originally Muzeina) and Khaleifa.

The ruling sheikhs come from the Najmat section, and the present chief sheikh is 'Ali, son of 'Alayan el-Qusair.

Another clan of the Laheiwat, the Safeiha, are descended from Safeih, cousin to Sa'ad Sadiq el-Wa'd, and live to the west of the Tiyaha in the 'Ain Sudr–Bir Mab'uq district. Muteir, the then sheikh of the Safeiha, was the man who decoyed Professor Palmer to his fate in 1822. Palmer wished to distribute gold to the Bedouin to keep them quiet during the English attack on Egypt, so Muteir by representing himself as sheikh of all the Laheiwat obtained considerable influence over the Professor, and arranged for his being kidnapped and held to ransom by a gang of brigands Dubur (Haweitat) and Terabin near 'Ain Abu Jarad. But when the ambush came off and Professor Palmer's party were captured, Muteir's son succeeded in escaping with all the money (£3,000 in gold) which Palmer had with him.

[1] All the eleven sections descended from Shufan are referred to generally as the Shuwafin.

Muteir, content with the plunder, refused to part with any of it to the brigands, whom he disclaimed entirely. Furious at being double-crossed, they murdered the Professor and his party by driving them over a precipice, hoping thereby to get Muteir into really good trouble with the future Government, whatever that might be. They succeeded so far that Muteir died in prison awaiting trial, while several of the others were hanged for the murder.

Masa'id.—When the original Masa'id split up ; the Laheiwat being left in Sinai and the Awlad Suleiman going on into Egypt, a small section were left behind who retained the original name of the tribe. They live due east of Qantara and number about one hundred souls under Sheikh 'Awda 'Atiya.

During the war, most of these Masa'id were as usual in Northern Sinai, with a few outlying families in the Egyptian province of Sharqiya. But the market at Salhiya in Egypt was attended every week by tribesmen from Sinai, who used to run the gauntlet of our lines on the Canal to buy coffee and sugar. Spying was not their object ; they would come down in the dark and float across the Canal on a blown-out waterskin. They used to cross the railway line when the sentry's back was towards them at the far end of his beat, and then disappear into the friendly reeds of Lake Menzala till daybreak. This caused a lot of annoyance, and Jennings Bramly was finally ordered to concentrate the whole tribe at Salhiya.

Qatawiya (Arabs of Qatia).—In and round the rich palmgroves of Qatia are ten small tribes of whom only two seem to be pure Arab, though the Hiteim certainly are of Arabian origin. Of the rest, a letter from an Egyptian officer says :

" Their way of talking is not that of true Bedouin, and most of them wear turbans like the *fellahin*. Very few of them have any knowledge of Bedouin Law. They cook their bread on iron, and not on a *qurs* as Arabs do, and use spices with their food after the Egyptian way. Many of them make formal contracts of marriage, and do not give the *qassala*. The women wear the jewels of the dead, and cover them with calico as the Egyptians do. The *burqu'* of their women is yellow, but twenty years ago it was black."

Some of them, like the Sa'adiyin, are believed to be the

descendants of *fellahin*, who came to Qatia as transport drivers with Muhammad 'Ali's Syrian expedition. Others may be a residue of the ancient population, since the Akharsa and the Bayadiyin, like the Suwarka, pay an annual ceremonial visit to the sea, which can hardly be a Bedouin custom.

(1) *Akharsa*, 250 souls under Sheikhs Ibrahim 'Atiya and Abd el-Aal Muhammad.

(2) *'Alawin*, a branch of the Haweitat from Midian.

(3) *'Aqeila*, Sheikh Atwan Sa'dun.

(4) *Awlad 'Ali*, Sheikh 'Omar Abi el-Hayat.

(5) *Bayadiyin*, 700 people, Sheikh Ibrahim Suleiman Marzuq. The present Governor of Sinai says of them[1] "There is one tribe in Sinai—the Bayadin—who are all lusty specimens of six feet or more, with huge patriarchal beards. Their origin is unknown, but their insistence on their pure Arab blood, and the application of Arab laws and ordinances to the tribe is so marked, that one feels they protest too much." Bramly says: "They are said to have come from Arabia, but not to be Bedouin."

(6) *Billi el-Barada*, 120 people under Sheikh Jeddawi Shelabi live in the vicinity of Maqeibra. They are probably an offshoot of the Arabian Billi and will not intermarry with the other Qatia tribes. Their women wear a red *burqu'*.

(7) *Dawaghra*, 300 people, Sheikhs 'Aid Suweilim and Salem Musabbah. They are Muteir, that is Hiteim in origin and used to pay tribute to the neighbouring Bedouin, but this has been stopped by Government. They cultivate the Zuqba district. Kennett (pp. 56–57) gives details of a quarrel between them and the Bayadiyin.

(8) *Sa'adiyin*, Sheikh Maqbul Nasr. These are said to have been Egyptian *fellahin*. Their women wear a curious yellow *burqu*.

(9) *Sam'ana*, 150 people under Sheikhs Muhammad Khudeir and Husein Shabana. They are said to have come from Syria and to be of Jewish origin.

(10) *Qatawiya*, a residue who have no other name than that of the place; a sure sign they are not of Bedouin origin. They live under Sheikh Sa'id Abu Batihan in the palm-groves at Qatia.

Of these tribes, the Akharsa, 'Aqeila, Awlad 'Ali, Bayadiyin and Sam'ana are also found in Sharqiya.

[1] Jarvis, 17.

ARABS OF SINAI

Suwarka.—The Suwarka, the most numerous tribe in Sinai, perhaps 4,000 strong, inhabit the coast of Sinai from Bir el-'Abd eastwards to the frontier, while their affiliated tribe Rumeilat live in the neighbourhood of Rafa.

The Suwarka, like the Luzd,[1] claim as their progenitor Okasha, one of the Prophet's companions, and relate that Nuseir and Mansur, two of his descendants, once came as guests to some Billi in Wadi Lif. Nuseir was already married, but his brother Mansur espoused one of the Billi girls, whose hair was streaked with grey. Nuseir's descendants are the 'Aradat, the ruling section, sometimes called " Ghoz el-'Arab " on account of their unusual cleanliness in food and dress, as compared to the rest of the tribe ; Mansur's children have multiplied into twelve sections : Duheimat (including Jerarat), Falafila, Khanasra, Mahafiz, Manaya, Maqata, Nimeilat, Rifai'a, Ruwashda, Waqaqda, Ziyud[2] and Zuweidiyin. The Ziyud section supplies the judges who decide camel-disputes throughout Sinai. These twelve sections are sometimes nicknamed " Awlad eth-Tharwa " or " children of the grey-haired woman," from their ancestress' peculiar hair.

The Jerarat are famous for their piety. " They own two saints, the living Abu Jureir by whose sleeve the Arabs take oaths, and the dead Abu Jureir who is buried in the town of El-'Arish."[3]

The ruling sheikh is Sheikh Sallam 'Arada of the 'Aradat. Their allies, the Rumeilat, are divided into 'Ajalin, 'Awabda, Busum, Sanana and Shartiyin and their present sheikh is Suleiman Ma'ayuf of the Busum, which is the largest clan. Formerly they lived near Khan Yunis, but were driven out by the Terabin, and later became affiliated to the Suwarka. Once famous for their aggressiveness, they are now the best-behaved tribe in Sinai, and have almost ceased to be nomads.

Terabin.—The Terabin (sing. Terbani) of Sinai are really part of the Naba'at division of the great tribe of Terabin, the most powerful in Southern Palestine. Their Sinai territory lies north of that of the Tiyaha from Jebel Maghara through Magdhaba and Wadi 'Amr to the frontier north of

[1] See p. 299.
[2] The Ziyud supply the judges who decide disputes about camels throughout Sinai. The Ziyud and Ruwashda recalled to MacMichael the Beni Rashid and Ziyud of Borku and Wadai. " In practically every Baqqara *nisba*, the ancestor of the Ziyud appears as a descendant of Rashid." He goes on to connect the whole lot with the Zebeidiya-Rashaida community of the Eastern Sudan. MacMichael, i, 297.
[3] Shuqeir, 121.

Qusaima; they rove also across the frontier north-eastwards through Bir es-Sani towards Beersheba and north towards Gaza.

Na'um Bey was told that the Terabin were originally descended from an ancestor called Najm, who came to Sinai with a companion called El-Wiheidi, " a descendant of Hasan, the brother of Husein." Both were guests of a great sheikh of the Beni Wasil, in the Sinai mountains. This sheikh had no sons, but two daughters, one with an ugly face and kinky hair, and the other a beautiful girl with fine hair. Najm was a great hero, but an ugly man, brown in colour, while the Wiheidi was a handsome youth with a fair complexion. The old sheikh gave his daughters in marriage to his guests, the ugly girl to Najm, and the other to the Wiheidi; and so Najm became the ancestor of the Terabin who are famous for their ugly faces and their bravery, while Wiheidi became the ancestor of the Wiheidat, who are renowned for their good looks. Najm was the son of Sheikh 'Atiya, who is buried in the wadi called after him near Ain Jozi."[1]

The Terabin usually visit his tomb every year and make sacrifices for him. They respect the Wiheidat, and usually go on the second day of the Qurban Bairam to congratulate the Sheikh of the Wiheidat as a mark of respect. These Wiheidat live in Southern Palestine, and are now generally reckoned as allies of the Tiyaha.

In 1815, the Terabin under their Sheikh Abu Jahama, raided into Egypt and plundered a pilgrim caravan on the Qift-Quseir road. But the Ma'aza, resenting this encroachment on their privileges, seized the sheikh and handed him over to the Pasha. He was imprisoned for a year, till he delivered part of his booty to the treasury of the Pasha.[2]

In 1856, a famous battle, called El-Maksar, between the Terabin and the Suwarka, ended in the total defeat of the latter. Many were killed, and others were driven for shelter into the fort at El-'Arish.

At one time the Terabin did a certain amount of carrying trade on the Gaza-Qantara and Hebron-Suez routes.

Sheikh Hammad es-Sufi is the paramount sheikh of all the Terabin, but his authority does not run in Sinai, though his opinion would be respected. Sheikh Shahuda ed-Daldul was created acting chief of the Sinai Terabin by the Turks

[1] Shuqeir, 116.   [2] Burckhardt, *Syria*, 462.

during their occupation. He came in reasonably soon after the Turkish retirement, and has been recognized as acting Chief Sheikh in place of Khidhr esh-Shenub, who had become too old for the post.

In Sinai, they are reckoned as 565 people, divided into the sections of Shubeitat, Jubeilat, and Hasabila. There is also an isolated clan, El-Utut near El-Giddi, and another Serai'a (of Hasabila origin) on the west coast north of Nuweiba. The Kasar section though living partly west of the frontier, is considered to belong to Palestine.

A few Terabin are to be found in Egypt at the village of Basatin, just south of Cairo, near El-Ma'adi. In fact most of the gardeners in that suburb come from the Terabin.

Tiyaha.—The Tiyaha (sing. Tihi), like the Terabin, are a tribe of whom the greater part live in Palestine. They are so called after the Jebel Tih, " The Hills of the wandering " (of Israel), where they first settled when they entered the Peninsula.

Both Terabin and Tiyaha are often reckoned offshoots from the Beni 'Atiya, but the Tiyaha claim as an ancestor one " Suleiman el-'Anud of the Beni Hilal ", and say that together with the Terabin they were driven out of the Hijaz by the Ma'aza. They then had a war with the Terabin as to which should inhabit Central Sinai, but finally made peace at Nekhl on the terms that the Tiyaha should have the " land of Jalad ", and the Terabin the " land of ed-Damath ".[1] Their territory in Sinai runs from Jebel Hilal in the north to Naqb er-Rakna in the south, and from Nekhl in the east to Jubeil Hasan in the west.

Colonel Parker made a sort of census of the Sinai Tiyaha about 1911, and found them to number 900 men. They are not all nomads, but attempt cultivation in Wadi Muweilih, Sabha, Qusaima, Seram, and most of the Wadi el-Arish.

The very numerous Palestine Tiyaha live to the east of Beersheba. In Prof. Palmer's time they were famous for their annual forays on the Ruala and other tribes of Northern Syria, sometimes raiding 400 miles north of Tadmor. Near Gaza, in 1875, Lieut. Conder's survey party was attacked by twenty horsemen of the Tiyaha, " all well mounted and armed with swords, guns, and pistols, and with great lances of cane with long iron heads and tufts of ostrich feathers."

[1] Shuqeir, 115

They left his party alone, when they found they were not Terabin, with whom the Tiyaha were then at war.[1]

Sections : 'Awamra, Banei'at, Bareikat,[2] El-'Imur, Naghamsha, Qedeirat (really a Palestine section from Tell esh-Shari'a), Shatiyat, and Sibabha. Of these the Bareikat are not true Tiyaha ; their ancestor Breik is buried at Mayein. The tribe is now divided into two ; a northern division under Sheikh Salem el-'Awamri, and a southern under the former Sheikh Hamd Muslih.

Towara.—The Towara (sing. Turi), or " Arabs of Tor ", that is to say, all the tribes living in the true Sinai Peninsula, south of the Jebel et-Tih, are a confederation of tribes, perhaps seven hundred and fifty tents strong, united not by blood relationship, but merely by community of interest. Confined within an Alpine labyrinth of jagged peaks and tortuous ravines, these mountaineers have lost, or perhaps, never gained the franker traits of the wanderers over the steppes. They may fairly be called shy, shifty and suspicious—especially of one another. He who will not trust others is seldom worthy of trust himself, yet in days gone by when I found it necessary to have considerable sums in gold brought long journeys, often by a single Bedouin, to pay the monthly hire of the caravan, there was never a piece lacking. In their continual wrangles about money, they lay hands on their swords and scream at one another like fox-terriers, but self-control is never really lost. Blows are not struck, nor is gross personal abuse exchanged.

Also the presence within their borders of a monastery which distributes free bread twice daily, and the tradition of centuries of extortion practised on pilgrims, have demoralized them from stalwart thieves to shameless beggars. The modern pilgrim to St. Catherine realizes this whenever his car halts in Wadi Feiran. Yet there is a sort of Irish charm about the Towara that endears them to everyone, who has known them well. In spite of what I have written above, I like the Towara. Perhaps Lupus the soldier, came to repent of the hasty judgment he scratched on the sandstone of Wadi Mukattab.[2] I hope he did.

Among themselves, they can distinguish each tribe and

---

[1] *Tent Work in Palestine*, ii, 171.
[2] " An evil race ! I, Lupus, a soldier wrote this with my hand." *Greek inscription in Wadi Mukkatab.*

PLATE XXVI

YOUNG ARAB OF THE 'ALEIQAT

ARABS OF SINAI

subtribe by their looks and dialects, but to a stranger the Towara seem much of a muchness, except that the 'Aleiqat, perhaps, are rather more like the North Sinai tribes.

Their traditions recount that the former inhabitants of the peninsula were the Beni Suleiman, the Hamada, and the Beni Wasil (these latter are an offshoot from the Beni 'Uqba), tribes now sunk to insignificance and incorporated in the others.

Not long after the Muhammadan conquest of Egypt, the Sawalha, or Arabs of Salhiya, and the 'Aleiqat originally from the Syrian desert, were living in the eastern districts of the Delta, whence they sallied in regular inroads into the Peninsula to carry off the date-harvest, or to graze their camels and goats there whenever rain fell or the Nile flood failed. At length leaving some of each clan behind in Sharqiya, the Sawalha and 'Aleiqat migrated in force into Sinai, where they succeeded in conquering the Beni Suleiman and the other tribes, some of whose families fled, others were exterminated, and the remnants absorbed by their conquerors. The 'Aleiqat and the Sawalha then engaged in mutual warfare, and a raiding party of the Sawalha, 250 strong, destroyed that of the 'Aleiqat, a hundred less in number, at Tor. They were encouraged to attack by a spy who crept into the 'Aleiqi camp by night and counted their camel-saddles. Victory was thus inclining towards the the Sawalha when there arrrived at Sherm, seven men of Muzeina, one of them a slave, with their families. They were flying from the effects of blood-revenge, and begged permission of the Sawalha to join them in their pastures. To this the Sawalha would only consent on condition of their paying a yearly tribute in sheep, a proceeding which reduces the tribe which pays it to the status of Hiteim or " outcast ". The Muzeina scornfully rejected this offer, and entered into alliance with the 'Aleiqat, who readily welcomed this addition to their strength, and admitted them to common rights in their grazing, etc. The 'Aleiqat, reinforced by Nafa'i horsemen from Cairo and by the seven Muzeina (or their descendants), now attacked their enemies at El-Watia. On seeing the Muzeina among their foes, the Sawalha thought they had to contend with more than one tribe, fell into confusion and were beaten. A compromise now took place, the Sawalha and the 'Aleiqat divided the fertile valleys of the country, and the Muzeina received one-third of their share from the 'Aleiqat. The Sheikh of the Sawalha was at the same time recognized as Sheikh of the whole peninsula.

At the present time the eastern half of the peninsula and the south of it up to Wadi Mi'r belong to the Muzeina; and all the country between Wadi Sidri and 'Ayun Musa, near Suez, to the 'Aleiqat.

Yet in pre-war days, when sharing the supply of camels to the outer world, the tribe of the Sawalha claimed half, while the tribes of 'Aleiqat and Muzeina had to be content with a quarter each. A still less equitable arrangement characterized the supply of camels to the Monastery, where the Sawalha[1] took their half, the Jebeliya (convent serfs) a quarter, the 'Aleiqat a fifth, and the largest tribe, the Muzeina, the remaining twentieth.

The 'Aleiqat and Sawalha seem to have occupied or retained raiding rights over the country between Cairo and Suez down to about 1820, for until then the carrying trade between those two cities was entirely in their hands. But about that time the merchants began also to employ the then recently arrived tribes of Ma'aza and Haweitat, and the Towara were greatly annoyed at this loss of support. To recompense themselves, the two tribes combined and plundered a large caravan laden with coffee and other merchandise, between Suez and Cairo, returning to their mountains with plenty of plunder. To a demand by the Pasha for the return of their booty, they replied laconically, "We were hungry and have eaten." Muhammad 'Ali immediately dispatched two or three thousand soldiers against them, and the Towara fortified Wadi Barq with a breastwork and prepared to defend it. But their position was easily outflanked by the troops who "crowned the heights" on either side, and the Towara were routed with little slaughter. The troops proceeded to the Convent, where the chief Sheikhs came in and surrendered. Peace was granted on condition that the Towara paid the expenses of the expedition. Since then they have lived in peaceful subjection to the Egyptian Government.

In 1904, the Arabian Haweitat of Abu Toqeiqa made war on the Billi and asked help from the Towara who were bound to them by an ancient offensive-defensive alliance.

---

[1] Only the 'Awarma and Wilad Sa'id divisions.

Sheikh Musa Nassir did not think fit to take part in a war from which he could gain no advantage, and replied (truthfully) that the Egyptian Government had forbidden the Arabs of Sinai to cross the frontier. Thereupon the Haweitat lampooned the Towara, saying :

"*Ahsabak, ya Turi, ti'izz el qabila,
Tarak huseini labid fi khamila.*"
" Turi, I thought you the honour of the land !
Fox, deserter, crouching in the sand ! "

More recently in 1932, when the combined Haweitat and Billi revolted against Ibn Sa'ud's government, the Towara were appealed to for help. Though some started out, they were all turned back at 'Aqaba, and Salem the son of Jebely, the ex-sheikh of the Muzeina, alone took part in the battle.

The office of supreme sheikh of the Towara continued with the Sawalha until the late war, when the Egyptian Government deposed Nassir Musa, of the Qararsha division of the Sawalha. The office has not been revived.

The general '*Aqid* of the Towara also came from their ranks, being supplied by the family of Tayima, from the 'Awarma division. The '*Aqid* is the general who conducts the expeditionary force of the tribe, in a raid or in war. But the 'Aleiqat and the Muzeina had also their own '*aqids*.

Tribal Subdivisions of the Towara

(1) *Sawalha* (245 tents). They are a confederation of three little tribes of obscure origin. Some Arabs alleged to Burckhardt that the Sawalha or " children of Sala " take their name from Nebi Sala, the principal *weli* of the Peninsula. But the Sawalha came into Sinai from Sharqiya, and the sheikh of the Wilad Sa'id says they are called Sawalha because they came from Salhiya in that province. Their subsections are:—

(*a*) '*Awarma* (59 tents). According to some, the 'Awarma are the original Sawalha of the Conquest, and this seems probable, because the Beni-Wasil who were conquered, are still affiliated to the 'Awarma, and further the 'Awarma are remarkable for possessing the right to supply the 'Aqid to the Sawalha, and, some say, to the whole of the Towara.

During the war, Suleiman Ghoneim, the then Sheikh of

the 'Awarma, accompanied the Austrian Gondos with a small party of Turks, who burnt Abu Zenima; Suleiman died in Palestine during the war, and Mubarak Said is now the Sheikh, and Mansur Abu Qurma, the judge.

Families: Fuwansa, Wilad Mubarak, Wilad Qurma, Mahasna,[1] Nuwasra, Talaiha, and the unrelated but affiliated Radhauna and Beni Wasil. Shuqeir gives also Rudeisat (including Wilad Shahin).

(*b*) *Qararsha* (95 tents). The Qararsha were among the richest of the Towara tribes (all are miserably poor), as they own the best of the palm-groves in Wadi Feiran, but a disastrous fire there in 1927 occasioned them much loss. Some claim relationship with the Qureish, or clan of the Prophet, but this is not seriously maintained. In Robinson's time (1838), the Qararsha were excluded from the ranks of *ghafirs* or protectors of the Convent (and so from the profits to be made out of camel-hire), on account of the following episode:

> "Yet the tradition is, that long ago the Kurrâshy shared in this right by sufferance, although not fully entitled to it; or, as our Arabs said, 'Not written in the book of the Convent.' But they lost the privilege in the following manner, according to the Arab story. One night seven of their leaders entered the Convent secretly by a back way; and in the morning presented themselves armed to the monks, demanding to be 'written in the book'. The monks, affrighted, said: 'Very well; but it must be done in the presence of witnesses from among the other protectors.' Witnesses were sent for; and on their arrival, being ordered to put aside their arms, were drawn up into the Convent. By a private understanding with the monks, however, they had arms concealed in the bags they brought with them. The monks were secretly armed; and upon a given signal, all fell upon the Kurrâshy and killed six outright. The remaining one was thrown from the Convent walls, and killed. Since that time the Kurrâshy have had no claim to any connection with the Convent."[2]

The Qararsha, and indeed all the Towara, were ruled for many years until 1912, by a remarkable character called Musa Nassir. Of his rise in the world, a tradition relates that in 1854, on the death of the Khedive Abbas I, work was

---
[1] The family of Tayima the 'Aqid is contained in the Mahasna.
[2] Robinson, *Researches in Palestine*, i, 204.

abruptly suspended on the palace that was being built for him near the Convent, and on the road leading to it from Tor. Money to pay off the workmen was sent from Cairo in a box, guarded by a clerk and four soldiers. One evening this party passed into the gorge of Wadi Sidri below the turquoise mines about the same time that Musa Nassir and a few friends passed into it from above. From that day to this, the box, the clerk, and the four soldiers have never been seen, but Musa and his associates suddenly became very rich.[1]

A few years later, he and another strong character, 'Awda ez-Zumeili, used to shoot ibex for the eccentric Major MacDonald, who attempted to open up the turquoise mines. " The Major was a good man, so good that we thought him insane," was the epitaph pronounced on this unfortunate officer by the grateful pair in later life. When 'Awda became Sheikh of the 'Aleiqat, Musa succeeded to the chieftaincy of the Qararsha; and the two resolved to make the pilgrimage to Mecca together. An opportunity was there afforded them to rob a Turkish merchant, and Musa, though welcoming the occasion, held that it cast a blemish on their sanctity, and refused the title of Hajji, which he earned by a second journey to Mecca. The Zumeili was not so punctilious, or thought that they were not likely to find another Turkish simpleton, so he assumed the rank of Hajji without more ado.

Musa now became respectable, so much so, that he was recognized as chief sheikh of all the Towara.[2] Haynes speaks of him as rendering some assistance in the search for the murderers of Prof. Palmer. He was one of the first sheikhs I met in Sinai in 1910, but died only two years afterwards.

His son, Nassir Musa, was foolish enough to join the Turks during the late war, so he was deposed, and the office of sheikh of the Towara has never been revived. The present sheikh of the Qararsha is El-Hajj Hamdan Abu Zeit who is also the judge, but he is old and infirm, and his son Masa'ud Hamdan acts for him.

---

[1] It is fair to Musa's memory to say that Col. Parker scouted the tale as a fabrication. It still persists, however, and I heard it again in 1933.
[2] Sala ibn Zubeir, the Sheikh of the Qararsha, was also Sheikh of the Towara in Burckhardt's time (1811).

Families : Nasaira, Wilad Budr, Hashashna, Naseirat, Shibaiba,[1] Wilad Jumei'a, Wilad 'Ayad, Haramsha, and Beni Suleiman, the remnant of a once powerful independent tribe of the same name.

(c) *Wilad Sa'id* (88 tents). Burckhardt rather ungratefully stigmatizes this tribe, his hosts, and gives a saying " *abeyt waheyd, wa la aned Oulad Sayd* ". That is, " camp by yourself, or with the Wilad Sa'id—you will get the same hospitality." [2] Since the Monastery falls inside their *darak*, they had at one time almost a monopoly of conveying tourists from Cairo to St. Catherine ; and their subsection, the Rizana, provides the servants of the mosques situated within the Monastery's walls. These Rizana are said by Burckhardt to be the descendants of some Turkish stragglers from the Hajj caravan of 1402.[3]

In appearance, the Wilad Sa'id are more Egyptian than Arab, and their dialect is also different to that of the other Sawalha. Fateih Sala is their sheikh and Musa Nassar the judge. Infirm and feeble-minded, he can still recall the great 1867 flood in Wadi Solaf, and is reckoned the oldest Arab in Sinai. Their territory includes Wadi esh-Sheikh, Wadi Solaf, and Wadi Hebran, while their section, the Zakheirat, own Wadi Mi'r, and share Wadi Rahaba with the Muzeina. Thus all the highest mountains of the Peninsula stand inside their boundaries.

Robinson seems to have confused them with these Zakheirat, for he says the "Awlad Sa'id" are a division of "Dhuheiry". The truth is that the Zakheirat were once an independent tribe. Their sheikh is also Sheikh ed-Deir, that is, he is the agent charged with the supply of camels to the Monastery. (The 'Awarma, 'Aleiqat, and Jebeliya have also each a Sheikh ed-Deir.)

Sections.—'Awamra, Bisharin, Farraja, Nakheilat, Rasheidat, Shararin, Wilad Seif, and Zakheirat. These last amount to about thirty-five tents and are subdivided again into 'Ajeilin, Hedeibat, and Rizana. Most of the Rasheidat and Shararin are settled in Suez.

Most of the Shararin and Rasheidat are settled in Suez.

---

[1] *Notes*, 197.
[2] *Syria*, 543.
[3] Descendants of the *weli*, Sheikh Abu Shebib.

ARABS OF SINAI

(2) *'Aleiqat*[1] (269 tents). According to their late Sheikh Mudakhil, the 'Aleiqat are an offshoot from the old Arabian tribe of Beni 'Uqba. They now inhabit the western coast of Sinai, but in earlier times their territory was in the east, between Ain Hadira and Nuweiba, in country now abandoned by them to the Muzeina. There are various colonies of the 'Aleiqat in the Nile Valley, notably at Shibin el-Qanatir and near Qus, while even further south they occupy as *fellahin* the whole Nile Valley between Seyala and Korosko, forming a buffer state as it were, between the Kunuz Nubians, and those of Dirr. This district is called after them Wadi el-'Arab, and their sheikh is the Omda of Malki. During the census of 1927, this old gentleman appeared at a conference of Bedouin sheikhs in Cairo, and on being twitted by me that none of his tribe had ever been seen in the desert, replied, " It is an ancient custom of our tribe to go into the desert whenever there is a census."

To return to Sinai, their chief sheikh is Zeidan Mudakhil, who generally resides at the mining settlement of Abu Zenima. His father, Mudakhil Suleiman, was an astute young fellow who was one of the camel-drivers in the caravan of the ill-fated Professor Palmer. So useful was his evidence at the trial of the murderers that Sir Charles Warren thought something should be done for him. He therefore deposed the then sheikh of the 'Aleiqat, El-Hajj 'Awda ez-Zumeili, for the reason that the murder had occurred in his area, and appointed Mudakhil in his stead. This provided the tribe with a standing quarrel between the family of the former sheikh the Khureisat or Zumeiliyin and the Awlad Selmi who have supplanted them.

During the Great War, Mudakhil was for a while the only sheikh in Sinai to remain loyal to the Egyptian Government, and the Zumeiliyin to a man joined the Turks hoping to obtain the chieftaincy. Some of them were among the party that besieged Tor in 1915, and lost their lives there.[2]

Old Mudakhil was on the *Minerva*, though he did not land, and so enjoyed a real triumph over his enemies.

As regards dialect, the 'Aleiqat are said to talk like the

---

[1] A movement has now originated with the Nile Valley 'Aleiqat to change the name of the tribe to 'Aqeilat. 'Aleiqat may indeed have an opprobrious meaning in Arabic, but since 'Aqeilat has hitherto been reserved for the itinerant camel-traders, always in Egypt Hiteim, they might have selected a better substitute.

[2] See pp. 169–170.

Terabin. Their families include Wilad Selmi, Sauwada (a remnant of their former allies the Nafei'at, Khureisat (or Zumeiliyin), Tleilat, Jarajira, and the Hamada, the descendants of the original inhabitants of the area. These last have a sheikh of their own, but he is an absentee landlord and lives at Zagazig.

Besides the above, the Hamaida family have deserted the Wilad Selmi section on account of a blood-feud, and are now *qusara* among the Muzeina. But to restore the balance, the Faranja have deserted the Abu Sabha section of the Muzeina and become *qusara* among the 'Aleiqat. There are also generally some 40 tents of the Terabin living in the coastal region of the 'Aleiqat area, south of 'Ayun Musa.

(3) *Muzeina* (600 tents). These are relatively late comers to Sinai. Their present Sheikh, 'Aweid Budr, says they are an offshoot of the great Arabian tribe of Harb; and Doughty does indeed give Muzeina as a clan of Harb. But most probably both these Muzeina remnants are descended from the independent clan of Muzeina, powerful in early Arabia.

Of them, it was written : " The tribes of the Arabs are seven, and whosoever is not included in them may lawfully be enslaved ; these are : Kenana, Muzayna, Guhayna, Ashga'a, Himyar, Ghafar, Kuraysh."[1]

According to the genealogists, they are descended from Muzeina bint Kalb, a descendant of Qahtan through Qudha'a, who married 'Amr ibn Odd, a Ma'addite ; that is, they are Qahtanid through their mother, and Ishmaelite through their father. But Robertson Smith, as we have already had occasion to remark,[2] has shown that the Qudha'a descent from Qahtan is probably forged, so in that case the distinction is immaterial, and we may conclude our Sinai Muzeina to be *arab el-must 'ariba* and not Yemenite at all.

The famous Sidi 'Uqba, who founded Qairwan in 677, and his one-eyed son Muslim, who sacked Medina in 683, were Muzeina according to Dozy. There was a Muzeini kingdom of Silves in the Algarve, the southernmost province of Portugal, which was extinguished by Mutadid, King of Seville, in 1052 or 1053.

Sir Richard Burton says of them : " Anyone who knows the Badawin can see the Muzaynah are pure blood. Their

---

[1] In an Arabic *nisba*, quoted by MacMichael, ii, 22. [2] p. 24.

PLATE XXVII

Musa Sofaran 'Aweid Budr

SHEIKHS OF THE MUZEINA

brows are broad, their faces narrow, their features regular, and their eyes of a moderate size ; whereas the other Tawarah (Sinaitic) clans are as palpably Egyptian."

According to their present sheikh, the ancestor who brought them to Sinai was 'Alwan, who is buried near a famous *weli*, Sheikh Faranja. The tribe is divided into three main divisions, descended from 'Alwan's two sons as follows :

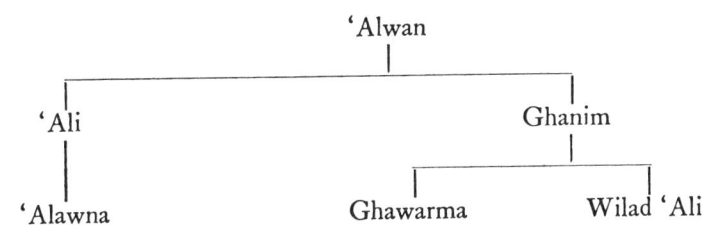

```
                        'Alwan
           ┌──────────────┴──────────────┐
         'Ali                         Ghanim
          │                  ┌───────────┴───────────┐
       'Alawna            Ghawarma              Wilad 'Ali
```

For some years after the war, Jebely Bareik, who had served some time with the Turks and been given a Turkish sword and decoration, was the chief sheikh, and Salem Anis, who has lost one hand from a leopard-bite, the *qadi*.

However, an old feud between the Muzeina and the 'Imran was then revived by the murder of an 'Imrani goat-buyer in Muzeina territory. The 'Imran affirm, and many Muzeina do not deny, that Jebely Bareik, their chief sheikh, directly instigated this, and the earlier raids by the 'Imran were directed against Jebely Bareik's family as a first objective. The northern subsections of the Muzeina bore no love to their sheikh for this, and some wanted to throw him off altogether.

Finally Jebely was deposed about 1928, and 'Aweid Budr became regent sheikh pending the majority of the son of their pre-war Sheikh Khidr. Later again, he was confirmed in office as sheikh, which he now holds. Many of the Muzeina have lately taken to fishing in the Gulf of 'Aqaba to supplement their gains from breeding camels and sheep.

Jebeliya.—The Jebeliya are the descendants of some Bosnian and Wallachian serfs, given by Justinian to the Monastery of St. Catherine. They look after the extra-mural gardens of the monks, and some are employed in the monastery as servants. They are despised as Hiteim by the Arabs, who will not intermarry with them. Nassir Musa, the sheikh of the Qararsha, to increase the importance of his small tribe, offered to remove this restriction during the Great War, but the concession, as might be expected, was repudiated by his tribesmen. In their dress and mode of living, the Jebeliya are in no way distinguishable from the other inhabitants of Sinai, though in features they preserve some trace of their foreign origin. The majority were converted to Islam in the seventh century by the Caliph 'Abd el-Malik ibn Merwan, but a few families remained Christian for a thousand years, the last, an old woman, dying in 1750.[1]

About twenty-five years ago, the monks of St. Catherine attempted to coerce the Jebeliya into giving up a garden which they had acquired by stopping their daily ration of bread. The Jebeliya complained to the Government, when it was found that this daily ration went back to Justinian's time and so had been established too long to be hastily done away with. An agreement was arrived at which satisfied both parties.

They suffered severely from the influenza epidemic after the War, and in 1929 numbered 420 souls, according to the Archbishop of Mount Sinai. Their Chief Sheikh is 'Awda Masa'ud.

Sub-divisions : (1) Wilad Masa'ud ; (2) Wilad Musa'ad ; (3) Wiheibat ; (4) Wilad Salim ; (5) Heimat ; (6) Wilad Gindi.

Burckhardt says that the Tabana in the gardens of Feiran, the Beziya in the gardens of Tor, and the Sattila elsewhere are all offshoots of the Jebeliya. There are also Mu'atira at Tor.

Ma'aza.—The Ma'aza, who now occupy the Eastern Desert of Egypt, from the North Galala mountains to the Gharqada ("Hurghada")-Qena road, are an offshoot from the tribe of the same name living in Midian between Petra and Tabuk. They came to Egypt in the course of the eighteenth century as a result of a quarrel with the Haweitat. Burckhardt says : " those who undertook the journey by land, were for the greater number killed during their passage through the territory of the Howeytats. Others came over by sea to Tor and arrived safely in Egypt."[2]

At the time of their leaving Arabia, they were 250 tents strong (according to their own computation) under a sheikh,

[1] Burckhardt, *Syria*, 564. [2] *Notes*, 225.

ARABS OF SINAI

Hamid Salem. Doughty says Ma'aza is another name for Beni 'Atiya, but they seem to be separate clans ('Atawna is a general name for the two), living side by side, with a common ancestry. Both claim to be descended from one Wa'il ibn Jebely,[1] who left two sons, Ma'az and 'Anaz (lit. " he-goat " and " she-goat "). From the former spring the Ma'aza, from the latter the 'Anaza, one of the most powerful clans of Northern Arabia. This genealogy appears too simple to be genuine. Another version declares that 'Anaz was so called because on the death of his mother he was suckled by a she-goat. If this version be accepted, the pair are the Arabian prototypes of Romulus and Remus. Hence Robertson-Smith wished to draw the inference that in the days of " ignorance " the goat was their totemic ancestor.

They have always been famous thieves. Sir Richard Burton calls them " turbulent and dangerous ; the men are professional robbers ; and their treachery is uncontrolled by the Bedawi law of honour. They will eat bread and salt with the traveller whom they intend to murder ".[2]

So highly was plunder esteemed among them that their young men were not allowed to shave the head (a sign of attaining manhood) till they had brought home some booty from an enemy.[3]

Perhaps the greatest feat achieved by the Ma'aza was the plundering of the Hajj caravan of Mecca pilgrims on the Qift–Quseir road. This occurred at the beginning of the nineteenth century, and the enormous booty taken, which included the Kiswa, popularly known as the " Holy Carpet ", and the large revenue sent annually to the Mosque at Mecca, was divided by the exultant tribesmen at a mountain still called Misikat el-Jukh. Muhammad 'Ali Pasha was not a man to pass this over lightly, and the sheikhs of the Ma'aza duly suffered for their sins.

A picturesque Arab account says :

" In Z'il Kada, 1221 H. (A.D. 1803), a caravan from the mountains in Upper Egypt arrived at the Capital with a lot of camels and goods, belonging to the Ma'aza Arabs, for trading, as is the custom of caravans. When this news reached Muhammad 'Ali, he at once got up at night, and while men were asleep he suddenly attacked

---
[1] Wa'il had a Qahtanid mother, so some of the Ma'aza call themselves 'arab el 'ariba, or Yemenites.
[2] *The Land of Midian*, i. 336.   [3] *Notes*, 133.

this caravan with his men, pillaging their camels, loads, and goods, even the sons, women, and daughters, and led them as prisoners inside the city. Then he started to sell them as he had previously done with the natives of Kafr Hakim and its neighbourhood." [1]

Among the Ma'aza the bride-price may range from £5 to £50, but a man can always get his *bint 'amm* cheaper than another girl. The blood-money is £200 in cash, not camels. Their clans (*'eila*) are given as :

'Adasin	Hammadiyin	Jideihat
Alamat	Hasaniya	Khamaisa
'Awanra	Hasasin	Mawadi
'Awdat	Hashaima	Museirat
Balanja	Hushman	Qisisat
Beit Sakr	'Iseifat	Subeihat
Durajin	Jibalat	Sudan
Hamadiya	Jibeilat	Tababna.

Their famous *'aqid* Rueishid came from the Qisisat.

Besides those of the Ma'aza who live in the desert, numerous colonies of them exist along the eastern fringe of the Nile cultivation, from Wadi Rishrash near es-Saff to nearly as far south as Qena. Their ruling sheikh of the Beit Sakr clan lives in Minya Province at Beni Mazar.

In bad years, some of the Ma'aza occasionally cross the Nile near Beni Suef and graze their camels between the Nile cultivation and that of the Faiyum. But they recognize the land there as belonging to the Mugharba (Western Arabs). One of these expressed great admiration to me of the unveiled women he saw among the Jawazi.

Hiteim.—Widely spread throughout Hijaz, Sinai, and Egypt are numerous nomad clans, both large and small, outwardly Arab in appearance, all called (though never to their faces) Hiteim. The Arabs despise these Hiteim, and will not intermarry with them. In Southern Sinai, the penalty for hitting or killing a Hiteimi used to be greater than that for a man, i.e. they were put in the category of women, slaves, and the like. In North Sinai, they are distinguished from the rest of mankind by their evil scent. To call a man a Hiteimi is an insult, even if he is one ; and if he is not, it is a serious slander to be expiated by a fine and the building of white cairns. For the most part, these Hiteim represent

[1] *Marvel of Antiquities.*

ARABS OF SINAI

ancient broken clans, who have lost their independence and been obliged to pay tribute to their conquerors. Some may contain non-Arab elements, but these must be rare. Nor do I fancy that religion has had anything to do with it, the Ma'aza of the Hijaz have a section Beni Sabt, who are supposed to have once been Christians, but this does not interfere with their tribal status. In the west, the distinction between Arab and Hiteim does not exist, and the converted Berber elements there, though they are despised for paying tribute, are esteemed for their piety.

In the Hijaz the Hiteim are reckoned better hunters than the Bedu, and their camels, especially those of the Shararat, are highly esteemed. Some of these are sold in Sinai, white camels with a marked yellowish tinge.

All the Hiteimi camel-brands have a certain resemblance
Zebeidiya ♀   Shararat ♀| Fehjat ♀

Doughty's Solubba, or Sleib, who have no domestic animals except asses but live only by hunting, cross rarely into Sinai. I saw four tents at Tor in 1933—the only time I have met them.

The Hijaz Shararat are a strong clan, now practically independent again, but " once a Hiteimi always a Hiteimi ". Some fifty years back they thought themselves strong enough to refuse to pay tribute to their masters, the Beni 'Atiya. Whereupon, in 1873, the Sinai Laheiwat who are of 'Atwani origin, prepared a great raid upon them, and raided Wadi Sirhan 250 strong (reinforced by Terabin, Tiyaha and Haweitat). The raiders were pursued by 500 Shararat, who after two rearguard actions at Sarw el-Qa' and Wada'at killed twenty Laheiwat and four of their allies. The victorious Hiteim recovered all their camels and captured some belonging to the raiders.[1]

There are Hiteim, called Rashaida, at Sherm near the tip of the Sinai Peninsula, and others, Dawaghra, in the palm-groves at Qatia. Also a few, Oreinat, live in Jebel Hilal among the Tiyaha. In Egypt there is a clan of Hiteim called Muteir living near Asyut, and two other clans, Azaiza and Qizaiza, are settled on the outskirts of the cultivation near Qena and Qift. They have been there some time, since Bruce noticed them there in 1765.

There used to be another clan of Rashaida living on the

[1] Shuqeir, 575.

shores of Foul Bay between Berenice and 'Aidhab, but after the murder of Lieut. Stewart, R.N., at Halaib in 1887, they were deported to south of Suakin. There are many Hiteim in the Sudan, notably Zebeidiya, and the large camel trade between Kassala and Egypt is in their hands.

These Zebeidiya are quite Arab in appearance, and are in fact recent immigrants from Arabia.[1] They are sometimes called 'Aqeil, an euphemism in Upper Egypt for Hiteim. There are other Hiteim long settled among the 'Ababda who have adopted Beja customs.

The 'Awazim, a tribe settled on the west bank of the Nile, between Isna and Farshut, are also of Hiteim origin and there is a well-known Hiteimi clan of the same name in the Hijaz.

[1] They arrived on the Atbara about 1903–4.

PLATE XXVIII

ARAB OF THE RASHAIDA (HITEIM)

[face p. 270

Chapter XVI
THE WESTERN BEDOUIN (EL MUGHARBA)[1]

" *The Moor is of a free and open nature.*"—Othello.

General Remarks—The Arab and the Libyan—The Sa'adi Tribes and the Murabitin—Bedouins of the Northern Littoral—Awlad 'Ali—Jawabis—Jumei'at—Samalus—Shiheibat.

Sinai has been called an " epitome of Arabia ", and the pilgrim certainly feels well on the way to Mecca as soon as he crosses the Suez Canal, but it is equally true that Algiers is not so very far west of the " Arab's Gate " at Alexandria. The skies of Mariut are coloured with much the same blue as those of Andalusia, and, though the Sierras are lacking, the historian instinctively begins to look for the Alhambra as soon as he crosses the causeway to Amriya. The reason is not so very far to seek, there is more of the Libyan than the Arab in the tribes that hardly a century ago flooded back into Egypt from Cyrenaica. Yet in spite of numerous resemblances, these two races are divided as the goats from the sheep by this essential difference that while the " Berbers "[2] are religious and often superstitious (traits of a converted race), his religion sits so lightly on the Arab that he has almost reverted to his early paganism. But though this is true, it is far from obvious, and a traveller will not find anyone in the Western Desert to admit that he is not of pure Arab descent.

This snobbishness was evident so long ago as the time of Ibn Khaldun (1332–1406), who found it advisable to represent the Tuareg, as descended from a respectable but mythical Arab conqueror, Ifrikias ibn Sufi. Ibn Khaldun asserts that when Ifrikias himself returned to Arabia, the Ketama and Sanhaja tribes remained behind and became absorbed in the people of the country. All this is pure

---

[1] Mugharba means literally " westerners ", and is used in Egypt to denote generally all the Bedouin west of the Nile. But there is a tribe in Cyrenaica who content themselves with this simple title, and so confuse the issue.

[2] All the indigenous races of North Africa are lumped together under this barbarian title by the Arab historians.

fiction, but it is interesting to read that, even in Ibn Khaldun's day, these Tuareg were known as " The Veiled Ones ".

The first Arab expedition to North Africa began in 643, two years after the conquest of Egypt, when 'Amr ibn el-'Asi invaded Cyrenaica and received the submission of the Luwata Berbers, whom he found in occupation of that country. Forty years later the conquerors had reached the Atlantic, but these early Moslem invaders mostly settled in the towns and left the open country to the Berbers. Their influence on the nomadic population was therefore trifling, and to-day need not be taken into account.

The eleventh century irruption from the east of the wild Bedouin tribes of Beni Hilal and Beni Suleim, who continued their nomadic existence after their conquest of the country, was one of the decisive factors in moulding the character of the present-day population ; a religious upheaval among the Berbers of Senegal the other. The Beni Hilal have indeed disappeared, but to-day all the independent tribes of Western Egypt, the Sa'adi, claim descent from the Beni Suleim, while their vassals all have the same title, Murabitin, as the adherents of the religious movement referred to above. Some historical explanation now becomes necessary and, since the vassals probably represent the aboriginal population more closely, we will first consider the Murabitin.

In the early days of Islam, volunteers constantly thronged to all the fighting fronts where the faith was being spread by the sword among the heathen. These were nicknamed *El-Murabitin*, which meant " pickets ", from the *ribat* or outposts (lit. " horse-lines ") in which they lived.

But in the eleventh century a violent religious movement among the Messufa and Lamtuna sections of the Sanhaja Tuareg appropriated the name to its followers, just as eight hundred year later the fanatics of the Eastern Sudan were known as *the* Dervishes of their time. Both upheavals began with a prophet on an island, and both spread northwards with terrifying rapidity. Yet the *Murabitin* of the Senegal were far more successful than their rivals on the Nile, and their title reached the height of its fame when a line of their kings, whose name the Spaniards corrupted to " Almoravides ", ruled over Andalusia till 1156.

Yet just as the original *Murabitin* were gaining their

THE WESTERN BEDOUIN

first successes in Senegal, the Beni Hilal and the Beni Suleim were being despatched by the Caliph Mustansir billah against Mu'izz ibn Badis, his rebellious viceroy in Tripoli. They sang of their conquest :

> " Great was the king, son of Badis, a mighty man of war !
> Yet we routed his thirty thousand men !
> We were but three thousand, yet the victory was ours, and ours the spoil !
> Their hearts were as water, not a man was in their ranks !
> We routed them and they fled far and wide ! "

These Beni Hilal, now extinct, are famous wherever Arabic is spoken for the exploits of their legendary hero Abu Zeid, while the Beni Suleim had helped the Prophet at the battle of Hunein, and are said by Hogarth to be the ancestors of the great modern tribe of Harb.[1]

The confusion of these two invasions caused the races of North Africa to become inextricably mixed. Both Arabs and Berbers spent their lives in the desert herding their flocks, and both were warlike. So it is natural that the intermarriages of a few generations should have made one people of them, and it is also natural that the conquered should claim relationship with the conquerors and not vice versa. But this aspiration of the Berbers has flooded their genealogies with so many lies that it is difficult to disentangle the truth.

The descendants of the original colonists, much mixed with Berber blood, still preserve their title of Murabitin, though no longer living in *ribat*, which soon lost their military character and were turned into *Zawia* " monasteries ", where the more peacefully inclined of the sect retired for religious teaching and contemplation. Later, when the *ribat* came to be deserted, the peaceful Murabitin, ill-fitted by their monastic habits for the resumption of an active nomadic life, sank into dependence on their warlike brethren the Sa'adi, and, among a primitive race, dependence means inferiority. Thus in Arabia any tribe that pays tribute to another is despised as Hiteim. And so the once proud title of " Murabitin " has simply come to mean " vassal " and nothing more.

[1] *History of Arabia*, 38.

The independent Saʻadi tribes fall into four groups :

1. The Jawazi, Fawayid, and Rammah, all of common origin with the ʻAwaqir of Cyrenaica.
2. The Harabi and Barʻasa, both of common origin with the ʻIbeidat of Cyrenaica.
3. The Hanadi, and
4. The Awlad ʻAli

The original ancestor whom these Saʻadi all claim is one Abu Dib, said to be of Suleim descent.

This sheikh was a real personage and a contemporary of Ibn Khaldun (who died in A.D. 1406). He was sheikh of the Beni Jaʻafir, and a man of great importance in Barka, the very place that the four tribes inhabited for centuries before they came to Egypt. Also the period of fifteen or sixteen generations, which the modern Bedouin assert to separate them from Abu Dib, agrees with this chronology well enough.[1]

Some are found to assert that their title of Saʻadi " helping " is derived from an ancestress called Saʻada, the wife of Abu Dib, or, according to a hostile account, of a Jew called Yana. But the real explanation of the term has already been given above.

At the present day a sort of feudal system prevails both in Egypt and Cyrenaica, by which families are *mrabit*,[2] or vassal families, not tribes to tribes ; thus the Qatʻan tribe of Murabitin is divided, one part vassal to a family of Awlad ʻAli el-Ahmar, another to the Sinaqra, and a third to the Sinana. For a tribute called " alms ", which by hereditary obligation each Mrabit family must pay, the Saʻadi family to which it is attached is bound to afford the Mrabit family protection in all minor difficulties of life, such as robbery by another family of Saʻadi, etc.

Thus a " Mrabit " family by paying tribute can herd its flocks in peace, calling upon the Saʻadi to see that justice is done them, but they are bound to join the Saʻadi to fight with them in any serious conflict with other tribes.

Among the " Mrabit " tribes of the present day are the Jumeiʻat, Qatʻan, and Awlad Suleiman, all claiming as common ancestor one Kaʻb, and feudal relations are

---

[1] The pedigrees of which these Western Bedouin are so proud can only be trusted so far back as the individual whose name a subdivision has adopted, such as Kharûf in the Awlad Kharûf pedigree. Taking them separately, the pedigrees will be found to dovetail into each other up to that point, but beyond it things become problematical.

[2] Sing. of " Murabitin ".

THE WESTERN BEDOUIN

maintained to this day in the desert between the last two and the Sa'adi, though they are relaxed in the cultivation.

The Jumei'at, who used to be "Murabitin" to the Beni 'Una, are now nominally so to the Awlad 'Ali, but are not required to pay tribute. Other tribes, such as the Jawabis and 'Awarma, are in an intermediate stage between the Sa'adi and the Murabitin. The Awlad 'Abd es-Sallam, the Samalus ed-Diminat, and perhaps the Fawakhir, call themselves " Murabitin bil Baraka ", a priestly caste which, in Tripoli, used to receive special privileges from the Turkish Government.

Though the Sa'adi tribes despise the Murabitin as serfs, they respect them for their piety and resort to them for the writing of charms.

While the Murabitin tribes generally may be suspected to contain more Libyan blood than the Sa'adi, there are other tribes such as the 'Amayim, the Jahama, and the Tarhuna, who have come to Egypt from further west than any of the above, and who seem to be quite definitely " Berber ", though, of course, none of them will admit it. These are known euphemistically as 'Arab el-Gharb.

Even some of the Juheina, settled east of the Nile in Sharqiya, are scorned by Klippel as " d'origine berbère, se pretendant section d'une tribu d'Arabie ".[1]

Awlad 'Ali.—This tribe, by far the most important of the Western Bedouin, occupies with its vassals the whole north coast of Egypt from Salum to Alexandria. Like the others, they claim descent from the Beni Suleim, alleging their ancestor 'Ali, son of 'Aqar, to be a grandson of that Dib, or Abu Dib, mentioned by Ibn Khaldun. Their enemies, however, allege that he was a Jew. " When the Arabs occupied the north coast of Africa, there was a notable, a Jew, who owned property at Saqiet el-Hamra in Morocco. This man welcomed and entertained the Arab sheikh Ez-Zanati. He became very popular with the sheikh, who gave him his daughter named Sa'ada, on condition that he embraced Islam before the marriage contract was made out."[2] Another version calls the Jew Yana, and says that he had two daughters. Of these Sa'ada was the

---

[1] E. Klippel, " Etudes sur le folklore Bédouin de l'Egypte," *Bull. Soc. Khédiv. de Géogr.*, vii, 10, Cairo, 1911.
[2] From information collected by Muhammad Bey Wasfi.

ancestress of the Awlad 'Ali and Hind of the Hanadi. (The Hanadi call their ancestress Hind, the daughter of Sallam.) These obvious fabrications only mean that their conventional genealogy is not believed outside the tribe. But the Awlad 'Ali themselves all agree that 'Ali was the son of 'Aqar bin Dib.

They are now a composite tribe made up of the descendants of 'Ali's three sons, and various fragments of broken tribes. The Awlad 'Ali lived for a long time in the "Green Mountain" of Cyrenaica, and about 150 years ago began to drift eastwards, called into Egypt by the Jumei'at to aid them against the Hanadi, who, with their subtribes, were then in possession not only of the north coast but were also settled all over the Beheira.

After the departure of the French in 1801, a firman was addressed to the sheikhs of the Hanadi, Afrad (a division of the Awlad 'Ali), Jumei'at, Beni 'Una, and other Arabs resident in Beheira, confirming them in their territories, but threatening them with expulsion and fine if they misbehaved themselves.[1]

By 1808, the Hanadi seem to have been quite driven out by the Awlad 'Ali, for in that year they bought their peace with Muhammad 'Ali and asked for the restitution of their lands in Beheira. The Pasha agreed to this and sent troops under Shahin Bey to chase the Awlad 'Ali out again. The Awlad 'Ali responded by offering 100,000 "tallaris" to be allowed to remain in the lands of the Hanadi—an offer which Muhammad Ali accepted. When they failed to pay up, troops were again sent to aid the Hanadi against them, but this combined force was completely defeated by the Awlad 'Ali near Hosh 'Isa.[2]

Of the events of 1810, Jabarti says :

"During his stay at Alexandria, he (Muhammad Ali) gave safe conduct to the chiefs of the Bedouins of the tribe of Awlad Ali who lived in the province of Beheira, and by this ruse enticed them to him ; but hardly had they arrived than he had them arrested, claimed large sums from them, and sent his soldiers to carry off their cattle ; their wives and their children were dishonoured. He then gave them robes of honour."[3]

Finally he exiled the Hanadi to Sharqiya, then a desert, and gave the Awlad 'Ali their lands on the coast and in Beheira.

[1] Jabarti, vii, 78–80.   [2] Jabarti, viii, 171 and 179–180.   [3] Jabarti, viii, 300.

THE WESTERN BEDOUIN

Had the Senussi been successful in the last war, they would no doubt have brought in the 'Ibeidat or the 'Awaqir from Cyrenaica to replace the Awlad 'Ali in Egypt.

At the present day the Awlad 'Ali, especially the eastern sections near the Nile Valley, have almost ceased to be nomadic, and only the old men have memories of their former warlike habits. They suffered considerably during the Great War, but are again becoming prosperous. They now own large comfortable tents, are beginning to build houses and clear out cisterns, and are also said to be increasing in numbers.[1] So civilized have they grown that my guides, one a Sinai Arab and the other an 'Abadi, concurred in calling them " green "—not real desert-worthy Bedouins.

Perhaps as a result of Libyan influence, or more probably the better nurture and climate, they are taller, heavier, stronger, and lighter-complexioned than the lightly built Arabs of Sinai and Hijaz. Also they are much franker and more straightforward than their shifty and suspicious eastern cousins, and altogether more trustworthy. Their women only veil themselves to strangers, and talk quite naturally and cheerfully to the men of their own tribe.

They cultivate as much barley as they can, using a primitive plough drawn by camels, in the clayey hollows scattered over their very stony limestone desert, but, as the rainfall is very uncertain, a good crop only occurs every five or six years. After harvest, they exchange some of their barley for maize, which the women grind to make bread as required, and some for dried dates. The seed for next year is buried in a hole lined with straw and covered with clay, and a year's forage for the animals is set aside. The rest of the crop goes to market, and for a short time the Arab has money to buy clothes for himself and his family and at utmost need to pay off some of the numerous debts he has inherited from his forefathers. Soon he is reduced again to the clothes he wears, the tent he sleeps in, and his animals grazing in the desert.

They are great breeders of camels and sheep, and a busy traffic in these goes on weekly in the markets of Hammam, 'Amriya, and the Beheira. So they have got into the habit

[1] At the 1927 census, the Western Desert Arabs, Awlad 'Ali, Jawabis, etc., numbered 38,928 souls exclusive of those settled in Beheira. But Pacho, 100 years ago, estimated them at 38,000 souls.

of thinking in money, and they reckon blood-money in cash (£300) and not in camels, as Bedouin should.

The more adventurous make, annually, long and waterless journeys to the oases of Siwa and Bahariya to remove the date crop, and, after their own wants are provided for, a good profit usually results from the sale of the remainder.

An Egyptian critic, who should know them only too well,[1] calls them "haughty, independent, and untrustworthy in character. They are dull and so abnormally lazy that they have no desire whatever to do more than they learnt (when young)". But he puts this down to the nature of the country; less generous critics ascribe the nature of the country to them!

Besides the descendants from 'Ali's three sons, 'Ali el-Abyad, 'Ali el-Ahmar, and Sineina, a large section called Sinaqra reckons its descent from Sinqir, a mysterious white man who was wrecked and washed up on the coast near Salum some time in the seventeenth century.[2] These are the true Awlad 'Ali, whose sections live mingled together in the most intricate fashion. Among them live also the Jumei'at, who invited them into the country, and various families of other *murabitin*, such as Qat'an, Awlad Suleiman, Hawara, Habun, etc. To distinguish themselves from their vassals, the Awlad 'Ali call themselves *hurr* free, and the *murabitin* are divided into various grades, according as they pay tribute or not.

The Awlad 'Ali are divided into three main divisions, with section (*badanat*) and subsections ('*eilat*) as follows. Some of these are so numerous that they practically constitute fresh tribes of their own.

I. Awlad Kharuf

These are the descendants of 'Ali el-Abyad ("The White"), the eldest son of 'Ali bin 'Aqar bin Dib, and are subdivided again into:

Section.	Subsections.
(1) 'Eilet Bu Hindi	'Eilet Bu Zayyana, 'Eilet Bahiya, 'Eilet Da'ud
(2) 'Eilet Bu Diya	'Eilet Ibrahim, 'Eilet Jereisat
(3) Awlad Mansur	El-Afrad, El-Tawa'il, 'Eilet 'Abd Allah

[1] Muhammad Bey Wasfi, for many years Inspector at Borg el-'Arab.
[2] Their sheikh told Hamilton in 1853, there were seven generations between him and Sinqir.

(SINAQRA)

The Sinaqra, or descendants of Sinqir, are also reckoned among the descendants of Ali the White, "because Sinqir married his daughter Khadija." They include:—

(4) Afrad　　　　　　Maghawra
(5) Azayim　　　　　'Eilet el-Abdi, Muwamna
(6) 'Eilet Eleura　　'Eilet Jeballa, 'Eilet Omar, 'Eilet Harun, 'Eilet Ajarma, 'Eilet Tahir.

II.

The descendants of 'Ali bin 'Aqar's second son, 'Ali el-Ahmar (" The Red ") are:—

(1) 'Esheibat　　　'Eilet ed-Dawi, 'Eilet el-Azraq, El-Wassafa, 'El-Lazumi
(2) Kimeilat　　　'Eilet el-Hajj Muhammad, El-Maharsa, 'El-Khadayij
(3) Jineishat [1]　'Eilet el-Majduba, Es-Samayil, Tabak

III. SINANA

The Sinana are the descendants of Sineina, the third son of Ali bin 'Aqar bin Dib. They include:—

(1) Mahafid　　　'Eilet Etman, 'Eilet el-Hammama, 'Eilet esh-Shimla
(2) Arawa　　　　'Eilet ez-Zireiriya, 'Eilet el-Ghazulat
(3) Qatifa　　　　'Eilet Nasralla, 'Eilet-Omar, Esh-Shawalha.
(4) Ijna

Jawabis.—The nomadic Jawabis (sing. Jibusi) are for the most part still settled in and around the Wadi Natrun, where General Andreossy found them in Napoleon's time. He calls them:

> "A hospitable tribe who lead a shepherd's life and encamp there every winter with their flocks. They are employed during this time carrying Natrun and prickly reeds; they also have some traffic in dates, which they fetch in caravans from Sioua in the Ammonian Oasis; it is a journey of twelve to fifteen days. These Arabs are *marabouths*, or peaceful people." [2]

He goes on to say they never make war, and only take up arms to defend themselves. In his time the tribe was composed of about 2,000 men, and possessed 60 horses. A little

---
[1] Kennett gives the three subdivisions of the Jineishat as Madi, Samayil, and Jabr.
[2] *Memoirs Relative to Egypt*, 288.

later Wilkinson estimated them at about 400 men near El Terrana and the Wadi Natrun.

At the present day they are still reckoned *Murabitin*, but, like the Jumei'at, are sufficiently independent not to have to pay tribute. They share with the Awlad 'Ali in the date traffic with Bahariya Oasis, where the produce of the village of Mandisha is reserved for them, and that from Bawitti for the Awlad 'Ali.

Kennett notes (p. 54) that they demand £400 for blood-money instead of £300, the usual price in the Western Desert, and alludes (p. 67) to :

> " The free and easy way in which the Gawabees tribe near the Wadi Natrun pack up their summer tents and leave them in situ while they themselves trek off with their winter tents into the open desert for the winter grazing is indicative of this code of honesty prevailing among them."

On page 101, he calls them " nearly all very small men, with strangely similar features and characteristics running through all the families of the tribe ".

Bramly has collected three pedigrees of the tribe all going back to Sheikh 'Abd el-Jawad el-Kassar. They state that they are an offshoot from the Qadadfa, and about 500 years ago left Saqiet el-Hamra in Morocco to settle in Egypt.

As a reward for " settling some affairs in the Wadi Natrun ", Muhammad 'Ali Pasha granted them the usual Bedouin privilege of exemption from military service. There are small colonies of them elsewhere among the Awlad Ali, while others are settled in the cultivated provinces of Giza, Beheira, Menufiya, and Gharbiya.

Jumei'at.—This tribe, possibly a remnant of the original Libyan inhabitants of Mariut, is of quite respectable antiquity, for Ibn Khaldun includes the Jumei'at as a subtribe of " Beni 'Ali ", themselves an offshoot from Beni Suleim. Whether his " Beni 'Ali " are the same as the modern Awlad 'Ali may be questioned, yet it is a reasonable assumption, for the exchange of the words " Beni " and " Awlad " in tribal names can be paralleled elsewhere.

The Jumei'at all agree that their remote ancestor, whom they share with the Awlad Suleiman and the Qat'an, was called Ka'b, and a Ka'b indeed appears in the pedigree ascribed

'Ilwani "Wanis"

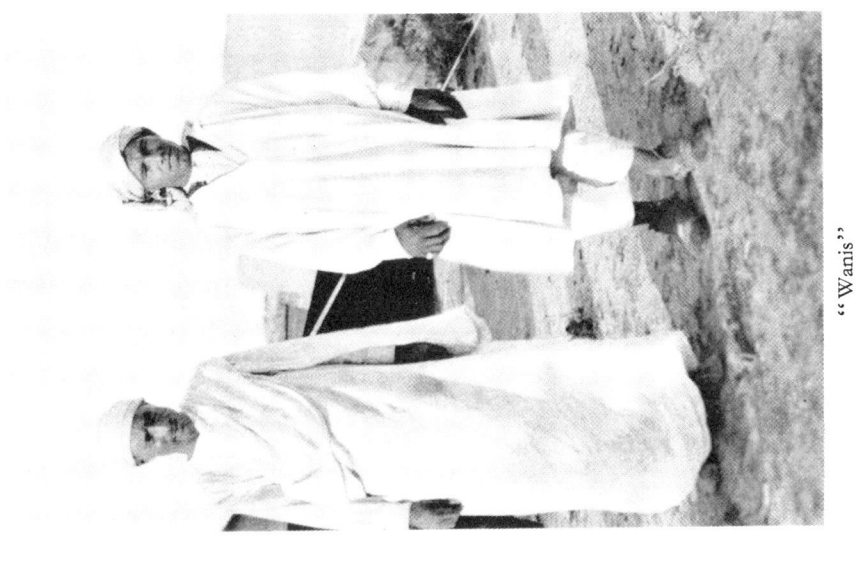

JUMEI'AT TYPES

[*face p.* 280

to Dib by Ibn Khaldun, who calls Dib a descendant of Ka'b, the great-grandson of Suleim.[1] If this be true, the Jumei'at must be an elder branch than any of the Sa'adi tribes, among whom the Awlad 'Ali are included. But in actual fact, the Awlad 'Ali do not consider the Jumei'at as of Sa'adi origin, that is, descendants of Abu Dib and his wife Sa'ada, but despise them as Murabitin or vassals, though they pay no tribute.

All this may be interpreted to mean that they are among the oldest inhabitants of Western Egypt. They have been in Egypt " seven hundred years " according to one of their sheikhs, Sa'ad Bey el-Masri, and a pedigree given me by another, Sheikh 'Ilwani Suleiman, who lives near Sidi 'Abd el-Rahman, runs :

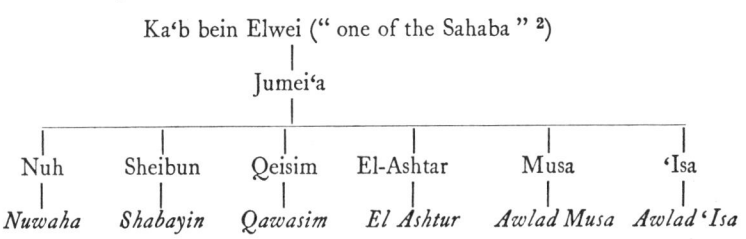

```
              Ka'b bein Elwei (" one of the Sahaba " [2])
                              |
                           Jumei'a
                              |
   ┌──────┬──────────┬─────────┬──────────┬──────────┐
  Nuh   Sheibun   Qeisim   El-Ashtar    Musa       'Isa
   |      |         |          |          |          |
 Nuwaha Shabayin Qawasim   El Ashtur  Awlad Musa Awlad 'Isa
```

The Jumei'at of Mariut are all descended from El-Ashtar, while the offspring of the other five sons are settled in Beheira, Gharbiya, and at Ramla near Alexandria.

It is, of course, possible that their eponymous ancestor, Jumei'a, was an Arab of Beni Suleim descent, who returned to Egypt from the " Green Mountain ", soon after the Beni Suleim invasion, and whose descendants became Murabitin by forming themselves into a religious community. But such religious fervour is not a Bedouin characteristic, but smacks rather of the fanaticism of the recently-converted, so I suspect the Jumei'at, in spite of their descent from Ka'b, to be mainly a remnant of the earlier Libyan population of the coast.

Prior to the arrival of the Awlad 'Ali, they were " Mrabit " to the Beni 'Una, and engaged in constant conflict with the Hanadi. Upon the rout and annihilation of the Beni 'Una, the Jumei'at were stirred up to revolt against the Hanadi by one of their holy men called Baqush. Outraged by their

---

[1] The more ignorant Awlad Suleiman have forgotten Ka'b's paternity, and confused him with the famous Arab poet Ka'b ibn Zuheir. See p. 287 for their version. And yet another Jumei'i version gives as their ancestor the Saint Ka'b el Ahbar.

[2] The " Friends " of the Prophet.

oppression, he gathered his people and delivered a fiery denunciation of his religion, during which he smashed his rosary into pieces and mixed it with his horse's fodder; Baqush then invited their kinsmen (?) the Awlad 'Ali, to come over from the " Green Mountain " and help them. To entice the Awlad 'Ali, he is said to have sent them samples of salt desert water and Nile water sweetened with sugar to illustrate the difference between the hardships of the desert and the comforts of the Rif.[1]

As recounted earlier, the Awlad 'Ali completely routed the Hanadi and their allies, and drove them from the desert. In the division of the conquered territory, the Jumei'at received a third, and, although they were still considered Murabitin, were released from the payment of tribute. They now live intermingled with the free sections of the Awlad 'Ali, all along the north coast of Egypt, and are numerous in Beheira, especially near Abu Hummus.

Samalus.—The Samalus are found scattered among the Awlad 'Ali on the northern coast and stranded among many of the Egyptian provinces. They once possessed a head sheikh Abu Sala at Minya, and colonies are recorded from Faiyum, Beheira, Menufiya, Gharbiya, and Sharqiya. An old paper from the Recruiting Department gives from seventeen villages in the Faiyum 775 mounted Samalus and 1,400 on foot, possessing 1,760 camels and 11,400 sheep. Two important groups of wells, both called " Sawani es-Samalus " exist on the north coast, one about 50 kilometres east of Salum, and the other 20 kilometres south of Dhab'a.

They say they came to Egypt, 400 strong, about 200 years ago, from the Wadi Samalus in the Jebel Akhdar, and their ancestor twelve generations ago was Nasr el-Hasani, of course an " Arab from Beni Suleim ".

In the *Description de l'Egypte*, P. D. Martin relates how in 1800 the Samalus of Faiyum were raided by a party of Ferjan, 200 strong, from Beheira.

Shiheibat.—These are a " Mrabit " tribe from the west with an unenviable reputation, living near the Wadi Natrun. Sayed Idris, the former Senussi leader, says of them : " Most

---

[1] Dumreicher, 16. This is probably the " Sheik Abdall Gawyal Bagooshi " who wrote to Sir Sydney Smith in March, 1801, warning him of the approach of the French from Damanhur. Wilson, *History of the British Expedition in Egypt*, 371. (Rif = cultivated area.)

THE WESTERN BEDOUIN

herds have a black goat or two—such are the Shiheibat." They are families of shepherds scattered amongst the Sa'adi families, and must not be confused with the 'Esheibat section of the Awlad 'Ali.

Dumreicher (pp. 52–7) gives a lively account of a quarrel between the Jawabis and the Shiheibat.

Chapter XVII
BEDOUIN SETTLED IN THE NILE VALLEY

"*Among the soldier-colonists of the Fayum and Upper Egypt, the papyri show a noticeable proportion of Cyreneans.*"—Bevan, *A History of Egypt under the Ptolemaic Dynasty.*

'Abs—'Afeinat—'Amayim—'Aqeila—'Atiyat—Awlad Suleiman—Bahja—Baraghith—Bar'asa—Beni 'Una—Beni Wasil—Billi—Dhu'afa—Fawakhir—Fawayid—Ferjan—Fezara—Hanadi—Harabi—Haruba—Hawara—Hawata—Hawazma—Ja'afira—Jahama—Jawazi—Jebeliya—Juheina—Luzd—Mugharba—Mujabara—Qadadfa—Qat'an—Tarhuna.

History has not repeated itself quite exactly since the days of the Ptolemies, for the Cyreneans referred to above were no doubt largely Greek by race, but the coincidence is striking, for the present-day population of Upper Egypt, and especially the Faiyum, has largely been reinforced in modern times from Cyrenaica.

There are also in Egypt offshoots from most of the Sinai tribes such as 'Ayaida, Haweitat, Sawalha, Sam'ana, Akharsa, Bayadiyin, with whom we have already dealt, and some fragments of tribes from Arabia itself such as Billi, Juheina, and 'Abs, and in Sharqiya a very important element has crossed over from the west, the Hanadi. Omitting the Sinai tribes, and reviewing the others in alphabetical order, we have:—

'Abs.—This tribe, famous in the days of "Ignorance" as that in whose bosom the hero 'Antar was nurtured, has sunk on such evil days that the name 'Absi is now applied as an insult equivalent to Hiteimi. This is the result of "giving a dog a bad name", for *'abs* may mean "filth", and when the 'Abs, a branch of Ghatafan, became weakened, their enemies no doubt lost no chance of punning on their name. Jennings Bramly met a few families of them in Sharqiya, and in Klunzinger's time there were 'Abs among the Arab fishermen settled on the coast at Queih and Safaja. These colonies have now disappeared. Burckhardt speaks of them as fishers on Hasani Island, and owning ships.

'Afeinat.—A section of this western tribe survives in Egypt, the Nejama, better known as the "Pyramid Arabs".

BEDOUIN SETTLED IN NILE VALLEY 285

'*Aqeila*.—These are stragglers from the society of 'Aqeil or 'Aqeilat, who are caravan-leaders and soldiers of fortune all over Arabia. They come through Sinai every week with

BEDOUIN TRIBES OF NORTHERN EGYPT.

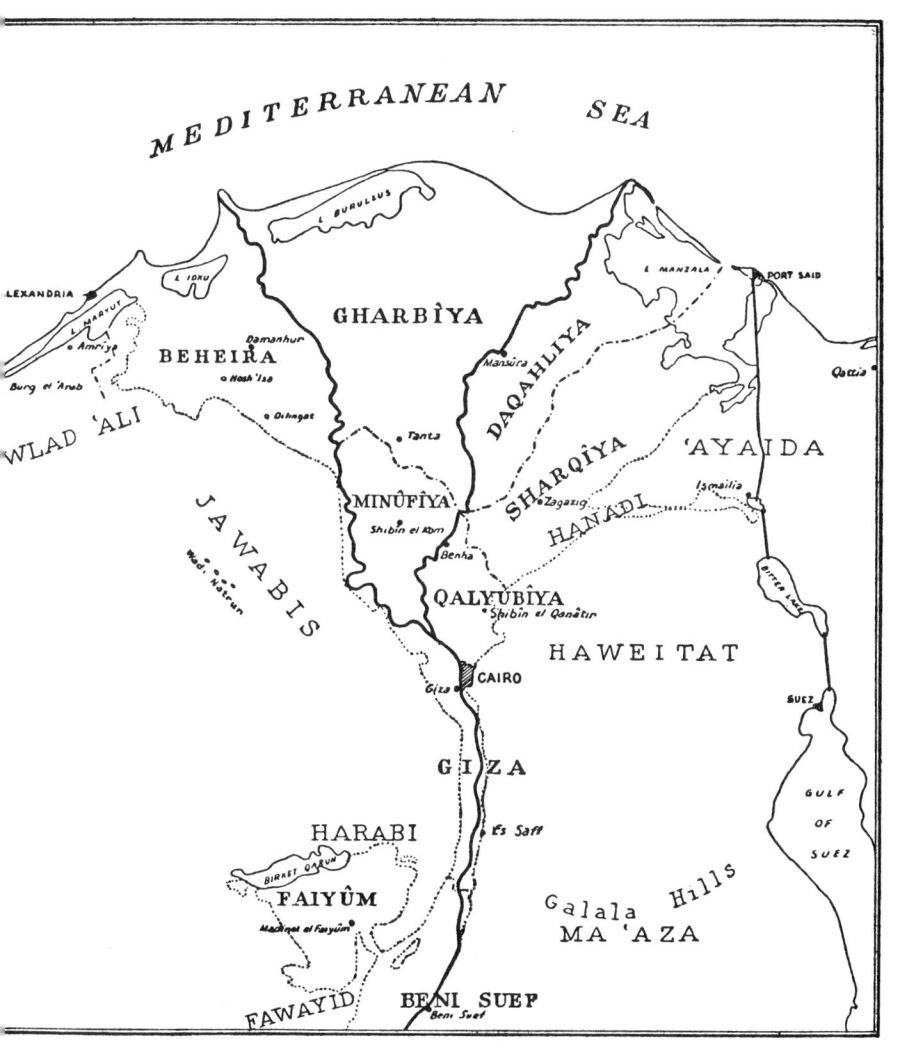

animals for sale in the Nile Valley, and a few have settled in Sharqiya. Nominally Arabs from Nejd, they are often really Hiteim, and call themselves " descended from the Beni Hilal ".

'Amayim.—Among the tribes of Berber origin settled on the desert edge near Manfalut are the 'Amayim, whose encampments are just south of those of the Jahama near the village of El-'Atamna. With the Jahama and Tarhuna, the 'Amayim are known collectively and euphemistically as " 'Arab el-Gharb ".

In company with the Billi from near Suhag, the 'Amayim are still accustomed to make an annual expedition of over 700 miles up the Darb el-Arba'in, the old slave traders' route through the oases of Kharga, Selima, and Laqiya to Bir Natrun in the Sudan. They there obtain natron which is sold on their return journey in Asyut for about 300 piastres a hundredweight. The Arab traveller, Et-Tunisi, met them on this errand between Selima and Laqiya in 1800. Their rivals, the Jahama, made a similar expedition in 1933, which resulted in a financial disaster, the natron only fetching P.T. 165 a hundredweight. They are exposed during the journey to raids by the Qura'n from Merga. The 'Amayim claim descent from Zoghb, a subtribe of the Beni Suleim, who are mentioned as taking part in the 1051 invasion.[1]

'Atiyat.—Vansleb met the 'Atiyat near Biba as long ago as 1673, and they are later referred to in the *Description de l'Egypte*,[2] compiled by the savants of Napoleon's expedition, as then forming the larger part of the population of the east bank of the Nile in the districts of 'Atfih, Ashmunein, and Manfalut, and to have only recently taken to cultivating the land. A letter from one of their headmen to the Recruiting Department asserts their descent from Beni 'Uqba, and says they have been in Egypt since the days of the first Moslem Conquest under 'Amr ibn el-'As. At the present time they are mostly settled round Abnub on the east bank near Asyut. They are undoubtedly of western origin, and some of them have lost their independence and, like the Sa'adna, become affiliated to the Jahama.

Awlad Suleiman.—Branches of a tribe of Murabitin, of considerable antiquity, settled in various parts of Egypt, though not now in the desert. In Maqrizi's time (1365–1441), they lived " between the great 'Aqaba and Suez ", that is to say, west of Salum.[3] Although reckoned Murabitin, the Awlad Suleiman of Cyrenaica are most warlike, and in Barth's

---

[1] Ibn Khaldun, i, 135.   [2] p. 275.   [3] Maqrizi, i, 42.

time raided as far as Lake Chad.[1] Once long ago, they practically exterminated the Jahama, and recently played a heroic part in the resistance to the Italian invasion.

A hundred years ago, Wilkinson gave them as 500 horsemen near Giza, "the rest not counted," and eighty Rabayi' (one of their subdivisions) near Beni 'Adi in Upper Egypt. These Rabayi' claim to have arrived in Egypt 1,800 strong from Tripoli under one Khalifa Balja. Like the Jumei'at and the Qat'an, the Awlad Suleiman claim descent from one Ka'b, whom some confuse with Ka'b ibn Zuheir, the famous Arab poet of antiquity. A version of their pedigree goes back seventeen generations, thus :—

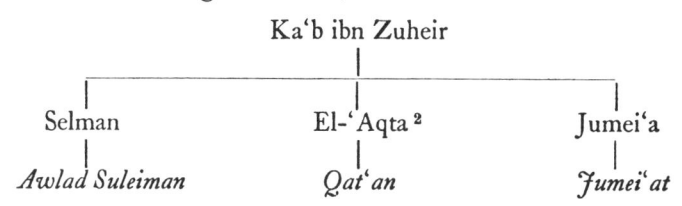

```
                    Ka'b ibn Zuheir
                           |
        _____|_____
        |                  |                  |
      Selman           El-'Aqta[2]          Jumei'a
        |                  |                  |
   Awlad Suleiman        Qat'an            Jumei'at
```

The Qadadfa, from whom the still nomadic Jawabis are an offshoot, are also said to be related to the Awlad Suleiman.

These Awlad Suleiman must not be confused with the eastern Awlad Suleiman, a division of the Masa'id settled in Sharqiya and the Hauran.

The modern Sohb, settled in the provinces of Giza, Qaliubiya, Gharbiya, Menufiya, Daqahliya, and Sharqiya, also give Awlad Suleiman as an alternative name for their tribe. But the historian Ibn Khaldun[3] says the Sohb are descended from Sohb ibn Fayid ibn Rafa' ibn Dibbab.

Bahja.—The Bahja, settled in Sharqiya and Gharbiya, claim descent from Beni Suleim, and give the following account of their origin :—

"When Obeidallah Ibn el-Hajjab was the ruler of Egypt, he asked Hashim ibn 'Abd el-Malek to send him some families from the tribe of Qeis, and in reply 3,000 men were sent about the year 728. The members of Beni Suleim emigrated, one after another, until none of them remained in Arabia. They resided in Upper Egypt

---

[1] He recounts the exploits of the "Weled Sliman" who, assisted by the Qadadfa, Ferjan, and other tribes, mustered 900 horsemen. They invaded Kanem, and in the course of two or three years stole "more than 30,000 camels" from the Tuareg. Their allies, however, deserted them, and proceeded home by way of Kufara. Left alone, the Awlad Suleiman were completely defeated by the Tuareg at Wadi Alala in 1850.
[2] Pronounced Laqta.   [3] Ibn Khaldun, i, 159.

during the period of the 'Ibadite dynasty, and migrated to the Maghreb, where the tents of the Awlad Sallam extended from Barka to the 'Aqaba el-Kubra (Salum), while from the 'Aqaba to Alexandria were the tents of the Awlad Muqdim comprising two batns, Awlad Turkiya and Awlad Fa'id. Both Awlad Muqdim and Awlad Sallam are descendants of Labeyid.

"The sheikh under whom the tribe migrated from Arabia was Ibn esh-Shedid es-Selmi, and when they went from Egypt to the west the sheikhs were Qaid Ibn Muqdim and Khalid Ibn Suleiman."

The Bahja, like the Beni 'Una and the Hanadi, form part of the first offshoot from Beni Suleim mentioned above, the Salalma or Awlad Sallam, for they claim that their ancestor Bahij was a son of Sallam. He is supposed to have founded Kom Bahij, beside Bahig station on the Mariut railway.

They migrated in the eighteenth century to Beheira, whence they were later expelled, with the other Salalma tribes, by Muhammad 'Ali to put a stop to their conflicts with the Awlad 'Ali.

Baraghith.—The descendants of Dib fall into two classes. The Baraghith, or descendants of Barghuth, include the Fawayid, Jawazi, Rammah, and the 'Orafa, while the 'Aqaqra, or descendants of 'Aqar, include the Harabi, the Bar'asa, and the Awlad 'Ali. The Fawayid and the Jawazi of Egypt are descended from Fayid and Jibrin, the sons of Barghuth, and until 500 years ago they constituted one tribe, but then in consequence of a family quarrel, followed by a great fight, they split into two divisions, the Awlad Fayid and the Awlad Jibrin. At the present day, these names are simply collective ; the Awlad Fayid consist of the Fawayid and the 'Orafa (the latter still in Cyrenaica), while the Awlad Jibrin are represented by the Jawazi in Egypt, and the Mujabra, 'Awaqir, and Mugharba, in the west.

These Awlad Fayid and Awlad Jibrin believe their ancestors to have lived near Bougie in Algeria, and Ibn Khaldun mentions a tribe of Beni Jibrin living at that very place.[1] He calls them a branch of Zuawa.

Bramly collected from them the following description of an old-time battle in the west :—

"On the day of Karkura the Baraghith and 'Aqaqra fought against each other, and he who caused the fight was Hamed Bayad

[1] i, 256.

BEDOUIN SETTLED IN NILE VALLEY

of the Bar'asa. The fight began before the rising of the sun, when the Arabs of Barka entrenched themselves. The foremost tribes of Barka were the Jawazi, after them the 'Awaqir, then the Mugharba, then the Fawayid. Of the Murabitin the most important were the Zuaya, the Fawakhir, and the Shiheibat, and the chief of them all was 'Abd en-Nebi Muteirid. Karkura, where this battle took place, is in the Barka el-Hamra. The women of both sides came out on camels to encourage the warriors, and she who beat the drum for the 'Aqaqra was Amina, and for the Baraghith, Habak beat the drum. When the son of Habak was slain, Amina sang: ' O Habak, it pleases me that your son is killed ! ' But Habak answered, ' My son's death is but a small thing, since 'Abd en-Nebi is still chief of Barka.' Then turning to her dying son, she said, ' Since 'Abd en-Nebi has won, rejoice in death ! ' Hamed Bayad was exulting in the powers of his son on this day, when he learnt of his death at the hands of 'Abd en-Nebi. After these events, the 'Aqaqra were completely beaten, and the victory remained in the hands of the Baraghith."

The Baraghith came to Egypt in company with the Hanadi in the eighteenth century in the great immigration under Yunis Ibn Mirdas es-Selmi. Later, when they joined that tribe in its war against the Awlad 'Ali, the Baraghith were driven from the desert.

During the wars of Muhammad 'Ali Pasha, 630 Fawayid are recorded as having accompanied him to the Sudan, and 153 to Syria. The corresponding figures for the Jawazi are 833 to the Sudan and 204 to the Hijaz.

When Sa'id Pasha attempted to conscript the Bedouin into his army, 'Omar Bey el-Masri, the Omda of the Jawazi, led an expedition which was intended to start a return migration to their ancestral home in Cyrenaica. But he was only able to collect some 200 men, seventy from his own tribe and the rest from the Berber tribes of 'Amayim, Tarhuna, and Jahama. After a brush at Balat in the Oasis of Dakhla with a party of other Bedouins sent in pursuit, they succeeded in crossing the frontier of the Vilayet of Tripoli, but the Turkish Government, unwilling to add to its responsibilities, obtained by negotiation with Sa'id Pasha their further exemption from military service, whereupon they returned and settled in the neighbourhood of the Faiyum.

'Omar Bey el-Masri remained in Tripoli till the time of Isma'il Pasha, who pardoned him and allowed him to return to his estates in Upper Egypt. Although doughty, he was a little man, and they tell of him that once as he lay asleep in a tent a woman asked another who he was. On being told it was 'Omar Bey el-Masri, she crept in and began to span him with her hand. 'Omar wakened when she reached his heart and cried, " Stop woman ! Don't you know a man's size is that of his heart ? "

Forms collected in 1909 gave 14,050 Fawayid settled in the provinces of Faiyum, Beni Suef and Minya, and 9,694 Jawazi, mostly in Minya. There is also a northern branch of the Fawayid in Beheira.

The head of the Fawayid is Sala Pasha Lamlum who owns a great deal of land on the desert edge of Minya Province due west of Maghagha. He is the brother-in-law of Sheikh 'Abd el-Qadir el-Kazza, the chief of the 'Awaqir in Tripoli, and acted as mediator between the 'Awaqir and the Awlad 'Ali in 1904 and 1905.

An important branch of the Fawayid is the Rammah, almost a separate tribe, who separated from them peaceably (without the usual quarrel) under an ancestor Zeidan. These live mostly in the Faiyum, but also in Beni Suef and Minya. Hamed Pasha el-Bassal, the well-known politician, belongs to this family.

The Jalalat, living in Minya Province, also claim descent from Barghuth.

Bar'asa.—The Bar'asa are an offshoot from Harb, for their founder Bar'as, son of Hamed, was a grandson of Harb, the common ancestor. The original Bar'asa are a large and important tribe settled in the " Green Mountain ", of whom the 'Eilet Khadra, the section now living in Egypt, once formed part. But about 1830, as the result of a battle at El-Abraq near Derna, the 'Eilet Khadra lost " 700 " men and were driven from Cyrenaica. Their conqueror, Abu Bakr Hadud, became chief of the Bar'asa, and later virtual governor of Barka.[1]

The 'Eilet Khadra live mostly in the Faiyum round the town of Sinaru. There are five subdivisions, viz. Halaliya, Khawalid, Mahafis, Shiteiwat, and Terada. (The Khawalid are mentioned in Wilkinson's list (1843) as 300 strong, living near Ishmant in Beni Suef Province.)

Suleiman Bey Bayad, the Omda, belongs to the same family as that ruling the Bar'asa in the west.

---

[1] James Hamilton, in his *Wanderings in North Africa*, describes this worthy.

Beni 'Una.—The Beni 'Una were formerly a division of the Salalma or Awlad Sallam branch of the Beni Suleim. They were the Sa'adi tribe to whom the Jumei'at were formerly *mrabit*. Driven from the desert by the Hanadi, they have become completely lost in the *fellahin* population.

Beni Wasil.—The Sawalha and the 'Aleiqat relate that when they came to Sinai, they found it inhabited by the Hamada and the Beni Wasil. The former are now only about twelve tents strong, and live mostly near Sarabit el-Khadim and Bir Nasb, where they are reckoned as part of the 'Aleiqat. In Sinai, the Beni Wasil are an even smaller sect, living near Tor—but on the maps of a century ago they are shown as inhabiting the whole Eastern Desert of Egypt north of the Qift–Quseir road. They were thus precursors of the Ma'aza. None of them now inhabit the Eastern Desert, but at various points in the Nile Valley one finds their colonies, notably near Akhmim, where their Omda, 'Abd er-Rasul, said : " Our tribe is descended from Beni 'Uqba, and formerly inhabited Aga and Salima in Arabia. Two hundred years ago the tribe migrated to Egypt to escape famine, and we think it then numbered about 600 men. The tribe lived in the Red Sea Hills opposite Girga Province and about a hundred years ago came down to the Nile, where most of them settled in the village of Akhmim."

Ibn Khaldun speaks also of the Beni Wasil of Egypt as " a branch of the Beni 'Uqba, son of Moghraba, son of Judham of the Qahtaniya ". If so, they are genuine Yemenites. The Beni 'Uqba were formerly a powerful tribe in Hijaz, but have suffered so severely at the hands of the Haweitat that they are now reduced to a few families living near Maqna.

Of their entry into Egypt, the Arab historian Hamadani says they emigrated from Syria at the invitation of the Emir Mu'izz et-Turkomani. But Burckhardt says they came from Barbary.[1] Certainly some of the Beni 'Uqba accompanied the Beni Hilal westwards, and Leo Africanus wrote of them : " They are a rude and wilde people, and in very deade estranged from all humanitie." [2]

There is a depression called Naqo Beni Wasil named after them not far east of Beni Suef ; while the village on the Nile opposite Beni Suef called Bayad en-Nasara is still inhabited by Beni Wasil.

[1] Burckhardt, ii, 12.   [2] Leo Africanus, i, 144.

Billi.—The Billi of Sinai and Egypt are offshoots from the great Arabian tribe of the same name descended from Qudhaʻa, who live on the coast of Arabia between Nuʼman I and the Wadi Hamdh. Sprenger thought they " came from Southern Arabia and exterminated the Thamudites ".[1] However that may be, they were prominent in the Conquest of Egypt, and ʻAmr said of them, " They have mostly been Companions of the Prophet, and their principal quality is that they are excellent cavaliers."

Twelve thousand of the *fellahin* in the provinces of Sharqiya and Qaliubiya claim descent from these conquerors. Of nomadic Billi, there is a small section, the Billi el-Barʻasa in North Sinai, and a colony in Upper Egypt, on the east bank of the Nile between Suhag and Baliana, under Sheikh Suleiman Muhammad. These ranged out into the Eastern Desert to Bir Sheitun in the old salt-smuggling days, and there is an important wadi named after them near the porphyry quarries. These Billi also combine with the ʻAmayim for the expedition to get natron from Bir Natrun in the Sudan. These Upper Egyptian Billi are recent arrivals from Arabia, for they recognize relationships with the ruling family there of Ibn Rifada. Perhaps they came over with the Arabs from Yambo to resist Napoleon's expedition. They are now in dress and appearance just like the Egyptian *fellahin.*

Dhuʻafa.—These Arabs, now settled in Egypt among the *fellahin* of Giza and Beni Suef, claim to be an offshoot of the ancient Arab tribe of Beni Tamim. They say the Beni Tamim came to Egypt with the first Muslim conqueror, Amr ibn-el-As, and afterwards invaded Tripoli, where their ranks were so reduced by fever that the tribe was nicknamed *El-Dhuʻafa* " the weaklings ". The well of Ain et-Tamimi in the " Green Mountain " is said to have been dug by them, and it still belongs to the Dhuʻafa living near Derna. In the time of Wali Pasha (A.D. 1713) "four thousand " of the tribe emigrated to Egypt under the leadership of Masaʻud ʻOmar and his sons Hamud and Muhammad. Wilkinson (1843) put them as 500 strong at Qiman el-ʻArus near Wasta. Bramly has a return giving them as 402 in Beni Suef Province.

Fawakhir.—The Fawakhir are another tribe of Murabitin from the west, who claim descent from a holy man, Sidi Fakhr et-Teir (commonly called *Et-Tiyyur* " the flier "), who

---

[1] In a letter to Sir R. Burton, see *The Land of Midian*, i, 296.

BEDOUIN SETTLED IN NILE VALLEY

is said to be buried at Barka el-Hamra near Benghazi. He, of course, was " one of the Beni Suleim ". While in Cyrenaica, they were allied to the 'Awaqir, but some time in the eighteenth century they emigrated " in families without a proper leader ", and settled in Egypt as " Mrabit " to the Hanadi. When the Awlad 'Ali came in at the invitation of the Jumei'at to expel the Hanadi, the Fawakhir were driven out too, and settled in Sharqiya. They now became " white " murabitin, that is, they ceased to pay tribute to their old masters.

Fawayid.—The Fawayid, or Awlad Fayid, are a subsection of the Baraghith, *q.v.*

Ferjan.—The Egyptian Ferjan claim descent from the Beni Suleim through " Barghuth, son of Abu Dib ", and came to Egypt with a great immigration in the eighteenth century under Yunis ibn Yahya ibn Mirdas es-Selmi, and these remained for thirty years in " uneasy peace " before they settled down. They claim to have assisted Muhammad 'Ali Pasha in his wars, and to have been granted the usual privileges. 'Eilet Ferjan still appears as the name of a sub-section of the Hasa tribe in Cyrenaica. The Egyptian Ferjan are found in Minya, Faiyum (where a century ago Wilkinson counted 220 near Sennures), and Gharbiya. Klippel calls them Berber.

Fezara.—The original Fezara, like 'Abs, were a section of Ghatafan, descendants of Qeis. By the time of the Prophet, they had become an independent tribe, living near Mecca. In the early days of Islam, they played a prominent part in the great feud between the Beni Kelb and the Beni Qeis. Some of them accompanied the Beni Hilal in their invasion of the Maghreb where, a century later, according to Idrisi, they had coalesced with the Berbers to such an extent as hardly to be distinguished from them.

Again, Maqrizi talks of Fezara in Upper Egypt, where there are still some in Beni Suef Province. There are also others at Qaliub in the Delta, but according to their Omda, these came to Egypt from the west, so it is better to assume that in them the Berber predominates rather than the Arab, indeed Jennings Bramly includes them among the Murabitin.

At one time, some of the Sudan tribes called themselves Fezara, and MacMichael [1] says of them :—

" The term Fezara is now no longer heard in the Sudan, but to the travellers of the eighteenth and nineteenth centuries, and

---

[1] MacMichael, i, 255.

perhaps even until the '*Mahdia*', it was the usual denomination of the largest group of camel-owning nomads of Kordofan and Darfur. These are now much more distinctly divided and each tribe is known by its own name."

He goes on to point out that these Sudan "Fezara" now claim descent from the Qahtanid Juheina, whereas the original Fezara, who invaded Egypt were, as stated above, descendants of Qeis and therefore Ishmaelites. That is to say, they have abandoned a claim to an ancient but forgotten lineage for something better-sounding.

Among these Sudanese "Fezara", we find the name Turshan as a subdivision of the Awlad Aqoi, and Tursha as a subdivision of Ferahna, both subtribes of Dar Hamid, one of the tribes into which the original Fezara have split up. In Egypt, Turshan occurs as the name of a section settled in Asyut Province and claiming common origin with the Tarhuna. Klippel stigmatizes the Turshan as Berbers, and he is probably right.

Hanadi.—The Hanadi are Salalma, that is they claim descent from Beni Suleim through Hind, daughter of Sallam. Before the rise of Muhammad 'Ali to power, the Hanadi were living in Beheira Province, where they were continually harassed and often defeated in fights by the Awlad 'Ali, who had been called in by the Jumei'at, a Mrabit tribe, to aid them against the Hanadi. Yadim Sultan, the sheikh of the Menasra section, was the head of the tribe at that time.

But Napoleon's savants give Musa Abu 'Ali as " the chief of the principal tribe of the Hanadi. They possess about three or four hundred horses and, with their allies, can muster from 900 to 1,000 cavalry.[1]

In the days of Muhammad 'Ali, the Awlad 'Ali completed their victory over the Hanadi by driving them out of Beheira. They moved to Sharqiya, where they were granted sixteen villages near the Wadi Tumeilat.

Burckhardt says of them at this period :—

"The Hanady, a tribe of Moggrebyn Bedouins, who have adopted the dress and customs of the Barbary and Libyan Arabs. They were formerly established in the Beheyre province of the Delta and in the desert extending from the Pyramids towards Alexandria. Having been overpowered by another Moggrebyn tribe of the same province, much superior to them in numbers,

[1] *Memoirs Relative to Egypt*, 298.

BEDOUIN SETTLED IN NILE VALLEY

they were obliged to abandon the right of tribute which they had exacted from the villages of the Beheyre, and leave it to their more powerful rivals. They retired across the River Nile towards the Sharkye where they now reside. From five to six hundred horsemen constitute the utmost forces of all these Sharkye tribes. Thirty years ago they were able to muster at least three thousand, *if we may believe their own reports*. The Pasha of Egypt levies a tribute on them at present, and observes their movements with so much vigilance that they are not permitted to make war against each other, the most galling predicament in which a Bedouin can possibly be placed." [1]

About this time, Shafei, the sheikh of the 'Elawat section, served with 200 of his men throughout the Syrian campaigns of Muhammad 'Ali,[2] and gained that viceroy's favour to such an extent, that on Yadim Sultan's death, he was appointed to control half the tribe, to the disgust of the Menasra section.

Shafei was succeeded as sheikh of half the Hanadi by his son Tahawi, by tradition a man of very strong character and turbulent temper, while Mahmud Sultan succeeded Sultan ibn Yadim as head of the Menasra half. But Tahawi's ardour would brook no opposition, and he began to usurp all authority. This led to a plot being formed against him, and he was murdered at a meeting of some of his tribe at Nesdiya in the tents of a family called Esh-Shiraji. Even though warned of treachery, he characteristically insisted on going to the meeting. Aided by Muhammad 'Ali's troops, Tahawi's brother 'Amir pursued the Menasra as far as Qatia and killed some of them there. The rest fled to Syria till a peace was patched up in which they had little faith. For on their return they avoided Sharqiya and settled in the province of Beni Suef, where they were included in the census of 1847.

In 1849, Muhammad 'Ali Pasha died, and under Abbas Pasha 'Amir esh-Shafei found himself out of favour. An informer called Nabeishi declared that 'Amir and the Hanadi were plotting to seize the country. Abbas determined to arrest the whole family and actually imprisoned two of its members, Feisal and Gharib, in the Citadel, while the rest fled to Syria.

Said Pasha released them and invited the Tahawi family

[1] *Notes*, 226.
[2] Altogether 1,154 Hanadi and 100 Bahja are recorded in the archives at the Citadel as having taken part in these campaigns between 1835–1840. Some of these remained after the campaigns and settled near Aleppo.

to return. Suleiman, the younger brother of 'Amir, was the first to come back to Egypt, and some of his lands in the Wadi Tumilat were restored.

Harabi.—The Harabi, like the Awlad 'Ali, claim descent from Dib through his son 'Aqar, and both they and the Bar'asa are of common origin with the 'Ibeidat of Cyrenaica. Their old home lay between Salum and Derna, from which they had driven out the Awlad 'Ali, who then settled in Egypt.

At the beginning of the nineteenth century, the Harabi also began to migrate to Egypt in very small numbers, so small that no member of their ruling family thought it worth while to accompany them. In fact their present Sheikh Riad el-Jibali is of Qat'an origin.

This Jibali family originally came from Aujila, and settled beside the Samalus ed-Daminat in the Beheira. For two generations they married Samalus women. The third generation married an Owakla woman (the Owakla are a sub-tribe of the Harabi) and had a son Husein; Husein married a Mifush woman (the Mifush are another sub-tribe of the Harabi), and their son was the Jibali to whom they owe their present importance.

Muhammad 'Ali recognized Jibali as sheikh of the small number of Harabi who were then settled in the Faiyum. Later on Muhammad 'Ali increased Jibali's authority until he became chief of all the Arabs in the Faiyum. His tribe then began to increase rapidly, until at present there are something like 30,000 " Harabi " (not all of course blood-relations) registered as living in Egypt.

The office of chief sheikh of the Harabi in Egypt has since remained in the Jibali family, although they are not really connected with the old ruling family of the tribe, the 'Eilet Gheith.

Two-thirds of the Egyptian Harabi live in the Faiyum, and are settled on the land, as is also the case with their colonies at Kafr ez-Zayat and Simbellawein. Some live in Mariut and further west among the Awlad 'Ali. These are nomadic, and take part in the carrying trade of Siwa.

Haruba.—A small tribe of Hiteim (?) living on the east bank opposite Baliana.

Hawara.—The Hawara Berbers have already been referred to in the second chapter.[1] Up to the eighteenth century

[1] p. 29.

PLATE XXX

BISHARIN TYPES

[face p. 296

they practically dominated Egypt south of Asyut and were famous horsemen and oppressors of the Copts. Their great sheikh Hamam, who ruled like a king, was killed by the Mamelukes, but the power of the tribe was not broken till the time of Muhammad 'Ali, when Ibrahim Pasha finally crushed it. In Upper Egypt, the Hawara are now lost in the *fellahin*.

In the west, a few Hawara families are still found in the desert as Murabitin to the Awlad 'Ali ; while in the Sudan the large and vigorous camel-owning tribe of the Hawawir (in Dongola) is also an ancient offshoot from the Hawara.

Hawata.—The Hawata are a tribe of Murabitin, "bil Baraka" living some in Beheira and others near Sennures in the Faiyum. They claim descent through Labeiyid from Suleim, and say they are allied to the Awlad 'Ali, Ferjan, and Samalus.[1]

Hawazim or *Hawazma.*—There are a few of these in Upper Egypt. Originally perhaps from Harb ; they form an important section of the Baqqara tribe in Kordofan.[2]

Ja'afira.—A branch of the Prophet's own tribe, the Qureish. Tradition has it that these, the descendants of Ja'afir ibn Abu Talib, were expelled from Mecca in the tenth century, and settled in Upper Egypt between Aswan and Qus. Others went further south into Mahass. They have long since become *fellahin* and town-dwellers.

Jahama.—Like the 'Amayim, the Jahama are of Tripolitan origin, and they relate that the males of their tribe were once exterminated by the Awlad Suleiman. Fortunately of the women who were spared, forty were pregnant, and from their offspring all the present Jahama are descended. Their eponymous ancestor, *the* Jahami, was so named "because he had luxuriant hair". They ascribe their origin to the Beni 'Ummayya, a branch of the Prophet's own tribe, the Qureish, but contain a great deal of Berber blood.

At one time they raided far and wide among the oases, and there was a colony of them settled in Kufara.

Nowadays they live for the most part in tents on the edge of the cultivation near Manfalut, though a few of the more wealthy have built houses and begun to cultivate. In the

---

[1] Bramly writes : " So holy do they esteem themselves that their Omda, when asked at Itai el-Barud to swear to the truth of a statement, burst into a roar of grief, to the astonishment of the Minister of War, who was present. He said he had never been so insulted before, and the other Omdas backed him up."

[2] s. MacMichael, i, 280–4.

autumn, some of them migrate into the oases, returning to the Nile in spring to avoid camel-fly. Not infrequently cattle are lifted by them and driven across to the Oasis of Dakhla, a long and thirsty journey. Others again, like the 'Amayim, make the long journey to the Sudan for natron.

The Jahama of our day have produced a really wonderful Arab traveller, Hajji Qwayatin,[1] a sort of illiterate Ibn Battuta, who, not content with performing the Mecca pilgrimage, visited Wadai and Sokoto, acted for some time as tax-collector among the Bedayat for 'Ali Dinar, the late Sultan of Darfur, lived for a long time with the Senussi at Kufara and disappeared two years ago on his return from a wild search for the mythical oasis of Zarzura. A large map, constructed from the information which he gave to Harding King, exists in the Survey of Egypt archives, which shows he had a remarkably correct mental picture of the Libyan Desert.

Among their sub-divisions are Zurg, No'om, Tallab (pl. Talalib), and, from affiliated tribes, 'Atiyat and Sa'adna.

Jawazi.—v. sub-*Baraghith*.

Jebeliya.—Some of the *fellahin* living near Tala in Menufiya province claim descent from an offshoot of the Beni Suleim going by this name, and assert that the rest of their tribe live in Tripoli. They must not be confused with the Jebeliya serfs of the Convent of St. Catherine in Sinai.

Juheina.—The Juheina were among the first to embrace Islam and to invade Africa. Six hundred of them took part in the first Libyan expedition in 647, and many of them joined the Rabi'a in their invasion of the Beja country in 869.

Ibn Khaldun describes them as conquering the Northern Sudan, succeeding to the chieftaincies of the Nuba tribes by marrying the kings' daughters, and living an uncivilized life " following the rainfall like the Arab of Arabia ". At the present day nearly every " Arab " of the Sudan has a fictitious pedigree going back to 'Abdalla el-Juhani.

Others were left behind, for Maqrizi, writing about 1400, calls them the most numerous tribe in Upper Egypt.

Nowadays they are lost in the *fellahin*, except for a small colony near Dishna. Some of them occasionally accompany a Ma'aza caravan into the desert; and I remember once comparing a Juheina lad from Dishna with some of his

---

[1] He was the brother of Mansur, the present chief of the tribe. Harding King has much to say about Qwayatin in his *Mysteries of the Libyan Desert*.

pearl-fishing cousins from Yambo. Beside them he seemed a true fellah.

The tribe is still powerful in Arabia, with its centre at Yambo. The pearl-fishers come north as far as Tor, where I counted twenty-three of their dug-out canoes at work off Jebel Hammam Saidna Musa in April, 1933.

Luzd.—A small tribe of Murabitin in Beheira. They claim as a member of their tribe the famous saint 'Okasha, buried at a hot spring in the Third Cataract region of the Sudan.

Mugharba.—Besides being a generic name for all western Bedouin, a considerable branch of the Awlad Jibrin (Baraghith) is so styled in Cyrenaica. There are few of them in Egypt.

Mujabra.—The Mujabra (sing. Majbari) are another offshoot of the Awlad Jibrin, occupying the oases of Aujila and Jalo in Cyrenaica. Hasanein Bey calls them "the merchant princes of the Libyan Desert. A Majbari boasts that his father died on the *basur* (camel's saddle) in the same way that a soldier boasts that his father died on the field of battle ".[1]

They used to be active slave-traders, and a small colony of them exists at Kirdasa, the village just north of the Giza Pyramids.

Qadadfa.—The Qadadfa are a Cyrenaican tribe, allied to the Awlad Suleiman and the Mawajir, possessing with the last a common ancestor, Mujir. A few of them are settled in Qaliubiya. The nomadic Jawabis are an offshoot from this tribe.

Qat'an.—Like the Awlad Suleiman and the Jumei'at, the Qat'an are descended from Ka'b bein Elwei, through his second son El-Aqta'. Most of them live west of the frontier, but those who live in Egypt are " mrabit " to the Awlad 'Ali. Curiously enough, one of their families, the 'Eilet Jibali, has become the chief family of the Harabi in Egypt. Their sub-divisions are Marirat, Sam'ana, and Bahamna.

Tarhuna.—The Tarhuna own land in Asyut Province, and a few of them are engaged in the carrying trade between the Nile Valley and the oases. A few of them accompanied 'Omar Bey el-Masri on his attempted return to Tripoli in Said Pasha's reign.

[1] *R.G.S. Journal*, Oct., 1923, 282.

Many of the tribe still live in Tunis and Tripoli, and those in Egypt declare they came there at the end of the Mameluke dynasty under the leadership of 'Omar Khalifa. Of the former, the Admiralty handbook says :

> " The Tarhuna, an ancient Berber tribe, is now much Arabized. Some 800 live a sedentary life at Kasr Tarhuna, the rest are for most part nomadic. Some live like the Gharian Berbers in underground dwellings. They are described as warlike and rebellious. The population includes both *marabut* and *sherif* elements." [1]

One of their *omdas* (in Egypt) traced his descent in fourteen generations to Tarhuni, while the *omda* of the allied Turshan gave twelve generations to the same ancestor. But the *omda* of the Andara, one of their subtribes, could only go back to ten generations, to " El-Hajj ".

They, of course, claim descent from the Beni Suleim, but are undoubtedly of Berber origin.

[1] *Handbook of Libya,* 1927, 45.

CHAPTER XVIII

THE BEJA

" *There is a difference of opinion as to the Kawahla, the sons of Kahil; some say they are among the descendants of the Jinn ; and some that they are the descendants of Zubeir ibn el 'Awwam ; God knows the truth best.*"—Old Sudan Nisba.[1]

General Remarks—The Beja a relic of the earliest invaders of the Nile Valley—The 'Ababda—The Hamedorab.

The African deserts east of the Nile and north of the Atbara are wandered over by different branches of one Hamitic race, who all speak the same language To Bdawi, or Bedauye as the Germans call it. From their isolation and their warlike character, they have for the most part resisted the infiltration of Arab manners and customs, though their most northern division, the 'Ababda, have learnt to talk Arabic.

An administrative line has been drawn between the countries so as to leave the Bisharin in the Sudan and the 'Ababda in Egypt. But if the arbitrary political frontier of lat. 22° be followed, the Hamedorab section of the Bisharin may be said to live in Egypt, and since I know them well, I have not scrupled to include them in this book.

Indeed, the 'Aliab and Hamedorab sections of this tribe do their shopping in Egypt, and a settlement of perhaps a hundred of the former forms the well-known " Bisharin camp " of Aswan, while there is a smaller Hamedorab colony at Daraw.

But before we deal with them in detail, a most interesting point, first called attention to by Professor Seligman,[2] falls to be considered. He showed quite definitely that the Beni 'Amir, the most southerly of the Sudanese Beja, possess a remarkable similarity to the old proto-Egyptians, while the Hadendawa, though probably of common origin, are a modified race, taller than the Beni 'Amir, and with broader skulls.

It was, therefore, most interesting to me to find when I began to make measurements of the 'Ababda, who live further north again in the deserts, immediately adjacent to Upper

[1] MacMichael, ii, 27. [2] Hamites, 610.

Egypt on the east, that they showed a marked resemblance to those made by Professor Seligman of the Beni 'Amir (and so to the proto-Egyptians), in spite of their separation from the Beni 'Amir by the Hadendawa and the Bisharin.[1] The Bisharin, and those 'Ababda who live in the hills, are much more truly nomadic than the people of Sinai or the Western Arabs. True, the Hamedorab cling rather closely to Jebel Elba, the reputed motherland of the whole Bisharin tribe, but the 'Aliab follow the rains between the Atbara and the Egyptian frontier, and though the 'Ababda recognize different areas for the different sections in time of drought, after the rain the desert becomes a vast playground, wherein anyone may range at will. There is very little rivalry between the tribal sections, or indeed, between the 'Ababda and the Bisharin. In fact, the 'Aliab and the Hamedorab have in the past asked to be transferred from the latter to the former. As Bramly wrote long ago:

" The Bisharin are as yet one big family, and the grazing is ample for all, so that the boundaries are very vague between the different tribes. Disputes of course do arise as to the possession of wadis, but I find that a week after a certain wadi has been allotted to one of the two tribes, both tribes are amicably grazing in it side by side without payment. The ownership of wells is more strictly defined."[2]

'Ababda.—The 'Ababda,[3] or children of 'Abad, like all the inhabitants of the Northern Sudan, are passionately anxious to claim descent from the Arabs of the Conquest. This they achieve by making their eponymous ancestor 'Abad, who is buried in Wadi 'Abad near Idfu, a descendant, through two earlier 'Abads, of the famous Zubeir ibn el 'Awwam, cousin of the Prophet and one of the first converts to Islam, who was slain in Iraq at the " battle of the Camel " in A.D. 656.

Twenty-one generations, according to their *nisba*, separate us from the earliest of these 'Abads, which gives an approximate date in the thirteenth century for his coming to Egypt. Besides the 'Azaz from whom the 'Ababda are descended, another of his sons was Kahil, the ancestor of the Kawahla, a tribe now in Kordofan.

---

[1] G. W. Murray, " The Northern Beja," *J.R.A.I.*, lvii, 1927.
[2] In a letter to Dr. Ball, quoted in *Geography and Geology of South-eastern Egypt*, 367 f.
[3] The name is Arabic, correctly formed from 'Abad, as 'Ayaida from 'Ayad.

PEDIGREE OF THE 'ABABDA.

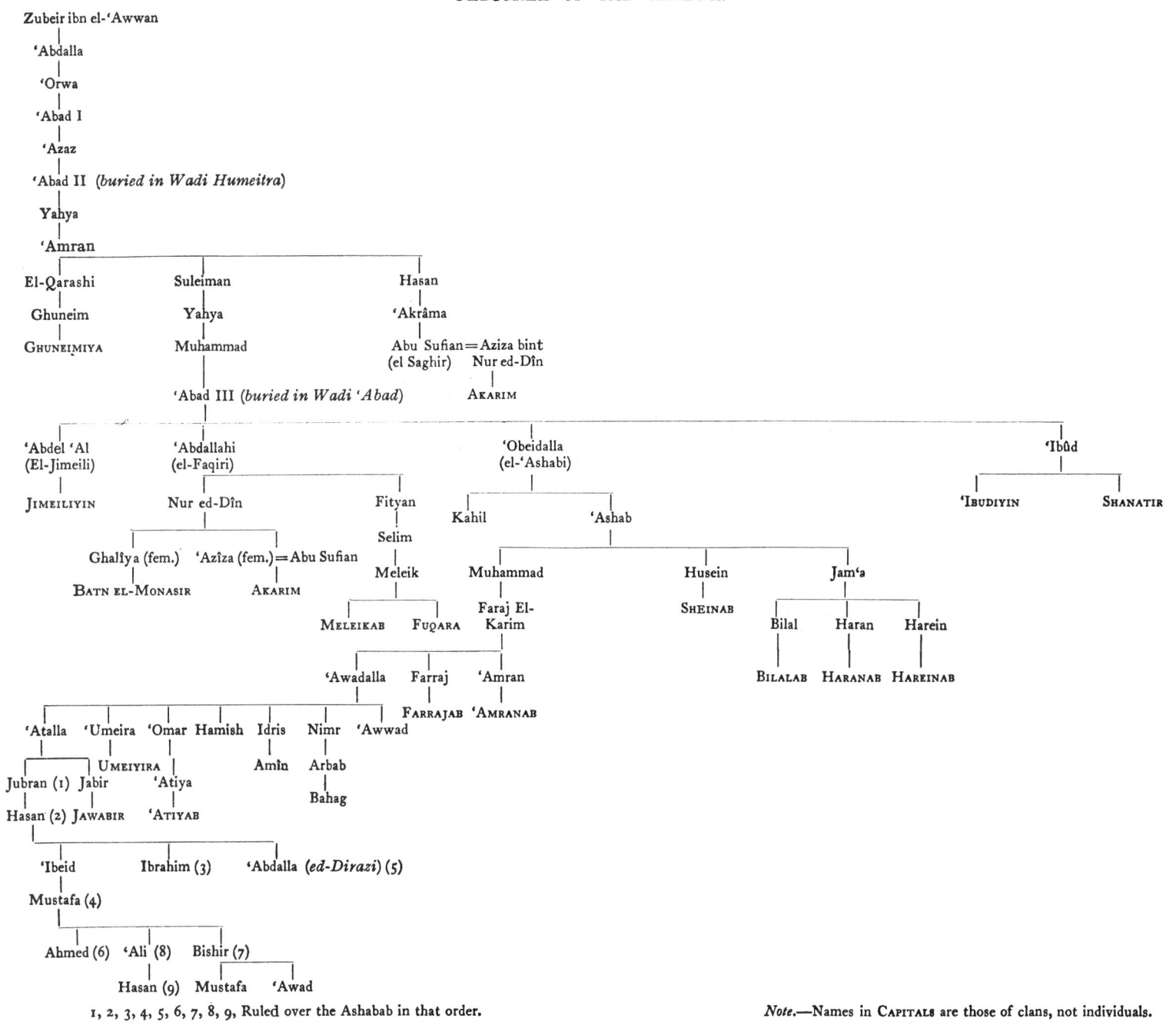

Zubeir ibn el-'Awwan
— 'Abdalla
— 'Orwa
— 'Abad I
— 'Azaz
— 'Abad II (*buried in Wadi Humeitra*)
— Yahya
— 'Amran
  - El-Qarashi
    - Ghuneim
      - GHUNEIMIYA
  - Suleiman
    - Yahya
      - Muhammad
        - 'Abad III (*buried in Wadi 'Abad*)
  - Hasan
    - 'Akrâma
      - Abu Sufian (el Saghir) = Aziza bint Nur ed-Dîn
        - AKARIM

'Abad III (*buried in Wadi 'Abad*)
- 'Abdel 'Al (El-Jimeili)
  - JIMEILIYIN
- 'Abdallahi (el-Faqiri)
  - Nur ed-Dîn
    - Ghalîya (fem.)
      - BATN EL-MONASIR
    - 'Azîza (fem.) = Abu Sufian
      - AKARIM
  - Fityan
    - Selim
      - Meleik
        - MELEIKAB
        - FUQARA
- 'Obeidalla (el-'Ashabi)
  - Kahil
  - 'Ashab
    - Muhammad
      - Faraj El-Karim
        - 'Awadalla
        - Farraj
          - FARRAJAB
        - 'Amran
          - 'AMRANAB
    - Husein
      - SHEINAB
    - Jam'a
      - Bilal
        - BILALAB
      - Haran
        - HARANAB
      - Harein
        - HAREINAB
- 'Ibûd
  - 'IBUDIYIN
  - SHANATIR

'Awadalla
- 'Atalla
  - Jubran (1)
    - Hasan (2)
      - 'Ibeid
        - Mustafa (4)
          - Ahmed (6)
          - 'Ali (8)
            - Hasan (9)
          - Bishir (7)
            - Mustafa
            - 'Awad
- 'Umeira
  - UMEIYIRA
  - Jabir
    - JAWABIR
- 'Omar
  - 'Atiya
    - 'ATIYAB
      - Ibrahim (3)
- Hamish
  - Amîn
- Idris
- Nimr
  - Arbab
    - Bahag
- 'Awwad
  - 'Abdalla (*ed-Dirazi*) (5)

1, 2, 3, 4, 5, 6, 7, 8, 9, Ruled over the Ashabab in that order.

Note.—Names in CAPITALS are those of clans, not individuals.

[*face p.* 302.

THE BEJA

Now, in 1353, the traveller Ibn Battuta found an encampment of "Awlad Kahil" on the Red Sea coast between Suakin and 'Aidhab, "mingled with the Beja and speaking their language.[1] That is to say, about a century after our assumed date for 'Abad, his descendants had already begun to coalesce with the Beja. Now we know from Maqrizi, that when the Arab tribes of Rabi'a and Juheina, invaded the Sudan, they married the daughters of the chiefs, and thereby secured to their descendants the chieftaincies of the Beja clans, since descent among the Beja was matrilineal. It seems, therefore, that 'Abad and his sons probably did likewise, and that the present-day "children of 'Abad" retain very little of the Arab blood of their ancestor.

For at the present day, the 'Ababda are not looked upon as Arabs by such true Arab tribes as Ma'aza and Juheina, who will not intermarry with them, and they themselves use the word "'Arab" to distinguish such tribes from themselves. In fact, we have seen from the preceding pages in dress, customs, and appearance they are racially not to be distinguished from the rest of the Beja.

One might even put it a little stronger than that, for, as their physical measurements show, they present a most striking resemblance to the pre-dynastic Egyptians, and one is tempted to believe that we possess in the desert-dwelling sections of the 'Ababda the purest blood in the area covered by our survey, and that they constitute, like the animals mentioned in the introduction, a remnant of the primitive population of the Sahara. Nowadays the 'Ashabab, the principal branch of the 'Ababda, occupy the whole of the eastern deserts of Egypt south of a line joining Qena to the oilfields of "Hurghada" (Gharqada) as far as the frontier of the Sudan. Colonies of them exist along the edge of the Nile cultivation from as far north as Qena to as far south as Korosko.

Another large branch, the Meleikab, is settled in the Sudan from Korosko to Berber, while a tribe, traditionally of the same origin, the Kawahla, possesses in Kordofan a subsection called 'Ababda. The Meleikab state that they were brought south by the Fung kings in the eighteenth century to safeguard the Sennaar caravan route from the Bisharin.

[1] Ibn Battuta, ii, 161.

They are a handsome race; Klunzinger recognized that when he described them as " dolichocephalous, orthognathous, with an oval face, large glowing eyes, nose straight, a little short and broad, hair smooth and jet black but not woolly, skin dark-brown verging on black, the expression of the face completely European (Caucasian), body remarkable for its beauty of form ".

Bruce mentions as chief of the tribe in 1765, one Nimr, with a son Ibrahim.[1] We learn from Linant de Bellefonds[2] that this Nimr was from the Fuqara (a section of the Meleikab) and that he was succeeded by a son whom he calls Sa'ad (Sadiq ?). A sheikh, Muhammad Khalifa, usurped the power from Sa'ad while the latter was young, and was of assistance to Ibrahim Pasha in his pursuit of the Mamelukes in 1811. But in 1828, he revolted against Khurshid Aga, the Governor-General of the Sudan, and lost his life in an attack upon Berber. In 1850 his son, Hasan Khalifa, who had been in charge of the main route to the Sudan from Korosko to Abu Hamed, was deposed and his brother Husein was appointed Mudir of Berber on 18th December, 1883, with the rank of Pasha; but on his way to Khartoum, General Gordon made the mistake of telling Husein and other sheikhs that he had come to evacuate the Sudan. The people consequently all went over to the Mahdi and Berber fell on 19th May, 1884. Husein Pasha Khalifa was brought to the Mahdi's camp at Rahad, where he became a fellow-prisoner with Slatin Pasha. His nephew, Hasan Khalifa, raided the Nile both north and south of Korosko in 1887, and in the following year one Bahr Karrar occupied the wells of Ongat and Haimur and raided Kalabsha. But in June, 1888, Bishir Bey, the Sheikh of the 'Ashabab, who had remained friendly to the Egyptian Government, turned the Meleikab out of Haimur. The Meleikab very soon deserted the Dervishes, and we find Sala, the son of Husein Pasha Khalifa, in command of an Egyptian outpost in Murrat in 1891. The 'Ababda friendlies occupied Berber on 31st August, 1897, a week before the arrival of the Anglo-Egyptian army. Sala was succeeded by Abd el-'Azim Bey, and he by the present sheikh of the Meleikab, Taha Bey Yasin. But the 'Ashabab are now the main branch, for the Meleikab after Nimr's time emigrated almost entirely to the Sudan.

[1] Bruce, *Travels to Discover the Source of the Nile.*   [2] L'Etbaye, 4.

PLATE XXXI

A BISHARI

The earliest sheikh of the 'Ashabab of whom we have any knowledge was Jubran, who flourished at the end of the eighteenth century and the beginning of the nineteenth. One of his great-great-grandsons, Taha, gave me the following information : Jubran had three sons, Hasan I, who succeeded him, Huseyn, and 'Omar. Of these, 'Omar was killed by the 'Atawna, and his death revenged on their sheikh by Huseyn. To Hasan succeeded his son Ibrahim, and his grandsons Mustafa and 'Abdalla ed-Dirazi. 'Abdalla reigned forty-five years and died about 1885. 'Abdalla was followed by two sons of his predecessor, Mustafa. Ahmed the elder had a very short reign, but his brother Bishir did good service to the Egyptian Government for twenty years in the Nile Campaigns, and was made a Bey for his services. He turned the dervishes out of Haimur and Ongat in 1888, and his lieutenant, Qarabawi, won a notable victory over one of their raiding parties at Meisa. Bishir died in 1905 and was succeeded by his brother, 'Ali Mustafa, who survived till 1915. Hasan, one of 'Ali's twelve sons, is the present sheikh.

The Qireijab fishers of the coast are not reckoned true 'Ababda—" for their ancestor was washed up on a plank ". They catch their fish with the spear and the throwing net, for they have neither boats nor canoes, and are afraid of venturing on the sea. Yet, living on fish, they remain strong and fat when the inland people are starving from lack of grain. Even their camels get fish to eat, and, unless the water is cold, wade out into the sea to eat mangrove leaves. These Qireijab, accustomed for generations to the saline water obtainable where the main wadis debouch on the sea, can drink water that no other human being could drink and survive.

In the north of Egypt there are about 800 'Ababda *fellahin* settled in the provinces of Sharqiya, Daqahliya, and Gharbiya.[1] The sheikh of these latter, Salem Hasan 'Awanat, states that they separated from the main stem in 925 A.H. (= A.D. 1519), that is just after the Turkish conquest of Egypt. This may perhaps mean that up to that time the 'Ababda held the whole Eastern Desert as far as Suez, and were then driven south. These northern 'Ababda have an Upper Egyptian look, but Hasan 'Ali Mustafa, the Omda of the 'Ashabab, despises them as Hiteim—not proper 'Ababda at all. At the 1927

---

[1] Subdivisions. 'Awanatiya, Jadad'a, Kerreirat, Qawatat, Ramadin, Rawashda, Shakamba.

census, 13,734 nomads were recorded from the 'Ababda territory in the Eastern Desert, north of the Sudan frontier, made up as follows :

1. *'Ashabab 'Ababda* (9,844 people) in two great subdivisions, and one small one.
    (*a*) Muhammadab (14 clans, 4,197 people).

'Abedeinab	Rahalab
'Amranab	Saadab
Edidanab	Shafab
Fiheidab	Shuweimab
Fisheijab	Sideinab
Jaralab	Silimayab
Najibab	Zeidin

    (*b*) *Jama'ab* (15 clans, 4,957 people).

'Abderigalab	Kirjab
'Amarab	Kiteita
'Amîrab	Mahmudab
Bakrab	Nifa
Bilalab	Rajabab
Hamudab	Saadallab
Haranab	Saidab (or Uqda)
Hareinab	

    (*c*) *Qireijab*, the " Icthyophagi " (690 people).

2. *Meleikab 'Ababda* (4 clans, 1,664 people).

Bedriab	Saad Hamidab
Meleikab	Yusfab

    The remainder of the Meleikab live in the Sudan.

3. *Bisharin* (8 clans, 1,661 people).

Abrihimab	Ilbab
'Abdelrahimab	Isa Hamidab
Ashwalab	Iseiyab
Ghamhatab	Nafab

    The majority of this great tribe live in the Sudan.

4. *Broken Tribes* (6 clans, 565 people).

Anqarab	Jahalab
Hamaj	Kimeilab
Hukm	Ismainiya

Bisharin.—Although the administration of the Bisharin is left to the Sudan Government, some of the sections live in Egyptian territory, and something may conveniently be said about them here.

Their progenitor Bishar, like 'Abad, is called " the son of Zubeir ibn el-'Awwam ", but of him nothing is known. His great-grandson Kuka was a holy man, who spent his summers on Jebel Elba, and his winters at the mouth of the Wadi 'Alaqi. Unfortunately his sister Fatma (some call her his wife) was seduced by a foreigner and fled to the 'Ababda country to give birth to a son, Anakw, who later, by three different wives, became the ancestor of the three main divisions of the Bisharin. One legend relates how Kuka disappeared on Jebel Elba and was "turned into stone", another that his tomb is in Wadi Eikidi near Ariab. In fact, memories of Abraham, Sarah, and Lot's wife all seem to have influenced this history which is designed to cover up the fact that the Bisharin tribes derive from female ancestors.

Anakw's chief wife, Umm Ali, had two sons, 'Ali the father of the 'Aliab, and Hamed who is only remembered by his son 'Ali Hassai, called Hamed Or, "son of Hamed," to distinguish him from his uncle. From him the Hamed-or-ab, "Hamed-son-ites" are descended.[1]

Hamedorab.—This section own the finest grazing of the Eastern Desert in the famous Jebel Elba and the coastal plain from Bir Shalatein on the administrative frontier southwards to Khor Ma'rob just south of latitude 22° N.

In summer this plain of El-Wadah is a desert, but sometimes after the winter rains, it becomes one grass field, nearly a hundred miles long by thirty broad, and all the Bisharin come down with their camels from the hills to graze.

Among the "tribe of the son of Hamed" are reckoned the allied tribes of 'Amrab and Jumhatab, while another section, the Ashshab, are reckoned half 'Ababda. Altogether they may number 4,000 souls, perhaps a quarter of the whole Bisharin nation. The ruling family call themselves Batranab, after the late Omda Batran Ali Tiut.

They possess an excellent breed of white sheep, but in spite of the good grazing their camels, though good, are certainly inferior to those of the 'Aliab.

They now pay an annual tax of £240 to the Sudan Government, but at one time in the past were sufficiently well organized to levy a tax of their own on shipping. Then there were markets at Shalatein, Adal Deib (a large one), and Mersa Olei (Halaib). Dhows paid 20 piastres a sack, and 50 piastres a slave. Dealers from the interior were also taxed.

Reports of this wealth of the Hamedorab attracted two Dervish raids, of which the first was successful, but the second, as we have told, came to an untimely end at Bir Meisa.

---

[1] This genealogical paragraph is compiled from Mr. G. E. R. Sandars' article on the "Bisharin" in *Sudan Notes and Records*, xvi, 2.

Physically, they have longer heads than the 'Aliab and so more closely approach the proto-Egyptians and the 'Ababda. These Hamedorab are the Bisharin, who were so hostile to Schweinfurth in 1865 and of whom he says [1]:

"The Bisharin are, like their related stock the 'Ababda, all dolichocephalic, and show it by elevated, yet very narrow, skulls. In the general expression of the face, there were more analogies with Europeans than with the Arabs and fellahin. There were Titus-heads, Schiller-noses, and Habsburg-foreheads; indeed, their features showed plenty of variety. The often astonishingly small lips limited the tightly closed, almost American, mouth, on which, as on their long necks, the hardships of their desert existence impressed itself. Remarkable appeared the particularly luxuriant muscular development, especially of their legs, which strongly differentiates them from the Berberines with their ape-like extremities. Every man's bearing is gracious and full of charm and dignity; their walk almost to be called bold. The shades of skin-colour range through all possible gradations between copper-red and the deepest brown-black. Whether this is the result of mixture with other races I dare not assert, but must refer to the fact that travellers speak of a similar variety of hue among the Ethiopian races."

Jebel Elba, the traditional place of origin of the Bisharin, is still holy ground to the tribe. A hundred years ago, Linant de Bellefonds was told a wonderful tale of the mountain, where Kuka, the tribal ancestor, sits turned to stone in a cave, from which a warm wind blew. Nobody would show him the spot. The Hamedorab in 1926, still believed in this cavern and called it "the nostrils of Elba". A fine spray is said to issue from two holes, and all the ground beneath them to be green with grass. A hunter, who had parked a dead ibex in one of the holes while he went after the rest of the herd, found on his return that Elba had sneezed the ibex to the other side of the ravine. But although they told me all this, nobody either could or would guide me to the place. I explored the mountain pretty thoroughly while mapping it, and climbed its two highest peaks, but had to retire with an open mind.

[1] *Auf unbetretenen Wegen in Aegypten*, 69.

CHAPTER XIX

EPILOGUE

"*The Bedawi is, indeed, the strangest of all mankind. His material civilization is about on a par with that of a bushman, yet his brain is as elaborately and subtly developed as that of any Englishman with a liberal education. There is no reasonable argument he cannot follow, no situation which he cannot immediately grasp, no man whom he cannot comprehend; yet there is no manual act he can perform.*—The Caliph's Last Heritage.—*Sir Mark Sykes.*

That acute Berber, Ibn Khaldun, saw all history as a sea of wild breakers, one ruling dynasty billowing in from the desert, smashing its virility on the cultivation, and making way for another in a century or less.

But his mediæval parallel is no longer quite exact; the forces of law and order are for the moment too strong for crude infiltration to continue. So that, in dry years like the present, the miserable Awlad 'Ali, now turned farmers, are denied their natural drift into Beheira, and obliged to starve in their barren fields. Scientific methods of agriculture may palliate this, and irrigation may yet help the district south of Lake Mariut.

Migration to the civilized world from the desert is terribly handicapped in these peaceful days by lack of education, without which even the most moderate amount of wordly success is hardly possible. Muhammad 'Ali Pasha, who learnt to read late in life and then seemed disappointed, was the last really heroic figure to succeed without literacy.

Town life appals anything of the nomad that may be left in their hearts. My worthy old marabout friend, 'Ilwani Suleiman, though living beside a railway line, does not permit even grown sons to visit Alexandria. His favourite " Wanis " saw Salum and the oases as a boy, but not till he was a married man was he allowed to depart with six camels to discover the Nile, and see what cultivation there might be at Hosh 'Isa.

There is most excellent raw material in these Bedouin, could their native *ghazu*-complex, the desire of getting something for nothing, be educated out of them. Nowadays it exhibits itself as mere smuggling or, still worse, the preying on tourists for bakshish. A hold-up on the Suez road, some year back, represented the last flicker of the Robin Hood spirit among the Ma'aza or the Haweitat.

Some of the Beja might fairly be called intellectual, and their perception of realities is very acute. 'Ali Kheir, the best map-reader I have known, at once comprehended the nature of an eclipse, while Muhammad Katul, a Bisharin, asked me at Jebel Zeit why the winter days there were shorter than in his home in the Etbai, five degrees of latitude farther south. This, from a man without a watch, was sufficiently amazing, but Katul had educated himself and surprised me even more, when prowling round the ruins of 'Aidhab, by quoting Ibn Battuta.

One more anecdote, the last, may indicate the channel into which the Sinai intellect, if ever educated, may direct itself. During the War, the Zumeiliyin family kidnapped one of Sabah Mudakhil's sisters, and he retorted in true Sinai fashion by capturing two of their maidens. These ladies were then exchanged, but Sabah went on with the affair, and, enticing the kidnapper to Abu Zenima, delivered him to the English as a spy. Whereupon the angry Zumeiliyin abducted the tribal judge Abu Diakul, and handed him over to the Turks at Beersheba.

There the matter might have rested, but the officious Abu Diakul paid £10 to the Turkish commandant and, returning to the land of the 'Aleiqat, demanded a return of his money. Young Sabah dismissed the old man's claim with scorn. " He was stolen, and you were stolen, and the matter was settled ! You should have remained stolen, and not come back here to start the thing over again ! This £10 is a private matter between you and the Turk at Beersheba ! " Thus non-suited for asserting an individual claim in an affair between families, the poor old judge knuckled under, and the matter was allowed to drop. An obvious future exists for such a Sinai youth, could he be educated, at the Bar.

His brother Zeidan has proved more of a statesman and has done much to relieve the distress of the Towara by persuading them to brush off what Amin Rihani calls the " mildew of Arab pride " so far as to work really hard in the manganese mines of Umm Bogma. As I write, the news comes that the company is about to make the experiment of working the mines with purely Bedouin labour. But Zeidan gets little thanks from his jealous tribesmen for this, who merely grudge him any worldly wealth he may have acquired.

Material help, short of altering the climate, can do little more than tide the Bedouin over a bad year now and then. Yet could learning bring to their logical minds some lesson more stirring than resignation to the will of God, I would not despair of the Bedouin.

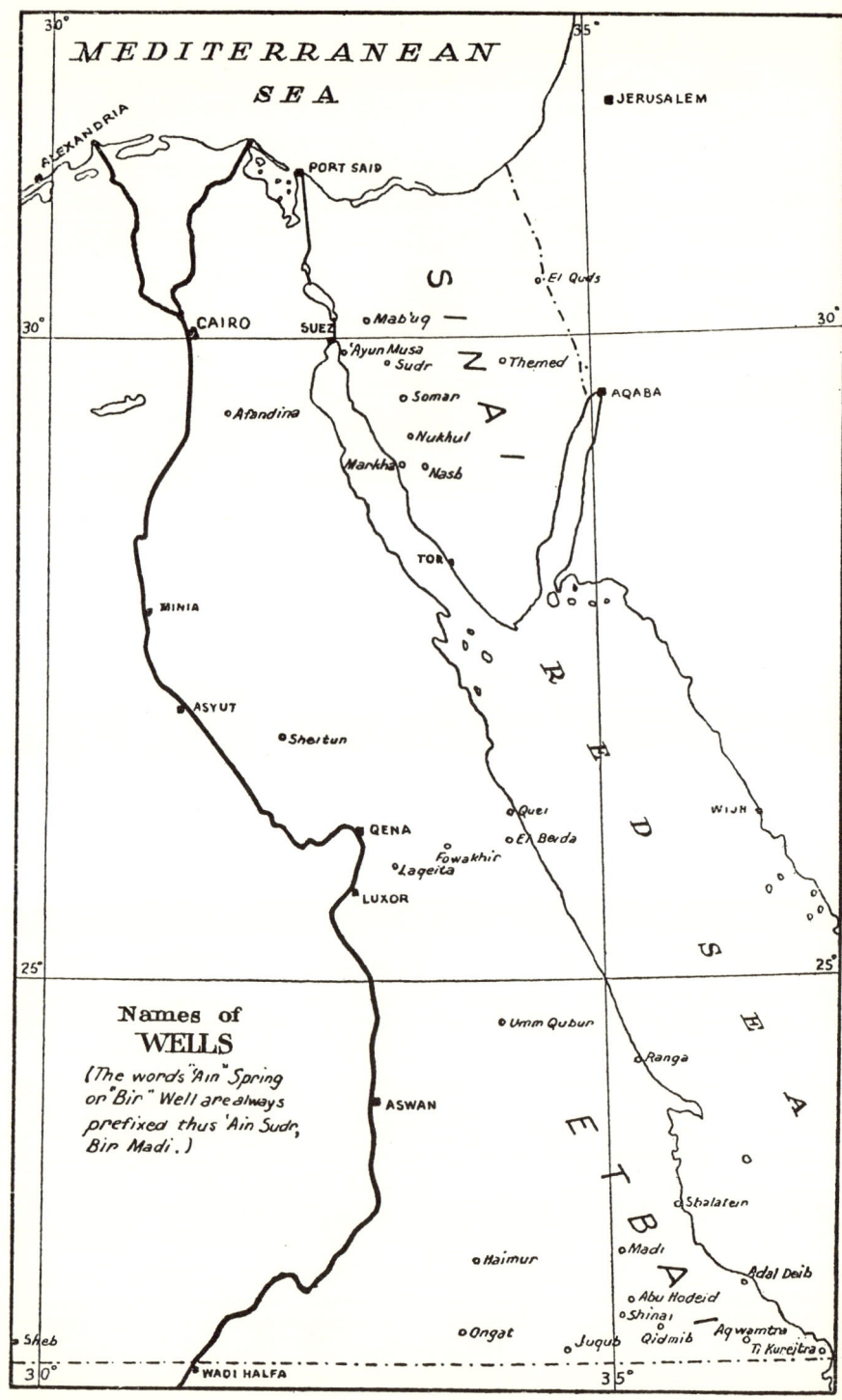

Desert Wells.

APPENDIX

WESTERN DESERT LAW

"*The Adyrmachidae are the people that dwell nearest to Egypt; they follow Egyptian usages for the most part, but wear a dress like that of other Libyans.*"
—Herodotus, iv, 168.

The Bloodwit—Difference between Intentional and Unintentional Killing—Killing of or by a Woman—Distribution of the Bloodwit—Taking Refuge (*Nazala*)—Outlawry—Oath to be Taken when Evidence is Lacking—Killing of a Mediator—Killing of a Thief—Killing of an Adulterer—Slaying by Contrivance—Instigation of Murder—Slaying by a Minor—Slaying of a Relative—Neglect of a Guest—Responsibility of a Host—Death in Prison—Death from Fright—Causing Miscarriage—Overlaying—Slaying by or of a Dangerous Animal—Rape—Assessment of Wounds—False Evidence—Stealing—Civil Claims—Land.

The customs of the Adyrmachidae, which included a *jus primae noctis*, have long since been supplanted by an unwritten code based on the Moslem *shara'*. Disputes must nowadays be notified to Government, and, when killing has occurred, the Government sees to it that the *nazala* or "taking refuge" with a neutral clan is properly carried out by the murderer's relatives. Although the original duration of this *nazala* was a year, in order to allow hot blood to cool down, a period of from three to six months is now usually sufficient for matters to be arranged amicably.

The basis of this chapter is a literal translation of an Arabic MS. dealing with the Awlad 'Ali code, which was very kindly obtained for me by Muhammad Bey Wasfi, formerly Inspector of the eastern district of the Western Desert Province and now Governor of Kharga Oasis. The original must have been taken down at an *'Urfi* court, and it bears the seals of twenty-two sheikhs to testify to its accuracy.

I have, however, edited it a little by amending some of the titles of the sections, and altering their order in some cases where a more logical rearrangement appeared desirable. The notes marked A. W. G. are those of A. W. Green Bey, Governor of the Western Desert Province, who has been good enough to revise the whole chapter.

Customs of the Awlad 'Ali and their Vassals (Murabitin).

The Bloodwit.—If one Arab kills another, it is the custom among them to summon him[1] to pay money or camels for such killing, and this payment is known as *diya*. The question of payment of *diya* among the Awlad 'Ali is generally settled by agreement between the two families according to the ability of him who has to pay it.

The *diya* for a free (not enslaved) Moslem killed unintentionally by a Bedouin (any inhabitant of the desert) is one hundred camels, divided in four parts, that is, twenty-five females of the first year, twenty-five females of the second year, twenty-five of the third year, twenty-five of the fourth year.[2]

If the people of the desert (*ahl el-badiya*) concerned have no camels, the value shall be paid in cash. The value shall be assessed at current market prices.[3]

Difference between Intentional and Unintentional Killing.—Intentional killing includes premeditation, concealment, and evil intent; unintentional killing differs from this and is dependent on the will of God. Any killing by means of stones and sticks shall be considered as unintentional, and shall be punished by the penalty for unintentional killing. But should killing take place by means of cutting instruments, as swords, knives, spears, or agricultural instruments, this shall be considered to be wilful murder and be punished as such.

The *diya* for a woman shall be assessed at half that for a man whether the slaying be unintentional or wilful murder.

Slaying of a Man by a Woman.—If a woman kills a man, he who is her heir-at-law in the event of her death, if she possesses property, shall comply with the payment of the *diya* after deducting her marriage-price from the amount of the *diya* itself. The *diya* in this case shall be considered as for unintentional killing.

---

[1] In reality, it is his *'eila* or family which is summoned.

[2] In the case of the first two sets of twenty-five, female camels are mentioned; of the last two, only the age is specified. The first year is known to the Awlad Ali as *bint* or *ibn makhadh*, the second *bint labun*, the third *huqqa*, and the fourth *jada'*.

[3] This custom has since been amended by mutual agreement between the clans and fixed at £300 for unintentional killing and £400 for wilful murder. The Arawa clan have now for some years been arguing that it is possible to collect the *diya* twice for the same man. One of their members first received a blow on the head which caused insanity, an injury which, as we shall see later, ranks as homicide, so a *diya* was duly awarded for this and paid. But when someone later accidentally killed the lunatic, he was surprised and annoyed to find the hucksters of the Arawa claiming another *diya* from him or rather his family. I will say no more, the matter is still *sub judice*, and long may it remain so.

Distribution of the Bloodwit.—The *diya* shall be distributed among the blood relations *awlia' ed-dam* as follows : half the *diya* to the sons of the murdered man, or to his brothers by the same mother ; the other half to the other persons with right to the bloodwit, provided they are on good terms with them and were wont to pay (fines) with him formerly.

Taking Refuge (Nazala).—If a slaying be committed by any members of a clan,[1] his clan at once seeks the protection of another clan to avoid the probable conflict between them and the clan of the man who was slain. Such clan shall stay with that other clan for a period not exceeding one year, during which the other clans may attempt to make peace between them. If peace be concluded, well and good ; but if not, the clans shall leave the opponents to act according to their discretion (or lack of it).[2]

Peace is usually concluded on the basis of the above-mentioned *diya*. But, if the family of the slain man attack the clan of the slayer during the course of the year during which they have taken refuge, and cause by such assault the death of a member of that slayer's clan within the region permitted to them to pasture and trade therein, then the clan committing the assault shall be obliged to pay a *diya* to the clan which has afforded its protection to the clan seeking refuge.

But if a member of the slayer's clan be killed outside the limits agreed upon beforehand, there shall be nothing due to the clan affording protection to the refugees, and this killing shall be considered as having put an end to the dispute between the first two clans (that of the slayer and that of the slain).

If a quarrel takes place between two clans, and a man of each is slain, each death shall be taken to compensate for the loss caused by the other, as it is ordained in the Holy Koran, " Soul for soul, but punishment for wounding."

Outlawry.—It might have been added that a clan may expel one of its members by a formal declaration in writing (called *barawa*) that they no longer recognize him as one of

---

[1] The word *qabila* "tribe" is used in this connection in the MS., but some smaller, division, such as *'eila*, is clearly meant. So I have translated it "clan" throughout.

[2] This is no longer the case. After Government has taken the matter in hand, revenge is discouraged. Although the killing of a man by the injured family would balance matters, the tribes have now accepted that such a killing entails payment of a fine of £100 if it takes place after Government has intervened. This was arranged by me in 1930.—A. W. G.

themselves and pay compensation for his misdeeds. Such a declaration cannot be retrospective. The individual thus expelled becomes outlaw, and his clan can claim no *diya* if he is killed. It usually happens that he clears out of the district.—A. W. G.

Lack of Evidence.—Should a killing take place by day or night, and there be no evidence or accusation against any definite person, then the suspected clan shall be obliged to take an oath *yemin allah*, and the clan of the murdered man shall have the right to pick out fifty-five persons (from that clan) to swear the oath, the text of which shall be : *Wa haqq haza el kitab wa el sheikh* . . . (naming one agreed upon by the two contending parties) *annana la qatalnahu wala tasabbabna fi qatlihi*, meaning, " By this book and Sheikh . . . we have not killed him nor did we cause his murder."[1] Should they fail to take the oath, they shall be obliged to pay the full *diya* for the murder.

Killing of a Mediator.—Should any person mediate to prevent quarrelling between clans, and be himself slain during the quarrel without his slayer being known, then both the clans that quarrelled shall share equally in the payment of the *diya* (for unintentional killing) after swearing the oath (that they had no part in the slaying).[2]

But if such mediator is only wounded, then he and the members of his clan shall, for the assessment of the wound, take an oath that he does not know the person that struck him, in which case the two contending clans shall equally partake in the payment of the damage for the wound as assessed. But should the person that struck him be known, then only the clan of him who wounded the mediator shall make the payment of the damage for the wound as assessed.

Killing of a Thief or Robber.—If anyone steal or rob property, whether camels or furniture or any other thing, and escape, and the owner of such things follow and kill the thief because he would not give them back, a *diya* of unintentional killing must be paid. But if the thief kill the owner, he must pay a *diya* of intentional killing and also return everything he stole. But if the thief abandon the stolen property, and

---

[1] Usually the man suspected of the murder swears an oath in the terms set out above and the other fifty-four swear as follows : *Wa haqq haza el talib el ghalib wa haza el sheikh mahallaf illi ala sadiqa.* By this searching and overcoming book (the Koran) and this sheikh who causes oaths to be taken truthfully.

[2] Should one of the clans fail to take the oath, it is obliged to pay the whole *diya*.

go away by himself, and be killed by the owner, then the latter must pay a *diya* for unintentional killing. The reasons (for such killings) must be proved by oath or by witness.

Slaying an Adulterer.—If a man enters his dwelling and finds another Arab in the act of adultery with his wife, and kills him in the act, the slayer shall pay the *diya* for unintentional killing after deducting the *mahr*, or bride-price, which he paid at the time of his marriage, and also a round figure of £50 as damages for trespass on his tent. But if he kills both man and woman, he must pay the *diya* which will be distributed as mentioned above.

Slaying by Contrivance.—If an Arab of the Awlad 'Ali cause the death of another by contrivance, as in the case when the deceased tumbled into a pit dug in the road intentionally by that Arab to cause hurt, then the contriver shall pay the *diya* for wilful murder. But if it was someone else that he intended to slay, the *diya* will only be that for unintentional slaying. In the event of such person being only wounded, the wound shall be assessed, and the causer thereof obliged to complete the payment for same. If the causer denies that he has done the deed, he is to swear the appropriate oath.[1] If, however, what was contrived was intended for gain or for good, and its contriver was ignorant that it might have caused hurt, he shall be quitted from payment.

Instigation of Murder.—If a man instigate another to kill a third person, the murderer shall bear the blame with one *diya* and the instigator with another *diya*, unless both the instigator and the murderer be of one clan, when they shall together be liable to pay one *diya* only. But if they belonged to different clans, then each clan shall pay a full *diya*, and, should either abstain, the sentence shall be death.

Slayer who is under Age.—If anyone who has not attained the age of puberty commit a slaying, his clan shall be liable to pay half a *diya* only,[2] and so also in the case of anyone insane, whose madness is proved. Excepting when these are induced by a third party to slay someone, when a full *diya* for unintentional killing shall be due.[3]

Slaying of a Relative.—If anyone slays his relative (that is one of his family who shares with him in the payment for

[1] There is a peculiar form of oath for slaying and another for bodily injury. (Green's authorities disagree with this and call both cases wilful murder.)
[2] Full *diya* for unintentional killing.—A. W. G.
[3] This should be " full *diya* for wilful murder ".—A. W. G.

blood), the slayer himself shall only be made to pay half a *diya* as penalty. He shall pay this to the brother of the deceased or to his father or to his son or to any next of kin. (This only applies if the slaying is unintentional. If it is wilful murder, the murderer himself must pay full *diya*.)

Neglect of a Guest or Refugee (Nazil).—If anyone residing with another clan, whether on his travels or otherwise, be in need for food and drink, and his state really necessitates support so that if he be denied food or drink he will perish, and (such a person) be not supported by him with whom he is residing, this refuser shall be obliged to pay a *diya* for unintentional killing. But he must be proved to have possessed food or drink and not to have supported such refugee, or to have offered it to him. Otherwise he will not be liable to any penalty.

Responsibility of a Host.—Should a thief become the guest of anyone in his dwelling, and this owner of a dwelling knew that this man was wont to steal, and supplied him with food and drink, or provided him with food for his journey, and should such a thief later steal from someone else, then the owner of the dwelling shall be liable to bear the penalty for the stolen property. But if the owner of the dwelling who sheltered the thief gave warning to his neighbours of the thief's character before any theft was committed, and also did not provide him with food and drink, he shall not be responsible for anything. But if he was ignorant that such a man was a thief or habitual criminal, and the thief later pilfered food and water and set out to steal animals or anything else, the owner of the dwelling shall not be responsible, provided he swears the oath, of which the text is, " By this book, I knew not that the man was a thief, and I did not provide him with food and drink . . ."[1]

If a man from any tribe other than the Awlad 'Ali and their vassals, sets out to visit a man of the Awlad 'Ali, and enquires for him, and falls in with a plunderer who robs him, then the prospective host shall have a right of damage against whoever attacked the man who came intending to visit him. The damages shall be assessed at £20 together with the return of the stolen property.

Death in Prison.—Should an Arab commit murder, and

---

[1] This oath would hardly suffice in a civilized court, where counsel would certainly inquire why he refused hospitality to his guest.

be arrested by Government, and sentence be passed on him in accordance with the penal code of Egypt, and the murderer die by any chance in prison, then his family shall have to pay £100 as difference between the penalty for wilful murder and " Death in Prison ", which is held to be equivalent only to the penalty for unintentional killing.[1] [2]

Death from Fright.—If anyone throw a snake on another, and the latter dies, the thrower shall pay a *diya* as he has caused the death of the other person, and the *diya* in such a case shall be that for unintentional killing ; similarly, if anyone point a firearm or draw a sword or dagger upon another, and the latter die from fear or affright on the spot, such person shall have to pay a *diya* for an unintentional killing.

Causing a Miscarriage.—If any member of a clan strike a woman that is pregnant and cause thereby the miscarriage of her burden, the *diya* for the miscarried child shall be assessed according to the consideration of the notables of the clans who have assembled to decide the case. This only applies when it cannot be distinguished whether the miscarried child be either male or female.

But if the miscarried child be " complete " (i.e. can be distinguished to be either male or female) then the *diya* shall be that for unintentional murder, should it be proved that the striking of such a woman was committed intentionally, but if it could be proved that the striking (beating) was committed without intention, then the *diya* shall be assessed at half the full rate, in which case the female child shall be reckoned as one-fourth of the *diya* for a (grown) man.

Overlaying.—Sayidna 'Ashab said that he heard Malek say about the woman that kills her child while she is asleep that, if her husband testify that she did it by mistake, she shall fast ten days, and also return half the bride-price to her husband.

Slaying by dangerous animals.—If an Arab of the Awlad 'Ali possess a savage dog, or a horse that kicks, or a camel that bites, or any animal that is wont to bite, and any man be bitten therefrom and die from the cause of such a bite, the owner of such animal together with his clan shall pay a *diya* of unintentional killing to the clan of him who was killed.

[1] That is, the term of imprisonment is held equivalent to the extra £100 penalty for wilful murder.
[2] If the murderer completes his term of imprisonment, full *diya* will be due from his family after his release.—A. W. G.

But if the animal concerned was not in the habit of biting previously, or if it cannot be proved that it had previously bitten someone, now, if it bites any person and he die therefrom, such an animal shall become the property of the relatives of the murdered man, but should such an animal cause only a wound the owner shall not be liable to anything.[1]

(In a case heard by Bramly, a man had been bitten in the arm by a dog, and Sheikh Miftah Dabun of the Sinaqra acted as assessor. " The assessor moved the arm about in every direction to acquire knowledge of the injury, and decided that the muscles of the forearm had been injured. The next point to be decided was whether it was the dog's first offence, as this would have made a considerable difference to the damages to be awarded. Various witnesses swore that the dog had bitten them, and that its fangs had not been drawn to prevent it biting others. (This is often done by the Arabs to save themselves from fines for their dogs' misbehaviour.) Finally he held that the muscles would always be contracted, and that the dog was of bad character. £15 were therefore to be paid as damages.")

Slaying of a dangerous animal ('ayil).—Anyone killing such an animal shall not be liable to any penalty, as in such case he shall be deemed to have been defending himself ; but if the beast be one that could be eaten after it has been killed, the owner shall be sent for to remove it, while the slayer shall take an oath that he did not intend to kill it except in self-defence. If this cannot be proved, he shall be obliged to pay its value according to current prices.

(Bramly writes, " Bedouin law is that if a man meets a camel that is furious and attempts to kill him, he may shoot it. If the animal is within the limits of its usual feeding grounds, then he must pay a price assessed at a low rate. If it is killed outside its usual feeding ground, there is no liability. The same law applies to a bad-tempered dog or a ram.")

Rape.—If someone assaults a woman in her dwelling and she finds no one with whom to seek protection, and such a man rapes her, he shall be made to pay a fine to be assessed by a special court. Such a fine is usually assessed at from £10 to £100.

---

[1] In English Law, such an animal used to be considered *deodand* or " given to God " in consequence of which it was forfeited to the king and sold for the benefit of the poor.

In earlier times a man was held personally responsible for the evil deeds of his animal. We find in the " Book of the Covenant " that " if the ox were wont to gore in time past, and it has been testified to his owner, and he has not kept him in, but he hath killed a man or woman, the ox shall be stoned, and *his owner* shall be put to death."—Exodus, xxi, 29.

WESTERN DESERT LAW

If he attack her in the open country, he shall be dealt with as having committed the offence within her dwelling. But if the assault was effected by her consent and surrender of her person, he shall be made to pay a small fine of £5 to £10.

But if the assault was on a virgin, and he deflowered her virginity, he shall be liable to pay a fine of £50 to £100 at the discretion of the court. If the virgin is deflowered with her consent, he shall be made to marry her and pay her bride-price in the way usually followed by her family.

Assessment of wounds.—The assessment of wounds among the Arabs of the Awlad 'Ali is in accordance with the Holy *Shara'*, and there are people among them who specialize in such assessment.[1] Assessment is usually made in the presence of a special court convened for the purpose, who swear an oath that none will assess the wound but with justice.

Of woundings, six (degrees) are within the jurisdiction of the court (without assessors) and the presiding officer shall be competent to distinguish them as follows. The damage is set down against each in dinars [2] approximately.

(1) *Ed-Damiya es-Sughra* : (" The lesser bleeding "), a wound such as that caused by a pebble on the head . $3\frac{1}{8}$ dinars
(2) *Ed-Damiya el-Kubra* : (" The greater bleeding "), a wound which opens the skin and cuts it . . . $6\frac{1}{4}$,,
(3) *El-Fakhira* : a wound which cuts the skin and scrapes the flesh . . . . $12\frac{1}{2}$,,
(4) *El-Badhi'a* : a wound which cuts the flesh on both sides, right and left . . . . 25 ,,
(5) *El-Mutlifa* : a wound which cuts the flesh more severely than the *Badhi'a* . . . . . . 30 ,,
(6) *El-Malta* : a wound which cuts the skin and flesh and reaches the fat near the bone . . . . 40 ,,

These six degrees do not necessitate the calling in of specialists, and the decision lies with the president of the court.

(7) *El-Muwaddhiha* : a wound which cuts the skin and flesh and the fat next to the bone and lays it open, is to be paid for by people owning camels as five camels and by people owning gold as 50 dinars.

(8) *El-Hashima* and (9) *El-Muqilna*. *Hashima* means a fracture of the bones of the head, and *Munqila* a fracture in which a piece of bone is detached (a comminuted

---

[1] A list of assessors to sit in the courts, chosen from the notables of each locality, is drawn up annually by the Governor.
[2] The "dinar" which is to be paid is nowadays assessed by the Awlad 'Ali as 5 piastres in Egyptian currency.

fracture). For these 150 dinars are to be paid. And the dinar in these two cases is assessed at 20 piastres (*double*) or fifteen camels.

(These nine degrees of wounding fall in the category of *salama* " healed-up wounds ".—A. W. G.)

(10) For *El-Maimuna*, a wound which cuts the scalp and reaches the skull, the compensation is 333⅓ dinars for those who own gold or alternatively 33 camels and one-third of a *ba'ir*, which amount is assessed at £100.[1]

Damage to hair.[2]—If an Arab cause another to be struck, and the hair of his head be scraped off, the striker shall pay one-third of the *diya*. In such a case the *diya* shall be assessed at £300, that is, the striker shall pay £100 only. Should the head recover and the hair grow again as it did before, then only the value of 20 *mithqal* is to be paid.

(But the MS. elsewhere quotes a leading case with a severer penalty.

" Yahya says that Muhammad ibn el-Muhallab said that (the Caliph) Mu'awiya ibn Sufian said that edh-Dhahhak decided in a case wherein a man had the hair of his head plucked in whole and never grew again that he should be compensated with full *diya* (1,000 dinars), and that if the whole of the hair be plucked and grew up again, only one-third of the *diya* need be paid.")

If the hair of the moustaches is plucked out, and as a consequence grows again sparsely, compensation shall only be paid for that which did not grow again. In all such cases, anything that is plucked out and does not grow again shall be compensated for proportionately from the *diya*.

Beard.—If the beard be plucked out and does not grow again and its place be vacant, then the full *diya* is due, viz. 1,000 dinars. But if the beard be plucked out and grow again without infirmity or deficiency, then only one-third of a *diya* is due, viz. 333⅓ dinars.

Eyelashes and eyebrows.—If the eyelashes be plucked out altogether and none of them grow again, one-third of a *diya* shall be due, that is 333⅓ dinars. If they be plucked out and grow again, then only 20 *mithqal* are due.

[1] The £100 is awarded as one-third of a *diya* for unintentional killing. Nowadays, no special assessment is made in either camels or " dinars " for *maimuna* wounds, which are classified as '*adam* " permanent injuries ".—A. W. G.

[2] No case of this has occurred within the memory of those now living. If it did happen it would be assessed according to the *Shari'a*.—A. W. G.

So, too, if the eyebrows are plucked out, and nothing of them grows again (one-third of a *diya* shall be due) ; but if the eyebrows are plucked out, and then grow again without defect or damage, then only 20 *mithqal* are due. So also any (hair) other than eyebrows that is plucked out shall be compensated for in like manner.

Hair of the nape of the neck.—If this is plucked out and never grows again, one-third of a *diya* shall be due, but if it grow again without defect or damage, then only 20 *mithqal* shall be due.

Fractures.[1]—Yahya says that (the Caliph) Mu'awiya ibn Sufian ordained that if the hand be broken and set again and repaired without defect or injury, 100 dinars should be due.

Yahya also says that if the arm be broken and the bone be set and repaired without injury, 100 dinars shall be due. Also fifty dinars for any bone of the arm or of the thigh, leg, or any projecting limb.

Yahya also says of the collar-bones, that if the two bones situated on the shoulders be broken, but afterwards set and repaired, 100 dinars shall be due, and for either of them separately only fifty dinars.

Dislocations.—Yahya says that if a limb be dislocated or severed, and later recover without defect or injury, fifty dinars shall be due, but if severed or disabled for good or paralysed, the compensation will be 500 dinars.

If the elbow is broken and repaired without damage (the compensation will be) 140 dinars for both (elbows) ; and fifty dinars for any part of the hips, if dislocated and then set or repaired without damage. Half the *diya*, that is 500 dinars, for the foot, if it is dislocated and does not recover and become useless ; but 100 dinars it it recovers without defect.

Gunshot Wounds.[2]—Yahya ibn Muhallab told us that Edh-Dhahhak said that (the Caliph) Mu'awiya ibn Sufian, in reviewing a case of piercing (*nafiza*), gave decision that if an organ be penetrated and recover without defect or damage, (the compensation shall be) 100 dinars, fifty for entering and fifty for passing out, but if it remains in the blood then the

---

[1] Fractures may be considered either as (1) *hashtma salama* (" healed fractures ", when repaired without defect. (Such are assessed at 150 dinars of 5 piastres each) ; or (2) *'adam* " permanent injuries ". If complete infirmity results, compensation is to be half a *diya*. Compensation for part of a limb is assessed in proportion to the number of parts in that limb.—A. W. G.

[2] Nowadays wounds caused by gunshots are assessed like other wounds, that is to say, either as *salama* " healed wounds " or as *'adam* " permanent injuries " as explained above.—A. W. G.

remaining portion shall be measured and deducted from the *diya*. If it be the leg that is penetrated, ten camels (shall be paid).

Loss of Fingers.—For the fingers of both hands, if cut off, 1,000 dinars, and for the fingers of one hand, 500 dinars, and for each finger amputated 100 dinars. If paralysed, since the fingers of the hands contain three joints but the thumbs only two, then $33\frac{1}{3}$ dinars shall be paid for each joint of the fingers, but fifty dinars for each joint of the thumbs.

We are also told by Yahya that (the Caliph) Mu'awiya ibn Sufian said that a wound on the body should be assessed at half the value of that wound on the head or face. For all bones of the body, great or small, if wounded (and recovered) without defect or damage, seventy-five dinars shall be due.

Loss of Toes.—If all the toes of both feet be cut off, 1,000 dinars, and for each toe-joint, if cut or disabled or paralysed, $33\frac{1}{3}$ dinars. Each of the big toes of the feet has two joints, and for each of these fifty dinars (shall be paid).

Nails.—If a nail be cut off, ten dinars. If the nail be injured so that its colour changes to black, three dinars.

Injuries to the Body.—Yahya says that if the neck be broken with all its bones and only the flesh be left, the full *diya* (1,000 dinars) shall be due, and if it suffers so that the owner cannot turn (his head) to right or left, 500 dinars only shall be due.

For a *munqila* injury to the neck, 150 dinars and sixteen dinars, and a half, and a sixth ($150 + 16 + \frac{1}{2} + \frac{1}{6} = 166\frac{2}{3}$) shall be due.

For a *hashima* injury in the neck, seventy-five dinars.

For a *muwadhdhiha* injury in the neck, twenty-five dinars.

For a *badhi'a* injury in the neck, twelve and a half dinars.

For a *damiya* injury in the neck, one and a half dinars.

Injuries to the Ears.—If the ears be torn off altogether, with loss of the sense of hearing, the full *diya* (1,000 dinars) shall be due, and for each ear separately 500 dinars. If the ear be injured and not recover, the wound shall be measured and estimated according to the remaining portion of the ear, or the part lost in proportion to the ear itself. If the ear be split or injured (and recover) without defect or damage, fifty dinars shall be due. But if the ear suffer damage and a little of the hearing remain, then comparison shall be made of the area from which he previously used to catch sounds and that remaining after the injury, and the damage assessed proportionately from the *diya*. Should the striker suspect that the injured man be pretending, then the injured man shall be detained till he is in need of sleep, when he shall be allowed to sleep. Then when he is asleep, drums are to be beaten above him. If he does not awake or seem to hear, then his hearing is lost. But if he starts up in horror, he is a liar.

The Eye.—Yahya says that if the sight be lost in whole, a full *diya* of 1,000 dinars shall be due, and if one eye only lose its sight, 520 dinars, and if the sight be lost in part, then the proportionate amount of the 500 dinars shall be paid.

Note.—Yahya says that the method of ascertaining how much sight has been lost is by making lines on an egg of a hen or on a white paper which is to be placed at a distance. When the patient closes his injured eye and looks with the good one, he is to be questioned as to the number of lines he can see on the egg or the paper. The egg or paper is then to be brought nearer to him little by little, until he can tell for certain the true number of the lines. Then he is to be ordered to close his good eye and look with the injured one, and the method repeated, and then the difference is to be measured between the distances.

If the eye be injured so that it lies askew, the slanting is to be measured, and compensation made from the *diya* by estimation.

The Nose.—Yahya says that if the whole nose be cut off or amputated a full *diya* of 1,000 dinars will be due, but if the flesh of the nose only be cut off, 100 dinars.

For a *nafiza* (piercing) of the nostrils in whole, 100 dinars, and for either nostril fifty dinars according to the appearance of the nose. If the bone of the nose be broken, and recover later without defect or damage, 100 dinars ; and for a *munqila* in the nose 100 dinars ; but if a big bone be removed from it, 150 dinars.

The Lips.—If the whole two lips be cut off, full *diya* will be due (1,000 dinars) and for the lips separately, if the upper one is cut off, one-third of the *diya* ; and if the lower one is cut off in whole, two-thirds of the *diya* will be paid, that is 666⅔ dinars.

For a *nafiza* in the lips, if the piercing is visible and its place is evident, fifty dinars according to the appearance of the mouth and lips (equivalent to *muwadhdhiha*), but if it be injured or split, then the compensation will be calculated from the *diya* for cutting off.

The Tongue.—Yahya says that if the tongue suffer and recover without defect or damage, 100 dinars shall be paid; but if it be all cut off, the full *diya* (1,000 dinars). If hurt be caused to the tongue, so that the owner cannot properly utter the letters, he is to be made to repeat the twenty-nine letters of the alphabet. Then the *diya* is to be divided according to the alphabet, so that the injured man is compensated for whatever letters he fails to recite or to pronounce properly.

Teeth.—Yahya says that for the whole of the teeth 1,000 dinars shall be due, and for each tooth separately fifty dinars, if it has been injured and fallen out.

For each tooth injured and split and its colour changed, fifty dinars. He also says that if a tooth fall off and be returned and fixed in its place firmly, the striker shall pay fifty dinars, and if the tooth be injured again after having been firmly stuck and grown in, the second striker shall also pay fifty dinars.

Loss of Mind.—If an Arab strikes another, whether intentionally or not, so that he goes out of his mind, the striker shall pay the full *diya* of 1,000 dinars. (The Caliph) 'Omar ibn el-Khattab decided a case in like manner.

If the mind is gone during only one day in a month, then one-thirtieth part of the full *diya* shall be due, and so on proportionately.

But if he (is partly mad and) recovers and then loses his mind for good, then the full *diya* and a tenth of the *diya* for that month shall be due.

It is also said that a *diya* (shall be due for the loss of) the mind, or the senses of hearing, sight, smell, taste, touch, or the sexual powers (in so far as) this can be felt or perceived on the outer body from its warmth and texture, or the reverse.

The Testicles.—For their cutting off or unsheathing, or retraction, 1,000 dinars, and for each separately, half the *diya*, and for their cutting off with the penis, 2,000 dinars.

For the cutting of a woman's womb a full *diya* is due if the bones become visible, and half *diya* only if they are not visible.

The Breasts.—If both breasts are cut off and milk cease, the full *diya* is due, and if only one is cut off, half the *diya*.

WESTERN DESERT LAW

But if the breasts are cut from an old woman, then the penalty shall be for wounding only, as the *diya* is only for the milk.

EVIDENCE

(1) No one is allowed to give evidence before special courts unless he be of good character, which is to be found out from his relatives' reports on him.
(2) Those under age cannot give evidence.
(3) No slave is allowed to give evidence.
(4) No drunkard is allowed to give evidence.
(5) No herdsman (*ra'i*) can give evidence for his master.
(6) No debtor can give evidence for his creditor.
(7) No artisan can give evidence for his master. (This case can hardly arise among Bedouin.)
(8) No brother or son or father-in-law can give evidence for his relative, nor a *nazil* (refugee) for his host, nor a son for his father, nor a brother for a brother, nor a foe for another between whom enmity is known, etc.

False Evidence.—If a witness give false evidence, void of truth, against another, and so cause the other man's imprisonment or subsequent death, or unmerited infliction of a fine, such witness shall be liable to pay the value of such a fine, or the amount of the *diya* in case of death.

Stealing.—If an Arab trespass on the dwelling of another and steal anything, he shall be obliged to return the same fourfold, that is, if he steal a camel he shall return four camels. But if he dispose of the stolen camel and be not in possession of any camels of his own, the camel shall be assessed in accordance with current market price, and he shall be made to pay four times that value. If the thief is poor and cannot pay the whole of the price, he may be made to pay three times the value of the camel only, while the fourth shall be paid by his clan.

A thief shall also be made to pay the fourfold value, or return four times the amount of the stolen property, if he steals a stray camel without herdsman (*ra'i*), whether he be aware whose camel it is or not, and in any way denies his theft.

And if he remove such a camel from its pasture or place of domicile to any other place, and he be proved to have acted with evil intent, the thief shall be made to pay its price only, and also return the camel if he be in possession of other camels.

Civil claims.—Claims are equivalent to debts among the Awlad 'Ali. If a creditor make a claim upon a debtor who is in possession of property, the debtor should settle the debt, and if he refuse, complaint is made to his relatives. If his relatives find no way to make him settle, then the creditor is free to plunder anything that the debtor may possess.[1]

Land.—The clans of the Awlad 'Ali are divided in Mariut and elsewhere among sections or plots or territories. Each clan has its own territory which it occupies to the exclusion of encroachment or invasion by others. They all admit that the land as a whole belongs to the Egyptian Government.

Should anyone encroach or trespass on the territory of another, the case shall be heard by a special court convened for the purpose, when evidence shall be taken from both parties, and also from the owners of the territories adjacent to the one in dispute, and in the end the court shall decide the case by means of oaths, for the Arabs of the Awlad 'Ali have great faith in an oath because it makes plain the true and condemns the false.

Cases relating to inheritance, wills, gifts, marriage, divorce, or other family connections used to be discussed by special courts, but since *shara'* courts have been established in the desert, we resort to them for the discussion and consideration of whatever befalls or happens in such cases and readily accept their decisions.

(Here follows the seals of twenty-two sheikhs testifying to the accuracy of the code set out above.)

---

[1] This custom is not followed nowadays, as all matters are now referred to Government when a debtor fails to settle his debt.

INDEX

Aamu, 14, 15, 79
'*Aba* (Arab cloak), 39, 71, 74
'Ababda (sing. 'Abadi), a Beja tribe, 11, 13, 31, 34, 36, 37, 42, 44, 48, 51; marriages are matrilocal, 54; do not address certain relatives by name, 55; 56; miners, 62; charcoal burners, 63; 64, 67, 68, 69; their dress, 73, 74; their weapons, 76, 78, 79; their food, 85, 87, 89, 90, 92; milking customs, 95–6; 97, 102; their camels, 113–15; 125; raids on and by, 139–143; their patron saint Shadli, 151; belief about animals, 154, 155; 157; serpent cult, 158; 162, 163; astronomy, 164, 166, 167; rites and ceremonies, 168, 169, 171, 172, 173, 176, 177, 178, 179, 180, 183, 184, 189, 190, 193–5, 198, 199; laws, 209, 211, 216, 217, 225, 231, 235; 241, 301; general account, 302–6; 307, 308
'Abad, ancestor of the 'Ababda, 151, 302, 303
'Abbas I, 260, 295
'Abbas (Hilmi) II, 152
'Abd, names beginning with, 174
   'Abd el-Hamid 'Ilwani, 199
   'Abd el-Jawad el-Kassar, 280
   'Abd el-Malik ibn Merwan, the Caliph, 266
   'Abd en-Nebi Muteirid, 289
   'Abd el-Qadir el-Kazza, 290
   'Abd er-Rahman, Sidi, 82, 152
   'Abd el-Wanis, 99, 100, 309
'Abdalla, a hunter, 120
'Abdalla ed-Dirazi, Sheikh of the 'Ababda, 142, 163, 305
'Abdalla Husein, a wizard, 142
Ablutions with sand, 169
'Abs, tribe, 284

Absha, chief of the Aamu, 14, 21
Abu Bakr Hadud, sheikh of the Bar'asa, 290
Abu Jureir, a saint, 228, 253
Abumina, or town of St. Menas, 19, 20, 172, 187 n.
Abu Diakul, a judge, 310
Abu Dib, sheikh of the Beni Ja'afir, 274, 275, 281, 288, 293, 296
Abu Hamed, town in the Sudan, 143, 304
"Abu Rusas", famous camel, 112
Abu Tuqeiqa, clan of Haweitat, 73, 246, 248, 258
Abu Zeid, mythical hero, 273
Abu Zeid ibn Wafi, 29
Abu Zena, legend of, 195–6
Abu Zenima, mining settlement, 144–6, 225, 263
Abyssinia, 11, 197
Acacias, burnt for charcoal, 63; good grazing for camels, 113
Addax antelope, 9, 124
Adultery, penalties for, 222–5, 317
Adyrmachidae, 313
Afrad, a clan of Awlad 'Ali, 276, 279
Afterbirth, disposal of, 172
Agatharchides, 18, 94, 197, 215, 225 n.
'Aidhab, medieval Red Sea port, 26, 27, 28, 270, 303, 310
'Aid, murderer of Mudakhil's father, 40, 206, 209
'Aid esh-Shilh, war-time sheikh of the Haweitat, 247
'*Ain* (spring), (all in Sinai):—
   'Ain Abu Jarad, 250
   'Ain Markha, 78
   'Ain el-Quds, 217
   'Ain Sudr, 224, 249, 250
   'Ain Sumar, 224
El-'Ain, at the mouth of Wadi Gemal, 51

INDEX

Akharsa, tribe, 44, 156, 252, 284
'*Alaq* ceremony, 155
'Alawin, a branch of the Haweitat, 252
'Alayan, ancestor of the Haweitat, 245, 248
'Aleiqat (sing. 'Aleiqi), tribe, 29, 33, 38, 40, 45, 46, 47, 49 n., 51, 105, 120, 134, 136; names of stars, 166; 179, 183; blood-money among, 204; 207, 208, 213; do not remarry a divorced wife, 226; 239, 243, 246, 257, 258, 259, 261; general account, 262–4; 291, 310
Alexander the Great, 19, 20
Alexandria, 5, 19, 32, 127, 152, 309
'Ali, a saint, 152
'Ali, of the Laheiwat, abducts a wife, 224
'Ali el-Abyad, 278
'Ali el-Ahmar, 274, 278, 279
'Ali Dinar, Sultan of Darfur, 289
'Ali Kheir, a guide, 60, 67, 68, 117, 118, 120, 122, 157, 161, 162, 170, 178, 310
'Ali Bey Mustafa, sheikh of the 'Ababda, 48, 102, 163, 305
'Ali Tiut Batran, sheikh of the Hamedorab, 142, 307
'Aliab, a clan of Bisharin, 92, 113, 209, 301, 302, 307, 308
Allah, 44, 149, 150, 161
Almasy, Count, 11
Almoravides, 41, 272
Amar Ar, a Beja tribe, 95, 141, 142, 162, 171 n., 189 n., 216, 221, 225
'Amayim, a Berber tribe in Upper Egypt, 33, 286, 289, 292, 297, 298
Amina, a heroine of the 'Aqaqra, 289
'Amir 'Ayyad the *mubasha'*, 234
'Amira, a female saint, 178
El-'Amri, a Sinai saint, 152
'Amriya, a village in Mariut, 60, 61, 271, 277
'Anafi breed of camel, 113
Anakw, a Bisharin ancestor, 307
'Anaza, a great Syrian tribe, 25, 134, 234, 267

Animals, domestic, 93–116
    ,,   dangerous, law about, 319–320
    ,,   wild, 117–132
Anqarab, a Beja tribe, 142, 306
'Antar, hero of Arab poetry, 157, 284
Antares, the star, 165
Ants, 88
'Antiu, 13
'Aqaba, town, 147, 224, 248, 249, 259
'Aqaba, Gulf of, 62, 248, 265
'Aqar bin Dib, ancestor of the tribes of Bar'asa, Harabi, and Awlad 'Ali, 275, 276, 288, 296; 'Aqaqra, his descendants, 288, 289
'Aqeila, or 'Aqeilat, camel traders, 252, 285
'*Aqid* or " raid-leader ", 42, 135, 136, 141, 259
'Aqliyin, small tribe in North Sinai, 44
Arabia, 1, 7, 8 n., 22, 27, 32, 33, 36, 39, 48, 51, 56, 59, 72 n., 85, 97, 104, 193, 195, 284, 285. *See also* Hijaz, Midian
'Arab el-Gharb, 286
Archers, 24, 137, 138
Ariel gazelle, 119
El-'Arish, town, 5, 134, 160, 200, 201, 225, 249, 254
" Armenoid " race, 10, 13
Armenti dogs, 99
'Ashabab, section of the 'Ababda, 142, 303–6
'*Ashura*, ceremony on the tenth day of the Moslem year, 25, 174
Ass, wild, 9, 89, 125
Assessment of wounds, 234–7, 321–7
Asyut, 29, 269, 286, 297
Aswan, 9, 24, 26, 28, 29, 78, 142, 179, 197, 297, 301
'*Atair*, 193
'Atalla, a guide, 241
'Atawna (sing. 'Atwani), an Arab tribe, 31, 140, 141, 198, 305
Atbara, battle of, 77; river, 125, 301
'Atiyat, tribe of Upper Egypt, 286
Atlas Mountains, 9
El-'Auja, Palestine frontier post, 152
Aujila, oasis in Cyrenaica, 292, 299

INDEX

Avoidance of relatives, 55, 56
'Awaqir, a tribe in Cyrenaica, 274, 277, 288, 289, 290
'Awarma (sing. 'Armi), a division of the Sawalha, 45, 46, 58, 145, 150, 259, 260
'Awazim, a tribe of Hiteim, 270
'Awda, a Muzeini, 159
'Awda Abu Tai, 199 n., 244, 245
'Awda ez-Zumeili, sheikh of the 'Aleiqat, 145, 209, 261, 263
'Aweid Budr, sheikh of the Muzeina, 264, 265
Awlad 'Abd es-Sallam, 275
Awlad 'Ali, a tribe of the Mediterranean littoral, 30, 37, 40, 44 n., 56, 57, 60, 67; dress, 74, 75; 80; tent, 81; 82, 83; food, 85, 88, 92; 96; dogs, 98; camels, 107, 113; hawking, 127, 130; 151; ceremonies, 172, 174, 191, 192; laws, 206, 210, 231, 313–328; general account, 275–9; 280, 281, 282, 283, 288, 289, 294, 296, 297, 299, 309
Awlad 'Ali, a small tribe of Sinai, 44, 252
Awlad Fayid, a division of the Baraghith, 288
Awlad Jibrin, a division of the Baraghith, 288, 299
Awlad Kahil, ancestors of the 'Ababda? 303
Awlad Kharuf, a division of the Awlad 'Ali, 40, 278
Awlad Sallam, or Salalma, 288, 291, 294
Awlad Suleiman, a Sinai tribe, 249, 287
Awlad Suleiman, Murabitin of Cyrenaica, 274, 278, 280, 286–7, 297, 299
'Ayaida, Arabs of Sinai and Eastern Desert, 43, 44, 105, 244, 284
'Ayun Musa (" Moses' Wells "), near Suez, 195, 207, 264
El-Azhar, Moslem University of Cairo 159

Badara, small Sinai tribe, 245
Bahariya Oasis, 85, 104, 111, 113, 278, 280

Bahig, 171, 288
Bahja, tribe of Western Arabs, 287–8
Bahnasa, town in Middle Egypt, 29
Baker, Sir Samuel, 83, 123, 171
Banas, a saint, 151
Banat Wudheiha, Arabian camels, 113
Baqqara, tribe of the Sudan, 142, 253 n., 297
Barabra, Nubians settled on the Nile, 96
Baraghith (" Sons of Barghuth "), tribe of Western Arabs, 288–290
Baraka or magical force, 160, 161, 196
Bar'asa, tribe of Western Arabs, 32, 290, 296
Barb horse, 101
Barbary sheep, 9, 124
Barghuth, ancestor of the Baraghith, 288, 293
Barth, Heinrich, 286
Baqush, a " marabout ", 281, 282
Bates, Oric, 91
Batn " belly ", used to denote a clan, 53, 288
Batn-el-Monasir, 53, 54
Bayadin, small tribe in North Sinai, 35, 44, 156, 252
Bdawi or Bedauye, the Beja language, 180, 301
Bedayat, tribe of the Sahara, 298
Beheira (" the lake "), province of the Western Delta, 33, 106, 152, 276, 277, 280, 281, 282, 294, 297, 299, 309
Beja, the descendants of the early Hamitic inhabitants of North-East Africa, 1, 11, 12, 14, 21, 22; resist the Arab invasion, 26; absorb their conquerors, 26–8; 29, 31, 34, 37; Arabs obtain the chieftaincies of the tribes, 54; avoid their mothers-in-law, 55; inhospitable, 60; dress, 74; weapons, 76, 79; hut and furniture, 81–4; food, 91, 92, 94; milking customs, 95, 96; dogs, 97; 100, 122, 161, 166; circumcision, 176; weddings, 182; blood-rite, 198; formerly Christian?, 199; laws, 209, 216, 217,

INDEX

225; Beja tribes, 301–8. *See also* 'Ababda, Bisharin, Beni 'Amir, Hadendawa

Bells, 199

Belzoni, 55

Beni 'Adi, town in Upper Egypt, carpets of, 61

"Beni 'Ali," name for Awlad 'Ali ?, 280

Beni 'Amir, a Beja tribe of the Sudan, 11, 13, 41, 52, 55, 56, 61, 95, 184, 192, 301, 302

Beni 'Atiya, a tribe of Northern Arabia, 25, 33, 72 n., 243, 248, 267

Beni Hilal, an ancient tribe of Arabia, invade North Africa, 25, 26, 27; 36, 272, 273, 293

Beni Kelb, an ancient tribe of Arabia, 36, 97, 293

Beni Mazar, a town of Middle Egypt, 268

Beni Sabt, a clan of the Ma'aza, formerly Christian ?, 269

Beni Sakhr or Sukhur, a tribe of Transjordania, 183, 193

Beni Suef, province of Middle Egypt, 268, 290, 291, 292, 293, 295

Beni Suleim, an ancient Arab tribe, ancestors of most of the Western Arabs of Egypt and Cyrenaica, 25, 26, 29, 33, 272, 273, 280, 281, 282, 287, 288, 291, 293, 294, 300

Beni Suleiman, an extinct Sinai tribe, 257

Beni Tamim, an ancient Arab tribe, 25, 292

Beni 'Ummayya, an ancient Arab tribe, 297

Beni 'Una, a tribe of "Murabitin", now settled in the cultivation, 29, 30, 275, 276, 281, 288, 291

Beni 'Uqba, an almost extinct Arab tribe, 25; their abasement by the Haweitat, 38, 39; supply the judges who try cases concerning women, 229; 245, 248, 249, 257, 263, 286, 291

Beni Wasil, an almost extinct tribe, 25, 31, 33, 140, 239, 254, 257, 259, 291

Bent, Theodore, Mrs., 61

Bent, Theodore, 74

Berber, town and province of the Sudan, 157, 303, 304

Berbers, the indigenous population of North Africa, 1, 17, 20, 22, 33, 150, 271, 272, 273, 293, 297, 300

Berenice, a ruined Red Sea port, 18, 270

Berenice's Bodkin, a peak, 5

Billi, an Arab tribe, 24, 25, 28, 29, 33, 72 n., 105, 133, 248, 253, 258, 284, 286, 292

Billi el-Barada, a small Sinai tribe, 252

Bir (well), nearly all in Eastern Desert
„ Abu Hodeid, 196
„ Adal Deib, 307
„ el-Beida, 102
„ Afandina, 121
„ Aqwamtra, 142, 143
„ Fowakhir, 141
„ Haimur, 142, 304, 305
„ Juqub, 110
„ Mab'uq (Sinai), 112
„ Madi, 196
„ Mashushenai, 110
„ Meisa, 142
„ Natrun (Sudan), 286, 292
„ Nasb (Sinai), 291
„ Nukhul (Sinai), 121
„ Ongat, 110, 142
„ Qidmib, 196
„ Quei, 25
„ Ranga, 158
„ Shalatein, 307
„ Sheb, 124
„ Sheitun, 292
„ Shinai, 196
„ Themed (Sinai), 249
„ Ti Kureitra, 196
„ Umm Qubur, 69

Birds, superstitions about, 92

"Birkil" (Col. Parker), 51, 58, 59

Birth ceremonies, 171–3

Bisharin, a Beja tribe, 5; speak a Hamitic language, 11; 34, 41; matrilocal marriages, 54; avoid their mothers-in-law, 55; 57; inhospitable, 60; their weaving, 61; 64; healthy, 67; weapons, 76,

INDEX 333

79; food, 82, 88–90; milking customs, 95, 96; their greyhounds, 99; their camels, 104, 106, 112, 113; 125, 126, 141, 142, 143; superstitions, 151, 154, 157, 160; rites, 169, 171, 172, 173, 176–180, 196; laws, 215, 225, 226; 301, 302; general account, 306–8, 310
Bishir Bey, sheikh of the 'Ababda, 142, 163, 304, 305
Bissel, battle in Arabia, 31
Bitter lakes, 115
Blackman, Miss, 56, 169 n., 170 n.
Blemmyes, 20, 21, 76; their raid on Tor, 136–8
Blind man, anecdote of, 69
Blood-covenant, 196, 197
Blood-customs, 196–9
Blood-money (*diya*), 37, 56, 97, 158 n., 203–210, 213, 219, 234, 235, 314–19
Boar, wild, 90, 124
Book of the Dead, 94
Bow, 76
Bramly, W. Jennings, v, 2, 55, 66, 89, 100, 101, 104, 107, 109, 115, 118, 120, 121, 125, 126; notes on falconry, 127–132; 156, 170, 172, 176, 184, 192, 200, 203, 209, 213, 217, 220, 221, 222, 233, 252, 280, 284, 302, 320
Bread, preparation of, 86, 87; essential to the marriage ceremony, 181 n.
Bruce, James, 39, 269, 304
Burckhardt, 36, 42, 60, 65, 66, 76, 92, 96, 110, 111, 112, 153 n., 157, 178, 181 n., 182, 183, 191, 198, 204, 210, 223, 232, 237, 244, 245, 248, 249, 250, 262, 266, 284, 291, 294, 295
Burghul, 86
Burqu' or mask, 73
Burton, James, 76
Burton, Sir Richard, 38, 45, 97, 179 n., 245, 264
Bustard, 127, 128, 130, 131

Cairo, 26, 45, 59, 106; Cairo–Suez road, 245, 310
Cairns, 194–6, 210

Cambyses, 196
Camels, 10, 17, 19, 20, 92, 96, 103–116, 136; sacrifices of, 153. *See* heliacal risings before men, 164
Canopus, 164–6
Castor-oil, 67
Cataract, First, 13, 20, 24
Cheetah, 9, 119, 124
Christianity, vestiges of, 199
Circumcision, 169, 174–9, 190
Cisterns, 3, 19, 20
Clayton, Lady, 124
Clayton, P. A., 124
Colocynth, 67, 84
Constellations, 164–7
Crocodile, 9, 162
Cromer, Lord, 162, 200
Crossland, Cyril, 177 n., 225
Crowfoot, J. W., 61, 164 n., 180 n., 216
Crowfoot, Mrs., 87
Cyrenaica, 8, 11, 21, 24, 30, 32, 33, 57, 61, 96, 99 n., 134, 195, 270, 272, 274, 276, 277, 284, 286, 288, 289, 290, 293, 296, 299
Cyrene, 19, 20

Dabb, spiny-tailed lizard, 90, 91
Dahab, harbour in the Gulf of 'Aqaba, 47
Dahiya, dance, 64, 65
Dances, 64, 65
Dakhil, right of, 210, 212–220
Dakhla Oasis, 11 n., 110, 123, 289, 298
Danakil, a tribe of Eritrea, 195 n.
Daqahliya Province, 124, 287, 305
Darb el-'Arba' in, 286
Daraw, town in Upper Egypt, 110, 157, 301
Darfur, 11
Dawaghra, clan of Hiteim, 252
Death from fright, law about, 319
Death in prison, law about, 318
Debt, recovery of, 238
Delta, Nile, 11, 13, 25, 92, 104, 113, 124, 293
Derna, town in Cyrenaica, 8, 290, 296
Dervishes, 272; defeated at Meisa and Murrat, 142–3; 304, 305

INDEX

Dhab'a, village in Mariut, 20, 199, 282
Dhiba, village in Arabia, 133
Dhu'afa, tribe, 292
Dhullam, tribe, 249
Dhureibi, or judge of appeal, 229
Dhuwi Hasan, tribe of Ashraf, 39, 40, 57, 174
Dib, *see* Abu Dib
Diboki, a drove of camels, 110
Dirwa, the Beja mop of hair, 73, 74, 178-9
Diseases prevalent in the desert, 67, 68
Dishna, town of Upper Egypt, 298
Divorce, 225-6
Diya, *see* blood-money
Dogs, 93, 97-100
Dogstar, 164
Dom-palm, 81, 82, 88
Domestic animals, 93-116
Dongola, province of the Sudan, 125, 297
"Dongola," i.e. Dongonab, 26, 28
Donkeys, 10, 101, 102, 104
Doughty, C. M., 59, 63, 73, 74 n., 91, 97, 110, 117, 133, 173, 193, 199, 267
Dugheim, tribe, 27
Dumreicher, André, 236 n., 283

Eckenstein, Miss, 136
Elephants, 9, 18
Elliot Smith, 1 n., 16 n.
Emeralds, 18, 21, 26
'Esheibat, section of the Awlad 'Ali, 279, 283
Etbai, or Red Sea Hills, 99, 113, 120, 310
Exemption from conscription, 31, 289
Exodus, the, 16; Book of Exodus, 71 n., 198, 230, 239, 320
Eye, evil, 114
Ezekiel, 71 n.

Faiyum, province, 21, 33, 57, 120
Falconry, Bramly's notes on, 127-132
Falls, Ewald, 88, 172, 176, 187 n., 191
Famine, expedients in time of, 90
Faranja, a section of the Muzeina, 40, 207, 208, 224, 225

Faranja, Sheikh, a saint, 153, 265
Farshut, 111, 270
Fawakhir, tribe, 292-3
Fawayid, tribe, 274, 288-290, 293
Feisal, King, 63
Ferjan, tribe, 282, 293, 297
Fezara, tribe, 293
Flint, implements, 8, 11; flint and steel, 70
Flintlock guns, 78
Frazer, Sir James, 93, 95
Fuad I, King, 152
Fuqara (of Arabia), 91
Fuqara, section of 'Ababda, 142, 304

Galala Mountains, 121, 244, 266
Gautier, E. F., 91
Galla, 96
Gaza, 69, 100, 152, 249
Gazelle, 118, 119, 121-3, 131, 154
Gharandel, a Sinai wadi, 246
Gharbiya Province, 124, 280, 281, 282, 287, 293, 305
Ghatafan, ancient tribe, 25, 284, 293
Ghouls, 118, 156
Ghurra, 203, 204, 206, 207
Gilf Kebir, 124
Giraffe, 9
Girga, town and province of Upper Egypt, 29, 171, 291
Giza Province, 29, 280
Goats, 49, 50, 63, 93
Gold-mines, 9, 16, 18
Gondos, an Austrian, 144, 146, 260
Graves, 192, 193
"Green Mountain" (Jebel Akhdar), 7, 11, 27, 276, 281, 282, 290, 292
Green, A. W., notes by, 313, 315, 317, 319, 322, 323
Greyhounds, 98-9, 120, 121
Griddle (*saj*), 86
Guests, 40, 59, 60
Guardian (*wasy*), 237-8
Gunpowder, 78
Gurkhas, 144, 145

Habab, a Beja tribe of Eritrea, 96, 199, 225
Habak, a heroine of the Baraghith, 289
Habun, a tribe of Murabitin, 278

INDEX

Hadahid, a Western tribe, 152
Hadendawa, a Beja tribe of the Sudan, 11, 61, 89, 95, 141, 169, 172, 177, 189 n., 301, 302
Hair ceremonies, 177–9
Halaib (Mersa Olei), Red Sea harbour, 270, 307
Halal, rite of, 88
Halenga, a Beja tribe of the Sudan, 198
Hamada, an old Sinai tribe, 120, 239, 257, 264, 291
Hamaida, clan of the 'Aleiqat, 40, 209, 264
Hamam, sheikh of the Hawara, 297
Hamd, Burckhardt's guide, 204
Hamda, an Arab girl, 49–51
Hamdan Abu Zeit, El-Hajj, sheikh of the Qararsha, 144, 145, 154, 261
Hamdan Himeid, a boy, 145
Hamed Pasha el-Bassal, 290
Hamed Bayad, a hero of the Bar'asa, 288–9
Hamedorab, section of the Bisharin, 142, 225, 301, 302, 307–8
Hamilton, James, 97, 99 n., 278 n., 286 n.
Hamilton, William, 197
Hamites, 1, 33, 94, 104, 203
Hamitic languages and culture, 2, 7, 10, 11, 12, 13, 14, 56
Hammam, a village of Mariut, 277
Hanadi, a Western tribe settled in Sharqiya, 16, 29, 30, 36, 53, 98, 99, 127, 274, 276, 281, 282, 288, 289; general account, 294–6
Harabi, a tribe of Western Bedouin, 40, 274, 296, 299
Haram, old political faction, 43, 44
Harb, tribe of Arabia, 48, 59, 134, 273, 290, 297
Harding King, 298
Hare, 89, 126
Hareinab, section of 'Ababda, 179
Haruba tribe, 296
Hasan 'Ali Mustafa, sheikh of the 'Ababda, 163, 305
Hasan, son of Jubran, 163, 305
Hasan el-Yasuri, 26
Hasan, sheikh of the Rashaida, 214

Hasanein Bey, 110, 299
Hasani, island off the Arabian coast, 284
Hasib = ambassador, 43
Hasib = refugee, 216–220
Hawara, a Berber tribe, 29, 33, 41; their dogs, 99, 278, 296, 297
Hawata, a tribe of Murabitin, 297
Hawawir, a tribe in Dongola; chase ostriches, 125–6; 297
Hawazim or Hawazma, 297
Haweit ibn Ham, an ancestor of the Haweitat, 245
Haweitat, a tribe of Arabia, Sinai, and Egypt, 33, 36; ill-treat the Beni 'Uqba, 38–9; 43, 44, 47, 51, 52; Haweitat women of Midian do not wear the *burqu'*,73; food, 87–8; 113, 120; rebel against Ibn Sa'ud, 133; raid the Muzeina, 146; circumcision rites, 175; marriage by capture, 183; mutilate the dead, 194; 227, 234, 243; general description, 245–8; 250, 258, 259, 266, 269, 284, 310. *See also* 'Imran
Hawking, 127–132
Haynes, 159, 261
Headrest, 81, 82
Hebrews, 2; their Exodus, 16; 20, 90, 94, 161, 166, 198, 200, 230
Henna, 99, 107
Henniker, Sir F., 38, 184, 197
Heriu-sha or "sand-dwellers", 13
Herodotus, 3, 7, 10 n., 158 n., 196, 198, 231, 313
Hida', 64
Hijaz, 56, 57, 73; camels from, 113; 200, 237, 243, 268, 269, 289
Hind, ancestress of the Hanadi, 36, 276, 294
Hiteim, outcaste tribes of Arabia and Egypt, 33, 38, 149, 251, 252, 257, 265, 268–270, 284, 285. *See also* Rashaida, Dawaghra
Holal, wooden hair-pin, 74
Horn of hair, women's, 72
Horse, 10, 14, 16, 100, 101, 125, 126
Hosh 'Isa, a town in Beheira, 30, 62, 74, 276, 309
Hospitality, 59, 60

INDEX

"Hurghada," a Red Sea oilfield, 303
Husein Pasha Khalifa, 304
Hyena, 119, 120, 155
Hyksos, 11, 14, 16, 20, 93

'Ibeidat, tribe of Cyrenaica, 32, 277, 296
Ibex, 9; tame; 14, 88, 89, 119, 121, 122, 154, 164
Ibn Battuta, 20 n., 27, 54, 92, 303, 310
Ibn Khaldun, 271, 272, 274, 275, 280, 281, 287, 288, 291, 298, 309
Ibn Sa'ud, 133, 200, 248
Ichthyophagi, descendants of, 92, 103, 158
'Id ed-Dahiya, or 'Id el-Kebir, 105, 153, 176, 179, 199
Idfu, or Edfu, a town of Upper Egypt, 26, 27, 67, 194, 302
"Ifrikias," 271
'Ilwani Suleiman, 48, 124; his wedding, 184-9, 199, 281, 309
'Imran, a section of the Haweitat, 135, 204, 248
Isalas the plasterer, 199
Ishmael, 8, 16, 26
Islam, 22, 23, 97, 149, 166, 207, 272
Isma'il Bey Shedid, sheikh of the Haweitat, 245, 248
Isma'il Pasha, 289
Isna, or Esna, town of Upper Egypt, 26, 29, 96, 111, 112, 270
Israelites, 2, 16, 20, 90, 94, 161, 166, 198, 200, 230

Ja'afira, Arabs settled in Upper Egypt, 96, 297
Ja'alin, a Sudan tribe, 142
Jabarti, Arab historian, 276
Jackal, 98, 112
Jahama, Berber tribe settled in Upper Egypt, 33, 286, 287, 297-8
Jalalat, 290
Jalo, oasis in Cyrenaica, 299
Jarvis, Major C. S., 35, 41 n., 121, 220, 233, 235 n., 252
Jaussen, Père, 37, 149, 156, 163, 170 n., 183 n., 193, 194, 199, 214, 232, 235 n., 237 n.

Jawabis, tribe of Murabitin, 35, 41, 111, 275, 279-280, 299
Jawazi, Western Arabs settled in Minya Province, 268, 274, 288-290
Jebel Abu Tiyur, 5
„ Akhdar, see " Green Mountain "
„ Asotriba, 9
„ Ejma, 5, 245
„ Elba, 5, 27, 80 n., 126, 142, 160, 302, 306, 307, 308
„ Fara'id (Pentadactylus), 5
„ Hamata, 5, 141
„ Hammam Saidna Musa, 144, 299
„ Hilal, 5
„ Maghara, in North Sinai, 121, 253
„ Mitiq, 141
„ Musa (Mount Sinai), 153, 154, 159
„ Raha, 156, 246
„ Shayib, 5
„ Sharr, 248
„ Shindeib, 125
„ 'Umm Rijlein, 120
„ 'Uweinat, 11
„ Zeit, 241, 310
Jebeliya, tribe settled in the Delta, 298
Jebeliya, serfs of the Monastery of St. Catherine, 180, 258, 265, 266, 298
Jebely 'Aid, 123, 146, 147, 183
Jebely Bareik, ex-sheikh of the Muzeina, 259, 265
Jemsa, 111, 144
Jerboa, 89, 126, 127
Jerusalem, 18, 28
Jews, 2, 16, 20, 90, 94, 161, 166, 198, 200, 230
Jibali, a sheikh of the Harabi, 296
Jidda, seaport of Mecca, 28, 39, 57
Jinn, 97, 155, 156
Jira, the camel paid as earnest of the blood-money, 221, 223
Jird, the toga of the Western Arabs, 74-6
Jubran, ancestor of the 'Ashabab 'Ababda, 305
Juheina, a famous Arab tribe, 24, 25,

INDEX

28, 33, 57, 60, 134, 179, 264, 275, 284, 294, 298–9, 303
Jumeiʻat, a tribe of Murabitin, 41, 48, 99, 176; a Jumeiʻat wedding, 184–9; 274, 275, 276, 278, 280–2, 294
Justinian, founder of the monastery of St. Catherine, 32, 265, 266

Kaʻb, the ancestor of the Murabitin; four worthies contend for this honour, viz. Kaʻb bein Elwei, 281, 299; Kaʻb el-Ahbar, 281; Kaʻb bin Suleim, 281; Kaʻb bin Zuheir, 281
Kaʻba, the, 155, 232
Kababish, an Arab tribe of the Sudan, 52, 142, 177
Kassala, a town of the Eastern Sudan, 110, 111, 270
Kanjar Aweib, the runaway stone, 157
Karait Batran, omda of the Hamedorab Bisharin, 160, 161, 225
Karkura, battle of, 288–9
Kawahla, a tribe of the Sudan, 301, 302
Kefiya, or Kerchief, 69, 70
Kemal ed-Din, Prince, 114, 121
Kennett, Austin, 35, 170, 206 n., 207, 221, 223, 233, 235, 236 n., 280
Ketama, a Berber tribe, 271
Kharga Oasis, 11, 21, 26, 286, 313
Khartoum, 104, 304
Khawalid, a section of the Barʻasa, 290
Khidr, sheikh of the Muzeina, 144, 265
Khor Arbaʻat, 9
Khuwa (blackmail), 38
Kinana, a noble Arab tribe, 25, 264
Klippel, E., 275, 294
Klunzinger, C. B., 74, 164 n., 170
Kom Ombo, town in Upper Egypt, 69
Koran, 37, 70, 155
Kordofan, 303
Korosko, village in Nubia, 303, 304
El-Kubri, ferry across the Suez Canal, 51
Kufara Oasis, 80 n., 110, 297, 298

Kuka, ancestor of the Bisharin, 5, 306, 307
Kurbeilab, section of the Bisharin, 196, 199

Laheiwat, a Sinai tribe, 25, 33, 43, 44, 100, 121, 126, 135, 183, 203, 204, 212, 224, 245, 248–251
Lamtuna, a Tuareg tribe, 200, 272
Lane, E. W., 44, 192
Laqeita wells, 141
Laqiya, oasis in the Sudan, 286
"Law of the Tent," 212–220
Lawrence, T. E., 134
Leopard, 9, 119
Leukos Limen, 18
Libyan Desert, so-named by Herodotus, 3, 298, 299
Libyans, 10, 11; invade Egypt, 17, 18; 19, 201 n.
Linant de Bellefonds, 114, 215, 304, 308
Lith, an Arabian harbour, 39
Looms, 61, 62
Luwata Berbers, 20, 21, 24, 26, 27, 29, 33, 272
Luzd, a Western tribe, 253, 299

Maʻaza, Arab tribe of the Eastern Desert, 25, 31, 33; dress, 71; tent, 81; food, 90, 91; raids, 138, 139; views on *jinn*, 156; rites, 95, 170, 172, 176–180, 182, 183; laws, 206, 212, 226, 234, 237, 243, 246; general account, 266–8; 269, 298, 303, 310
MacDonald, Major, 261
MacMichael, H. A., 253 n., 293, 301 n.
Madigan, J., 196
Maghara, turquoise mines of, 9, 13, 62
Maghra, uninhabited oasis in the Western Desert, 87, 119, 124
Malaria, 67
Mamelukes, 28, 29, 30, 31, 197, 297, 304
Manfalut, town in Upper Egypt, 29, 286, 297
Maqrizi, Arab historian, 27, 54, 294, 303
Mareotis (Mariut), Lake, 19, 309

z

INDEX

Mariut, coastal district west of Alexandria, 85, 92, 99, 106, 127, 280, 296, 328
Marmarica, 3
Marqub, story of the, 215, 217–220
Marriages, 179–191 ; of first cousins, 179, 180 ; " by capture," 180, 182, 183
Masai, 12, 174, 177, 193, 197
Mas'ud, Arab historian, 91
Matchlocks, 78
Matriarchate, 53, 54
Matting huts, 81, 82
Mazices, 20, 21
Mazzaloth (the planet Venus), 166
Mecca, pilgrimage, 27, 28, 32, 42, 114, 200 ; the town of, 97, 157, 174, 245
Megabari, 21
Meinhof, 94
Meir, 14
Meisa, skirmish at the well of, 142, 143, 193, 305
Meleikab, division of the 'Ababda, 143, 303, 304, 306
Menasra, section of the Hanadi, 295
Menufiya Province, 29, 124, 280, 282, 287, 298
Menzala, Lake, 251
Merenptah, 17
Merga, oasis in the Sudan, 286
Mersa Wadi Lahami, 103
Meshwesh, 17
Messufa, a tribe of Tuareg, 54, 272
Midian, 33, 35, 73, 87, 234, 266
Milking customs, 95–7
Milky Way, 167
Miller, J. W., 57, 216
Millet, 87, 118
Minya Province, 268, 282, 290
Millstones, 82, 86
Moab, 121, 154 n., 156, 163, 170, 183, 222, 229 n., 235
Monasir, tribe in the Sudan, 54 ; their camels, 112
Monsoon, discovery of the, 18
Moon, 165
Mosaic Code, 16, 239
Moses, 153
Mother-in-law, avoidance of, 55, 56

Mount Sinai, 153, 159, *and see* Jebel Musa
Mubasha', 151, 161, 232–4, 244
Mu'awiya, the Caliph, 322, 323, 324
Mudakhil, sheikh of the 'Aleiqat, 40, 51, 144, 145, 206, 207, 208, 209, 224, 225
Mudar, ancient Arab tribe, 25
Mugharba, a Western tribe, 288, 299
Mugharba, general name for Western Arabs, 268, 271–283
Muhammad, the Prophet, 22, 37, 53, 90, 155, 174, 184
Muhammad 'Ali, the Great, 18, 30, 31, 248, 252, 258, 267, 280, 288, 289, 293, 294, 295, 296, 297, 309
Muhammad 'Arif, a sheikh of the Harb, 39–40, 57
Muhammad Buleib, a Bishari, 92
Muhammad Katul, a Bishari, 199, 310
Muhammad Abu Rumeil, a raid-leader, 146
Muhammad Bey Wasfi, Governor of Kharga, 278 n., 313
Mu'izz, the Caliph, 26
Mu'izz ibn Badis, 27, 273
Mu'izz et Turkomani, 291
Mujabra, a Western tribe, 288, 299
Munshid, judge of honour, 53, 210, 229
Munzinger, W., 56, 184, 192
Murabitin, the descendants of the early Arab invaders of the West, 41, 89, 150, 174, 272–5, 279, 280, 281, 282, 286, 289, 291, 292, 293, 297, 299
Murrat wells, 143, 304
Mursi 'Abdu, 194
Musa ibn Nuseir, the leader of the first invasion of North Africa, 25
Musa Nassar, the old judge of the Wilad Sa'id, 233, 234
Musa Nassir, the Sheikh of all the Towara, 153, 259, 260, 261
Musa Sofaran, a sheikh of the Muzeina, 153
Musabbah, a saint, 152
Mushahira, an imaginary disease, 169, 176

INDEX

Musil, Alois, 154 n., 156, 175, 179, 199 n.
Mustansir, the Caliph, 26, 273
Muteir, a tribe of Hiteim, 248, 249, 269
Muteir, a sheikh of the Laheiwat, involved in Prof. Palmer's murder, 250, 251
Muweila, a port of Arabia, 233
Muzeina, an ancient tribe of Arabia with an offshoot settled in Sinai, 33, 35, 40, 45, 46, 53, 62; women's dress, 72, 73; 89, 119, 123; raided by the Haweitat, 146–7; 153; belief in 'Umm el-Gheith, 156; rites, 171, 172, 178, 182, 183; law, 209, 228, 241, 243, 250, 257, 258; general account, 264–5

Names, 173–4
Nasamonians, 231
Nassar, a Bedouin sheikh, 45
Nassir Musa, sheikh of the Qararsha, 44, 144, 259, 261, 265
Naʻum Bey Shuqeir, 44, 65, 72, 160, 175, 194, 197, 210, 220–1, 234, 245, 253, 254, 255, 260
Nebi Harun, 153
„ Musa, 153
„ Sala, 153, 259
Nebk, a harbour in the Gulf of ʻAqaba, 51
Nekhl, a former station on the pilgrimage route, 58, 146, 160, 200, 249; people of Nekhl, 77
Nimr, sheikh of the ʻAbabda, 304
Nobadae, 20, 21
Nubia, 8, 9, 33
Nubians, 11, 24, 26, 67, 170

Oases, 5, 9, 17, 20, 29, 32, 298, 309. See also Bahariya, Dakhla, Kharga, Kufara, Laqiya, Merga, Selima, Siwa
Oaths, 151, 153, 159, 230–4, 316, 317
ʻOkasha, a saint, 253, 299
Okeil and Fatma, anecdote of, 221–2
ʻOmar, the Caliph, 22, 24, 44, 326
ʻOmar Toussoun, Prince, 124

ʻOmar Khalifa, sheikh of the Tarhuna, 300
ʻOmar Bey el-Masri, 289, 290, 299
ʻOrafa, a tribe of Cyrenaica, 288
Orion, 164, 166
Oryx, 9, 14
Ostrich, 9, 125, 126
Ox, 13, 93, 95

Palestine, 76, 86, 100, 104, 133, 156, 196, 200, 208, 224
Palgrave, W. G., 149
Palmer, Prof. E. H., 72, 90, 97, 151, 170, 171, 175, 176, 181 n., 192, 195, 196 n., 217, 233, 246, 250, 251, 261
Pariah dogs, 98
Parker, Col. (" Birkil "), 51, 58, 59, 144
Penfield, F. C., 179
Persians, 18, 104
Petrie, Sir Flinders, 163
Pharan (Feiran), 137, 138
" Pharaoh's bells," 199
Philby, H. St. J. B., 8 n., 114
Piankhi, Ethiopian conqueror of Egypt, 92
Placenta, disposal of the, 172
Pleiades, 164, 166
Plowden, W. C., 96, 225
Poets, 63, 64
Psoes, a monk of Sinai, 137, 138
Ptolemy the geographer, 19
Ptolemy II (Philadelphus), 18
Punt, 12, 14

Qadadfa, a tribe of Murabitin, 280, 287, 299
Qadi, or tribal judge, 42, 200–2
Qahtan, ancestor of the true Arabs, 24, 36, 264
„ a tribe of Arabia, 199
Qahtanid tribes, 24, 291, 294
Qairwan, a town of Tunis, 27, 264
Qaliub, a town of the Delta, 25, 248, 293
Qaliubiya Province, 245, 292
Qantara, 251
Qarabawi, an ʻAbadi, 142, 143
Qararsha, a division of the Sawalha,

58, 144, 145, 207, 208, 259, 260, 261, 265
Qarina, female attendant spirit, 159, 169, 170
Qassala, green twig, 180
Qassas, assessor, 229, 234–6
Qatʻan, a tribe of Murabitin, 274, 278, 280, 287, 296
Qattara Depression, 3, 4, 8, 124, 194
Qatawiya, or Arabs of Qatia, 251–2
Qatia, oasis in Northern Sinai, 5, 85, 90, 243, 249, 251, 252, 269, 295
Qeis ʻAilan, an ancient Arabian tribe, 25, 293, 294
Qena, town and province of Upper Egypt, 5, 18, 111, 112, 139, 268, 269, 303
Qift, a village of Upper Egypt, 18, 102, 269
Qift–Quseir road, 26, 141, 254, 267, 291
Qireijab, section of the ʻAbabda, 158, 305
Quail, 127
Qudhaʻa, a descendant of Qahtan, 24, 264, 292
Qunfuda, a port of Arabia, 39
Qurʻan, a tribe of the Libyan Desert, 286
Qurein ʻAtut, a hill in Sinai, 139
Qureish, the tribe of the Prophet, 25, 36, 260, 297
Qus, a village of Upper Egypt, 18, 26, 27, 263, 297
Qusaima, a Sinai frontier post, 217, 234, 254, 255
Qusara, or squatters, 40, 264
Quseir, an Egyptian port on the Red Sea, 5, 113, 141, 150, 151
Qwayatin, Hajji, 298

Rababa or viol, 63, 64 n.
Rabayiʻ section of Awlad Suleiman, 287
Rabiʻa, an ancient tribe of Arabia, 25, 26, 28, 33, 298, 303
Rabugh, an Arabian harbour, 59
Rafa, a Sinai frontier post, 127, 160, 253
Rafiq, or "wayfellow", 37–8, 146, 173, 197

Rahat, a leather girdle, 74
Raʻi, or herdsman, 114
Raiding, 133–147
Rainfall, 8, 19, 20
Raithou (Tor), 136–8
Ramadan, 238
Rammah, a branch of the Fawayid, 274, 290
Rape, penalties for, 220, 221, 320, 321
Ras Muhammad, the tip of Sinai, 150
Ras Rawaya, 92
Ras Banas, a peninsula, 151
Ras Shukheir, 139
Rashaida, a tribe of Hiteim, 214, 269
Rats, desert, 89, 127
Ravens, 92, 127, 155
Reclus, Elisée, 52
Red Sea, 11, 122
Reinach, Salomon, 93
Renaud de Chatillon, 27
Rizana, section of Wilad Saʻid, 262
Robertson Smith, W., 24 n., 36, 37, 53, 91 n., 216, 237 n., 264, 267
Robinson, E., 88, 138, 260
Romans, 20, 21, 177
Rowaja, a tribe settled in Upper Egypt 96
Ruala, an Arab tribe of Syria, 179, 193, 255
Rueishid, a raid-leader, 179
Rumeilat, a Sinai tribe, 44, 253

Saʻad, political faction, 43, 44
Saʻad Abu Nar, sheikh of the Haweitat, 247
Saʻad Abu Sulb, 217
Saʻad Bey El-Masri, 281
Saʻad Sadiq el-Waʻd, ancestor of the Laheiwat, 250
"Saʻada, wife of Abu Dib," 274, 281
Saʻadi tribes, 41, 272–5, 281, 283, 291
Saʻadiyin, 251, 252
Sabah Agha, a policeman, 144–5
Sabah Mudakhil, 51, 105, 114, 118, 150, 179, 207–8; steals Selim's wife, 224–5; plunders a wreck, 239–240; 310
Sabah Musa, 45, 57
Saddles, 101; for camels, 115, 116

INDEX

Safaja, 124, 284
Said Pasha, 289, 295, 299
Sa'id 'Ali, a wizard, 142–3
Sa'ida, wife of Selim, 224–5
St. Antony, monastery of, 125, 140
St. Catherine, monastery of, 5, 31, 38, 76, 89, 153, 239, 243, 260, 261, 265, 266
St. Nilus, 105, 197
Sala Bey Khalifa, a sheikh of the 'Ababda, 143
Sala Pasha Lamlum, Sheikh of the Fawayid, 290
Salem Anis, judge of the Muzeina, 119
Salem Faraj, a Ma'azi sheikh, 90, 156, 240
Salam Jebely, a Muzeini, 133
Salalma, or Awlad Sallam, 288, 291, 294
Salih, Arabian prophet, 105
Saliva, magical use of, 197
Sallam, story of, 207–8
Saluki dogs, 98, 99
Salum, western frontier post, 127, 288, 309
Salhiya, a town in Sharqiya, 251, 259
Samalus, a Western tribe, 40, 282, 296, 297
Sam'ana, a small Sinai tribe, 44, 252, 284
Samir, a dance, 65–6
Sandals, 71
Sanhaja, a tribe of Tuareg, 271, 272
Saqiet el-Hamra, a Moroccan religious centre, 275, 280
Sarabit el-Khadim, an Egyptian temple in Sinai, 163, 291
Sawalha, a Sinai confederation, 29, 33, 45, 46, 49 n.; dress, 70, 145; beliefs, 152; 183; laws, 226, 234, 239; 244; warfare with the 'Aleiqat, 257–8; general account, 259–262; 284, 291. *See also* 'Awarma, Qararsha, Wilad Sa'id
Schiaparelli, 166
Schweinfurth, 160, 308
Scorpion, 155
Scorpion device on sword, 78, 197
Scorpion, Arab constellation of the, 165–6

Seligman, Professor C. G., v, 52, 56, 95 n., 123, 170, 172, 174 n., 177 n., 301, 302
Selim Abu Radi, 224–5
Selima Oasis, 286
Semerkhet, Pharaoh of Dynasty I, 9, 13
Senna, 67, 68
Senussi sect, 32, 277, 298
Serpent-cult, vestiges of a, 158
Serpent-device on swords, 77–8
Shablaq, a spy, 247
Shadli, Moslem saint, 27, 96, 151, 155, 173
Shadli 'Alayan, a sheikh of the Haweitat, 248
Shaiqia, a Sudan tribe, 142
Shara', the (Islamic code of law), 57, 201 n., 313, 321
Shararat, an Arabian tribe of Hiteim, 114 n., 149, 183, 269
Sharqiya Province, 106, 124, 127, 129, 244, 245, 251, 257, 276, 282, 284, 285, 292, 294, 295, 305
Sheep, 92, 117, 121, 152, 257
Sheep, wild, 9, 124
Sheikh, powers of, 41, 42
Sheikh Abu Khalaifa, 162
Sheikh = saint
  ,, Banas, 151
  ,, Faranja, 153, 265
  ,, Hashash, 151
  ,, Jureir, 228, 253
  ,, Shadli, 27, 96, 151, 155, 173
  ,, Shebib, 151, 229
Sherifs (*Ashraf*), 2, 39, 40
Sherm, a Sinai harbour, 257, 269
Sheshenq, or Shishak, 18, 54
Shibeika, virgin's ornament, 49–51, 72, 181
Shields, 79, 143
Shiheibat, the " black sheep " of the Murabitin, 282, 283, 289
Sidi 'Abd er-Rahman, a saint, 82, 152
Sidi Fakhr et-Teir, a saint, 292
Silko, King of the Nobadae, 21
Simoons, 164
Sinana, division of the 'Awlad Ali, 274, 279

INDEX

Sinaqra, descendants of Sinqir, 274, 278, 279, 320
Sineina, ancestor of the Sinana, 278, 279
Sinkwab, 189
Sinqir, ancestor of the Sinaqra, 40, 278
Sisters, marriages with, 184
Siwa, oasis and town therein, 19, 85, 104, 113, 197, 278, 279, 296
Slatin Pasha, 89, 113, 304
Slaves, 56–8
Smallpox, 68
Sohb, a Western tribe settled in the Delta, 287
Solubba, gipsies of Arabia, 117, 269
Somalis, 36
Stars, 163–6
Strabo, 9, 13, 21, 214 n., 215
Suakin, 5, 28, 92, 270, 303
Suakin el-Qadim ('Aidhab), 27–8
Sudan, 11, 31, 57, 76, 78, 83, 104, 113, 115, 161, 168, 177, 190, 270, 289, 292, 293, 294, 297, 298, 299, 301, 302, 303, 304
Sudan Government, 306, 307
Suez, 26, 45, 63, 78, 134, 139, 141, 143, 200, 239, 258, 262
Suez Canal, 5, 51, 68, 134, 244, 271
Suez, Gulf of, 5, 139, 144, 197, 200
Suez–Tor road, 38, 195
Sukhur or Beni Sakhr, a Syrian tribe, 183, 193
Suleiman Ghoneim, sheikh of the 'Awarma, divides the money, 46–7; views on slaves, 58–9; on malaria, 67; burns Abu Zenima, 145–6; views on God, 150; dies in Palestine, 259, 260
Suleiman ibn Jad, a Haweiti sheikh, 245
Suleiman Selmi, an 'Aleiqi, 134
Sun, 166, 167; avoidance of, 190
Suwarka, a tribe of North Sinai, 43, 44, 156, 194, 229, 232, 253
Swords, 76, 77, 79

Tabana, cultivators in Wadi Feiran, 233, 266
Tahawi, a Hanadi sheikh, 36, 295
Tahawiya, his descendants, 36, 295
Tamarisks, 160
Tanib (refugee), 40
Tarbul el-Fellah, a hill, 140
Tarhuna, a Berber tribe, 33, 286, 289, 299, 300
El-Teb, battle of, 79
Tebu, a negroid Saharan folk, 17, 81 n.
Tehenu (Libyans), 17
Temehu, 17
Tents, 80–1
Terabin (sig. Terbani), a North Sinai tribe, 25, 33, 43, 44, 146, 147, 183, 194, 204, 249, 253–5, 264
Terebinths, superstition about, 160
Thamud, ancient Arabian tribe, 105, 292
Eth-Tharwa, anecdote of, 253
Thebes, 20
Throwing-stick, 14, 79
Tih escarpment, 5, 67
Tiyaha (sing. Tihi), an Arab tribe of North Sinai, 25, 33, 43, 44, 59; their camels, 114, 115; raids, 134, 139, 143; 183; laws, 203, 204, 214, 223, 243, 245, 254; general account, 255–6; 269
Tobacco-pipes, 84
Tor, fishing village and quarantine station, 21, 38, 58, 59, 62; raided by Blemmyes, 136–8; 139; battle of, 143–5, 193, 201, 202, 240, 257, 263, 266, 269, 299
Towara (sing. Turi), or Arabs of South Sinai, 35, 43, 44, 63, 71, 88, 90; raids, 138, 139; rites, 170, 171, 174, 175; laws, 204, 248; general account, 256–265. *See also* 'Aleiqat, Muzeina, Sawalha.
Tracking, 117–19
Trees, sacred, 159–161
Tripoli, 27, 62, 273, 287, 289, 299, 300
Tripoli dogs, 98
Tristram, Canon, 121
Troglodytes, 13, 94, 197, 215, 225 n.
Tuareg, 1, 40, 54, 91, 271, 272, 287 n.
Tunis, 27, 62, 75, 300
Et-Tunisi, Arab traveller, 286

INDEX

Turkana, East African tribe, 123 n., 197
Turks, 68, 143–7, 224, 248
Turquoise-mine, 58, 62, 207
Turshan, section of the Fezara, 294, 300
Twins, turn into cats, 96

'Umani camels, 113, 114
Umm Bogma, manganese mines, 62, 310
Umm-el-Bulis, anecdote of, 59
Umm el-Gheith, " mother of rain," 156
'Uqba, the conqueror of North Africa, 22, 264
'Uqbi, or judge of women, 53, 224, 226
'Urfi, or Arab law, 201, 210
'Uweinat, Jebel, 11

Van Gennep, 168, 182
Vansleb, 125, 140, 286
Venus, the planet, 166, 182
Viol, 63
Viper, horned, 127, 158, 159

Wad Hajj Sa'ad, a Dervish raider, 142
El-Wadah, a plain, 307
El-Wadi, a palm grove at Tor, 144
Wadi 'Abad, 302
„ 'Alaqi, 142, 158, 306
„ Amur (Sudan), 132
„ el-'Araba, 248, 249
„ el-'Arish, 5, 44
„ Baba, 146
„ Barq, 258
„ Biyar lil 'Ain, 152
„ Budra, 208
„ Butum, 160
„ Eikidi (Sudan), 307
„ Feiran, 67, 70, 85, 137, 144, 151, 152, 233, 244, 260
„ Hamdh (Arabia), 292
„ Hebran, 119, 262
„ Gemal, 51, 57, 231
„ Gir (Algeria), 9
„ Ibib, 157
„ Iqna, 194
„ Isla, 59, 209

Wadi Kajuj, 157
„ Kharit, 154, 157
„ Khashir, 157
„ Lahian, 120
„ Matalla, 146
„ Mishiti, 152
„ Mi'r, 262
„ Mukattab, 256
„ Murr, 224
„ Natrun, 20, 124, 279, 280, 282
„ Nukhul, 146
„ el-'Obeiyid, 152
„ O Sir Eirab, 152
„ Rahaba, 51
„ Romit (" of the Romans "), 178
„ Sahu, 151
„ Salib el-Azraq, 193
„ esh-Sheikh, 262
„ Sidri, 207, 208, 258, 261
„ Sirhan (Arabia), 269
„ Solaf, 153, 244, 262
„ Sudr, 194
„ Tayiba, 146
„ Tumilat, 16; settled by the Hanadi, 294–6
„ Zaghra, 153
„ Abu Ziran, 141
„ Zubeir, 120
Wahabis, 31, 149, 248
Wa'il, ancestor of the Ma'aza, 243, 267
Wasm, or tribal mark, 44, 45
El-Watia, a pass in Sinai, 257
Waterskins, 83, 84, 156
Weaving, 60–2
Weli (pl. *awliya*), 150–5, 158, 216
Wellhausen, 193
Westermarck, 194
Wheel-trap, 12, 76, 122, 123
Wiheidat, 254
El-Wijh, Arabian port, 57, 63, 179, 200
Wilad Sa'id, a division of the Sawalha, 45, 153, 230, 233, 236
Wilkinson, Sir Gardner, 76, 99, 280, 290, 292
Witnesses, 229–231
Withaqa, a legal right, 211, 238
Wizards, 142, 143, 161, 162
Wounds, assessment of, 234–7, 321–7

344 INDEX

Yadim Sultan, 294–5
Yaghuth, pagan deity, 25
Yahya, a jurist, 322–6
Ya'uq, pagan deity, 25
Yambo, Arabian port, 292, 299
Yana, a Jew, 274, 275
Yunis ibn Mirdas, 289

Zab, an Algerian oasis, 9
Zaid, the Prophet's slave, 56
Zareiqa, anecdote of, 114
Zarzura, mythical oasis, 298
Zebeidiya, a tribe of Hiteim, 269, 270

Zeidan, Sheikh of the 'Aleiqat, 144, 213, 263, 310
Zibid ('Aidhab), 28
Zidem (Jidda), 28
Ziyadi, or judge of camels, 229, 238
Ziyud, section of the Suwarka, 229, 253
Zizyphus trees, 159, 160
Zoghb, an ancient tribe, 286
Zuaya, a Western tribe, 289
Zuawa, an ancient tribe, 288
Zubeir ibn el 'Awwam, a hero of the Conquest, 24, 301, 302, 306
Zumeiliyin, section of the 'Aleiqat, 263, 264, 310